PRIMER ON ERISA FIDUCIARY DUTIES

Dana J. Domone
Editor
BNA's Compensation and Benefits Guide
formerly Staff Editor
BNA Pension Reporter

BNA BOOKS

The Bureau of National Affairs, Inc., Washington, D.C.

To my husband, Peter, for his love and understanding

Library of Congress Cataloging-in-Publication Data

Domone, Dana J.
Primer on ERISA fiduciary duties / Dana J. Domone.
p. cm.
Includes bibliographical references and index.
ISBN 0-87179-809-3
1. Pension trusts—Law and legislation—United States. 2. Trusts and trustees—United States. I. Title.
KF3512.D66 1994
343.7306'4—dc20
[347.30364] 94-23864
CIP

Published by BNA Books
1250 23rd St., N.W., Washington, D.C. 20037

PRIMER ON ERISA FIDUCIARY DUTIES

Preface

The Employee Retirement Income Security Act of 1974 (ERISA) was designed to protect retirement benefits. It was passed after the failure of a number of large manufacturers had left thousands of workers without retirement benefits, because those benefits had been promised but not funded.

ERISA contains elements of both labor and tax law. The labor provisions govern the conduct of the pension and welfare plan fiduciaries by providing general fiduciary standards of conduct and prohibiting fiduciaries from engaging in certain transactions with certain parties, called "parties in interest," who have relationships with the plans. The tax portion amends the Internal Revenue Code, governing the conduct of "disqualified persons" (similar to parties in interest) and assessing excise taxes on disqualified persons who violate the "prohibited transaction" rules. Civil penalties may be assessed under the labor provisions of ERISA on fiduciaries who breach their duty.

The fiduciary rules are an integral part of the protection established by ERISA. These rules require that the individuals who control plan assets use these assets solely in the interest of plan participants and beneficiaries, for the exclusive purpose of providing benefits to participants and beneficiaries, while paying reasonable expenses under the plan. Fiduciaries are personally liable for any losses they cause a plan to experience through breach of their duties; fiduciaries may lose their personal assets to repay these losses. In addition, fiduciaries may be liable for actions of co-fiduciaries.

This book will help readers determine whether they are ERISA fiduciaries, subject to the prohibited transaction requirements, and personally liable for plan losses. It will explain who fiduciaries are, how they must act, and the consequences of their failure to act prudently. While case law may be used as examples of fiduciary liability, this book is not intended as a legal treatise. Some discussion is simplified and the actual law paraphrased to help readers with little or no familiarity with ERISA and the fiduciary rules. However, full text of the relevant provisions of ERISA, the Internal Revenue Code, and Labor Department and Treasury regulations appear in the appendices.

The fiduciary rules apply to all employee benefit plans (both retirement and health and welfare). They do not apply to government, church, unfunded deferred compensation (plans for executives that offer benefits beyond what the qualified plans offer), or plans whose participants are primarily nonresident aliens.

The short citations are used in the text, with a references section at the end of each chapter. Case information appears in the Table of Cases. Further reading and resources are suggested at the end of the Glossary.

The first chapter, "What Is ERISA?," sets the stage with an explanation of the federal law's structure, regulation by the three agencies, preemption of state laws, and broad coverage of employee benefit plans. For more information, readers should consult *Primer on ERISA*, also published by BNA Books.

The second chapter, "Fiduciaries, Trustees, and Liability," identifies plan fiduciaries and trustees and the liabilities they may incur for breaching their duties.

The third chapter, "Investment of Plan Assets," explains the trust and handling requirements for plan assets, and their investments.

The fourth chapter, "Fiduciary Duties," explains the duties in detail, as well as the consequences of breaching those duties.

The fifth chapter, "Prohibited Transactions," identifies the transactions specifically forbidden between plans and those with financial interests in the plans.

The sixth chapter, "Prohibited Transaction Exemptions," identifies the exemptions to prohibited transactions included in the statute as well as granted individually or in a class by the Labor Department.

The Glossary explains common pension and benefit terms

used in this book. The Bibliography refers readers to books, articles, publications, organizations, and conferences that may be useful. The appendices offer full text of relevant portions of ERISA and the Internal Revenue Code, accompanying regulations, and important cases and exemptions. Finally, the Table of Cases provides case citations, including citations to BNA's Employee Benefit Cases (EBC).

CONTENTS

APPENDICES

1

What Is ERISA?

The Employee Retirement Income Security Act (ERISA) is a comprehensive federal law covering nearly all employee benefit plans. ERISA was passed by Congress in 1974 to ensure that benefits promised to employees would be paid. In the past, some companies promised retirement benefits, but either did not fund those benefits or used the plan assets for other purposes. When employees retired, some companies did not have the money to pay the benefits.

The term "employee benefit plans" includes pension plans and welfare plans. "Pension plans" are defined by ERISA as plans that provide retirement income or defer income until the employment is terminated. (ERISA Sec. 3(2)) "Welfare plans," which are also called health and welfare plans, provide medical, surgical, or hospital care or benefits; benefits to cover sickness, accident, disability, death or unemployment; vacation benefits; scholarship, training, and apprenticeship programs; and day care. (ERISA Sec. 3(1))

Employers that establish pension plans qualified under Internal Revenue Code (IRC) Section 401(a) may make limited tax-deductible contributions to the plans. These contributions are held in trust. Interest earned on the plan contributions is tax-deferred until the plan's assets are distributed to participants and beneficiaries. Employers are not required to offer their employees employee benefit plans, as the system is voluntary. However, once plans are established, they must be operated using the high standards set by ERISA and the tax code.

The tax code sets minimum requirements for plans to maintain their favorable tax status. Plans that meet those standards are "qualified," which means that contributions to the plans are tax deductible for the employer, the earnings on the assets within the plans are tax-deferred, and taxes on the benefits are deferred until distributions are made to participants. One of the most important of the minimum standards is the nondiscrimination rule of IRC Section 401(a)(4), which requires that a plan's benefits, contributions, rights and features, and amendments may not discriminate in favor of highly compensated employees.

ERISA further protects the interests of participants in private pension plans by requiring the plans to "vest" the benefits (i. e., to give employees the rights to the benefits that cannot be taken away), to fund the benefits, and to insure a basic level of benefits if the plan is a defined benefit plan that terminates with insufficient assets to pay the promised benefits.

ERISA also requires plan sponsors to report to the government and disclose to participants and beneficiaries financial and other important plan information, and requires plan fiduciaries to meet standards of conduct and responsibility. ERISA also provides for remedies, sanctions, and access to federal courts when plan sponsors and fiduciaries do not meet the standards set for them.

Health and welfare plans are subject to similar reporting and disclosure requirements as pension plans, and, of course, to the fiduciary responsibility provisions. However, most substantive regulation of health and welfare plans is on the tax side, which contains provisions relating to the tax exclusion for contributions and benefits, nondiscrimination, and funding rules. Both ERISA and the tax code offer parallel provisions for continuation of health care following certain events (known as COBRA, after the law that enacted it, Consolidated Omnibus Budget Reconciliation Act). The Internal Revenue Service has primary responsibilities for interpreting and enforcing COBRA.

STRUCTURE OF ERISA

ERISA regulates the organization and operation of private sector employee pension and health and welfare plans. The law is divided into four sections or titles:

- Title I, Labor—Covers the protection of employee benefit rights, including general definitions used in ERISA, the duty of the plan to report on its operations to the government, the duty of the plan to disclose information to participants and beneficiaries, fiduciary responsibility, enforcement provisions and penalties for failure to comply with ERISA, continuation coverage under group health plans (COBRA), and, as to pension plans, rules on which employees must be covered under the plan (participation), rules on when participants have the rights to their benefits (vesting), and how the benefits must be funded (funding). The rules that relate to pension plans parallel rules contained in the IRC.
- Title II, Tax—Amends the IRC provisions relating to pension and benefit plans. Generally, tax-related provisions are referenced to the tax code rather than this title.
- Title III, Administration—Coordinates jurisdiction among the federal agencies responsible for its enforcement (Labor Department, Internal Revenue Service, and Pension Benefit Guaranty Corporation). It also establishes the Joint Board for the Enrollment of Actuaries, requiring examinations and special training for actuaries who perform required duties of ERISA plans.
- Title IV, Pension Insurance—Establishes the Pension Benefit Guaranty Corporation, a quasi-governmental agency that collects premiums from defined benefit pension plans to pay a basic level of pension benefits to participants if their plans are terminated with insufficient assets to pay the benefits promised.

(See the index to the tax code and ERISA, as well as their related regulations in Appendix 1.)

Scope of ERISA

The scope of ERISA is very broad, covering all employee benefit plans (pension and welfare), established or maintained by an employer or employee organization (union) engaged in, or affecting, interstate commerce. (ERISA Secs. 3(1), 3(2), and 3(3)) The term "employee benefit plan" is defined in ERISA Section 3(3) to describe either a pension plan or a welfare plan.

A "pension plan" is described in ERISA Section 3(2) as any plan, fund, or program established and maintained by an employer or a union, or both, to provide retirement income or to defer income until after employees terminate their employment. However, certain severance plans and plans that supplement pensions with cost of living increases are treated as "welfare plans" under ERISA.

A "welfare plan" is defined in ERISA Section 3(1) as any plan, fund, or program established and maintained by an employer, or a union, or both, to provide through the purchase of insurance or otherwise,

- medical, surgical, or hospital care or benefits;
- benefits in the event of sickness, accident, disability, death, or unemployment;
- vacation benefits, apprenticeship or training programs;
- day-care centers, scholarship funds, or prepaid legal services; or
- any bargainable benefit (other than pension or death benefits) that is described in Section 302(c) of the Labor Management Relations Act (LMRA).

Plans Exempt From ERISA

ERISA generally covers employee benefit plans in the "private sector," which means plans sponsored by businesses or unions, or both. Some employee benefit plans are exempted from ERISA requirements, including its fiduciary standards (ERISA Sec. 4(b)):

- **Federal, state, or local government plans.** (ERISA Sec. 3(32)) Some of these plans, however, may have to meet tax standards applicable to qualified plans, such as nondiscrimination rules. In addition, many of these "public" plans have adopted fiduciary standards that are similar to ERISA's fiduciary standards.

- **Church plans.** These plans are established and maintained for members and employees of tax-exempt churches or by associations of churches, and are exempt from ERISA. However, a plan covering church employees who conduct unrelated trade or business would not qualify as a church plan, and church plans may elect to be treated as ERISA plans. (ERISA Sec. 3(33))
- **Workers' compensation.** Plans maintained solely to comply with laws on worker's compensation, unemployment compensation, or disability insurance are also exempt from ERISA coverage. (ERISA Sec. 4(b)(3))
- **Nonresident alien plans.** Plans maintained outside the United States primarily for the benefit of employees who are substantially nonresident aliens are exempt. (ERISA Sec. 4(b)(4))
- **"Top hat" plans.** These plans are unfunded deferred compensation plans for a select group of managers or highly compensated employees. Top hat plans are exempt from most of ERISA, but are subject to limited reporting requirements. Pursuant to departmental regulations they first must file a simple notice to the Labor Department to alert the government to their existence. Many of the protections afforded to participants in ERISA plans, such as the reporting and disclosure provisions, are not afforded participants in these plans because it is assumed that their participants are highly knowledgeable and sophisticated in the area of compensation and deferred compensation.

Preemption

ERISA Section 514 generally "preempts" or supersedes all state laws that relate to employee benefit plans, especially state-mandated benefit laws. While insurance companies must meet state insurance requirements, companies that "self-insure" their plans are exempt from those requirements under ERISA. Some courts have found that if the defendant is not an ERISA fiduciary, then state law claims are not preempted. (*Quigley v. Unum Life Ins. Co.; Jordan v. Reliable Life Ins. Co.*) However, the U.S. Supreme Court has held that state law claims of bad faith brought against an insurer of a welfare benefits plan are preempted under ERISA without any determination that the insurer was an ERISA fiduciary. (*Pilot Life Ins. Co. v. Dedeaux*)

Some state law claims may not be preempted, however. The Maryland Court of Appeals held that ERISA does not preempt professional malpractice law claims, even if they relate to an employee benefit plan. In that case, a participant in a pension plan asked the contract administrator for advice on borrowing from the plan. The participant received a written response that did not include the tax consequences to the participant of the plan loans, which included excise taxes for early withdrawal of the benefits and reporting of the loans as income for tax purposes. Over a two-year period, the participant borrowed from the plan without realizing the loans had to be reported. After paying income taxes, interest, and penalties on the loans, the participant sued the administrator in state court alleging malpractice, breach of fiduciary duty, and breach of various obligations under the plan document. The case originally was dismissed as being preempted by ERISA, but on appeal the court found that ERISA did not preempt the state law claims because those claims were made by a plan participant for damages (income taxes, interest, and penalties) unrelated to plan benefits. (*Shofer v. Stuart Hack Co.*)

Fiduciary Duties

ERISA's fiduciary requirements are designed to ensure that a qualified plan's assets may be used only to pay benefits to participants and beneficiaries and to pay the reasonable expenses of maintaining a plan. Therefore, ERISA lists the duties of those who control and manage plan assets—the fiduciaries.

Briefly, there are two types of fiduciaries. One is a "named fiduciary," who is the person named in the plan document responsible for the plan. The second type is a person who has discretionary authority on the management or administration of a plan, or discretion to manage and invest the plan assets, or give advice with respect to such investments. (See Chapter 2 for a complete definition of a fiduciary, Chapter 3 for a discussion of plan assets, and Chapter 4 for a description of fiduciary duties.)

A plan may have more than one fiduciary. For example, a plan may have a plan administrator who has discretion in the administration of the plan and a trustee who is responsible for investment decisions.

Plans also have "trustees" who have authority over plan assets held in trust. Trustees may be directed by fiduciaries named in the plan or by investment managers who are fiduciaries. If these directions are proper, in accordance with plan terms, and not in violation of ERISA, and to the extent they follow such directions, the plan trustees generally are not liable for actions taken by those fiduciaries or investment managers. Trustees generally are held to the same fiduciary standards as fiduciaries. (ERISA Sec. 403(a)(1))

(See Appendix 2 for definitions relating to plans and Appendix 10 for a chronology of amendments to ERISA.)

REFERENCES

Pension Plans: ERISA Section 3(2)
Welfare Plans: ERISA Section 3(1)
Employee Benefit Plan: ERISA Section 3(3)
Plans Exempt From ERISA: ERISA Section 4(b)
Preemption: ERISA Section 514
Fiduciaries: ERISA Section 3(21)
Directed Trustees: ERISA Section 403(a)(1)

2

FIDUCIARIES, TRUSTEES, AND LIABILITY

Fiduciaries generally are defined functionally by reference to their authority with respect to management and investment of plan assets, and their authority and responsibility with respect to plan administration. A trustee is a type of fiduciary. Fiduciaries and trustees are personally liable for their own actions and for actions of co-fiduciaries and co-trustees. Personal liability means that if a fiduciary "breaches" or fails in his or her duty to the plan and thereby causes the plan to lose assets, then the personal assets of the fiduciary could be taken by a court to repay the plan's loss. This is why it is important for individuals working in employee benefits to understand whether they may be considered fiduciaries or trustees, and if they are, to know their obligations to plans and their participants.

Plan assets usually are required to be held in trust by one or more trustees and include participant and employer contributions and earnings on those contributions. Plan trustees are fiduciaries under ERISA and are generally subject to all of ERISA's fiduciary requirements plus some provisions applicable only to trustees. In some cases, the plan assets may include the underlying assets of the entities in which plans invest. (See Chapter 3 for a discussion of plan assets and investment of those assets.)

FIDUCIARIES AND TRUSTEES

Each plan must have a least one "named fiduciary" who is designated in the plan document as being responsible for the plan and, if plan assets are held in trust, at least one trustee. ERISA provides that the written plan document must include one or more "named fiduciaries" who control and manage the plan's operation and administration. (ERISA Sec. 402(a)(2))

The named fiduciary is either identified by name in the plan or by a plan procedure to identify the named fiduciary. For example, the plan document may say the named fiduciary of this plan is John Smith. Or it may say the named fiduciary is an administrative committee appointed by the employer's board of directors. Because specifying the individuals by name would require plans to be amended each time the individual specified leaves the position, most plans designate the position. Furthermore, that position need not be designated as being the "named fiduciary" by the plan document. It is sufficient if the plan document describes the position as responsible for carrying out the functions that would make one a named fiduciary. These functions are the "authority to control and manage the operation and administration of this plan." Typically, plan administrators and trustees are named fiduciaries.

While the plan document *must* identify the named fiduciaries, it has the option to include various provisions relating to the duties of named fiduciaries. (ERISA Sec. 402(c)) A plan may provide that:

- Any person may serve in more than one fiduciary capacity (including service as both trustee and administrator);
- A named fiduciary, or a fiduciary designated by the named fiduciary according to plan procedures, may employ people to give advice on any responsibility the fiduciary has under the plan; or
- A named fiduciary may appoint an investment manager to manage, acquire, and sell any plan assets.

In addition to the "named fiduciary," an individual who performs certain plan management functions is treated as a plan fiduciary. (ERISA Sec. 3(21)(A), ERISA Interpretive Bulletin 75-5) These functions include:

- Exercising any discretionary authority or control in managing the plan or in acquiring or selling plan assets;
- Rendering investment advice for a fee or other compensation, direct or indirect, with respect to any money or other plan property; or
- Having any discretionary authority or responsibility in plan administration.

Individuals who have no power to make any decisions on plan policy, interpretations, practices, or procedures, but who perform administrative functions for the plan are not fiduciaries.

Trustees

Plans subject to ERISA generally are required to be held in trust, managed by trustees either named in the trust instrument or appointed by the plan's named fiduciary, and who have accepted such position. (ERISA Sec. 403) Trustees have exclusive authority to manage and control plan assets, except when a plan expressly provides that:

- The trustees are subject to the direction of the named fiduciary, or
- The authority is delegated to properly appointed investment managers.

Trustees subject to the direction of the named fiduciary are called "directed trustees." Directed trustees will not be liable for following the instructions of the named fiduciary, as long as those instructions are in accordance with the plan document and not contrary to ERISA. (ERISA Sec. 403(a)(1); 29 C.F.R. Sec. 2509. 75-8 FR-14) Where plan assets are held in more than one trust, trustees are liable only for the management and control of assets in their own trusts. (ERISA Sec. 405(b)(3)(A)) However, where two or more trustees govern one trust, trustees share co-trustee responsibility and each trustee must use reasonable care to prevent the other trustees from breaching their duties. (ERISA Sec. 405(b)(1)(A)) The trustees of the plan must be either named in the trust instrument, in the plan instrument, or appointed by a named fiduciary. (ERISA Sec. 403(a))

The requirement that plan assets be held in trust does not apply to all plans with plan assets. For instance, custodial accounts (individual retirement accounts, plans for the self-employed, or tax-deferred annuities held by banks or brokerage firms), and plans funded solely by insurance contracts are not covered. (ERISA Sec. 403(b))

Fiduciary by Function

In addition to the named fiduciary, a person who performs certain plan functions is treated as a plan fiduciary. (ERISA Sec. 3(21)(A); DOL Regulation, 29 C.F.R. 2510.3-21) These functions may be summarized as follows:

- Exercising any discretionary authority or control in managing the plan or in acquiring or selling plan assets;
- Offering investment advice for a fee or other compensation, direct or indirect, with respect to any money or other plan property; or
- Acting with discretionary authority or responsibility in plan administration.

As an example of a fiduciary by function, the wife of a pension plan fiduciary executed documents on behalf of her husband and signed her name as a plan trustee even though she had not been appointed formally as a plan fiduciary or trustee. Using the "duck" test—"if it walks like a duck and quacks like a duck, it is a duck"—an appeals court found her to be a fiduciary because she exercised discretionary authority over plan assets. (*Donovan v. Mercer*)

A corporate officer who is not designated as a named fiduciary under the plan may nevertheless assume a fiduciary status by performing fiduciary functions. (ERISA Interpretive Bulletin 75-8). A corporation as an entity may be a plan fiduciary. Also, individuals within the corporation who exercise the type of authority or control described in ERISA Section 3(21)(A) will themselves be plan fiduciaries. (*Freund v. Marshall & Ilsley Bank*)

For example, a company backdated an amendment to exclude motorcycle accidents from coverage under its health plan after an employee had a motorcycle accident. Although the benefits supervisor knew the company had amended the plan after the date of the accident, the supervisor was instructed by the plan administrator to deny the claim. The benefits supervisor was not a fiduciary of the plan, the court held, adding therefore that the supervisor did not share the liability with the plan administrator. (*Confer v. Custom Eng'g Co.*)

Shared liability goes the other way as well. As a result of individuals in other companies breaching their fiduciary duties, corporate entities employing those individuals may be held accountable for their actions. For example, a brokerage firm was liable for the acts of a stockbroker it employed. The broker was a fiduciary because she exercised control and authority over plan assets by investing those assets. (*Stanton v. Shearson Lehman Am. Express*)

Nonfiduciary Functions

Functions that are administrative and do not involve discretionary authority or control over plan assets are not fiduciary functions (ERISA Interpretive Bulletin 75–5). The Labor Department lists the following functions as being nonfiduciary administrative functions:

- Application of rules determining eligibility for participation or benefits;
- Calculation of services and compensation credits for benefits;
- Preparation of employee communications material;
- Maintenance of participants' service and employment records;
- Preparation of reports required by government agencies;
- Calculation of benefits;
- Orientation of new participants and advising participants of their rights and options under the plan;

- Collection of contributions and application of contributions as provided in the plan;
- Preparation of reports concerning participants' benefits;
- Processing of claims; and
- Making recommendations to others for decisions with respect to plan administration.

Thus, mere administrative responsibilities—such as calculating benefits or processing claims—do not make an individual a fiduciary. However, in one instance an employee with administrative responsibilities who also had authority to write checks for a company acted on the direction of a company officer to withdraw thousands of dollars in plan assets as "loans" made to company officers either for their personal use or to keep the company solvent. The loans were never repaid. The company officers, who were named fiduciaries, were found liable for breach of duty. The employee also was held to be a fiduciary because of his check-writing powers, since he had discretion over plan assets. The attorney who counseled the employee on the withdrawals was not held to be a fiduciary (see Service Providers below for a discussion of the fiduciary status of service providers). (*Yeseta v. Baima*)

(For more information on DOL regulations relating to fiduciaries, see Appendix 4.)

Investment Advisers

As noted above, a plan trustee must control assets unless a named fiduciary does so or an investment manager is appointed. The responsibility for plan investments can be delegated only if the plan permits it and if the trustees properly retain an "investment manager," who acknowledges in writing its ERISA fiduciary status and responsibility. An investment manager is defined under ERISA Section 3(38) as any fiduciary (other than a trustee or named fiduciary) who:

- Has the power to manage, buy, or sell any plan asset;
- Is registered as an investment adviser under the Investment Advisers Act of 1940, or is a bank, or is an insurance

company licensed to do business in more than one state; and
- Has acknowledged in writing that it is a fiduciary with respect to the plan.

Once an investment manager is appointed, the plan trustee or named fiduciaries may no longer, for example, decide how to vote the proxies of stock in the investment manager's portfolio. (Avon letter, Appendix 5) The plan trustees and fiduciary are relieved of their fiduciary responsibilities for the assets allocated to that investment manager as long as the fiduciaries do the following:

- Are prudent in their selection of manager by investigating the investment manager's background, experience with investment for similarly sized plans, reputation, credentials (such as registration with the Securities and Exchange Commission), past performance with similar investments, fee structure compared with other investment managers, and the type and frequency of reports to trustees;
- Establish prudent guidelines on investments, with limits on risk, allocation, types of investments, and expected rates of return; and
- Monitor the investment manager on a regular basis to ensure the plan's investment guidelines are being followed.

For example, in one case an employee stock ownership plan (ESOP) trustee was found to have breached his fiduciary duty in choosing an investment management company, because he allowed his co-fiduciary to suggest someone without checking the background of the person or finding out anything about him or the company he managed. The trustee delegated the responsibility of investing plan assets to this investment management company. However, the company did not meet ERISA's definition of an investment manager: it did not acknowledge in writing its fiduciary status and it was not registered as investment advisers under the Investment Advisors Act of 1940. The ESOP trustee and plan sponsor were found to be personally and jointly liable for the trustee's violation of fiduciary duty in choosing that manager and in failing to monitor the plan investments. (*Whitfield v. Cohen*)

Service Providers

Those individuals or companies that provide services to employee benefit plans—such as lawyers, accountants, third party administrators, and actuaries—are usually not plan fiduciaries as long as they stay within professional boundaries. For instance, a lawyer giving legal advice to a plan may not be a fiduciary until he or she begins to offer investment advice as well.

In one case, a plan borrowed money from a bank to purchase employer stock. The loan was made in an "arm's-length transaction," which means that it was made on the same terms as used with other commercial borrowers. The employer declined financially, eventually going bankrupt. When the plan defaulted on the loan, the bank converted the stock given as collateral for the loan. The court held that neither the bank nor the attorney advising the plan was a fiduciary with respect to the plan and neither could be held liable for the loss of plan assets. (*Useden v. Acker*)

Plan fiduciaries must ensure that fees paid to service providers are reasonable compared to the services received, and that the services provided are appropriate to the plan. (29 C.F.R. 2509.75-5) The Labor Department's enforcement program has been focusing on service providers who do not provide the services paid for, or provide unnecessary or duplicative services with unreasonable compensation and kickbacks. (Chicago Deputy Area Director, Pension and Welfare Benefits Administration, Steve Haugen speech to WEB, Inc., Apr. 30, 1992)

Persons Prohibited From Serving as Fiduciaries

Convicted criminals are prohibited from being fiduciaries, administrators, plan officers, plan employees, plan consultants, or taking any position involving the authority and control of plan assets, for 13 years after the conviction or end of imprisonment, whichever is later. The sentencing court may reduce the 13-year prohibition to a minimum of 3 years.

The prohibition applies to people committing robbery, bribery, extortion, embezzlement, fraud, grand larceny, burglary, arson, felony drug crimes, murder, rape, kidnapping, perjury, assault with intent to kill, and racketeering. (ERISA Sec. 411(a)) Any person who hires for a plan a person he or she knows is a convicted criminal may be fined $10,000 and imprisoned for five years. (ERISA Sec. 411(b))

If a fiduciary is convicted of criminal mishandling of fund assets, for example, for receiving kickbacks in violation of the Racketeering Influenced Corrupt Organizations Act (RICO), the plan cannot withhold the pension benefits of the criminal to offset personal liability to the fund, a court has held. ERISA Section 206(d)(1) prohibits the assignment or alienation of pension benefits. This antialienation prohibition must apply even though protecting the benefits of a convicted criminal with an outstanding debt to the fund is an "unpalatable result." (*Coar v. Kazimir*)

FIDUCIARY LIABILITY

Fiduciaries who breach their duties are personally liable to restore any plan losses and to return any profits improperly gained from the plan. (ERISA Sec. 409(a)) For example, a pension fund trustee was a full-time paid union business manager and fund administrator who "self-dealt" plan assets by designing his own employment contract for a second full-time salary as plan administrator. While ERISA allows plans to pay reasonable compensation to fiduciaries for services rendered, the fiduciary was already receiving full-time compensation as a union business manager. As a correction, the court required him to repay to the fund the salary he received as plan administrator plus interest and required the contract to be rescinded. (*Gilliam v. Edwards*)

Fiduciaries generally are not liable for losses caused by breaches of duty that occurred before they became fiduciaries, as long as they take reasonable steps to correct the problems. (ERISA Sec. (409(b)) Reasonable steps might include establishing a record of objection to the act in a trustees' meeting, withdrawing plan assets from a questionable investment, or seeking legal advice on how to recapture losses from a breach.

Fiduciary Damages

In addition to liabilities to restore losses and return profits, a fiduciary may be subject to further damages for committing a breach of duty on behalf of the plan, including:

- **Equitable or remedial relief.** Under this relief a court may remove a fiduciary and appoint an independent fiduciary or require other appropriate relief.
- **Punitive damages.** These monetary damages are not expressly provided for in ERISA, but may be added by the courts to stop additional breaches of duty.
- **Civil penalty.** The Labor Department assesses penalties against plan fiduciaries who breach their duties. (ERISA Sec. 502) Plan administrators may be assessed up to $1,000 per day from the date of failure to file the Form 5500 annual report; $100 per day from the date of failure to disclose information to plan participants; $1,000 per violation for a failure to respond to a request for information necessary to comply with the Medicare and Medicaid Coverage Data Bank requirements of ERISA Section 101(f); and up to 20 percent of amounts recovered from the fiduciaries in court orders or in Labor Department settlements. The 20-percent penalty may be waived by the department or may be reduced by excise taxes required to be paid for prohibited transactions (see Chapter 5 for information on prohibited transactions).
- **Criminal penalty.** This penalty, which applies only to reporting and disclosure violations, may impose up to $5,000 and/or one year's imprisonment on individuals or $100,000 on companies, for convictions of willful violations of fiduciary duty. (ERISA Sec. 501) Any person who intentionally and knowingly hires a person who has been convicted of a felony crime may be fined $10,000 and/or imprisoned for five years.

Co-Fiduciary Liability

A fiduciary has a lot to worry about—not just his or her own conduct, but that of other fiduciaries of the plan. In fact, one fiduciary may be personally and jointly liable for loss to the plan and excise taxes resulting from breaches of fiduciary duty caused by other plan fiduciaries. (ERISA Sec. 405(a))

However, before a fiduciary will be held responsible for the acts of another, the court must find that she or he:

- Knew that an act or a failure to act by a co-fiduciary was a breach of duty and tried to cover up the breach;
- Did not comply with fiduciary requirements and allowed a co-fiduciary to commit a breach of duty; or
- Knew about a co-fiduciary's breach and failed to correct it.

If a co-fiduciary has established a pattern of violations and that pattern is noticed by a fiduciary, then the fiduciary still may be held accountable for the co-fiduciary's actions. This is true even if the fiduciary does not know the details of a co-fiduciary violation.

In particularly egregious cases, some courts have stretched to allow a recovery even without finding fiduciary status. For example, in one case a court decided that a bank was not liable for breach of duty as a co-fiduciary, but could be liable as a nonfiduciary. In this case, a plan's investment manager defrauded a plan using mortgage loans. The investment manager operated through a bank that was a fiduciary to the plan for short-term investments, but not for long-term mortgage investments. The bank did not have discretionary authority for the mortgage investments, but because the bank aided the investment manager in a breach of duty, the bank could be liable for the mortgage fraud as a nonfiduciary. (*Mid Jersey Trucking Indus. Pension Fund v. Omni Funding Group*)

However, the U.S. Supreme Court decided that nonfiduciaries who knowingly participate in a breach of fiduciary duties are not liable for monetary damages under ERISA for losses that the plan suffered as a result of the breach. (*Mertens v. Hewitt Assocs.*) In *Mertens,* a class of former salaried employees of Kaiser Steel Co. sued the plan's actuary, Hewitt Associates, for causing plan losses when the actuary failed to change the plan's actuarial assumptions to reflect additional costs imposed by the early retirement of many participants. The former employees alleged that the actuary was liable because it allowed Kaiser to select the actuarial assumptions and did not disclose the plan's funding shortfall. The plan was taken over by the Pension Benefit Guaranty Corporation because of underfunding. The former employees asked that ERISA Section 502(a)(3) be interpreted to require Hewitt to pay monetary damages as "equitable relief."

The Supreme Court held that monetary damages assessed against a nonfiduciary do not constitute the "equitable relief" noted under ERISA Section 502(a)(3). This case has significant implications for actuaries, lawyers, and consultants who are often placed in the role of nonfiduciary advisers to retirement plans. This decision insulates these advisers from monetary damages, even if they knowingly participate with a fiduciary in a breach of his or her fiduciary duty. However, Congress may overturn the *Mertens* decision through legislation.

REFERENCES

Definition of Fiduciary: ERISA Section 3(21)

Trustees: ERISA Section 403(a)

Nonfiduciary Functions: ERISA Interpretive Bulletin 75-5

Definition of Investment Manager: ERISA Section 3(38)

Persons Prohibited as Fiduciaries: ERISA Section 411

Civil Penalties: ERISA Section 502; ERISA Section 502(c)(4), as added by the Omnibus Budget Reconciliation Act (OBRA) of 1993, Section 4301(c)(2)

Medicare and Medicaid Coverage Data Bank: ERISA Section 101(f), as added by OBRA 1993, Section 4301(b)(1)

3

Investment of Plan Assets

Plan assets generally are required to be held in trust and include participant and employer contributions and earnings on those contributions. In some cases, the plan assets may include the underlying assets of the entities in which plans invest.

PLAN ASSETS

Determining what is a plan asset and when a contribution becomes an asset is very important because ERISA fiduciaries generally are liable only for their actions relating to plan assets. Under ERISA, plan assets must be held in trust (unless fully funded by insurance contracts or annuities) and diversified to minimize risk. Holding assets in trust segregates them from the employer's other accounts and protects them from creditors.

Participant Contributions

When participants make contributions to qualified plans—whether paid directly or through withholding by the employer—

the contributions must be segregated from the employer's general assets within a "reasonable" time, but no later than 90 days from the date of contribution. Segregation cannot be made earlier than the date of contribution.

As the following examples illustrate, determining what is reasonable depends on the facts and circumstances of each employer (Labor Dep't Regulation 24 C.F.R. 2310.3–102(B)). For example, Employer A is a large national corporation with several payroll centers and different pay periods. Each payroll center promptly forwards figures representing its total payroll deductions for each plan for each month to a central location. The central office totals the contributions due the plan and sends the plan a check every month. Plan assets include the participant contribution as of the date on which the employer issues the check to the plan. Because of the size of the employer, monthly segregation of employee contributions from employer assets is reasonable.

However, Employer B is a small company with a few employees at a single payroll location. Employer B maintains a contributory profit-sharing plan. Employer B commingles accumulated participant contributions with general assets and makes plan contributions only once a quarter. Because of the small number of employees paid at a single payroll center, quarterly segregation is unreasonable. Instead, Employer B could reasonably be expected to transmit participant contributions to a trust within 10 days of the close of each pay period. The plan assets in this case would include the participant contributions attributable to the date 10 days after the pay period closes.

Employer Contributions

Employer contributions to plans become plan assets when they are segregated and deposited into the trust. Determining when this actually occurred or should have occurred may have legal consequences if there is a default. For example, a company president failed to make health care contributions to a multiemployer health plan before the company went bankrupt. The plan trustees sued the company president, alleging that he breached his fiduciary duty by not making plan contributions. The court held that until the money was actually paid to the plan, the money owed was a debt unregulated by ERISA rather than a plan asset. Furthermore, the president was not a fiduciary with respect to the contribution since it was not yet a plan asset. Had the money been withheld from employees rather than paid totally by the employer, the contribution would have constituted plan assets when withheld. Had the president been considered to be a fiduciary, then he would have been personally liable for the plan contributions. (*Mine Workers v. Powhatan Fuel Co.*)

Underlying Investments

A plan's investment in an entity generally includes the investment but not the assets underlying the entity. For example, if a plan purchases the stock of a publicly traded corporation, that stock is a plan asset. No other assets of that corporation are treated as plan assets except the particular stock bought by the plan. This is important because decisions made about the other nonplan assets of the corporation do not affect the plan.

However, under certain circumstances, the assets underlying the entity are considered plan assets, such as when:

- The securities are not publicly offered (e.g., a family-owned firm);
- The securities are not issued by a registered investment company; or
- The entity is not an "operating company" that is primarily engaged in the production or sale of a product or service other than the investment of capital.

If a plan's investment does include underlying assets, that plan is called a "benefit plan investor," and anyone exercising authority or control over the management or disposition of those underlying assets, and anyone providing investment advice concerning those assets for a fee (direct or indirect), is a fiduciary of the investing plan. (Labor Department regulation 29 C.F.R. 2510.3–101)

ERISA Section 401(b)(2) says that in the case of a plan to which a guaranteed benefit policy is issued by an insurer, the assets of the plan include the policy but not the assets of the insurer. The term "insurer" generally means an insurance company, insurance service, or insurance organization qualified to do business in a state. The term "guaranteed benefit policy" means an insurance policy or contract that provides for benefits guaranteed by the insurer. The term includes any surplus in a separate account, but excludes any other portion of a separate account.

The Department of Labor does not consider general account assets of insurance companies to be plan assets. However, the U.S. Supreme Court expanded the term "plan assets" under ERISA to hold that an insurance company is a fiduciary with respect to non-guaranteed assets held in a group annuity contract. (*John Hancock Mutual Life Ins. Co., v. Harris Trust & Savings Bank*)

In deciding whether the non-guaranteed portion of a group annuity account was a plan asset subject to ERISA's fiduciary requirements, the Supreme Court discarded the Labor Department's view. The Court said Congress had rejected a provision that would have exempted all general account assets from the reach of the fiduciary rules. Instead, Congress excluded guaranteed benefit policies from the definition of plan assets, but did not specifically exempt non-guaranteed assets.

To fund a retirement plan, a corporation entered into a group annuity contract with John Hancock. Under the contract, the insurer provided guaranteed benefits to the company's retirees. However, a portion of the group annuity contract assets, known as "free funds," was not guaranteed by the insurer. Instead of being converted to fixed, guaranteed obligations, these funds were subject to fluctuation based on the insurer's investment performance, according to the appeals court. Harris Trust and Savings Bank, as the trustee of the company's retirement plan, filed suit in federal district court after the insurer discontinued paying non-guaranteed benefits to the plan. According to Harris, the insurer's elimination of the non-guaranteed benefit payments prevented the trustee from withdrawing any of the increasing free funds without first terminating the annuity contract and causing the purchase of new annuities at inflated prices.

Specifically, the trustee charged that the insurer breached its fiduciary duties under ERISA by improperly administering the free funds portion of the contract. The district court dismissed the complaint, but the appeals court reversed, finding that the free funds were plan assets and therefore were not included within the guaranteed benefit policy exception to ERISA's fiduciary duty provisions.

The Supreme Court affirmed the 1992 federal appeals court ruling by a vote of 6–3. The dissenters said the holding disrupts settled expectations among buyers and sellers of group annuity contracts and would prohibit:

- An insurer's investment in stock issued by any of the employers whose pension plans the insurer funds;
- A lease of a building owned by the insurer to one of those employers; or
- The purchase of goods or services from any of those employers.

PLAN INVESTMENTS

Once assets are held in trust, ERISA requires they be invested and diversified to minimize large losses. Plan investments must be prudent, made solely in the interest of plan participants and beneficiaries, and in accordance with the plan document. The interest earned on the assets of qualified pension plans is tax free until benefits are distributed to the plan participants. An investment of plan assets in tax-free securities is one example of an imprudent investment because tax-free securities offer lower yields than other investments.

A plan's named fiduciary—the person named in the plan document as the individual who manages and controls the plan operation and administration—may appoint investment managers to manage plan assets. Such investment managers generally will be plan fiduciaries if they acknowledge this status in writing. (ERISA Sec. 3(38)) (See Chapter 2 for a discussion of named fiduciaries and investment managers.)

How plan assets are invested also depends on whether the plan is a pension plan or a health and welfare plan. A pension plan is funded over the long term, with contributions of perhaps

40 years before any benefit is paid out. Health and welfare plans, however, are usually operated on a calendar year pay-as-you-go basis. They are considered to operate on the short term. The types of plans are discussed below.

- A **defined benefit pension plan** offers a benefit at retirement that is determined by a formula based on the number of years of service with the employer and the employee's average pay at retirement. In this type of plan, a participant's benefit is funded over the long term from the date of plan participation until the participant retires or leaves the job (separation from service). The funding consists of employer contributions plus investment experience, pooled into one trust. In some cases, employee contributions may be required. If the plan's investment experience does not live up to expectations, then the plan sponsor will have to make additional contributions. The health of the industry and relative ages of plan participants also affect how plan assets are invested.
- A **defined contribution plan** offers individual accounts in a trust. In this type of plan, a participant's benefit is the amount in the individual account for that participant, made up of employer and employee contributions plus investment gains or minus investment losses. Unlike a defined benefit plan where poor investment performance means the plan sponsor must make additional contributions to fund the benefit, the defined contribution plan puts the risk of investment losses on the plan participant. The losses reduce the value of the individual account and therefore the individual's benefit. If the plan is an ERISA Section 404(c) plan, which allows participants to direct the investments of their own accounts, then plan fiduciaries generally are not liable for any investment decision made by the participant. Of course, the choices of investment offered are still a fiduciary decision.
- In **fully insured pension plans,** the plan obtains a contract with an insurance company or purchases an annuity for a fixed interest rate that is paid until the contract expires.

- **Health and welfare plans** generally need cash for the short term, so their assets are invested in money market accounts or other "liquid" investments. Some plans may use very short-term bonds to diversify their cash holdings.

As described in "Diversification of Plan Assets" below, these types of plans make a variety of investments, depending on the plan's cash flow needs; the "time horizon," which is the time from the date of contribution until the benefits are paid out; inflation rate; and risk tolerance.

Diversification of Plan Assets

ERISA requires plans to diversify plan investments to minimize the risk of large losses, unless under the circumstances it is clearly prudent not to do so. (ERISA Sec. 404 (a)(1)(C)) The law does not establish actual percentage limits for plan investments, although some defined contribution plans cannot invest more than 10 percent of plan assets in employer securities. (ERISA Sec. 407(a))

In determining whether assets are diversified, plan fiduciaries should examine:

- The purpose of the plan;
- The amount of plan assets;
- The cash flow needs of the plan;
- The geographic area covered by the plan;
- The type of investment;
- The dates of maturity of investment types; and
- The composition of the plan's investment portfolio as a whole. (ERISA legislative history)

(See Appendix 11 for the Labor Department's Interpretive Bulletin on economically targeted plan investments.)

Identifying how much of a plan's assets can be invested into any one type of investment depends on the facts and circumstances. In the following cases, pension plan fiduciaries were charged with failing to diversify their plans' assets:

- An investment manager put 70 percent of plan assets in 30-year government bonds and 15 percent in 25-year bonds, despite the high cash needs of the plan. Early redemption of the bonds to pay benefits caused a loss to the plan. (*GIW Indus. v. Trevor, Stewart, Burton & Jacobsen, Inc.*)

- A plan attempted to invest 23 percent of its assets in a single loan for a highly risky real estate time-sharing venture. (*Marshall v. Glass/Metal Ass'n & Glaziers*)
- A plan invested 36 percent of its assets in a risky gambling venture, despite the limit of 25 percent for any one investment specified in the plan document. In this case, the fiduciary was charged with failing to adhere to the terms of the plan document, as well as failing to diversify plan assets. (*Marshall v. Teamsters Local 282 Pension Trust Fund*)
- A plan invested 65 percent of its assets in real estate. The Labor Department warned it to reduce the investment to 30 percent, or be sued for failing to diversify. When the plan did not comply, suit was filed and the court concluded that the fiduciaries had failed to diversify plan investments. (*Brock v. Citizens Bank of Clovis*)

Risk and Return

"Risk" in investment terms is the likelihood of loss. Generally speaking, the more risky an investment, the greater the return. For example, junk bonds, which are low-quality bonds that were popular as an investment in the 1980s, achieved high rates of return. However, the bonds also carried a high level of risk because of their poor quality. In the recession of the early 1990s, many investors in junk bonds saw their holdings become worthless.

Insurance companies were among those who had invested heavily in junk bonds. Some insurers (Executive Life and Mutual Benefit Life) were in such financial trouble as a result of their junk bond investments that they were taken over and declared insolvent by state insurance regulators. Some of the failed insurers were unable to pay the promised benefits from the guaranteed investment contracts (GICs) and annuities. Fiduciaries who had purchased annuities and GICs from these insurers found themselves being charged with breaches of their duty because they had bought from financially unsound companies.

TYPES OF INVESTMENTS

Generally, plans invest their assets in stocks, bonds, cash, insurance products (such as annuities or guaranteed investment contracts), and real estate. Plan assets are "allocated" among these options according to the need to diversify, the risk and return on the options, the liquidity and cash flow needs of the plan (the liquidity means how easily an investment is converted to cash), and the asset management strategies established by the plan trustees and named fiduciaries.

Stocks or Equity Investments

Equities generally are common or preferred stock. Common stock is a security representing ownership in a company. The stock is accompanied by voting rights for the board of directors of the company and variable dividends. Preferred stock has a fixed dividend rate and a senior claim over common stock if the company were to be liquidated.

Equities are very "volatile," meaning that they are very sensitive to market changes, but generally out-perform bonds and other investments in the long run. Volatility is not the same as "risk," which is the chance of loss. The risk of investing in any particular stock depends on the financial markets, current economics, and the financial health of the company. A company's financial health may be assessed by its annual shareholder report.

Investment managers use several strategies to invest in equities, but usually are more concerned with how the stocks fit into the investment portfolio rather than whether one stock is better than another.

Bonds

A corporate, municipal, government, or government agency bond is a promissory note for an amount to be paid at a certain time and rate. To own a corporate bond is to be owed a debt by the company. This aspect of "debt" is different from corporate "equity," which are essentially entitlements to corporate assets. Bonds are traded on most exchanges or over the counter. If interest rates rise after a bond is bought, then that bond would be sold at a discount. If interest rates fall, then a bond would be sold at a premium.

A number of corporations rate bonds on their investment quality. For example, Standard & Poor's Corporation grades bonds as follows:

- A1+, highest grade;
- A1, high grade;
- A, upper medium grade;
- B1+, medium grade;
- B, speculative;
- C+ and C1, very speculative;
- C, bonds paying no interest, and the best defaulted bonds;
- D1, in default; and
- D, little recoverable value.

Bond portfolios may be "immunized" against interest rate changes by buying long- and short-term bonds. This means that as rates rise, maturing bonds with lower rates may be sold and bonds with higher rates purchased. Bond values are inversely proportional to interest rates, so that as interest rates rise, bond values drop. Bond portfolios also may be "dedicated," where specific bond maturities are matched to particular plan liabilities.

Real Estate

Pension plans may invest in real estate by acquiring actual property, by investing in equities through real estate investment trusts (REITs), or by investing in real estate funds offered by insurance companies. Traded real estate and mortgage-backed securities are the most liquid, while buying whole mortgages, property partnerships, and whole properties are the least liquid. Real estate differs from other investments because each property is unique and ownership rights are not easily divided, information on transactions is not freely available, no national market or exchange exists, compared with stock or bonds markets, and there is no assurance that prices paid reflect fair value.

According to real estate experts, investment in real estate should be coordinated from a strategic plan developed by the plan sponsor, its consultant, and a real estate adviser. The strategic plan should spell out the pension plan's investment criteria and risk tolerance levels, performance goals, and funding requirements. Among the criteria to consider when investing in real estate are diversification of risk, inflation, volatility, total structure of investment portfolio, liquidity, class of property, and geographic location.

Insurance Products

The most popular insured investments are guaranteed investment contracts (GICs). In a GIC, the insurance company issues an annuity contract where the principal and interest payments are guaranteed by the insurer. GIC contracts are nontransferable and often have maturity dates of four years or longer.

GICs gained popularity in the 1980s when used as an option for a tax code Section 401(k) plan because GICs offered higher yields than Treasury securities and were considered very safe. However, the reliance by some insurers on junk bonds and the poor financial condition of other insurers put some GICs into jeopardy. In response, many employers are planning to diversify among GIC issuers when their current contracts expire, rename GICs to be called a fixed income fund, or switch to investments that offer the same yield as GICs, but with less risk. The move to rename GICs stems from confusion caused by the word "guaranteed" in the GIC name. Some plan participants thought that meant they could never suffer losses with a GIC. (Alexander Consulting Group survey, *Defined Contribution Plans and Investment in GICs*)

The Labor Department may exempt a plan sponsor from the prohibited transaction requirements of ERISA to allow the sponsor to advance cash to its pension plan to cover losses from a GIC purchased from a failed insurer.

Cash

Cash or cash equivalents may be kept in plans to meet immediate payment needs. Cash equivalents include bank certificates of deposit, commercial paper, and Treasuries (bills, bonds, and notes). Treasury bills are the safest and most liquid investment next to cash. To be "liquid" means to be easily sold and converted to cash. They are short-term obligations of the U.S. government and are usually issued with maturities of three months, six months, or one year. Treasury bonds and notes are also very liquid government-guaranteed investments.

Mutual Funds

A mutual fund is an investment company that invests assets on behalf of individuals or pension plans. Every fund has an investment objective described in the fund's "prospectus," which is an information document the Securities and Exchange Commission requires be given to investors. A fund's goals may include:

- Stability, where the amount invested is protected from loss;
- Growth, where the value of the amount invested is increased; and
- Income, where a constant flow of income is generated from dividends.

Mutual funds may be attractive to small plans that cannot participate in bank-sponsored pooled investment services. Mutual funds offer plans professional money managers, adherence to defined investment policy, diversification, liquidity, and ease of administration.

A number of kinds of funds are available, including income, growth, balanced, international, municipal bond, corporate bond, and money market funds. The Investment Company Institute, the trade association of mutual funds, divides mutual funds into 22 categories of investment objectives. For pension plans, however, the most common is the balanced fund, which diversifies its investments among common and preferred stocks and corporate bonds.

Mutual funds often charge fees, called "loads."

- A front-load fund charges fees when the securities are bought, and some also charge for reinvesting dividends.
- A back-load fund charges a fee when shares are redeemed, expressed either as a dollar amount or as a percentage of the redemption price.
- A contingent deferred sales charge is a back-load fee charged by some funds when sales are redeemed during the first few years of ownership. This sales charge usually is reduced over a specific period of time (one to six years) and may be expressed as a percentage of the purchase price or the redemption proceeds.
- A no-load fund is one that sells directly to investors for a small fee or no fee. Funds with sales charges, front- or back-loaded, are usually sold by brokers or salespeople.
- A "12b-1 fee" is another fee distinct from loads, named for the Securities and Exchange Commission rule that permits a fund to use up to 1.25 percent of its assets for distribution expenses. These expenses relate to advertising and dealer compensation.

Before investing plan assets in mutual funds, the plan trustees and fiduciaries should look at a fund's prospectus. According to the Investment Company Institute, investors should look for the following information in Part A of the prospectus:

- What is the fund's investment objective and how is it achieved?
- What is the name and address of the investment adviser, and what experience does the adviser have?
- What level of risk is the fund willing to assume in achieving its investment objective?
- What investments will the fund not make (such as real estate)?
- What are the tax consequences of the investment for the shareholder?
- How are the fund shares purchased, and what is the cost of investing?

- What other services are provided, such as automatic reinvestment of dividends?
- How has the fund performed over the last 10 years, as explained in a table called "Per Share Income and Capital Changes"?
- What fees are charged by the fund, and how do they affect earnings over time?

Part B of the prospectus offers additional information on lists of a fund's securities investments, lists of directors and fund officers, information about 5-percent shareholders, and the fund's audited financial statements.

ADMINISTRATION OF INVESTMENTS

Before choosing investment managers and strategies for plan investments, plan trustees and fiduciaries usually identify their policies on investment by answering such questions as the following:

- **What is the purpose of the plan?** All plans exist to pay retirement or health and welfare benefits to participants and beneficiaries. However, some plans—especially public and multiemployer plans—engage in economically targeted or social investing. This means they invest with certain goals in mind, in addition to return on the money. For example, a building trades plan might invest in real estate construction ventures.
- **How will a portfolio be diversified?** Except for limits on employer securities, there are no set limits on how much of a plan may be invested in any one investment vehicle. Instead, ERISA requires only that the assets be invested to minimize the risk of large losses.
- **When will cash be needed to pay out benefits and to pay for plan administration?** Plan cash flow needs vary. Health and welfare plans generally pay out benefits in the same year that contributions are received. Pension plans may receive contributions for 40 years for a participant, before paying out benefits. Cash flow depends on

the type of plan and the relative ages of participants. In one case, for example, an investment company put 70 percent of a plan's assets into long-term government bonds, without taking into account the cash-flow needs of the plan. After having to sell some bonds at a loss to meet cash needs to pay benefits, the investment company was held liable for failing to diversify plan assets. (*GIW Indus. v. Trevor, Stewart, Burton & Jacobson, Inc.*)

- **How will the expected investment return be linked with the plan's funding objectives?** Trying for a maximum return is not always the best policy, according to pension investment experts. If the principal participant in a small defined benefit plan is within five years of retirement, the investment manager may want to move out of equity and into high quality corporate bonds; because the stock market fluctuates so much, the plan could suffer a big loss if it stayed in equities or it could experience a large gain that could result in excise taxes from excess distributions.
- **How much risk is acceptable?** The investment risk and return for a transaction should be examined individually and in the aggregate looking at its effect on the portfolio as a whole.

Whatever investment policy is chosen should be put in writing, to help successor trustees and fiduciaries maintain the policy. Some experts recommend keeping written notes of all meetings and decisions. This paper trail is helpful in reviewing why investment decisions were made and could help in defending against future complaints that fiduciaries breached their responsibility in investment actions.

Asset Allocation

"Asset allocation" is the process of deciding how much of plan assets should be invested in the different types of investments to meet plan objectives. Asset allocation may be one of the chief concerns of plan administrators.

In allocating assets, plans must decide how much risk is tolerable; the investment return over long- and short-term periods; the rates of return adjusted for inflation; the correlation of risk and return of different investments; and changes to the allocation in response to short-term changes in the market.

The major factors affecting the asset allocation decision include the following:

- The time horizon, which is the time from the date of contribution until the benefits are paid out. The horizon for pension plans is longer than for health plans, for example.
- The rate of inflation, as fixed income (bond) investments are very sensitive to interest rate increases.
- Liquidity requirements, as the need for major cash flows must be taken into account.
- Risk tolerance, including financial and "psychological risk." Psychological risk refers to investor reactions to short-term market changes. While most investors recognize that pension plans should be invested for the long run and that equities historically have out-performed bonds and other investments over many years, a temptation of investors is to react to short-term market fluctuations.

Investment Managers

Generally, when plan trustees and fiduciaries choose investment managers, they have already decided on their plan's investment policy, asset allocation, and desired strategies to implement the policy. Because of the cyclical nature of investments, past performance of managers is not a guarantee of future performance. However, data of past performance may be compared with "benchmarks" for that asset class to see if the manager did well because of strategy or whether that class did very well anyway.

A "benchmark," also called an index, is a standard against which to measure investment performance. For example, a benchmark for common stock is the Standard & Poor's (S&P) 500 market index. S&P averages the returns on investment in common stock of the 500 companies in its index. These benchmarks are then compared with the fund's stock performance for a quarter, a year, and 10 years.

REFERENCES

Definition of Plan Assets: 29 C.F.R. 2510.3-101

Investment Managers: ERISA Section 3(38)

Diversification: ERISA Section 404(a)(1)(C)

Reading a Mutual Fund Prospectus: *The Mutual Fund Fact Book,* published annually by the Investment Company Institute, an association of mutual fund companies, Washington, D.C.

Asset Allocation: *Greenwich Report,* a survey of plan administrators published annually by Greenwich Associates, Greenwich, Connecticut.

4

FIDUCIARY DUTIES

Plan fiduciaries must act solely in the interest of plan participants and beneficiaries, for the exclusive purpose of providing benefits to participants and beneficiaries while defraying reasonable plan expenses. Fiduciaries also must (1) act prudently, using the care and skill that an expert would use under similar circumstances; (2) diversify plan investments to minimize large losses; and (3) act according to the plan document, as long as it is consistent with ERISA.

While meeting these requirements, fiduciaries must adhere to the prudence standard—known as the "prudent man" rule. In enforcing the prudent man rule, the Labor Department emphasizes "procedural prudence," which is the process of making certain fiduciary decisions are made in the best interests of participants and beneficiaries, rather than focusing only on the results of decisions. (ERISA Sec. 404(a)(1))

PRUDENT MAN RULE

The prudent man rule of ERISA requires the fiduciary to act with the care, skill, prudence, and diligence under the circumstances that a prudent man acting in a similar capacity and familiar with such matters would use in a similar project with the same goals. (ERISA Sec. 404(a)(1)(B))

Fiduciaries have an active duty under ERISA to understand what is going on. Fiduciaries without sufficient understanding of an area have the responsibility to hire people with the background and experience to give appropriate advice. They cannot blindly follow the advice of advisers, but rather should ask questions, consider the advice, and then act reasonably. (Former Pension and Welfare Benefits Administration administrator Jeffrey Clayton, in speech to International Foundation of Employee Benefit Plans, 1990)

For example, as discussed in Chapter 2, a fiduciary of an employee stock ownership plan (ESOP) was found to have breached his duty of prudence in choosing an investment management company. He chose a company suggested by a co-fiduciary without checking the background of the investment manager or finding out anything about him or the company he managed. The fiduciary delegated the responsibility for investing plan assets to the investment company. However, the company did not meet ERISA's definition of an "investment manager": the company did not acknowledge its fiduciary status in writing and it was not registered as an investment adviser under the Investment Advisors Act of 1940. The ESOP fiduciary and co-fiduciary were found by the courts to be personally and jointly liable for the choice of the manager and the failure to monitor the plan investments made by the manager. (*Whitfield v. Cohen;* see the discussion on "Investment Advisers" in Chapter 2.)

The prudence standard is basically one of "procedural prudence." Procedural prudence emphasizes the process of fiduciary decisions over the results. While no one can predict exactly what investments will out-perform other investments, prudence requirements may be met by a process that requires all investments to be examined for the risk of loss, the opportunity for return, diversification, liquidity, current return, and projected return.

To prove procedural prudence, fiduciaries should document everything, including minutes of all meetings and discussions, the advice received from experts, any legal opinions, deliberations on the advice, and the action eventually taken. Other important documents to be reviewed by fiduciaries include financial statements, auditor reports, administrative management reports on fund operations, and actuarial reports. (Clayton, *supra*)

EXCLUSIVE BENEFIT RULE

Plan fiduciaries must act for the exclusive purpose of providing benefits to participants and beneficiaries. This "exclusive benefit rule," which embodies the duty of loyalty, must be met by ERISA plans and by tax-qualified retirement plans. (ERISA Sec. 404(a)(1)(A))

The exclusive benefit rule of ERISA requires that:

- The cost of plan assets not exceed the fair market value at the time of purchase;
- The return on the investment be a fair one compared with the market rate;
- The plan maintain enough liquidity to pay out benefits; and
- A plan adopt safeguards and diversity of a prudent investor.

Exceptions to the Exclusive Benefit Rule

With a few exceptions, plan assets cannot be used by employers beyond providing benefits to participants and beneficiaries and defraying the reasonable expenses of the plan. (ERISA Sec. 403(c)(2)) The exceptions include:

- A contribution made by mistake of fact by an employer to a single-employer plan, where the contribution is returned within a year of being made.
- A contribution made by mistake of fact or law by an employer to a multiemployer plan, where the contribution is returned within six months of the plan administrator's determination that the contribution was a mistake.

- A contribution conditioned on the initial qualification of the plan may be returned to the employer if the plan receives an adverse determination letter.
- A contribution conditioned on its deductibility to the employer may be returned within one year after the disallowance of the deduction.
- Assets from a terminated welfare plan may be allocated according to the terms of the plan.
- Assets from an underfunded plan terminated by the Pension Benefit Guaranty Corporation (PBGC) go to the PBGC to defray the cost of paying the guaranteed minimum benefits.
- Excess assets from a pension plan may be used to pay current liabilities for retiree health care, under a tax code provision that expires in 1995. (Internal Revenue Code Sec. 420)

Diversification of Plan Assets

ERISA requires plans to diversify plan investments to minimize the risk of large losses, unless under the circumstances it is clearly prudent not to do so. (ERISA Sec. 404(a)(1)(C)) The law does not establish actual percentage limits for plan investments, although some defined contribution plans cannot invest more than 10 percent of plan assets in employer securities. (ERISA Sec. 407 (a)) (For more information, see the discussion in Chapter 3.)

(See Appendix 5 for the text of *Donovan v. Bierwirth*, the seminal case on procedural prudence in plan investments.)

DENIAL OF BENEFITS

A plan administrator denying a claim for benefits is functioning as a fiduciary and must comply with the fiduciary standards mentioned above. In addition to meeting other fiduciary responsibilities, a plan administrator denying a benefit claim must notify the participant of the following information:

- The specific reason for denial;
- The provision of the benefit plan document justifying the denial of benefits;
- A description of the organization's complaint and grievance procedures; and
- Any additional information that the participant must provide the plan when requesting reconsideration of the decision to deny coverage and the reason such information is necessary. (ERISA Sec. 503(*l*))

Strict adherence to these requirements may help a plan fiduciary to avoid liability for punitive damages if the participant alleges that the decision to deny benefits was made in bad faith and this is upheld by a court.

Appeals Procedure

An appeals procedure for every ERISA plan must allow claimants to appeal a denied claim to a designated plan fiduciary. The appeals procedure at a minimum must allow claimants to submit a written appeal of a denied claim to a fiduciary, review pertinent plan documents, and file written comments or explanations of issues. A plan may establish a time limit for appeal of not less than 60 days after a benefit denial. (ERISA Sec. 503(2))

MEDICAL CHILD SUPPORT ORDERS

Plan administrators are acting as fiduciaries when they determine whether an order or decree by a domestic court to cover a child under a group health plan is qualified and should be paid. A qualified medical child support order (QMCSO) is an order that creates or recognizes the existence of an "alternate recipient's" right to receive benefits for which a participant or beneficiary is eligible under a group health plan. An "alternate recipient" means any child of a participant who is recognized under a medical child support order as having a right to enrollment under a group health plan with respect to that participant.

A QMCSO cannot require a plan to offer any benefit or form of benefit not otherwise provided under the plan beyond providing the medical child support. The plan administrator must maintain written procedures on determining the qualified status of orders. At the time an order is received, the administrator must notify the participant and each alternate recipient that the order has been received, determine the qualification of the order within a reasonable time, and then notify the participants and alternate recipients of the determination.

QMCSO provisions were added to ERISA by the Omnibus Budget Reconciliation Act (OBRA) of 1993. (ERISA Sec. 609) ERISA Section 609(a)(6) states: "If a plan fiduciary acts in accordance with part 4 of this subtitle [the fiduciary rules of ERISA] in treating a medical child support order as being (or not being) a qualified medical child support order, then the plan's obligations to the participant and each alternate recipient shall be discharged to the extent of any payment made pursuant to such act of the fiduciary." These provisions were effective August 10, 1993, although plans did not have to be amended to include this information until January 1, 1994.

MEDICARE/MEDICAID COVERAGE DATA BANK

ERISA was amended by OBRA 1993 to require employers and plan administrators to contribute certain group health plan information to a Medicare and Medicaid data bank. This data bank is administered by the Department of Health and Human Services (HHS). ERISA allows small employers (under 50 employees) to have the data furnished by third party administrators or insurers directly to HHS. (ERISA Sec. 101(f)) The disclosure requirements are effective January 1, 1994.

The purposes of the data bank are to identify and collect payments from third parties responsible for payment for health care items and services furnished to Medicare beneficiaries, and to assist in identifying the third parties responsible for the reimbursement of costs incurred by any state plan under Medicaid. Employer-sponsored group health plans generally are primary payers for Medicare and Medicaid. This means that group health plans pay claims first, and any claims amounts unpaid (e.g., for deductibles) may be reimbursed by Medicare or Medicaid.

The type of information that employers must report to the data bank (and that group health plan administrators, plan sponsors, insurers, or other persons must disclose to requesting employers) includes:

- The names and taxpayer identification numbers (TINs) of employees enrolled in the group health plan maintained by one or more employers;
- The type of group health plan coverage (single or family) elected by each employee;
- The name, address, and identifying number of the group health plan elected by the employee;
- The name and TIN of each other individual covered under the group health plan;
- The period during which the coverage is elected; and
- The name, address, and TIN of the employer.

Any plan sponsor, plan administrator, health care provider, insurer, or employer must provide information about participants in group health plans to the data bank. Health care providers or administrators *may* file directly with HHS, rather than going through the employer, but *must* do so for employers with fewer than 50 employees if those employers so request. Information that cannot be disclosed to the data bank includes participant and beneficiary health status, coverage costs, or limitations on coverage specific to individuals. Failure to report to the data bank results in a penalty of $1,000 per violation beginning January 1994.

COURT REVIEW

ERISA allows participants to bring claims disputes to federal court after all possibilities for relief have been exhausted under the plan's appeals process. In *Pilot Life Insurance Co. v. Dedeaux,* the U. S. Supreme Court held that ERISA is the exclusive remedy for participants seeking redress for the denial of benefits under an ERISA-covered plan. The Court held that all state law causes of action are preempted.

Case precedent or "common law" generally requires that federal courts adhere to a particular "standard of review" for cases involving ERISA plan benefit denial. Until the Supreme Court's 1989 ruling in *Firestone Tire & Rubber Co. v. Bruch,* courts generally used the "arbitrary and capricious" standard of review. In *Firestone,* however, the Court said review under the de novo standard was appropriate, except in cases where the plan document grants to the administrator discretionary decision-making authority. In such cases, an "abuse of discretion" standard is applied.

The de novo standard allows the court to review a benefits claim dispute "from the beginning," as if no decision had been made yet. The court decides the dispute based on the merits of each side's argument, rather than only reviewing whether someone else's decision was "arbitrary and capricious."

The arbitrary and capricious standard, which is now referred to as the abuse of discretion standard, allows the court to defer to the administrator's denial of benefits as long as there is a reasonable basis for such decision. The courts look at whether the fiduciary acted reasonably and rationally, fraudulently or in bad faith, under the plan terms and ERISA, or based on substantial evidence.

PROXY VOTING BY PLAN FIDUCIARIES

The voting of common stock held by the plan is a fiduciary function subject to the fiduciary provisions of ERISA. Fiduciaries must exercise the right to vote proxies for the benefit of plan participants. As in other areas, the responsible fiduciary should investigate where the plan's interests lie, analyze the risks and rewards of alternative actions relative to those interests, and act accordingly. (Letter from Alan D. Lebowitz, deputy assistant secretary, Labor Department, to Avon Products, Inc., Feb. 23, 1988; see Appendix 6)

Companies that issue the stock in which the plan invests hold annual stockholders meetings. At those meetings, stockholders vote on a board of directors for the company and major decisions affecting the value of the stock. Although some stockholders attend the annual meeting in person, many vote by "proxy." A proxy is a piece of paper stating the number of shares owned and the number of votes available to the owner of the stock. The proxy usually is mailed to an independent third party (such as an accounting firm) that is responsible for counting the votes.

The plan trustees usually have the authority to vote the stock. When the trustees are subject to the nontrustee named fiduciary, then the named fiduciary votes the stock. Where the named fiduciary has delegated responsibilities to an investment manager (ERISA Sec. 403), the investment manager makes the proxy voting decision. Some plan fiduciaries have been aggressive in voting the proxies, for example, supporting attempts to limit "excessive" executive compensation or fighting antitakeover proposals for companies that are takeover targets.

PARTICIPANT-DIRECTED ACCOUNTS

A plan fiduciary generally is not liable for losses relating to investments made by participants in participant-directed individual account plans under ERISA Section 404(c). However, the choice of investments made available to plan participants is a fiduciary decision.

To comply with ERISA Section 404(c), plans must meet very specific disclosure requirements concerning information that must be provided automatically to plan participants and information that must be provided upon request. Compliance with Section 404(c) is optional and plans that do not comply do not violate ERISA. However, noncompliance means that plan fiduciaries continue to be responsible under the law for participant-directed investments.

A final rule (DOL Regulation, 29 C.F.R. 2550.404c) effective for plan years beginning January 1, 1994, spells out the Section 404(c) requirements. The final rule requires plans to offer participants a broad range of investment alternatives, which give the participants the opportunity to:

- Affect substantially the potential return on those assets;
- Choose from at least three investment alternatives, each of which is diversified and has materially different risk and return characteristics; and
- Diversify investments to minimize the risk of large losses.

Plans may impose reasonable restrictions on the frequency with which participants may give investment instructions. However, participants must be permitted to give instructions with a frequency that is appropriate in light of the market volatility of the investments. The opportunity to direct investments must be available at least as frequently as once within any three-month period.

Employers must provide participants with a description of confidentiality procedures and the identity of the fiduciary responsible for monitoring compliance, especially when employer securities are one of the investment options.

Participants must have information to make informed investment decisions. Information that must be furnished automatically to participants includes:

- An explanation that the plan is intended to be an ERISA Section 404(c) plan and that fiduciaries may be relieved of liability for any losses that are the result of participant investment instructions;
- A description of the investment alternatives available under the plan and, with respect to each designated investment alternative, a general description of the investment objectives and risk return characteristics of the alternative;
- Identification of any designated investment manager;
- An explanation of the circumstance under which participants may give investment instructions and an explanation of any specified limitations on such instructions;
- A description of any transaction fees and expenses that affect the participant's account balance in connection with the purchase or sale of interests in an investment alternative;

- Identification of the plan fiduciary who is responsible for providing disclosure information on request and description of the information that is available on request; and
- A description of the confidentiality procedures and the identification of the fiduciary responsible for monitoring compliance with those procedures, in the case of a plan that offers investments in employer securities.

Optional information, or information to be furnished only on request includes:

- A description of the annual operating expenses of a designated investment alternative that reduces the rate of return and the aggregate amount of such expenses expressed as a percentage of average net assets;
- A list of assets comprising the portfolio of designated investment alternatives that constitute plan assets and the value of each asset;
- Information concerning the value of shares or units in designated investment alternatives, as well as the past and current investment performance of the alternative, determined on a reasonable and consistent basis; and
- Information concerning the value of interest in designated investment alternatives held in the account of the participant.

(See Appendix 7 for an analysis of ERISA Sec. 404(c).)

OTHER FIDUCIARY CONCERNS

ERISA provides guidance on other fiduciary issues such as a prohibition on "exculpatory" provisions, permission to obtain fiduciary liability insurance, requirements for bonding, indemnification insurance, and the statute of limitations relating to breach of fiduciary duty.

Exculpatory Provisions

Plan provisions that seek to "exculpate" or free plan fiduciaries from responsibility or liability are void under ERISA as being against public policy. However, plan provisions that allocate responsibilities among named fiduciaries or delegate responsibility to investment managers are not treated as exculpatory provisions. (ERISA Sec. 410(a))

Fiduciary Liability Insurance

An employer may purchase insurance for its fiduciaries or for itself to cover liability or losses occurring from the act or omission of a fiduciary, as long as the insurance permits recourse by the insurer against the fiduciary in the case of a breach of duty. Fiduciaries may purchase insurance to cover their own liability, as may employers or unions to cover potential liability of fiduciaries. (ERISA Sec. 410(b))

Bonding

Every fiduciary and every person who handles funds or other plan property must be bonded. (ERISA Sec. 412) Called "fidelity bonds," these bonds protect the plan against fraud and dishonesty by employees. The bond may name specific individuals or may be a blanket bond covering plan officials and employees in general. A plan official required to be bonded violates ERISA by receiving, handling, disbursing, or otherwise controlling or taking custody of employee benefit funds without the proper bond. The bonding trigger of a person handling plan funds includes:

- Physical contact with plan property or funds, except when these duties are performed by persons under close supervision;
- The opportunity to obtain physical possession of property;
- The power to transfer plan property to oneself or a third party;
- The power to disburse plan funds and sign checks; and
- Supervisory or managerial control over persons who obtain, transfer, and disburse plan assets.

The bond must provide for recovery by the plan even if the individuals acting fraudulently or dishonestly do not gain from their acts nor are subject to criminal punishment. Bond amounts are set at 10 percent of the money handled for the plan during the previous year, with a minimum of $1,000 and a maximum of $500,000. A bond may be purchased with plan assets, but not by a party in interest, except for an insurer who provides other insurance to the plan.

No bonding is required for plans where the only assets from which benefits are paid are the general assets of the employer. Banks, trust companies, and insurers that meet certain capitalization requirements and that are bonded under state law also may be exempt from fiduciary bonding requirements.

Indemnification

As with exculpatory provisions, plans cannot indemnify fiduciaries against breach of fiduciary duty. (ERISA Sec. 410(a)) However, a plan may purchase insurance covering itself or fiduciaries from fiduciary liability and may pay all reasonable costs incurred by fiduciaries in litigation or settlement, as long as the fiduciaries did not breach their duty. One court prohibited a plan from paying the fiduciary's legal fees where the fiduciary was acquitted of criminal charges but was found to have civil liability resulting from a breach of duty.

Statute of Limitations

ERISA Section 413 limits the time period during which actions may be taken against fiduciaries who breached their duty to the earlier of:

- Six years after the date the breach occurred or, in the case of an omission, the latest date the breach could have been cured; or
- Three years after the earliest date on which the plaintiff had actual knowledge of the breach.

In the case of fraud or concealment, however, action is limited to six years after the date of discovery of the breach or violation.

Indicia of Ownership

ERISA Section 404(b) prohibits fiduciaries from moving the "indicia of ownership" of plan assets outside the jurisdiction of the U.S. district courts, except as authorized by Labor Department regulations. These regulations offer exceptions for certain foreign securities and currency managed and controlled by U.S. banks, insurance companies, or investment advisers.

MULTIEMPLOYER PLANS

Multiemployer plan fiduciaries must meet the same requirements as fiduciaries of single-employer plans. In addition, however, the collection of employer contributions is also held to be the responsibility of plan fiduciaries. This collection may take the form of requests by letter, employer audits, or taking of legal action. This Section expands on the fiduciary duty concepts explained earlier in this chapter by showing particular concerns of multiemployer plans.

"Multiemployer plans" generally are collectively bargained pension or health and welfare plans where more than one employer contributes to a plan maintained by a union or industry. Also known as Taft-Hartley trusts, the plans are characterized by a joint board of trustees—that is, equal numbers of trustees appointed by management and by the union. When serving as trustees, both union and management representatives must be sure to wear their "fiduciary hats" and to make sure they are acting in the best interests of participants and beneficiaries, rather than in the interests of the employers or unions. Taft-Hartley trustees are named fiduciaries.

Collection of Contributions

ERISA Section 515 requires employers to make contributions to multiemployer plans under the terms of the plan or of the collective bargaining agreement. A failure to collect contributions was treated as a prohibited transaction for extending credit to a party in interest and for failing the exclusive benefit requirement.

In 1976, however, the Labor Department issued a final class exemption from the prohibited transaction requirements—PTE 76-1—exempting the employer's failure to make the contribution or the trustees' failure to collect the entire contribution. To be eligible for the class exemption, a plan must establish a written procedure for collecting delinquent contributions.

The written procedure must expressly state the plan's policy of collecting employer contributions in a systematic and reasonable manner. The policy may state that if contributions are not received by the due date, the plan administrator will send the employer a letter reminding it of its obligations.

Follow-up letters may warn of impending legal action if contributions are not made. The trustees may request an audit of employers to ensure that the proper amount of contributions are made to the plan. Finally, trustees may sue employers to be awarded delinquent contributions, attorneys' fees, interest, and damages.

For the trustees to accept employers' contributions and pay out benefits, the Taft-Hartley Act requires employers to have a written collective bargaining agreement between the employer and the plan. The agreement must include the rate of contribution that employers pay, how the contributions are computed (such as a percentage of hours worked), and how the contributions are to be collected. (*Moglia v. Geoghegan*)

REFERENCES

Prudent Man Rule: ERISA Section 404(a)(1)(B)

Procedural Prudence: Jeffrey Clayton, of Callister, Duncan & Nebeker, Salt Lake City, and former Pension and Welfare Benefits Administration administrator, speech to International Foundation of Employee Benefit Plans, Oct. 1990.

Exclusive Benefit Rule: ERISA Section 404(a)(1)(A)

Exceptions: ERISA Section 403(c)(2)

Diversification: ERISA Section 404(a)(1)(C)

Employer Securities: ERISA Section 407(a)

Benefit Denial Procedure: ERISA Section 503(1)

Denial Appeals Procedure: ERISA Section 503(2)

Qualified Child Medical Support Orders: ERISA Section 609, as added by the Omnibus Budget Reconciliation Act (OBRA) of 1993, Section 4301(a)

Medicare Data Bank: ERISA Section 101(f), as amended by the OBRA 1993 Section 13581

Proxy Voting: Letter from Alan D. Lebowitz, deputy assistant secretary, Labor Department, to Avon Products Inc., February 23, 1988. (See Appendix 6 for the full text of the letter.)

Relief From Liability Under Participant-Directed Accounts: ERISA Section 404(c)

Allocation of Responsibility: ERISA Section 410(a)

Fiduciary Liability: ERISA Section 410(b)

Bonding: ERISA Section 412

Indemnification: ERISA Section 410(a)

Indicia of Ownership: ERISA Section 404(b)

Collection of Contributions: ERISA Section 515

5

PROHIBITED TRANSACTIONS

ERISA Section 406 specifically prohibits certain transactions, known as "prohibited transactions," between plans and "parties in interest." Parties in interest include fiduciaries, employer or union plan sponsors, participants and beneficiaries, people who provide services to plans, and their relatives. Prohibited transactions include:

- The sale, exchange, or lease of property;
- The lending of money or extending of credit;
- The furnishing of goods, services, or facilities; or
- The acquisition of too much employer stock or other securities.

If a party in interest enters into a prohibited transaction with a plan, the party in interest is assessed with civil and tax penalties of 5 percent of the amount of the transaction. The tax rises to 100 percent if the transaction is not corrected.

ERISA Section 408 offers statutory exemptions to the prohibited transaction rules. In addition, the Labor Department exempts certain classes of entities—usually relating to plan investments—

and individual parties in interest upon application. The Labor Department enforces the prohibited transaction rules, but coordinates with the Internal Revenue Service for assessment of tax penalties on those transactions.

Plan fiduciaries, who manage and control plan assets, must avoid causing those plans over which they have fiduciary responsibility from entering into prohibited transactions. (See Chapter 2 for a discussion of who is a plan fiduciary.)

PARTY IN INTEREST

ERISA Section 3(18) defines who is a party in interest for purposes of the prohibited transaction rules. A similar concept appears in the Internal Revenue Code (IRC) Section 4975 under "disqualified persons." The definitions differ slightly, and transactions between plans and disqualified persons are subject to significant excise taxes. Transactions between plans and parties in interest also may be subject to Labor Department penalties if the party in interest knew or should have known that the transaction was prohibited; however, those penalties may be offset by the excise taxes.

ERISA's Definition

ERISA Section 3(18) defines a party in interest to a plan as the following:

- A) Any fiduciary (including, but not limited to, any administrator, officer, trustee, or custodian), counsel, or employee of the plan;
- B) A service provider to the plan;
- C) An employer whose employees are covered by the plan;
- D) An employee organization (union) whose members are covered by the plan;
- E) A direct or indirect owner of 50 percent of:
  - 1) the combined voting power of all the voting stock or the value of all stock in the corporation;

2) the capital interest or the profits interest of a partnership; or
3) the beneficial interest of a trust or unincorporated enterprise, which is an employer whose employees are covered by the plan or an employee organization whose members are covered by the plan;

F) A linear relative, which is a spouse, grandparent, child, or child's spouse (but not brother, sister, or brother- or sister-in-law) of the above-described fiduciaries, service providers, employers, or 50-percent owners;
G) A corporation, partnership, or trust which is 50-percent or more owned by fiduciaries, service providers, employers, unions, or 50-percent owners of the stock or capital.
H) An employee, officer, director (or an individual having powers similar to those of officers or directors), or a 10-percent or more shareholder, of a service provider, employer, union, or 50-percent owners (individuals or organizations); or
I) A 10-percent or more partner or joint venturer of a service provider, employer, union, or 50-percent owner (individual or organizations).

Disqualified Person

The excise tax provisions of the tax code use the term "disqualified person" rather than party in interest. (IRC Sec. 4975) The tax code definition differs from the ERISA party in interest in that a fiduciary acting in a fiduciary capacity is not a disqualified person in a prohibited transaction, and therefore not subject to excise taxes.

A nonfiduciary disqualified person who participates in a prohibited transaction is subject to the excise tax. Under ERISA, a party in interest—fiduciary or not—is liable for penalties if the party in interest knew or should have known the transaction was prohibited. The tax code does not include this "knowledge" test.

(See Appendix 3 for excerpts of the tax code relating to prohibited transactions.)

PROHIBITED TRANSACTIONS

ERISA Section 406(a) prohibits a plan fiduciary from entering into a transaction that is a direct or indirect:

- Sale or exchange, or leasing, of any property between a plan and a party in interest;
- Lending of money or extension of credit between the plan and a party in interest;
- Furnishing of goods, services, or facilities between the plan and a party in interest;
- Transfer to, or use by or for the benefit of, a party in interest, of any plan assets; or
- Acquisition, on behalf of the plan, from a party in interest.

These prohibitions are discussed below. ERISA Section 406(b) adds further fiduciary prohibitions:

- Self-dealing with plan assets;
- Representing interests other than those of participants and beneficiaries; and
- Receiving any consideration from any party dealing with the plan in transactions using plan assets.

ERISA Section 407(a) places strict requirements on how much and what type of employer stock can be bought and held by plans. Violating these requirements is a prohibited transaction.

ERISA Section 407(b) restricts the amount and type of real property that plans purchase and lease to their plan sponsors. Violating these restrictions is a prohibited transaction.

Sale, Exchange, or Lease

ERISA provides that the sale, exchange, or lease of property between a plan and a party in interest is a prohibited transaction. As noted above, it is possible to be exempted from a transaction on individual application. For example, the Labor Department issued an individual prohibited transaction exemption for the cash sale of a vacant lot owned by an individual retirement account (IRA) to a disqualified person with respect to the IRA.

The exemption was issued because the sale was made at a price the plan would have received in an "arm's-length transaction," which means a transaction between two unrelated parties.

In addition to the typical concept of sale, a transfer of real or personal property by a party in interest to a plan will be treated as a sale or exchange if the property is subject to a mortgage or similar lien that the plan assumes or if it was placed on the property within a 10-year period ending on the date of the transfer. (IRC Sec. 4975(c)(1)(A))

A contribution of real or personal property to a plan may or may not be a prohibited transaction. According to the U.S. Supreme Court, if the contribution is made to satisfy a plan funding obligation, then the transaction is prohibited because the contribution is the economic equivalent of a sale or exchange. (*Commissioner v. Keystone Consol. Indus.*)

However, if the contribution is voluntary (meaning that it is not made to satisfy a plan funding obligation), then the contribution is not a prohibited transaction unless mortgaged properties are involved. (IRC Sec. 4975(f)(3))

Loans

Generally, the prohibited transaction rules forbid plans from extending credit or making loans to parties in interest. For example, a profit-sharing plan trustee and administrator were found to have violated both their fiduciary duties and prohibited transaction provisions by failing to collect loans long in default, by causing the plan to loan to the trustee sums exceeding allowable amounts and time limits, by failing to recover benefit overpayments, and by causing the plan to transfer assets to the bankrupt plan sponsor. (*Brock v. Ardito*)

However, an exception explained in a Labor Department regulation (29 C.F.R. 2550.408b-1) permits plans to make loans to plan participants if the following conditions are satisfied:

- The plan makes loans available to all participants and beneficiaries on a reasonably equivalent basis;
- The loans are not made to highly compensated employees in amounts greater than the amounts available to other employees;

- The loans are made in accordance with specific provisions set forth in the plan document;
- The loans bear a reasonable rate of interest; and
- The loans are adequately secured.

The conditions for plan loans are contained in final regulations issued by the Labor Department. Under these rules, loans made or renewed after October 18, 1989, must be made available to plan participants without regard to an individual's race, color, religion, age, sex, or national origin. The plan's approval of loan applications should be based on the type of factors normally considered by a commercial lender in the business of making similar loans.

Plans may establish loan minimums, but otherwise cannot unreasonably withhold loans from any participant. For example, a physician and an associate were the only participants in a pension plan sponsored by a corporation of which the physician was the sole owner and president. Over a period of years, the plan made substantial loans to the physician, all at a 10 percent annual interest rate. The plan made no loans to the associate, but the physician did make personal loans to the associate bearing a 12 percent interest rate. Based on these facts, a federal tax court ruled that the plan had unreasonably withheld loans from a participant in violation of the rules governing participant loans. (*Kadivar v. Commissioner*)

Provision of Goods, Services, or Facilities

ERISA Section 406(a)(1)(C) prohibits the furnishing of goods, services, or facilities between a plan and a party in interest. This prohibition does not pertain, however, to a contract or reasonable arrangement with a party in interest for office space or for services necessary for the plan. This exemption in ERISA Section 408(b)(2) requires that:

- The office space or service be necessary for the establishment or operation of the plan;
- The office space or service be furnished under a reasonable contract or arrangement; and

- The plan pay no more than reasonable compensation for the office space or services.

For example, a court found that trustees of a construction trade pension fund did not violate the prohibited transaction provisions by constructing a building (employing actual fund participants) with the intention of landing the participating union as the major tenant, and by entering into a lease arrangement with the union. The trustees met the exemption because the arrangement ensured the plan received reasonable compensation for the lease, could terminate the lease on short notice, and maintained records to verify compliance. (*Donovan v. Walton*)

A contract may be reasonable if it allows the plan to cancel without penalty on reasonably short notice. Such cancellation privileges prevent the plan from being locked into a disadvantageous arrangement. A provision in the contract that reasonably compensates the service provider or lessor for loss upon early termination is not a penalty.

Also, a party in interest may receive reasonable compensation for services to the plan, unless that person is already receiving full-time pay from the plan sponsor. For instance, trustees of collectively bargained pension and welfare plans were receiving full-time pay from contributing employers and unions. These trustees committed prohibited transactions diverting plan assets to parties in interest and self-dealing because they authorized for each other monthly payments from plan assets as compensation for their services as trustees, a court found. In addition, they authorized the plans to make contributions on their behalf so as to make each other eligible for the receipt of plan benefits. (*Donovan v. Daugherty*)

The exemption for the provision of services or office space does not apply where the plan fiduciaries do not act solely in the interest of participants and beneficiaries. If a fiduciary uses influence or control of plan assets to cause the plan to pay additional fees to the fiduciary, then even if a second fiduciary has approved the transaction, the fiduciary has committed a prohibited transaction. For example, a company manager was a fiduciary of the company pension plan. He hired his son to provide for a fee various administrative services necessary for the operation of the plan. Even if the provision of services was exempt, the father committed a prohibited transaction. The son is a person in whom the father had an interest, which could affect the father's judgment as a fiduciary. (29 C.F.R. Sec. 2250.408(b)-2(f), Example 6)

Transfer of Assets

ERISA prohibits plan assets or income from being transferred to or used by a party in interest. For example, a pension plan fiduciary violated ERISA's fiduciary duties and prohibited transaction provisions by using plan assets to further his own corporate expansion goals. The fiduciary failed to reexamine or independently examine further investment in a target corporation before liquidating the plan's portfolio to buy the target's stock. The fiduciary violated ERISA by using plan assets to benefit himself and an affiliated company that was also a party in interest. (*Sandoval v. Simmons*)

EMPLOYER SECURITIES AND REAL PROPERTY

ERISA Section 407(a) allows plans to acquire and hold only "qualified employer securities." Fiduciaries who cause a plan to buy and hold nonqualifying employer securities commit prohibited transactions. The amount of qualifying employer securities and real property that may be held by the plan differs depending on the type of plan.

Defined benefit plans and "hybrid plans" are limited to holding qualifying employer securities and real property equaling 10 percent of the fair market value of plan assets. Hybrid plans, which have features that resemble both defined contribution and defined benefit plans, are not treated as defined contribution plans for the purposes of these limits. The 10 percent limit does not apply to defined contribution plans—also known as individual account plans—such as stock bonus, profit-sharing, and employee stock ownership plans (ESOPs).

The term "qualifying employer real property" means parcels (there must be more than one) of employer real property dispersed geographically, suitable (or adaptable without excessive cost) for more than one use. The plan owns the properties and leases them back to the employer or an affiliate of the employer. Qualifying employer real property must be more than one parcel (ERISA Advisory Opinion Letter 77-16).

The term "qualifying employer security" means employer stock or marketable obligations, or an interest in a publicly traded partnership existing in 1987. An employer security includes stock, bonds, debentures, subscription rights, and warrants. (ERISA Sec. 407(d)(1))

The tax code Section 4975 does not impose an excise tax on the prohibited transaction of acquiring and holding nonqualified employer securities and real property. However, excise taxes could be imposed on other prohibited transactions relating to the acquisition of employer securities and real property. Such transactions might include purchase from a party in interest or extension of credit (see above).

Qualifying employer securities must be marketable obligations. Nonmarketable stock is qualifying only for "eligible" individual account plans. Eligible individual account plans include profit-sharing, stock bonus, thrift, savings, and employer stock ownership plans (ESOPs).

The eligible plans must explicitly provide for the acquisition and holding of qualified employer securities and real property. While eligible individual account plans do not have to meet ERISA's diversification rules, fiduciaries still must be prudent overall.

Adequate Consideration

The fiduciary rules require that adequate consideration be paid for plan purchase of employer securities and real property. Without such a rule, the plans could be taken advantage of by selling a property for less than its worth or by paying too much when buying a property, compared with transactions where the seller or buyer is an unrelated third party. (ERISA Sec. 3(18)) This provision on adequate consideration applies whether the plan is investing in only a few shares or is an ESOP investing primarily in employer securities. Fiduciaries can meet their burden of proving that they purchased employer stock for adequate consideration by showing that they arrived at their determination of fair market value by way of a prudent investigation into the circumstances then prevailing.

For example, ESOP fiduciaries were found to have breached their duties since they were unable to establish that they paid adequate consideration for employer stock. The fiduciaries failed to conduct a sufficient investigation to determine whether past appraisal of employer stock remained a reasonable approximation of fair market value, since two critical assumptions made by the appraisal—the employer's growth projection and absence of an ESOP—were no longer valid at the time of their decision. (*Donovan v. Cunningham*)

In a more recent case, *Reich v. Valley Nat'l Bank of Ariz.*, a district court agreed with the Labor Department that the trustee of an ESOP breached its fiduciary duty by causing the plan to buy stock in the employer without determining the fair market value of the stock and without conducting a good faith independent investigation of the leveraged buyout. The court granted summary judgment to the Labor Department and awarded damages of $17.5 million to the department for the benefit of participants and beneficiaries.

The court found that the bank trustees did not understand the complicated leveraged buyout transaction and did not assess the transaction independently. This assessment should have covered the employer's ability to meet its debt payments in the face of increased competition and declining sales, the court said. The bank trustees relied upon a financial report prepared by management. Another department in the same bank had declined to participate as an investor in the buyout because that department did not believe the employer had the cash flow to repay the debt. That department apparently did not communicate its concerns to the trust department.

In the buyout, the ESOP paid $5.92 per share for 6 million shares of class A stock, for a total investment of $35.5 million. Non-management, management, and outside investors bought lower classes of stock for $1.125 per share. The employer paid $17.5 million in contributions to the ESOP until declaring bankruptcy. During these proceedings, the ESOP sold its employer stock to an outside investor for $250,000 under a Bankruptcy Court order.

The Labor Department alleged that the bank trustee had caused the ESOP to engage in prohibited transactions by causing the plan to purchase employer stock for more than adequate consideration. The trustee failed to conduct an independent, good faith inquiry and therefore the plan did not pay fair market value for the stock, and suffered a $17.5 million loss.

An analysis of the decision published by *BNA's Tax Management* made the following suggestions for fiduciaries considering investments in privately held companies:

- Conduct a diligent, independent investigation of the company, including a visit to company premises, a review of relevant corporate governance documents and management interviews.
- Hire outside advisors rather than accepting advisors picked by management.
- Participate in the price and terms negotiation rather than relying on advisors to negotiate.
- Have, or obtain, the experience and knowledge to understand the nature of the investment.
- Analyze the terms of the ESOP loan and other financing arrangements independently from the management analysis.
- Scrutinize and question the work and conclusions drawn by advisors.
- Furnish any relevant information to the advisors.
- Investigate the solvency of the corporation.
- Do not reject a potential independent advisor because of anticipated difficulties in negotiations, because to do so may predispose that a deal would be accepted as presented by management.

ENFORCEMENT

ERISA is enforced by three agencies: the Labor Department, the Internal Revenue Service (IRS), and the Pension Benefit Guaranty Corporation (PBGC). Plan information is reported to these agencies on a combined Form 5500, but enforcement of ERISA compliance is left to each agency. All three agencies use plan audits as their primary enforcement tool.

IRS has the primary responsibility for enforcing the Title II provisions of ERISA: minimum participation, vesting, distributions, and funding rules of qualified plans. It also assesses excise taxes and penalties on ERISA violations. IRS examines plans' operational compliance and offers several programs to correct defects without disqualifying plans.

The Labor Department enforces the Title I provisions of ERISA, which include reporting information to the federal government, disclosing plan information to participants and beneficiaries, prohibited transactions, and fiduciary responsibility. The department's Pension and Welfare Benefits Administration (PWBA) targets its enforcement to compensation paid to plan service providers, such as third party administrators or insurance brokers, and on financial institutions that offer multiple services to plans.

The PBGC enforces the Title IV provisions of ERISA, which require defined benefit plans sponsored by single and multiple employers to pay premiums for termination insurance. PBGC guarantees a basic level of benefits to participants should a plan terminate with insufficient assets to pay its benefits liabilities. PBGC audits terminated plans to ensure that proper benefit levels were paid to participants and ongoing plans to ensure proper premium payments.

Labor Department Enforcement

The Labor Department's PWBA has a field investigative staff of several hundred people to investigate hundreds of thousands of retirement plans. PWBA directs its limited resources at areas found to have the most potential for abuse: providers of services to plans (such as accounting, actuarial, legal, investment, and insurance services) and financial institutions that provide multiple services to plans (such as banking, custodial, investment management, and trustee services).

This type of enforcement is known as "targeted enforcement." Generally targeted enforcement leads to "limited review" cases, where investigators audit plans only for a specific violation. The information sources for the targeted enforcement include:

- Review and analysis of the Form 5500;
- Prohibited transaction exemption applications, complaints under the civil enforcement provisions of ERISA, and internal PWBA sources;
- Other agencies, including IRS, the Securities and Exchange Commission, and state insurance commissions;
- Nongovernment sources, such as newspapers, industrial journals, and leads from knowledgeable sources; and
- Complaints from participants, fiduciaries, and informants.

PWBA develops compilations of selected plans or service providers using the sources above. To obtain additional information, before opening a limited review case, PWBA area offices may send out "inquiry letters" to plan officials or service providers. These letters may request additional information, but may not violate the Paperwork Reduction Act.

Limited Review Cases

After a limited review case is opened, the field office may send detailed inquiry letters to plan officials or service providers. These detailed letters may request much more information than the other inquiry letters because they are not subject to the Paperwork Reduction Act.

Limited review cases inquire into one or more specific issues or aspects of the plan or service provider operations. The review allows the investigators to explore specific matters quickly to see if fiduciary investigations are warranted. Except for stating that the purpose of the limited review is to determine whether a violation of ERISA Title I has or is about to occur, PWBA's policy is to not inform the plan officials or providers as to the basis of its investigations.

In addition to inquiry letters, the investigators conducting the limited review examine reports and returns filed with the national office, exemption application files, advisory opinion letters, and Solicitor of Labor information. These cases may be resolved in three ways:

- No violation found. The PWBA area director sends a letter to the plan or service provider noting that no violations have been found. The case is then closed.
- Violations are found and corrections requested. The PWBA sends a letter to the plan or provider with the requested corrections. The case may be recharacterized as a fiduciary duty case, with the department launching into a full plan audit (see "Full Investigation," below) and sharing the information with IRS for the assessment of penalties.
- Apparent criminal violations are found. The PWBA sends a letter noting the civil violations and requesting correction, recharacterizes the case as a fiduciary duty case as above, and then refers the criminal violations to the Department of Justice.

Full Investigation

In the full plan investigation, PWBA investigators examine and verify employee benefit plan financial activity, including review of contributions, investment income, other income and assets, accounts payable and accrued liabilities, benefit payments and related disbursements, and administrative expenses. The investigators look over canceled checks for proper signatures and endorsements. They also analyze disbursements to affiliated organizations, with particular emphasis on transfers of funds to plan sponsors.

In checking whether fiduciaries are properly bonded, investigators examine surety bonds and schedules of names, positions covered, and the amount of coverage. They compare this information with trust records to determine who handles plan assets, and then develop a "bonding computation" of assets, receipts, and disposals for the beginning and ending of each fiscal period.

Other areas covered in a full investigation are actuarial considerations, insurance information in fully insured plans, funding agents for defined contribution plans, custodial accounts, deficient or delinquent reporting, disclosure to participants, and benefit claims disputes.

Agency Coordination

PWBA coordinates in enforcement with IRS and other agencies. PWBA completes a checklist for IRS when a violation may result in excise taxes or penalties. IRS in turn refers information to PWBA when its own examinations turn up prohibited transaction or fiduciary violations.

In addition to IRS, PWBA has information-sharing agreements with the PBGC, Department of Justice, Office of Inspector General, Office of Labor Racketeering, Federal Reserve Board, Federal Deposit Insurance Corporation, and other federal financial regulatory authorities.

PENALTIES

IRS taxes disqualified persons engaging in prohibited transactions, based on the amounts involved in the transaction. The excise tax is in two levels, with the higher level triggered only if the transaction remains uncorrected.

The Labor Department may impose civil and criminal penalties on parties in interest involved in prohibited transactions. These penalties may be waived or reduced by the amount of excise taxes assessed by the IRS.

Some plans, such as individual retirement accounts, may be disqualified for engaging in prohibited transactions. The consequence of disqualification is that contributions are no longer deductible and plan benefits are taxed in current income. Disqualification is such a harsh penalty, with individual participants being penalized for actions of the fiduciaries, that IRS uses disqualification only as a last resort.

IRS Excise Taxes

The IRS imposes two tiers of excise taxes on disqualified persons engaging in prohibited transactions. The first tier is 5 percent of the "amount involved" in the transaction. If the transaction is not "corrected" within the "taxable period," IRS assesses a second tier of tax equal to 100 percent of the amount involved. Both tiers of taxes are to be paid by any disqualified persons who committed the prohibited transaction. However, if a fiduciary was acting solely in the capacity of a fiduciary, then the fiduciary is not liable for either tier of the excise tax.

The "amount involved" in a prohibited transaction, except for service providers, is the amount of money and the fair market value of the property given or received. In the case of service providers, the amount involved is equal to the excess compensation received.

To "correct" a transaction means to undo it to the extent possible, and to put the plan in a financial position that is as good as it would have been had the disqualified person acted under the highest fiduciary standards.

The "taxable period" is the period that begins on the date the prohibited transaction occurs and ends on the earliest of:

- The date IRS mails a notice of tax deficiency;
- The date on which the excise tax is assessed; or
- The date on which correction of the prohibited transaction is completed.

Civil Penalty

In addition to the tax penalty, ERISA allows the Labor Department to assess both civil and criminal penalties for violation of the fiduciary rules, including the prohibited transaction rules. The civil penalty for prohibited transactions for welfare plans mirrors the penalty of the excise tax imposed on retirement plans. The department may assess the party in interest a penalty of 5 percent of the amount involved (see "IRS Excise Taxes," above). If the transaction is not corrected within 90 days from the date the 5 percent penalty was assessed, then the penalty rises to 100 percent of the amount involved.

A different civil penalty may be assessed on fiduciaries or co-fiduciaries for breaches of their fiduciary duty. This penalty is equal to 20 percent of the amount recovered from the fiduciary as the result of a court order or settlement agreement with the department. The Labor Department may waive or reduce the penalty if the department determines that a fiduciary acted reasonably and in good faith or that the fiduciary could not restore all plan losses without severe financial hardship. This penalty on fiduciaries may be reduced by other civil penalties or by any excise taxes imposed for violation of the prohibited transaction rules.

Criminal Penalty

Any person who willfully violates any ERISA provision relating to the filing of annual reports, such as failing to describe on Form 5500 prohibited transactions entered into, may be convicted of a criminal offense. The penalties for an individual criminal conviction are $5,000, or one year's imprisonment, or both. The penalty for a conviction of an entity, such as a company or a union, is a fine of up to $100,000.

REFERENCES

Prohibited Transactions: ERISA Section 406

Party In Interest: ERISA Section 3(18)

Disqualified Person: IRC Section 4975

Adequate Consideration: ERISA Section 3(18); Analysis of *Reich v. Valley National Bank of Arizona,* "Kroy Decision—A Reality Check for ERISA Fiduciaries," by Gregory K. Brown, John E. Curtis, Jr., and Marilyn H. Marchetti, *Tax Management's Weekly Report.*

Enforcement: Clayton, Jeffrey, N., "The DOL, the IRS and Fiduciary Responsibility," *Trustee Handbook,* International Foundation of Employee Benefit Plans, 1990, pp. 89–91

Audit Reports: Ronald Allen, Michael Auerbach, Pension and Welfare Benefits Administration (PWBA), speech to 1993 Enrolled Actuaries Meeting

PWBA Audit Process: *PWBA Enforcement Manual,* 1987

6

PROHIBITED TRANSACTION EXEMPTIONS

ERISA offers statutory exemptions to the prohibited transaction rules. In addition, the Labor Department exempts certain classes of entities—usually involved in investment of plan assets—and individual parties in interest upon application.

Individual and class exemptions are not listed specifically but are issued by application to the Labor Department. The criteria for the class or individual exemptions are whether they are administratively feasible, and whether an exemption is in the interest of, and protective of the rights of, the plan and its participants and beneficiaries.

STATUTORY EXEMPTIONS

Statutory exemptions are specifically listed in ERISA. These include:

- Plan loans,
- Office space,
- Employee stock ownership plan loans,

- Investment in the bank by a plan covering the bank's employees,
- Certain insurance or annuity contracts,
- Some ancillary services,
- Securities conversion,
- Asset allocation,
- Certain aspects of multiemployer benefit plan mergers, and
- Certain transfers of excess pension assets to fund retiree health liabilities.

Owner-employees do not have statutory exemptions for plan loans, receipt of compensation from the plan for services rendered, or purchase of property to and from the plan.

(See Appendix 8 for a list of class exemptions and Appendix 9 for an index of exemptions.)

Plan Loans

ERISA Section 408(b)(1) exempts from the prohibited transaction penalties any loans made by the plan to parties in interest who are participants or beneficiaries of the plan under certain conditions. Such loans must be available to all such participants and beneficiaries on a reasonably equivalent basis, must not be made available to highly compensated employees in an amount greater than made available to other employees, must be made under specific provisions in the plan, must bear a reasonable rate of interest, and must be adequately secured.

Office Space

ERISA Section 408(b)(2) permits plans to contract with or make reasonable arrangements with a party in interest for office space or legal, accounting, or other services necessary for the establishment and operation of the plan. Such contracts will not be prohibited transactions if no more than "reasonable compensation" is paid.

A contract may be reasonable if it allows the plan to cancel without penalty on short notice. Short notice cancellation prevents the plan from being locked into disadvantageous arrangements. The exemption permits the plan to pay for loss on early termination of the contract, however.

ESOP Loans

Under ERISA Section 408(b)(3), a loan to an employee stock ownership plan (ESOP) is not a prohibited transaction if the loan is primarily for the benefit of participants and beneficiaries and bears a reasonable interest rate. An ESOP is a defined contribution pension plan that invests primarily in employer securities. A "leveraged" ESOP (IRC Sec. 409) is one where the plan borrows money from a bank to buy company stock and the loan is guaranteed by the employer. The employer makes its contributions to the plan and the plan uses the contributions to make payments on the loan. As the loan is repaid, employer stock is allocated to participants' accounts.

Under the prohibited transaction exemption, if a plan gives a party in interest collateral for an ESOP loan, that collateral must be in the form of qualifying employer securities. (See Chapter 4 for a discussion of qualifying employer securities.)

Bank Deposits

ERISA Section 408(b)(4) permits plans to hold assets in bank accounts bearing reasonable rates of interest where the bank is a plan fiduciary, if the plan covers only bank employees or affiliates, or if the plan document or named fiduciary expressly provides for the investments.

Insurance Contracts

ERISA Section 408(b)(5) allows plans to contract for life insurance, health insurance, or annuities with insurers (qualified by the state), as long as the plan pays no more than adequate consideration and the insurer is either the employer maintaining the plan or is a party in interest owned by the employer maintaining the plan. The premiums or annuities written to the employer by the plan cannot exceed 5 percent of the total premiums and annuities written for all lines of insurance.

Ancillary Bank Services

Under ERISA Section 408(b)(6), a bank or financial institution that is a plan fiduciary may provide ancillary services, such as cash management programs to the plan if the bank has adopted adequate internal safeguards. These safeguards should ensure sound banking and financial practices. Also, the ancillary service must be provided through specific guidelines that preclude the bank from providing services in an excessive or unreasonable manner that is inconsistent with the best interests of plan participants and beneficiaries.

Conversion of Securities

Under ERISA Section 408(b)(7) a plan may exercise its privilege to convert securities from one type of stock to another, but only if the plan receives adequate consideration. Fiduciaries may prove that the plan received adequate consideration by showing that they arrived at their determination of fair market value using a prudent investigation of the purchase, comparing it with comparable investments, before the conversion occurred.

Pooled Investment Funds

Under ERISA Section 408(b)(8), certain plan transactions with trust funds or pooled investment funds (mutual funds) maintained by a regulated bank or trust company party in interest are exempt from prohibited transaction rules if:

- The transaction is a sale or purchase of an interest in the fund;
- The bank, trust company, or insurance company receives reasonable compensation; and
- The transaction is expressly permitted by the plan document or by a fiduciary (other than the bank or trust com-

pany) who has the authority to manage and control plan assets.

Fiduciary Receipt of Benefits

The prohibited transaction provisions of ERISA Section 408(c) do not prohibit a fiduciary from:

- Receiving any benefit as a participant or beneficiary in the plan, so long as the benefit is computed and paid on the same terms as the benefits of others in the plan;
- Receiving any reasonable compensation for services rendered, or for the reimbursement of expenses properly and actually incurred (although reimbursement is unavailable for a person receiving full-time pay from an employer or union whose employees or members are participating in the plan); or
- Serving as a fiduciary in addition to being an officer, employee, agent, or representative of a party in interest.

Termination Distribution

Under ERISA Section 408(b)(9), a transaction is not prohibited where a plan fiduciary distributes the assets of a terminated plan in accordance with the terms of the plan as long as the assets are allocated according to ERISA Section 4044.

In a terminating single-employer plan, the plan administrator must allocate the assets available to provide benefits among the participants and beneficiaries in the following order:

- To that portion of each individual's accrued benefit that is derived from the participant's contributions to the plan that were not mandatory contributions;
- To that portion of each individual's accrued benefit that is derived from the participant's mandatory contributions;
- To benefits in pay status for the three years before the plan termination, where benefits are paid as annuities;
- To benefits guaranteed by the Pension Benefit Guaranty Corporation (PBGC);

- To all other nonforfeitable benefits under the plan; and then
- To all other benefits under the plan.

If any assets remain, they may revert to the employer if all plan liabilities to participants and beneficiaries have been satisfied, if the distribution of assets does not violate any law, and if the plan provides for such a distribution and reversion. Excise taxes on reversions do apply.

Merger of Multiemployer Plans

Under ERISA Section 408(b)(11), a merger of multiemployer plans, or a transfer of assets or liabilities between such plans, may be exempt from the prohibited transaction provisions if:

- The plan sponsors notify the PBGC of a merger with or a transfer of assets or liabilities to another multiemployer plan at least 120 days before the effective date of the transfer or merger;
- No participant's or beneficiary's accrued benefit will be lower immediately after the effective date of the merger or transfer than immediately before that date;
- The benefits of participants and beneficiaries are not expected to be suspended because the plan is financially unable to pay benefits; and
- An actuarial valuation of the assets and liabilities of each affected plan has been performed during the plan year preceding the effective date of the merger or transfer, based on the most recent data available before the start of the plan year, or other valuation or plan assets and liabilities.

Transfer of Assets for Retiree Health Accounts

Transfers of excess pension assets from defined benefit plans to retiree health accounts are exempt from the prohibited transaction rules under ERISA Section 408(b)(13) and IRC Section 420, as long as the transfers are qualified. The exemption is available through 1995. To be qualified, a transfer must be used to pay only current retiree health liabilities for employees other than key employees.

Only one transfer is permitted each year. The amounts transferred to a health plan are not includable in the employer's gross income, but they are subject to the 20 percent excise tax on the reversion of excess pension assets to employers. However, these excess amounts are not subject to the excise tax of 50 percent of a reversion generally applied to reversions where no successor plan is established. Any assets not used to satisfy health liabilities must be transferred back to the original plan.

CLASS EXEMPTIONS

In addition to the blanket exemptions established by ERISA, the Labor Department offers prohibited transaction exemptions to "classes" of transactions, as long as members of the class meet prescribed conditions. The first class exemptions were issued jointly by IRS and the Labor Department in 1975. After the reorganization of the administration of ERISA in 1978, the Labor Department took full authority in issuing exemptions.

The relief offered by class exemptions is limited to the transaction described in the exemption and is available only when certain conditions are met. If conditions in the class exemption cannot be met, plans or parties in interest may apply for individual exemptions. (For further information, see *ERISA Class Exemptions,* published by BNA Books, excerpts of which appear in Appendixes 8 and 9).

Particular Industries

Particular industries are targeted in some class exemptions:

- Securities industries (Prohibited Transaction Exemption (PTE) 86-128);
- Plan investment in mutual funds (PTEs 77-3 and 77-4);
- Plan investment in insurance company products (PTEs 81-82 and 90-1); and

- Collective investment funds maintained by banks (PTE 80-51).

Types of Transactions

Types of transactions are also treated as class exemptions:

- Plan purchases of employer customer notes (PTEs 79-9 and 85-68);
- The use of proceeds from the sale of securities to reduce or retire debt (PTE 80-83);
- Securities lending (PTEs 81-6 and 82-63);
- Short-term investments (PTE 81-8); and
- Investments in mortgages or mortgage pools (PTEs 83-1 and 85-59).

Special Plan Concerns

Special plan concerns also are treated in class exemptions, such as:

- Multiemployer plans (PTEs 76-1, 77-10, and 78-5), and
- Large plan investments using qualified professional asset managers (PTE 84-14).

INDIVIDUAL EXEMPTIONS

While a class exemption applies to any party in interest within the class, individual exemptions apply only to the specific party in interest named or defined in the exemption. Either the plan or the party in interest may apply for exemptions. (29 C.F.R. 2570.30)

According to its regulations, the Labor Department will not consider applications for exemptions that:

- Do not include all the required information;
- Are the subject of an investigation for possible violations of the reporting and disclosure rules or fiduciary responsibilities; or

- Are the same type of transactions under consideration for class exemptions.

APPLYING FOR EXEMPTIONS

To be considered by the Labor Department (29 C.F.R. 2570.30), all applications for exemption (both class and individual) must contain the following information:

- The name(s) of the applicant(s);
- A detailed description of the exemption transaction and the parties in interest for whom an exemption is requested, including a description of any larger integrated transaction of which the exemption transaction is a part;
- Whether the plan and parties in interest will be represented by the same person on the exemption application;
- Reasons a plan would have for entering into the exemption transaction;
- The prohibited transactions provisions from which exemptive relief is requested and the reason why the transaction would violate such provision;
- Whether the exemption transaction is customary for the industry or class involved;
- Whether the exemption transaction is or has been the subject of an investigation or enforcement action by the Labor Department or IRS;
- The hardship or economic loss, if any, that would result to the person for whom the exemption is sought, to affected plans, and to their participants and beneficiaries from denial of the application;
- A statement explaining why the requested exemption would be administratively feasible, in the interests of plans and their participants and beneficiaries, and protective of their interests;
- A list of people interested in the exemption that the applicant will notify, the manner that notice will take, and an estimate of time the applicant needs to notify people following publication of the proposed exemption in the Federal Register;

- If an advisory opinion has been requested with respect to any issue relating to the exemption transaction, a copy of the request or the department's letter if action has been taken;
- If an application is signed by anyone other than the party in interest, a provision explaining who the signer is and the relationship to the party in interest; and
- A declaration to be signed by the applicant, officer, or plan fiduciary, which states: "Under penalty of perjury, I declare that I am familiar with the matters discussed in this application and, to the best of my knowledge and belief, the representations made in this application are true and correct."

An application for exemption may also include a draft of the requested exemption which defines the transaction and parties in interest for which exemptive relief is sought and the specific conditions under which the exemption would apply.

Additional Requirements for Individuals

Applications for individual prohibited transaction exemptions must include not only the required information listed above, but also the following:

- The name, address, telephone number, and type of plans to which the requested exemption applies;
- The Employer Identification Number (EIN) and the Plan Number (PN) used by the plans in reporting and disclosure;
- Whether the plan or trust affected by the requested exemption has ever been found to have violated the exclusive benefit or prohibited transaction rules;
- Whether any prohibited transaction relief has been sought or granted to the plan or party in interest;
- Whether the applicant or any party in interest involved in the exemption transaction is now or has been in the past five years a defendant in a lawsuit or criminal action concerning fiduciary conduct;

- Whether the applicant or any party in interest has, within the last 13 years, been convicted of any crime listed in ERISA Section 411—which prohibits persons convicted of a number of felony crimes from serving as fiduciaries, plan administrators, or any officer, employer, or representative of the plan;
- Whether the plan or party in interest has been or continues to be examined, investigated, or in dispute with the Labor Department, IRS, PBGC, or the Federal Retirement Thrift Investment Board. If so, copies of correspondence with the agencies must be included;
- Whether the plan has ever experienced a "reportable event," such as plan termination, plan amendments that decrease benefits, a reduction in active participants, plan failure to meet minimum funding standards or pay benefits when due, certain distributions greater than $10,000 to substantial owners, plan mergers or consolidations, or any other event which requires PBGC to terminate the plan;
- Whether the plan has filed notice of intent to terminate;
- Names, addresses, and taxpayer identification numbers of all parties in interest involved in the transaction;
- The estimated numbers of participants and beneficiaries in each plan affected by the requested exemption as of the date of the application;
- The percentage of the fair market value of the total assets of each affected plan that is involved in the transaction;
- Whether the transaction has been made or will be made only if the exemption is granted;
- If the transaction already has been made, the circumstances that resulted in plan fiduciaries causing the plan to enter into the transaction without an exemption, whether the transaction has been terminated, whether it has been corrected, whether IRS Form 5330, Return of Excise Taxes Related to Employee Benefit Plans, has been filed with IRS and whether any excise taxes have been paid;
- The name of every person with investment discretion over plan assets involved in the transaction and their

relationships to the party in interest requesting the transaction;

- Whether the plan assets are invested in loans, leases, or employer securities to the parties in interest, identifying the type of investment, aggregate fair market value, percentage of the plan's investment in this type, and any statutory or administrative exemptions covering these investments;
- The approximate aggregate fair market value of the total assets of each affected plan;
- The person who will bear the costs of the exemption application and of notifying interested persons; and
- Whether an independent fiduciary will be involved in the transaction and, if so, who will pay the fee to the fiduciary.

Documents

Every application for exemption must include certified copies of all contracts, deeds, agreements, and instruments, as well as portions of plan documents, trust agreements, and any other documents relating to the transaction.

The application must also include a discussion of the facts relevant to the exemption transaction that are reflected in the documents submitted and an analysis of their bearing on the requested exemption. The most recent financial statements of each plan affected by the exemption request should also be included in the application.

Applications for exemption should be mailed or delivered to Exemption Application, Pension and Welfare Benefits Administration, Office of Exemption Determinations, Division of Exemptions, U.S. Department of Labor, 200 Constitution Ave., N.W., Washington, DC 20210.

REFERENCES

Prohibited Transaction Exemptions: ERISA Section 408

Individual Exemptions: Pension and Welfare Benefits Administration Procedures: 29 C.F.R. 2570.30

Class Exemptions: see *ERISA Class Exemptions,* by Donald J. Myers, 1991, BNA Books

Appendix 1

Index to Relevant Sections of ERISA, Internal Revenue Code, and ERISA Regulations

	Law		Regulations	
	ERISA	IRC	26 CFR (Treas. reg.)	29 CFR (DOL, PBGC, EEOC)
***				
Fiduciary				
Actions under Title IV	4023			
Breach				
Co-fiduciary liability	405			2509.75-5, -8
Knowing participation in	502(l)			**p**2560.502(l)-1
Liability for	409			
Penalty for	502(l)			**p**2560.502(l)-1
Statute of limitations	413			
Definition	3(21)	4975(e)(3)		2509.75-4, -8
				2510.3-21
Duties of	404			2550.404a-1
Exculpatory provisions	410			
Felon prohibited as	411			
Insurance or indemnification	410(b)			2509.75-4
Prohibited transactions (*see* Prohibited transactions)				
***				
Prohibited transactions				
Agency coordination	3003			
Church plans		503	1.503	
Civil penalty	502(i)			2560.502i-1
Procedures for assessment				2570.1 to .12
Contributed property	406(c)	4975(f)(3)		
Criminal offenses (*see* Criminal offenses)				
Definition of	406	4975(e)		
Employee-pay-all plans		503	1.503	
Employer real property	406(a)(2)			
	407			2550.407a-1 to -4
Employer securities	406(a)(2)			
	407			2550.407a-1 to -4
				2550.407c-3
				2550.407d-5

Note: Regulation index is included for researching convenience, cited as the regulations appear in the 1993 edition of *ERISA Regulations* (BNA Books). The prefix **p** indicates a proposed regulation. An * indicates material located in the supplement section of that edition. Text of most sections listed appears in Appendix 2 (ERISA), 3 (IRC), and 4 (29 CFR).

	Law		Regulations	
	ERISA	**IRC**	**26 CFR (Treas. reg.)**	**29 CFR (DOL, PBGC, EEOC)**
Excise tax		4975(a)-(b)		
Exemptions				
Application for				2570.30 to .52
Bank ancillary services	408(b)(6)	4975(d)(6)		2550.408b-6
Bank common or collective trust	408(b)(8)	4975(d)(8)		
Bank deposits	408(b)(4)	4975(d)(4)		2550.408b-4
Class exemptions	408(a)	4975(c)(2)		2570.30 to .52
Conversion of securities	408(b)(7)	4975(d)(7)		
Employee or officer of party in interest	408(c)(3)	4975(d)(11)		
Employer securities	408(e)			2550.408e
ESOPs	408(b)(3)	4975(d)(3)		2550.408b-3
Fiduciary as participant	408(c)(1)	4975(d)(9)		
Fiduciary compensation	408(c)(2)	4975(d)(10)		2550.408c-2
Individual exemptions	408(a)	4975(c)(2)		2570.30 to .52
Insurance company plan	408(b)(5)	4975(d)(5)		
Insurance company pooled investment fund	408(b)(8)	4975(d)(8)		
IRA, inapplicable to	408(d)	4975(d)		
Loans to participants	408(b)(1)	4975(d)(1)		2550.408b-1
Merger, multiemployer plans	408(b)(11)	4975(d)(15)		
Multiemployer withdrawal liability	408(b)(10)	4975(d)(14)		
	4219 (d)			
Owner-employee	408(d)	4975(d)		
Services	408(b)(2)	4975(d)(2)		2550.408b-2
Shareholder employee	408(d)	4975(d)		
Termination, pension plan	408(b)(9)	4975(d)(12)		
Fiduciary, transaction involving	406(b)	4975(c)(1)(E)-(F)		2550.408b-2(e)
Government plans		503	1.503	
IRAs		408(e)(2)	1.408-1(c)(3)	
	408	4975(c)(3)		
		4975(d)		
Party in interest transaction	406(a)(1)	4975(c)(1)(A)-(D)		
Penalties (*see also* Criminal offenses)				
Civil penalty	502(i)			2560.502i-1
Excise tax		4975(a)-(b)		
Procedure for assessment of civil penalty				2570.1 to .12
Supplemental unemployment benefit (SUB) plans		503	1.503	

***

APPENDIX 2

SELECTED TEXT OF ERISA

Contents

Section

U.S.C. ERISA

Title I—Protection of Employee Benefit Rights

Subtitle A—General Provisions

***

Part 4—Fiduciary Responsibility

Part 5—Administration and Enforcement

Title I—Protection of Employee Benefit Rights

SUBTITLE A—GENERAL PROVISIONS

FINDINGS AND DECLARATION OF POLICY

Sec. 2. (a) The Congress finds that the growth in size, scope, and numbers of employee benefit plans in recent years has been rapid and substantial; that the operational scope and economic impact of such plans is increasingly interstate; that the continued well-being and security of millions of employees and their dependents are directly affected by these plans; that they are affected with a national public interest; that they have become an important factor affecting the stability of employment and the successful development of industrial relations; that they have become an important factor in commerce because of the interstate character of their activities, and of the activities of their participants, and the employers, employee organizations, and other entities by which they are established or maintained; that a large volume of the activities of such plans is carried on by means of the mails and instrumentalities of interstate commerce; that owing to the lack of employee information and adequate safeguards concerning their operation, it is desirable in the interests of employees and their beneficiaries, and to provide for the general welfare and the free flow of commerce, that disclosure be made and safeguards be provided with respect to the establishment, operation, and administration of such plans; that they substantially affect the revenues of the United States because they are afforded preferential Federal tax treatment; that despite the enormous growth in such plans many employees with long years of employment are losing anticipated retirement benefits owing to the lack of vesting provisions in such plans; that owing to the inadequacy of current minimum standards, the soundness and stability of plans with respect to adequate funds to pay promised benefits may be endangered; that owing to the termination of plans before requisite funds have been accumulated, employees and their beneficiaries have been deprived of anticipated benefits; and that it is therefore desirable in the interests of employees and their beneficiaries, for the protection of the revenue of the United States, and to provide for the free flow of commerce, that minimum standards be provided assuring the equitable character of such plans and their financial soundness.

(b) It is hereby declared to be the policy of this Act to protect interstate commerce and the interests of participants in employee benefit plans and their beneficiaries, by requiring the disclosure and reporting to participants and beneficiaries of financial and other information with respect thereto, by establishing standards of conduct, responsibility, and obligation for fiduciaries of employee benefit plans, and by providing for appropriate remedies, sanctions, and ready access to the Federal courts.

(c) It is hereby further declared to be the policy of this Act to protect interstate commerce, the Federal taxing power, and the interests of participants in private pension plans and their beneficiaries by improving the equitable character and the soundness of such plans by requiring them to vest the accrued benefits of employees with significant periods of service, to meet minimum standards of funding, and by requiring plan termination insurance.

DEFINITIONS

Sec. 3. For purposes of this title:

(1) The terms "employee welfare benefit plan" and "welfare plan" mean any plan, fund, or program which was heretofore or is hereafter established or maintained by an employer or by an employee organization, or by both, to the extent that such plan, fund, or program was established or is maintained for the purpose of providing for its participants or their beneficiaries, through the purchase of insurance or otherwise, (A) medical, surgical, or hospital care or benefits, or benefits in the event of sickness, accident, disability, death or unemployment, or vacation benefits, apprenticeship or other training programs, or day care centers, scholarship funds, or prepaid legal services, or (B) any benefit described in section 302(c) of the Labor Management Relations Act, 1947 (other than pensions on retirement or death, and insurance to provide such pensions).

(2)(A) Except as provided in subparagraph (B), the terms "employee pension benefit plan" and "pension plan" mean any plan, fund, or program which was heretofore or is hereafter established or maintained by an employer or by an employee organization, or by both, to the extent that by its express terms or as a result of surrounding circumstances such plan, fund, or program—

(i) provides retirement income to employees, or

(ii) results in a deferral of income by employees for periods extending to the termination of covered employment or beyond, regardless of the method of calculating the contributions made to the plan, the method of calculating the benefits under the plan or the method of distributing benefits from the plan.

(B) The Secretary may by regulation prescribe rules consistent with the standards and purposes of this Act providing one or more exempt categories under which—

(i) severance pay arrangements, and

(ii) supplemental retirement income payments, under which the pension benefits of retirees or their beneficiaries are supplemented to take into account some portion or all of the increases in the cost of living (as determined by the Secretary of Labor) since retirement, shall, for purposes of this title, be treated as welfare plans rather than pension plans. In the case of any arrangement or payment a principal effect of which is the evasion of the standards or purposes of this Act applicable to pension plans, such arrangement or payment shall be treated as a pension plan.

(3) The term "employee benefit plan" or "plan" means an employee welfare benefit plan or an employee pension benefit plan or a plan which is both an employee welfare benefit plan and an employee pension benefit plan.

(4) The term "employee organization" means any labor union or any organization of any kind, or any agency or employee representation committee, association, group, or plan, in which employees participate and which exists for the purpose, in whole or in part, of dealing with employers concerning an employee benefit plan, or other matters incidental to employment relationships; or any employees' beneficiary association organized for the purpose in whole or in part, of establishing such a plan.

(5) The term "employer" means any person acting directly as an employer, or indirectly in the interest of an employer, in relation to an employee benefit plan; and includes a group or association of employers acting for an employer in such capacity.

(6) The term "employee" means any individual employed by an employer.

(7) The term "participant" means any employee or former employee of an employer, or any member or former member of an employee organization, who is or may become eligible to receive a benefit of any type from an employee benefit plan which covers employees of such employer or members of such organization, or whose beneficiaries may be eligible to receive any such benefit.

(8) The term "beneficiary" means a person designated by a participant, or by the terms of an employee benefit plan, who is or may become entitled to a benefit thereunder.

(9) The term "person" means an individual, partnership, joint venture, corporation, mutual company, joint-stock company, trust, estate, unincorporated organization, association, or employee organization.

(10) The term "State" includes any State of the United States, the District of Columbia, Puerto Rico, the Virgin Islands, American Samoa, Guam, Wake Island, and the Canal Zone. The term "United States" when used in the geographic sense means the States and the Outer Continental Shelf lands defined in the Outer Continental Shelf Lands Act (43 U.S.C. 1331-1343).

(11) The term "commerce" means trade, traffic, commerce, transportation, or communication between any State and any place outside thereof.

(12) The term "industry or activity affecting commerce" means any activity, business, or industry in commerce or in which a labor dispute would hinder or obstruct commerce or the free flow of commerce, and includes any activity or industry "affecting commerce" within the meaning of the Labor Management Relations Act, 1947, or the Railway Labor Act.

(13) The term "Secretary" means the Secretary of Labor.

(14) The term "party in interest" means, as to an employee benefit plan—

(A) any fiduciary (including, but not limited to, any administrator, officer, trustee, or custodian), counsel, or employee of such employee benefit plan;

(B) a person providing services to such plan;

(C) an employer any of whose employees are covered by such plan;

(D) an employee organization any of whose members are covered by such plan;

(E) an owner, direct or indirect, of 50 percent or more of—

(i) the combined voting power of all classes of stock entitled to vote or the total value of shares of all classes of stock of a corporation,

(ii) the capital interest or the profits interest of a partnership, or

(iii) the beneficial interest of a trust or unincorporated enterprise, which is an employer or an employee organization described in subparagraph (C) or (D);

(F) a relative (as defined in paragraph (15) of any individual described in subparagraph (A), (B), (C), or (E);

(G) a corporation, partnership, or trust or estate of which (or in which) 50 percent or more of—

(i) the combined voting power of all classes of stock entitled to vote or the total value of shares of all classes of stock of such corporation,

(ii) the capital interest or profits interest of such partnership, or

(iii) the beneficial interest of such trust or estate, is owned directly or indirectly, or held by persons described in subparagraph (A), (B), (C), (D), or (E);

(H) an employee, officer, director (or an individual having powers or responsibilities similar to those of officers or directors), or a 10 percent or more shareholder directly or indirectly, of a person described in subparagraph (B), (C), (D), (E), or (G), or of the employee benefit plan; or

(I) a 10 percent or more (directly or indirectly in capital or profits) partner or joint venturer of a person described in subparagraph (B), (C), (D), (E), or (G).

The Secretary, after consultation and coordination with the Secretary of the Treasury, may by regulation prescribe a percentage lower than 50 percent for subparagraph (E) and (G) and lower than 10 percent for subparagraph (H) or (I). The Secretary may prescribe regulations for determining the ownership (direct or indirect) of profits and beneficial interests, and the manner in which indirect stockholdings are taken into account. Any person who is a party in interest with respect to a plan to which a trust described in section 501 (c)(22) of the Internal Revenue Code of 1954 is permitted to make payments under section 4223 shall be treated as a party in interest with respect to such trust.

(15) The term "relative" means a spouse, ancestor, lineal descendant, or spouse of a lineal descendant.

(16)(A) The term "administrator" means—

(i) the person specifically so designated by the terms of the instrument under which the plan is operated;

(ii) if an administrator is not so designated, the plan sponsor; or

(iii) in the case of a plan for which an administrator is not designated and a plan sponsor cannot be identified, such other person as the Secretary may by regulation prescribe.

(B) The term "plan sponsor" means (i) the employer in the case of an employee benefit plan established or maintained by a single employer, (ii) the employee organization in the case of a plan established or maintained by an employee organization, or (iii) in the case of a plan established or maintained by two or more employers or jointly by one or more employers and one or more employee organizations, the association, committee, joint board of trustees, or other similar group of representatives of the parties who establish or maintain the plan.

(17) The term "separate account" means an account established or maintained by an insurance company under which income, gains, and losses, whether or not realized, from assets allocated to such account, are, in accordance with the applicable contract, credited to or charged against such account without regard to other income, gains, or losses of the insurance company.

(18) The term "adequate consideration" when used in part 4 of subtitle B means (A) in the case of a security for which there is a generally recognized market, either (i) the price of the security prevailing on a national securities exchange which is registered under section 6 of the Securities Exchange Act of 1934, or (ii) if the security is not traded on such a national securities exchange, a price not less favorable to the plan than the offering price for the security as established by the current bid and asked prices quoted by persons independent of the issuer and of any party in interest; and (B) in the case of an asset other than a security for which there is a generally recognized market, the fair market value of the asset as determined in good faith by the trustee or named fiduciary pursuant to the terms of the plan and in accordance with regulations promulgated by the Secretary.

(19) The term "nonforfeitable" when used with respect to a pension benefit or right means a claim obtained by a participant or his beneficiary to that part of an immediate or deferred benefit under a pension plan which arises from the participant's service, which is unconditional, and which is legally enforceable against the plan. For purposes of this paragraph, a right to an accrued benefit derived from employer contributions shall not be treated as forfeitable merely because the plan contains a provision described in section 203(a)(3).

(20) The term "security" has the same meaning as such term has under section 2(1) of the Securities Act of 1933 (15 U.S.C. 77b(1)).

(21)(A) Except as otherwise provided in subparagraph (B), a person is a fiduciary with respect to a plan to the extent (i) he exercises any discretionary authority or discretionary control respecting management of such plan or exercises any authority or control respecting management or disposition of its assets, (ii) he renders investment advice for a fee or other compensation, direct or indirect, with respect to any moneys or other property of such plan, or has any authority or responsibility to do so, or (iii) he has any discretionary authority or discretionary responsibility in the administration of such plan. Such term includes any person designated under section 405 (c)(1)(B).

(B) If any money or other property of an employee benefit plan is invested in securities issued by an investment company registered under the Investment Company Act of 1940, such investment shall not by itself cause such investment company or such investment company's investment adviser or principal underwriter to be deemed to be a fiduciary or a party in interest as those terms are defined in this title, except insofar as such investment company or its investment adviser or principal underwriter acts in connection with an employee benefit plan covering employees of the investment company, the investment adviser, or its principal underwriter. Nothing contained in this subparagraph shall limit the duties imposed on such investment company, investment adviser, or principal underwriter by any other law.

(22) The term "normal retirement benefit" means the greater of the early retirement benefit under the plan, or the benefit under the plan commencing at normal retirement age. The normal retirement benefit shall be determined without regard to—

(A) medical benefits, and

(B) disability benefits not in excess of the qualified disability benefit.
For purposes of this paragraph, a qualified disability benefit is a disability benefit provided by a plan which does not exceed the benefit which would be provided for the participant if he separated from the service at normal retirement age. For purposes of this paragraph, the early retirement benefit under a plan shall be determined without regard to any benefit under the plan which the Secretary of the Treasury finds to be a benefit described in section 204(b)(1)(G).

(23) The term "accrued benefit" means—

(A) in the case of a defined benefit plan, the individual's accrued benefit determined under the plan and, except as provided in section 204(c)(3), expressed in the form of an annual benefit commencing at normal retirement age, or

(B) in the case of a plan which is an individual account plan, the balance of the individual's account.

The accrued benefit of an employee shall not be less than the amount determined under section 204(c)(2)(B) with respect to the employee's accumulated contribution.

(24) The term "normal retirement age" means the earlier of—

(A) the time a plan participant attains normal retirement age under the plan, or

(B) the later of—

(i) the time a plan participant attains age 65, or

(ii) the 5th anniversary of the time a plan participant commenced participation in the plan.

(25) The term "vested liabilities" means the present value of the immediate or deferred benefits available at normal retirement age for participants and their beneficiaries which are nonforfeitable.

(26) The term "current value" means fair market value where available and otherwise the fair value as determined in good faith by a trustee or a named fiduciary (as defined in section 402(a)(2)) pursuant to the terms of the plan and in accordance with regulations of the Secretary, assuming an orderly liquidation at the time of such determination.

(27) The term "present value", with respect to a liability, means the value adjusted to reflect anticipated events. Such adjustments shall conform to such regulations as the Secretary of the Treasury may prescribe.

(28) The term "normal service cost" or "normal cost" means the annual cost of future pension benefits and administrative expenses assigned, under an actuarial cost method, to years subsequent to a particular valuation date of a pension plan. The Secretary of the Treasury may prescribe regulations to carry out this paragraph.

(29) The term "accrued liability" means the excess of the present value, as of a particular valuation date of a pension plan, of the projected future benefits cost and administrative expenses for all plan participants and beneficiaries over the present value of future contributions for the normal cost of all applicable plan participants and beneficiaries. The Secretary of the Treasury may prescribe regulations to carry out this paragraph.

(30) The term "unfunded accrued liability" means the excess of the accrued liability, under an actuarial cost method which so provides, over the present value of the assets of a pension plan. The Secretary of the Treasury may prescribe regulations to carry out this paragraph.

(31) The term "advance funding actuarial cost method" or "actuarial cost method" means a recognized actuarial technique utilized for establishing the amount and incidence of the annual actuarial cost of pension plan benefits and expenses. Acceptable actuarial cost methods shall include the accrued benefit cost method (unit credit method), the entry age normal cost method, the individual level premium cost method, the aggregate cost method, the attained age normal cost method, and the frozen initial liability cost method. The terminal funding cost method and the current funding (pay-as-you-go) cost method are not acceptable actuarial cost methods. The Secretary of the Treasury shall issue regulations to further define acceptable actuarial cost methods.

(32) The term "governmental plan" means a plan established or maintained for its employees by the Government of the United States, by the government of any State or political subdivision thereof, or by any agency or instrumentality of any of the foregoing. The term "governmental plan" also includes any plan to which the Railroad Retirement Act of 1935 or 1937 applies, and which is financed by contributions required under that Act and any plan of an international organization which is exempt from taxation under the provisions of the International Organizations Immunities Act (59 Stat. 669).

(33)(A) The term "church plan" means a plan established and maintained (to the extent required in clause (ii) of subparagraph (B)) for its employees (or their beneficiaries) by a church or by a convention or association of churches which is exempt from tax under section 501 of the Internal Revenue Code of 1954.

(B) The term "church plan" does not include a plan—

(i) which is established and maintained primarily for the benefit of employees (or their beneficiaries) of such church or convention or association of churches who are employed in connection with one or more unrelated trades or businesses (within the meaning of section 513 of the Internal Revenue Code of 1954), or

(ii) if less than substantially all of the individuals included in the plan are individuals described in subparagraph (A) or in clause (ii) of subparagraph (C) (or their beneficiaries).

(C) For purposes of this paragraph—

(i) A plan established and maintained for its employees (or their beneficiaries) by a church or by a convention or association of churches includes a plan maintained by an organization, whether a civil law corporation or otherwise, the principal purpose or function of which is the administration or funding of a plan or program for the provision of retirement benefits or welfare benefits, or both, for the employees of a church or a convention or association of churches, if such organization is controlled by or associated with a church or a convention or association of churches.

(ii) The term employee of a church or a convention or association of churches includes—

(I) a duly ordained, commissioned, or licensed minister of a church in the exercise of his ministry, regardless of the source of his compensation;

(II) an employee of an organization, whether a civil law corporation or otherwise, which is exempt from tax under section 501 of the Internal Revenue Code of 1954 and which is controlled by or associated with a church or a convention or association of churches; and

(III) an individual described in clause (v).

(iii) A church or a convention or association of churches which is exempt from tax under section 501 of the Internal Revenue Code of 1954 shall be deemed the employer of any individual included as an employee under clause (ii).

(iv) An organization, whether a civil law corporation or otherwise, is associated with a church or a convention or association of churches if it shares common religious bonds and convictions with that church or convention or association of churches.

(v) If an employee who is included in a church plan separates from the service of a church or a convention or association of churches or an organization, whether a civil law corporation or otherwise, which is exempt from tax under section 501 of the Internal Revenue Code of 1954 and which is controlled by or associated with a church or a convention or association of churches, the church plan shall not fail to meet the requirements of this paragraph merely because the plan—

(I) retains the employee's accrued benefit or account for the payment of benefits to the employee or his beneficiaries pursuant to the terms of the plan; or

(II) receives contributions on the employee's behalf after the employee's separation from such service, but only for a period of 5 years after such separation, unless the employee is disabled (within the meaning of the disability provisions of the church plan or, if there are no such provisions in the church plan, within the meaning of section 72(m)(7) of the Internal Revenue Code of 1954) at the time of such separation from service.

(D)(i) If a plan established and maintained for its employees (or their beneficiaries) by a church or by a convention or association of churches which is exempt from tax under section 501 of the Internal Revenue Code of 1954 fails to meet one or more of the requirements of this paragraph and corrects its failure to meet such requirements within the correction period, the plan shall be deemed to meet the requirements of this paragraph for the year in which the correction was made and for all prior years.

(ii) If a correction is not made within the correction period, the plan shall be deemed not to meet the requirements of this paragraph beginning with the date on which the earliest failure to meet one or more of such requirements occurred.

(iii) For purposes of this subparagraph, the term "correction period" means—

(I) the period ending 270 days after the date of mailing by the Secretary of the Treasury of a notice of default with respect to the plan's failure to meet one or more of the requirements of this paragraph; or

(II) any period set by a court of competent jurisdiction after a final determination that the plan fails to meet such requirements, or, if the court does not specify such period, any reasonable period determined by the Secretary of the Treasury on the basis of all the facts and circumstances, but in any event not less than 270 days after the determination has become final; or

(III) any additional period which the Secretary of the Treasury determines is reasonable or necessary for the correction of the default, whichever has the latest ending date.

(34) The term "individual account plan" or "defined contribution plan" means a pension plan which provides for an individual account for each participant and for benefits based solely upon the amount contributed to the participant's account, and any income, expenses, gains, and losses, and any forfeitures of accounts of other participants which may be allocated to such participant's account.

(35) The term "defined benefit plan" means a pension plan other than an individual account plan; except that a pension plan which is not an individual account plan and which provides a benefit derived from employer contributions which is based partly on the balance of the separate account of a participant—

(A) for the purposes of section 202, shall be treated as an individual account plan, and

(B) for the purposes of paragraph (23) of this section and section 204, shall be treated as an individual account plan to the extent benefits are based upon the separate account of a participant and as a defined benefit plan with respect to the remaining portion of benefits under the plan.

(36) The term "excess benefit plan" means a plan maintained by an employer solely for the purpose of providing benefits for certain employees in excess of the limitations on contributions and benefits imposed by section 415 of the Internal Revenue Code of 1954 on plans to which that section applies, without regard to whether the plan is funded. To the extent that a separable part of a plan (as determined by the Secretary of Labor) maintained by an employer is maintained for such purpose, that part shall be treated as a separate plan which is an excess benefit plan.

(37)(A) The term "multiemployer plan" means a plan—

(i) to which more than one employer is required to contribute,

(ii) which is maintained pursuant to one or more collective bargaining agreements between one or more employee organizations and more than one employer, and

(iii) which satisfies such other requirements as the Secretary may prescribe by regulation.

(B) For purposes of this paragraph, all trades or businesses (whether or not incorporated) which are under common control within the meaning of section 4001(b)(1) are considered a single employer.

(C) Notwithstanding subparagraph (A), a plan is a multiemployer plan on and after its termination date if the plan was a multiemployer plan under this paragraph for the plan year preceding its termination date.

(D) For purposes of this title, notwithstanding the preceding provisions of this paragraph, for any plan year which began before the date of the enactment of the Multiemployer Pension Plan Amendments Act of 1980, the term "multiemployer plan" means a plan described in section 3(37) of this Act as in effect immediately before such date.

(E) Within one year after the date of the enactment of the Multiemployer Pension Plan Amendments Act of 1980, a multiemployer plan may irrevocably elect, pursuant to procedures established by the corporation and subject to the provisions of sections 4403 (b) and (c), that the plan shall not be treated as a multiemployer plan for all purposes under this Act or the Internal Revenue Code of 1954 if for each of the last 3 plan years ending prior to the effective date of the Multiemployer Pension Plan Amendments Act of 1980—

(i) the plan was not a multiemployer plan because the plan was not a plan described in section 3(37)(A)(iii) of this Act and section 414(f)(1)(C) of the Internal Revenue Code of 1954 (as such provisions were in effect on the day before the date of the enactment of the Multiemployer Pension Plan Amendments Act of 1980); and

(ii) the plan had been identified as a plan that was not a multiemployer plan in substantially all its filings with the corporation, the Secretary of Labor and the Secretary of the Treasury.

(F)(i) For purposes of this title a qualified football coaches plan—

(I) shall be treated as a multiemployer plan to the extent not inconsistent with the purposes of this subparagraph; and

(II) notwithstanding section 401(k)(4)(B) of the Internal Revenue Code of 1986 may include a qualified cash and deferred arrangement.

(ii) For purposes of this subparagraph, the term "qualified football coaches plan" means any defined contribution plan which is established and maintained by an organization—

(I) which is described in section 501(c) of such Code;

(II) the membership of which consists entirely of individuals who primarily coach football as full-time employees of 4-year colleges or universities described in section 170(b)(1)(A)(ii) of such Code; and

(III) which was in existence on September 18, 1986.

(38) The term "investment manager" means any fiduciary (other than a trustee or named fiduciary, as defined in section 402(a)(2))—

(A) who has the power to manage, acquire, or dispose of any asset of a plan;

(B) who is (i) registered as an investment adviser under the Investment Advisers Act of 1940; (ii) is a bank, as defined in that Act; or (iii) is an insurance company qualified to perform services described in subparagraph (A) under the laws of more than one State; and

(C) has acknowledged in writing that he is a fiduciary with respect to the plan.

(39) The terms "plan year" and "fiscal year of the plan" mean, with respect to a plan, the calendar, policy, or fiscal year on which the records of the plan are kept.

(40)(A) The term "multiple employer welfare arrangement" means an employee welfare benefit plan, or any other arrangement (other than an employee welfare benefit plan), which is established or maintained for the purpose of offering or providing any benefit described in paragraph (1) to the employees of two or more employers (including one or more self-employed individuals), or to their beneficiaries, except that such term does not include any such plan or other arrangement which is established or maintained—

(i) under or pursuant to one or more agreements which the Secretary finds to be collective bargaining agreements,

(ii) by a rural electric cooperative, or

(iii) by a rural telephone cooperative association.

(B) For purposes of this paragraph—

(i) two or more trades or businesses, whether or not incorporated, shall be deemed a single employer if such trades or businesses are within the same control group,

(ii) the term "control group" means a group of trades or businesses under common control,

(iii) the determination of whether a trade or business is under "common control" with another trade or business shall be determined under regulations of the Secretary applying principles similar to the principles applied in determining whether employees of two or more trades or businesses are treated as employed by a single employer under section 4001(b), except that, for purposes of this paragraph, common control shall not be based on an interest of less than 25 percent,

(iv) the term "rural electric cooperative" means—

(I) any organization which is exempt from tax under section 501(a) of the Internal Revenue Code of 1954 and which is engaged primarily in providing electric service on a mutual or cooperative basis, and

(II) any organization described in paragraph (4) or (6) of section 501(c) of the Internal Revenue Code of 1954 which is exempt from tax under section 501(a) of such Code and at least 80 percent of the members of which are organizations described in subclause (I), and

(v) the term "rural telephone cooperative association" means an organization described in paragraph (4) or (6) of section 501(c) of the Internal Revenue Code of 1986 which is exempt from tax under section 501(a) of such Code and at least 80 percent of the members of which are organizations engaged primarily in providing telephone service to rural areas of the United States on a mutual, cooperative, or other basis.

(41) Single-Employer Plan.—The term "single-employer plan" means an employee benefit plan other than a multiemployer plan.

[*Editor's Note:* Subsection 3(41) below was added by OBRA 1990 Subsection 12002(b)(2)(C) without renumbering or removing Subsection 3(41) above.]

(41) The term "single-employer plan" means a plan which is not a multiemployer plan.

COVERAGE

Sec. 4. (a) Except as provided in subsection (b) and in sections 201, 301, and 401, this title shall apply to any employee benefit plan if it is established or maintained—

(1) by any employer engaged in commerce or in any industry or activity affecting commerce; or

(2) by any employee organization or organizations representing employees engaged in commerce or in any industry or activity affecting commerce; or

(3) by both.

(b) The provisions of this title shall not apply to any employee benefit plan if.

(1) such plan is a governmental plan (as defined in section 3(32));

(2) such plan is a church plan (as defined in section 3(33)) with respect to which no election has been made under section 410(d) of the Internal Revenue Code of 1954;

(3) such plan is maintained solely for the purpose of complying with applicable workmen's compensation laws or unemployment compensation or disability insurance laws;

(4) such plan is maintained outside of the United States primarily for the benefit of persons substantially all of whom are nonresident aliens; or

(5) such plan is an excess benefit plan (as defined in section 3(36)) and is unfunded.

Part 4—Fiduciary Responsibility

COVERAGE

Sec. 401. (a) This part shall apply to any employee benefit plan described in section 4(a) (and not exempted under section 4(b)), other than—

(1) a plan which is unfunded and is maintained by an employer primarily for the purpose of providing deferred compensation for a select group of management or highly compensated employees; or

(2) any agreement described in section 736 of the Internal Revenue Code of 1954, which provides payments to a retired partner or deceased partner or a deceased partner's successor in interest.

(b) For purposes of this part:

(1) In the case of a plan which invests in any security issued by an investment company registered under the Investment Company Act of 1940, the assets of such plan shall be deemed to include such security but shall not, solely by reason of such investment, be deemed to include any assets of such investment company.

(2) In the case of a plan to which a guaranteed benefit policy is issued by an insurer, the assets of such plan shall be deemed to include such policy, but shall not, solely by reason of the issuance of such policy, be deemed to include any assets of such insurer. For purposes of this paragraph:

(A) The term "insurer" means an insurance company, insurance service, or insurance organization, qualified to do business in a State.

(B) The term "guaranteed benefit policy" means an insurance policy or contract to the extent that such policy or contract provides for benefits the amount of which is guaranteed by the insurer. Such term includes any surplus in a separate account, but excludes any other portion of a separate account.

ESTABLISHMENT OF PLAN

Sec. 402. (a)(1) Every employee benefit plan shall be established and maintained pursuant to a written instrument. Such instrument shall provide for one or more named fiduciaries who jointly or severally shall have authority to control and manage the operation and administration of the plan.

(2) For purposes of this title, the term "named fiduciary" means a fiduciary who is named in the plan instrument, or who, pursuant to a procedure specified in the plan, is identified as a fiduciary (A) by a person who is an employer or employee organization with respect to the plan or (B) by such an employer and such an employee organization acting jointly.

(b) Every employee benefit plan shall—

(1) provide a procedure for establishing and carrying out a funding policy and method consistent with the objectives of the plan and the requirements of this title,

(2) describe any procedure under the plan for the allocation of responsibilities for the operation and administration of the plan (including any procedure described in section 405(c)(1)),

(3) provide a procedure for amending such plan, and for identifying the persons who have authority to amend the plan, and

(4) specify the basis on which payments are made to and from the plan.

(c) Any employee benefit plan may provide

(1) that any person or group of persons may serve in more than one fiduciary capacity with respect to the plan (including service both as trustee and administrator);

(2) that a named fiduciary, or a fiduciary designated by a named fiduciary pursuant to a plan procedure described in section 405(c)(1), may employ one or more persons to render advice with regard to any responsibility such fiduciary has under the plan; or

(3) that a person who is a named fiduciary with respect to control or management of the assets of the plan may appoint an investment manager or managers to manage (including the power to acquire and dispose of) any assets of a plan.

ESTABLISHMENT OF TRUST

Sec. 403. (a) Except as provided in subsection (b), all assets of an employee benefit plan shall be held in trust by one or more trustees. Such trustee or trustees shall be either named in the trust instrument or in the plan instrument described in section 402(a) or appointed by a person who is a named fiduciary, and upon acceptance of being named or appointed, the trustee or trustees shall have exclusive authority and discretion to manage and control the assets of the plan, except to the extent that—

(1) the plan expressly provides that the trustee or trustees are subject to the direction of a named fiduciary who is not a trustee, in which case the trustees shall be subject to proper directions of such fiduciary which are made in accordance with the terms of the plan and which are not contrary to this Act, or

(2) authority to manage, acquire, or dispose of assets of the plan is delegated to one or more investment managers pursuant to section 402(c)(3).

(b) The requirements of subsection (a) of this section shall not apply—

(1) to any assets of a plan which consist of insurance contracts or policies issued by an insurance company qualified to do business in a State;

(2) to any assets of such an insurance company or any assets of a plan which are held by such an insurance company;

(3) to a plan—

(A) some or all of the participants of which are employees described in section 401(c)(1) of the Internal Revenue Code of 1986; or

(B) which consists of one or more individual retirement accounts described in section 408 of the Internal Revenue Code of 1986,

to the extent that such plan's assets are held in one or more custodial accounts which qualify under section 401(f) or 408(h) of such Code, whichever is applicable.

(4) to a plan which the Secretary exempts from the requirement of subsection (a) and which is not subject to any of the following provisions of this Act;

(A) part 2 of this subtitle,

(B) part 3 of this subtitle, or

(C) title IV of this Act; or

(5) to a contract established and maintained under section 403(b) of the Internal Revenue Code of 1954 to the extent that the assets of the contract are held in one or more custodial accounts pursuant to section 403(b)(7) of such Code.

(6) Any plan, fund or program under which an employer, all of whose stock is directly or indirectly owned by employees, former employees or their beneficiaries, proposes through an unfunded arrangement to compensate retired employees for benefits which were forfeited by such employees under a pension plan maintained by a former employer prior to the date such pension plan became subject to this Act.

(c)(1) Except as provided in paragraph (2), (3), or (4) or subsection (d), or under section 4042 and 4044 (relating to termination of insured plans) or under section 420 of the Internal Revenue Code of 1986 (as in effect on January 1, 1991), the assets of a plan shall never inure to the benefit of any employer and shall be held for the exclusive purposes of providing benefits to participants in the plan and their beneficiaries and defraying reasonable expenses of administering the plan.

(2)(A) In the case of a contribution, or a payment of withdrawal liability under part 1 of subtitle E of title IV

(i) if such contribution or payment is made by an employer to a plan (other than a multiemployer plan) by a mistake of fact, paragraph (1) shall not prohibit the return of such contribution to the employer within one year after the payment of the contribution, and

(ii) if such contribution or payment is made by an employer to a multiemployer plan by a mistake of fact or law (other than a mistake relating to whether the plan is described in section 401(a) of the Internal Revenue Code of 1954 or the trust which is part of such plan is exempt from taxation under section 501(a) of such Code), paragraph (1) shall not prohibit the return of such contribution or payment to the employer within 6 months after the plan administrator determines that the contribution was made by such a mistake.

(B) If a contribution is conditioned on initial qualification of the plan under section 401 or 403(a) of the Internal Revenue Code of 1986, and if the plan receives an adverse determination with respect to its initial qualification, then paragraph (1) shall not prohibit the return of such contribution to the employer within one year after such determination, but only if the application for the determination is made by the time prescribed by law for filing the employer's return for the taxable year in which such plan was adopted, or such later date as the Secretary of the Treasury may prescribe.

(C) If a contribution is conditioned upon the deductibility of the contribution under section 404 of the Internal Revenue Code of 1954, then, to the extent the deduction is disallowed, paragraph (1) shall not prohibit the return to the employer of such contribution (to the extent disallowed) within one year after the disallowance of the deduction.

(3) In the case of a withdrawal liability payment which has been determined to be an overpayment, paragraph (1) shall not prohibit the return of such payment to the employer within 6 months after the date of such determination.

(d)(1) Upon termination of a pension plan to which section 4021 does not apply at the time of termination and to which this part applies (other than a plan to which no employer contributions have been made) the assets of the plan shall be allocated in accordance with the provisions of section 4044 of this Act, except as otherwise provided in regulations of the Secretary.

(2) The assets of a welfare plan which terminates shall be distributed in accordance with the terms of the plan, except as otherwise provided in regulations of the Secretary.

FIDUCIARY DUTIES

Sec. 404. (a)(1) Subject to sections 403(c) and (d), 4042, and 4044, a fiduciary shall discharge his duties with respect to a plan solely in the interest of the participants and beneficiaries and—

(A) for the exclusive purpose of:

(i) providing benefits to participants and their beneficiaries; and

(ii) defraying reasonable expenses of administering the plan;

(B) with the care, skill, prudence, and diligence under the circumstances then prevailing that a prudent man acting in a like capacity and familiar with such matters would use in the conduct of an enterprise of a like character and with like aims;

(C) by diversifying the investments of the plan so as to minimize the risk of large losses, unless under the circumstances it is clearly prudent not to do so; and

(D) in accordance with the documents and instruments governing the plan insofar as such documents and instruments are consistent with the provisions of this title and title IV.

(2) In the case of an eligible individual account plan (as defined in section 407(d)(3)), the diversification requirement of paragraph (1)(C) and the prudence requirement (only to the extent that it requires diversification) of paragraph (1)(B) is not violated by acquisition or holding of qualifying employer real property or qualifying employer securities (as defined in section 407(d)(4) and (5)).

(b) Except as authorized by the Secretary by regulation, no fiduciary may maintain the indicia of ownership of any assets of a plan outside the jurisdiction of the district courts of the United States.

(c) In the case of a pension plan which provides for individual accounts and permits a participant or beneficiary to exercise control over assets in his account, if a participant or beneficiary exercises control over the assets in his account (as determined under regulations of the Secretary)—

(1) such participant or beneficiary shall not be deemed to be a fiduciary by reason of such exercise, and

(2) no person who is otherwise a fiduciary shall be liable under this part for any loss, or by reason of any breach, which results from such participant's, or beneficiary's exercise of control.

(d)(1) If, in connection with the termination of a pension plan which is a single employer plan, there is an election to establish or maintain a qualified replacement plan, or to increase benefits, as provided under section 4980(d) of the Internal Revenue Code of 1986, a fiduciary shall discharge the fiduciary's duties under this title and title IV in accordance with the following requirements:

(A) In the case of a fiduciary of the terminated plan, any requirement—

(i) under section 4980(d)(2)(B) of such Code with respect to the transfer of assets from the terminated plan to a qualified replacement plan, and

(ii) under section 4980(d)(2)(B)(ii) or 4980(d)(3) of such Code with respect to any increase in benefits under the terminated plan.

(B) In the case of a fiduciary of a qualified replacement plan, any requirement—

(i) under section 4980(d)(2)(A) of such code with respect to participation in the qualified replacement plan of active participants in the terminated plan.

(ii) under section 4980(d)(2)(B) of such Code with respect to the receipt of assets from the terminated plan, and

(iii) under section 4980(d)(2)(c) of such Code with respect to the allocation of assets to participants of the qualified replacement plan.

(2) For purposes of this subsection—

(A) any term used in this subsection which is also then used in section 4980(d) of the Internal Revenue Code of 1986 shall have the same meaning as when used in such section, and

(B) any reference to this subsection in the Internal Revenue Code of 1986 should be a reference to such Code as in effect immediately after the enactment of the Omnibus Budget Reconciliation Act of 1990.

LIABILITY FOR BREACH BY COFIDUCIARY

Sec. 405. (a) In addition to any liability which he may have under any other provision of this part, a fiduciary with respect to a plan shall be liable for a breach of fiduciary responsibility of another fiduciary with respect to the same plan in the following circumstances:

(1) if he participates knowingly in, or knowingly undertakes to conceal, an act or omission of such other fiduciary, knowing such act or omission is a breach;

(2) if, by his failure to comply with section 404(a)(1) in the administration of his specific responsibilities which give rise to his status as a fiduciary, he has enabled such other fiduciary to commit a breach; or

(3) if he has knowledge of a breach by such other fiduciary, unless he makes reasonable efforts under the circumstances to remedy the breach.

(b)(1) Except as otherwise provided in subsection (d) and in section 403(a)(1) and (2), if the assets of a plan are held by two or more trustees—

(A) each shall use reasonable care to prevent a co-trustee from committing a breach; and

(B) they shall jointly manage and control the assets of the plan, except that nothing in this subparagraph (B) shall preclude any agreement, authorized by the trust instrument, allocating specific responsibilities, obligations, or duties among trustees, in which event a trustee to whom certain responsibilities, obligations, or duties have not been allocated shall not be liable by reason of this subparagraph (B) either individually or as a trustee for any loss resulting to the plan arising from the acts or omissions on the part of another trustee to whom such responsibilities, obligations, or duties have been allocated.

(2) Nothing in this subsection shall limit any liability that a fiduciary may have under subsection (a) or any other provision of this part.

(3)(A) In the case of a plan the assets of which are held in more than one trust, a trustee shall not be liable under paragraph (1) except with respect to an act or omission of a trustee of a trust of which he is a trustee.

(B) No trustee shall be liable under this subsection for following instructions referred to in section 403(a)(1).

(c)(1) The instrument under which a plan is maintained may expressly provide for procedures (A) for allocating fiduciary responsibilities [(other than trustee) responsibilities] among named fiduciaries, and (B) for named fiduciaries to designate persons other than named fiduciaries to carry out fiduciary responsibilities (other than trustee responsibilities) under the plan.

(2) If a plan expressly provides for a procedure described in paragraph (1), and pursuant to such procedure any fiduciary responsibility of a named fiduciary is allocated to any person, or a person is designated to carry out any such responsibility, then such named fiduciary shall not be liable for an act or omission of such person in carrying out such responsibility except to the extent that—

(A) the named fiduciary violated section 404(a)(1)—

(i) with respect to such allocation or designation,

(ii) with respect to the establishment or implementation of the procedure under paragraph (1), or

(iii) in continuing the allocation or designation; or

(B) the named fiduciary would otherwise be liable in accordance with subsection (a).

(3) For purposes of this subsection, the term "trustee responsibility" means any responsibility provided in the plan's trust instrument (if any) to manage or control the assets of the plan, other than a power under the trust instrument of a named fiduciary to appoint an investment manager in accordance with section 402(c)(3).

(d)(1) If an investment manager or managers have been appointed under section 402(c)(3), then, notwithstanding subsections (a)(2) and (3) and subsection (b), no trustee shall be liable for the acts or omissions of such investment manager or managers, or be under an obligation to invest or otherwise manage any asset of the plan which is subject to the management of such investment manager.

(2) Nothing in this subsection shall relieve any trustee of any liability under this part for any act of such trustee.

PROHIBITED TRANSACTIONS

Sec. 406. (a) Except as provided in section 408:

(1) A fiduciary with respect to a plan shall not cause the plan to engage in a transaction, if he knows or should know that such transaction constitutes a direct or indirect—

(A) sale or exchange, or leasing, of any property between the plan and a party in interest;

(B) lending of money or other extension of credit between the plan and a party in interest;

(C) furnishing of goods, services, or facilities between the plan and a party in interest;

(D) transfer to, or use by or for the benefit of, a party in interest, of any assets of the plan; or

(E) acquisition, on behalf of the plan, of any employer security or employer real property in violation of section 407(a).

(2) No fiduciary who has authority or discretion to control or manage the assets of a plan shall permit the plan to hold any employer security or employer real property if he knows or should know that holding such security or real property violates section 407(a).

(b) A fiduciary with respect to a plan shall not—

(1) deal with the assets of the plan in his own interest or for his own account,

(2) in his individual or any other capacity act in any transaction involving the plan on behalf of a party (or represent a party) whose interests are adverse to the interests of the plan or the interests of its participants or beneficiaries, or

(3) receive any consideration for his own personal account from any party dealing with such plan in connection with a transaction involving the assets of the plan.

(c) A transfer of real or personal property by a party in interest to a plan shall be treated as a sale or exchange if the property is subject to a mortgage or similar lien which the plan assumes or if it is subject to a mortgage or similar lien which a party-in-interest placed on the property within the 10-year period ending on the date of the transfer.

10 PERCENT LIMITATION WITH RESPECT TO ACQUISITION AND HOLDING OF EMPLOYER SECURITIES AND EMPLOYER REAL PROPERTY BY CERTAIN PLANS

Sec. 407. (a) Except as otherwise provided in this section and section 414:

(1) A plan may not acquire or hold—

(A) any employer security which is not a qualifying employer security, or

(B) any employer real property which is not qualifying employer real property.

(2) A plan may not acquire any qualifying employer security or qualifying employer real property, if immediately after such acquisition the aggregate fair market value of employer securities and employer real property held by the plan exceeds 10 percent of the fair market value of the assets of the plan.

(3)(A) After December 31, 1984, a plan may not hold any qualifying employer securities or qualifying employer real property (or both) to the extent that the aggregate fair market value of such securities and property determined on December 31, 1984, exceeds 10 percent of the greater of—

(i) the fair market value of the assets of the plan, determined on December 31, 1984, or

(ii) the fair market value of the assets of the plan determined on January 1, 1975.

(B) Subparagraph (A) of this paragraph shall not apply to any plan which on any date after December 31, 1974, and before January 1, 1985, did not hold employer securities or employer real property (or both) the aggregate fair market value of which determined on such date exceeded 10 percent of the greater of—

(i) the fair market value of the assets of the plan, determined on such date, or

(ii) the fair market value of the assets of the plan determined on January 1, 1975.

(4)(A) After December 31, 1979, a plan may not hold any employer securities or employer real property in excess of the amount specified in regulations under subparagraph (B). This subparagraph shall not apply to a plan after the earliest date after December 31, 1974, on which it complies with such regulations.

(B) Not later than December 31, 1976, the Secretary shall prescribe regulations which shall have the effect of requiring that a plan divest itself of 50 percent of the holdings of employer securities and employer real property which the plan would be required to divest before January 1, 1985, under paragraph (2) or subsection (c) (whichever is applicable).

(b)(1) Subsection (a) of this section shall not apply to any acquisition or holding of qualifying employer securities or qualifying employer real property by an eligible individual account plan.

(2) Cross References.

(A) For exemption from diversification requirements for holding of qualifying employer securities and qualifying employer real property by eligible individual account plans, see section 404(a)(2).

(B) For exemption from prohibited transactions for certain acquisitions of qualifying employer securities and qualifying employer real property which are not in violation of the 10 percent limitation, see section 408(e).

(C) For transitional rules respecting securities or real property subject to binding contracts in effect on June 30, 1974, see section 414(c).

(c)(1) A plan which makes the election, under paragraph (3) shall be treated as satisfying the requirement of subsection (a)(3) if and only if employer securities held on any date after December 31, 1974 and before January 1, 1985 have a fair market value, determined as of December 31, 1974, not in excess of 10 percent of the lesser of—

(A) the fair market value of the assets of the plan determined on such date (disregarding any portion of the fair market value of employer securities which is attributable to appreciation of such securities after December 31, 1974) but not less than the fair market value of plan assets on January 1, 1975, or

(B) an amount equal to the sum of (i) the total amount of the contributions to the plan received after December 31, 1974, and prior to such date, plus (ii) the fair market value of the assets of the plan, determined on January 1, 1975.

(2) For purposes of this subsection, in the case of an employer security held by a plan after January 1, 1975, the ownership of which is derived from ownership of employer securities held by the plan on January 1, 1975, or from the exercise of rights derived from such ownership, the value of such security held after January 1, 1975, shall be based on the value as of January 1, 1975, of the security from which ownership was derived. The Secretary shall prescribe regulations to carry out this paragraph.

(3) An election under this paragraph may not be made after December 31, 1975. Such an election shall be made in accordance with regulations prescribed by the Secretary, and shall be irrevocable. A plan may make an election under this paragraph only if on January 1, 1975, the plan holds no employer real property. After such election and before January 1, 1985 the plan may not acquire any employer real property.

(d) For purposes of this section—

(1) The term "employer security" means a security issued by an employer of employees covered by the plan, or by an affiliate of such employer. A contract to which section 408(b)(5) applies shall not be treated as a security for purposes of this section.

(2) The term "employer real property" means real property (and related personal property) which is leased to an employer of employees covered by the plan, or to an affiliate of such employer. For purposes of determining the time at which a plan acquires employer real property for purposes of this section, such property shall be deemed to be acquired by the plan on the date on which the plan acquires the property or on the date on which the lease to the employer (or affiliate) is entered into, whichever is later.

(3)(A) The term "eligible individual account plan" means an individual account plan which is (i) a profit-sharing, stock bonus, thrift, or savings plan; (ii) an employee stock ownership plan; or (iii) a money purchase plan which was in existence on the date of enactment of this Act and which on such date invested primarily in qualifying employer securities. Such term excludes an individual retirement account or annuity described in section 408 of the Internal Revenue Code of 1954.

(B) Notwithstanding subparagraph (A), a plan shall be treated as an eligible individual account plan with respect to the acquisition or holding of qualifying employer real property or qualifying employer securities only if such plan explicitly provides for acquisition and holding of qualifying employer securities or qualifying employer real property (as the case may be). In the case of a plan in existence on the date of enactment of this Act, this subparagraph shall not take effect until January 1, 1976.

(C) The term "eligible individual account plan" does not include any individual account plan the benefits of which are taken into account in determining the benefits payable to a participant under any defined benefit plan.

(4) The term "qualifying employer real property" means parcels of employer real property—

(A) if a substantial number of the parcels are dispersed geographically;

(B) if each parcel of real property and the improvements thereon are suitable (or adaptable without excessive cost) for more than one use;

(C) even if all of such real property is leased to one lessee (which may be an employer, or an affiliate of an employer); and

(D) if the acquisition and retention of such property comply with the provisions of this part (other than section 404(a)(1)(B) to the extent it requires diversification, and sections 404(a)(1)(C), 406, and subsection (a) of this section).

(5) The term "qualifying employer security" means an employer security which is—

(A) stock

(B) a marketable obligation (as defined in subsection (e)), or

(C) an interest in a publicly traded partnership (as defined in section 7704(b) of the Internal Revenue Code of 1986), but only if such partnership is an existing partnership as defined in section 10211(c)(2)(A) of the Revenue Act of 1987 (Public Law 100-203).

After December 17, 1987, in the case of a plan other than an eligible individual account plan, an employer security described in subparagraph (A) or (C) shall be considered a qualifying employer security only if such employer security satisfies the requirements of subsection (f)(1).

(6) The term "employee stock ownership plan" means an individual account plan—

(A) which is a stock bonus plan which is qualified, or a stock bonus plan and money purchase plan both of which are qualified, under section 401 of the Internal Revenue Code of 1954, and which is designed to invest primarily in qualifying employer securities, and

(B) which meets such other requirements as the Secretary of the Treasury may prescribe by regulation.

(7) A corporation is an affiliate of an employer if it is a member of any controlled group of corporations (as defined in section 1563(a) of the Internal Revenue Code of 1954, except that "applicable percentage" shall be substituted for "80 percent" wherever the latter percentage appears in such section) of which the employer who maintains the plan is a member. For purposes of the preceding sentence, the term "applicable percentage" means 50 percent, or such lower percentage as the Secretary may prescribe by regulation. A person other than a corporation shall be treated as an affiliate of an employer to the extent provided in regulations of the Secretary. An employer which is a person other than a corporation shall be treated as affiliated with another person to the extent provided by regulations of the Secretary. Regulations under this paragraph shall be prescribed only after consultation and coordination with the Secretary of the Treasury.

(8) The Secretary may prescribe regulations specifying the extent to which conversions, splits, the exercise of rights, and similar transactions are not treated as acquisitions.

(9) For purposes of this section, an arrangement which consists of a defined benefit plan and an individual account plan shall be treated as 1 plan if the benefits of such individual account plan are taken into account in determining the benefits payable under such defined benefit plan.

(e) For purposes of subsection (d)(5), the term "marketable obligation" means a bond, debenture, note, or certificate, or other evidence of indebtedness (hereinafter in this subsection referred to as "obligation") if—

(1) such obligation is acquired—

(A) on the market, either (i) at the price of the obligation prevailing on a national securities exchange which is registered with the Securities and Exchange Commission, or (ii) if the obligation is not traded on such a national securities exchange, at a price not less favorable to the plan than the offering price for the obligation as established by current bid and asked prices quoted by persons independent of the issuer;

(B) from an underwriter, at a price (i) not in excess of the public offering price for the obligation as set forth in a prospectus or offering circular filed with the Securities and Exchange Commission, and (ii) at which a substantial portion of the same issue is acquired by persons independent of the issuer; or

(C) directly from the issuer, at a price not less favorable to the plan than the price paid currently for a substantial portion of the same issue by persons independent of the issuer;

(2) immediately following acquisition of such obligation—

(A) not more than 25 percent of the aggregate amount of obligations issued in such issue and outstanding at the time of acquisition is held by the plan, and

(B) at least 50 percent of the aggregate amount referred to in subparagraph (A) is held by persons independent of the issuer; and

(3) immediately following acquisition of the obligation, not more than 25 percent of the assets of the plan is invested in obligations of the employer or an affiliate of the employer.

(f)(1) Stock satisfies the requirements of this paragraph if, immediately following the acquisition of such stock—

(A) no more than 25 percent of the aggregate amount of stock of the same class issued and outstanding at the time of acquisition is held by the plan, and

(B) at least 50 percent of the aggregate amount referred to in subparagraph (A) is held by persons independent of the issuer.

(2) Until January 1, 1993, a plan shall not be treated as violating subsection (a) solely by holding stock which fails to satisfy the requirements of paragraph (1) if such stock—

(A) has been so held since December 17, 1987, or

(B) was acquired after December 17, 1987, pursuant to a legally binding contract in effect on December 17, 1987, and has been so held at all times after the acquisition.

(3) After December 17, 1987, no plan may acquire stock which does not satisfy the requirements of paragraph (1) unless the acquisition is made pursuant to a legally binding contract in effect on such date.

EXEMPTIONS FROM PROHIBITED TRANSACTIONS

Sec. 408. (a) The Secretary shall establish an exemption procedure for purposes of this subsection. Pursuant to such procedure, he may grant a conditional or unconditional exemption of any fiduciary or transaction, or class of fiduciaries or transactions, from all or part of the restrictions imposed by sections 406 and 407(a). Action under this subsection may be taken only after consultation and coordination with the Secretary of the Treasury. An exemption granted under this section shall not relieve a fiduciary from any other applicable provision of this Act. The Secretary may not grant an exemption under this subsection unless he finds that such exemption is—

(1) administratively feasible,

(2) in the interests of the plan and of its participants and beneficiaries, and

(3) protective of the rights of participants and beneficiaries of such plan. Before granting an exemption under this subsection from section 406(a) or 407(a), the Secretary shall publish notice in the Federal Register of the pendency of the exemption, shall require that adequate notice be given to interested persons, and shall afford interested persons opportunity to present views. The Secretary may not grant an exemption under this subsection from section 406(b) unless he affords an opportunity for a hearing and makes a determination on the record with respect to the findings required by paragraphs (1), (2), and (3) of this subsection.

(b) The prohibitions provided in section 406 shall not apply to any of the following transactions:

(1) Any loans made by the plan to parties in interest who are participants or beneficiaries of the plan if such loans (A) are available to all such participants and beneficiaries on a reasonably equivalent basis, (B) are not made available to highly compensated employees (within the meaning of section 414(q) of the Internal Revenue Code of 1986) in an amount greater than the amount made available to other employees, (C) are made in accordance with specific provisions regarding such loans set forth in the plan, (D) bear a reasonable rate of interest, and (E) are adequately secured.

(2) Contracting or making reasonable arrangements with a party in interest for office space, or legal, accounting, or other services necessary for the establishment or operation of the plan, if no more than reasonable compensation is paid therefor.

(3) A loan to an employee stock ownership plan (as defined in section 407(d)(6)), if—

(A) such loan is primarily for the benefit of participants and beneficiaries of the plan, and

(B) such loan is at an interest rate which is not in excess of a reasonable rate.

If the plan gives collateral to a party in interest for such loan, such collateral may consist only of qualifying employer securities (as defined in section 407(d)(5)).

(4) The investment of all or part of a plan's assets in deposits which bear a reasonable interest rate in a bank or similar financial institution supervised by the United States or a State, if such bank or other institution is a fiduciary of such plan and if—

(A) the plan covers only employees of such bank or other institution and employees of affiliates of such bank or other institution, or

(B) such investment is expressly authorized by a provision of the plan or by a fiduciary (other than such bank or institution or affiliate thereof) who is expressly empowered by the plan to so instruct the trustee with respect to such investment.

(5) Any contract for life insurance, health insurance, or annuities with one or more insurers which are qualified to do business in a State, if the plan pays no more than adequate consideration, and if each such insurer or insurers is—

(A) the employer maintaining the plan, or

(B) a party in interest which is wholly owned (directly or indirectly) by the employer maintaining the plan, or by any person which is a party in interest with respect to the plan, but only if the total premiums and annuity considerations written by such insurers for life insurance, health insurance, or annuities for all plans (and their employers) with respect to which such insurers are parties in interest (not including premiums or annuity considerations written by the employer maintaining the plan) do not exceed 5 percent of the total premiums and annuity considerations written for all lines of insurance in that year by such insurers (not including premiums or annuity considerations written by the employer maintaining the plan).

(6) The providing of any ancillary service by a bank or similar financial institution supervised by the United States or a State, if such bank or other institution is a fiduciary of such plan, and if—

(A) such bank or similar financial institution has adopted adequate internal safeguards which assure that the providing of such ancillary service is consistent with sound banking and financial practice, as determined by Federal or State supervisory authority, and

(B) the extent to which such ancillary service is provided is subject to specific guidelines issued by such bank or similar financial institution (as determined by the Secretary after consultation with Federal and State supervisory authority), and adherence to such guidelines would reasonably preclude such bank or similar financial institution from providing such ancillary service (i) in an excessive or unreasonable manner, and (ii) in a manner that would be inconsistent with the best interests of participants and beneficiaries of employee benefit plans.

Such ancillary services shall not be provided at more than reasonable compensation.

(7) The exercise of a privilege to convert securities, to the extent provided in regulations of the Secretary, but only if the plan receives no less than adequate consideration pursuant to such conversion.

(8) Any transaction between a plan and (i) a common or collective trust fund or pooled investment fund maintained by a party in interest which is a bank or trust company supervised by a State or Federal agency or (ii) a pooled investment fund of an insurance company qualified to do business in a State, if—

(A) the transaction is a sale or purchase of an interest in the fund,

(B) the bank, trust company, or insurance company receives not more than reasonable compensation, and

(C) such transaction is expressly permitted by the instrument under which the plan is maintained, or by a fiduciary (other than the bank, trust company, or insurance company, or an affiliate thereof) who has authority to manage and control the assets of the plan.

(9) The making by a fiduciary of a distribution of the assets of the plan in accordance with the terms of the plan if such assets are distributed in the same manner as provided under section 4044 of this Act (relating to allocation of assets).

(10) Any transaction required or permitted under part 1 of subtitle E of title IV.

(11) A merger of multiemployer plans, or the transfer of assets or liabilities between multiemployer plans, determined by the Pension Benefit Guaranty Corporation to meet the requirements of section 4231.

(12) The sale by a plan to a party in interest on or after December 18, 1987, of any stock, if—

(A) the requirements of paragraphs (1) and (2) of subsection (e) are met with respect to such stock,

(B) on the later of the date on which the stock was acquired by the plan, or January 1, 1975, such stock constituted a qualifying employer security (as defined in section 407(d)(5) as then in effect), and

(C) such stock does not constitute a qualifying employer security (as defined in section 407(d)(5) as in effect at the time of the sale).

(13) Any transfer in a taxable year beginning before January 1, 1996, of excess pension assets from a defined benefit plan to a retiree health account in a qualified transfer permitted under section 420 of the Internal Revenue Code of 1986 (as in effect on January 1, 1991.)

(c) Nothing in section 406 shall be construed to prohibit any fiduciary from—

(1) receiving any benefit to which he may be entitled as a participant or beneficiary in the plan, so long as the benefit is computed and paid on a basis which is consistent with the terms of the plan as applied to all other participants and beneficiaries;

(2) receiving any reasonable compensation for services rendered, or for the reimbursement of expenses properly and actually incurred, in the performance of his duties with the plan; except that no person so serving who already receives full-time pay from an employer or an association of employers, whose employees are participants in the plan, or from an employee organization whose members are participants in such plan shall receive compensation from such plan, except for reimbursement of expenses properly and actually incurred; or

(3) serving as a fiduciary in addition to being an officer, employee, agent, or other representative of a party in interest.

(d) Section 407(b) and subsections (b), (c), and (e) of this section shall not apply to any transaction in which a plan, directly or indirectly—

(1) lends any part of the corpus or income of the plan to;

(2) pays any compensation for personal services rendered to the plan to; or

(3) acquires for the plan any property from or sells any property to;

any person who is with respect to the plan an owner-employee (as defined in section 401(c)(3) of the Internal Revenue Code of 1954), a member of the family (as defined in section 267(c)(4) of such Code) of any such owner-employee, or a corporation controlled by any such owner-employee through the ownership, directly or indirectly, of 50 percent or more of the total combined voting power of all classes of stock entitled to vote or 50 percent or more of the total value of shares of all classes of stock of the corporation. For purposes of this subsection a shareholder employee (as defined in section 1379 of the Internal Revenue Code of 1954) as in effect on the day before the date of enactment of the Subchapter S Revision Act of 1982 and a participant or beneficiary of an individual retirement account or individual retirement annuity described in section 408 of the Internal Revenue Code of 1986 or a retirement bond described in section 409 of the Internal Revenue Code of 1954 (as effective for such obligations issued before January 1, 1984) and an employer or association of employers which establishes such an account or annuity under section 408(c) of the Internal Revenue Code of 1986 shall be deemed to be an owner-employee.

(e) Sections 406 and 407 shall not apply to the acquisition or sale by a plan of qualifying employer securities (as defined in section 407(d)(5)) or acquisition, sale or lease by a plan of qualifying employer real property (as defined in section 407(d)(4))—

(1) if such acquisition, sale, or lease is for adequate consideration (or in the case of a marketable obligation, at a price not less favorable to the plan than the price determined under section 407(e)(1)),

(2) if no commission is charged with respect thereto, and

(3) If—

(A) the plan is an eligible individual account plan (as defined in section 407(d)(3)), or

(B) in the case of an acquisition or lease of qualifying employer real property by a plan which is not an eligible individual account plan, or of an acquisition of qualifying employer securities by such a plan, the lease or acquisition is not prohibited by section 407(a).

(f) Section 406(b)(2) shall not apply to any merger or transfer described in subsection (b)(11).

LIABILITY FOR BREACH OF FIDUCIARY DUTY

Sec. 409. (a) Any person who is a fiduciary with respect to a plan who breaches any of the responsibilities, obligations, or duties imposed upon fiduciaries by this title shall be personally liable to make good to such plan any losses to the plan resulting from each such breach, and to restore to such plan any profits of such fiduciary which have been made through use of assets of the plan by the fiduciary, and shall be subject to such other equitable or remedial relief as the court may deem appropriate, including removal of such fiduciary. A fiduciary may also be removed for a violation of section 411 of this Act.

(b) No fiduciary shall be liable with respect to a breach of fiduciary duty under this title if such breach was committed before he became a fiduciary or after he ceased to be a fiduciary.

EXCULPATORY PROVISIONS; INSURANCE

Sec. 410. (a) Except as provided in sections 405(b)(1) and 405(d), any provision in an agreement or instrument which purports to relieve a fiduciary from responsibility or liability for any responsibility, obligation, or duty under this part shall be void as against public policy.

(b) Nothing in this subpart shall preclude—

(1) a plan from purchasing insurance for its fiduciaries or for itself to cover liability or losses occurring by reason of the act or omission of a fiduciary, if such insurance permits recourse by the insurer against the fiduciary in the case of a breach of a fiduciary obligation by such fiduciary;

(2) a fiduciary from purchasing insurance to cover liability under this part from and for his own account; or

(3) an employer or an employee organization from purchasing insurance to cover potential liability of one or more persons who serve in a fiduciary capacity with regard to an employee benefit plan.

PROHIBITION AGAINST CERTAIN PERSONS HOLDING CERTAIN POSITIONS

Sec. 411. (a) No person who has been convicted of, or has been imprisoned as a result of his conviction of, robbery, bribery, extortion, embezzlement, fraud, grand larceny, burglary, arson, a felony violation of Federal or State law involving substances defined in section 102(6) of the Comprehensive Drug Abuse Prevention and Control Act of 1970, murder, rape, kidnaping, perjury, assault with intent to kill, any crime described in section 9(a)(1) of the Investment Company Act of 1940 (15 U.S.C. 80a-9(a)(1)), a violation of any provision of this Act, a violation of section 302 of the Labor-Management Relations Act, 1947 (29 U.S.C. 186), a violation of chapter 63 of title 18, United States Code, a violation of section 874, 1027, 1503, 1505, 1506, 1510, 1951, or 1954 of title 18, United States Code, a violation of the Labor-Management Reporting and Disclosure Act of 1959 (29 U.S.C. 401), any felony involving abuse or misuse of such person's position or employment in a labor organization or employee benefit plan to seek or obtain an illegal gain at the expense of the members of the labor organization or the beneficiaries of the employee benefit plan, or conspiracy to commit any such crimes or attempt to commit any such crimes, or a crime in which any of the foregoing crimes is an element, shall serve or be permitted to serve—

(1) as an administrator, fiduciary, officer, trustee, custodian, counsel, agent, employee, or representative in any capacity of any employee benefit plan,

(2) as a consultant or adviser to an employee benefit plan, including but not limited to any entity whose activities are in whole or substantial part devoted to providing goods or services to any employee benefit plan, or

(3) in any capacity that involves decisionmaking authority or custody or control of the moneys, funds, assets, or property of any employee benefit plan, during or for the period of thirteen years after such conviction or after the end of such imprisonment, whichever is later, unless the sentencing court on the motion of the person convicted set a lesser period of at least three years after such conviction or after the end of such imprisonment, whichever is later, or unless prior to the end of such period, in the case of a person so convicted or imprisoned (A) his citizenship rights, having been revoked as a result of such conviction, have been fully restored, or (B) if the offense is a Federal offense, the sentencing judge or, if the offense is a State or local offense, the United States district court for the district in which the offense was committed, pursuant to sentencing guidelines and policy statements under section 994(a) of title 28, United States Code, determined that such person's service in any capacity referred to in paragraphs (1) through (3) would not be contrary to the purposes of this title. Prior to making any such determination the court shall hold a hearing and shall give notice to such proceeding by certified mail to the Secretary of Labor and to State, county, and Federal prosecuting officials in the jurisdiction or jurisdictions in which such person was convicted. The court's determination in any such proceeding shall be final. No person shall knowingly hire, retain, employ, or otherwise place any other person to serve in any capacity in violation of this subsection. Notwithstanding the preceding provisions of this subsection, no corporation or partnership will be precluded from acting as an administrator, fiduciary, officer, trustee, custodian, counsel, agent, or employee of any employee benefit plan or as a consultant to any employee benefit plan without a notice, hearing, and determination by such court that such service would be inconsistent with the intention of this section.

(b) Any person who intentionally violates this section shall be fined not more than $10,000 or imprisoned for not more than five years, or both.

(c) For the purpose of this section:

(1) A person shall be deemed to have been "convicted" and under the disability of "conviction" from the date of the judgment of the trial court, regardless of whether that judgment remains under appeal.

(2) The term "consultant" means any person who, for compensation, advises or represents an employee benefit plan or who provides other assistance to such plan, concerning the establishment or operation of such plan.

(3) A period of parole or supervised release shall not be considered as part of a period of imprisonment.

(d) Whenever any person—

(1) by operation of this section, has been barred from office or other position in an employee benefit plan as a result of a conviction, and

(2) has filed an appeal of that conviction, any salary which would be otherwise due such person by virtue of such office or position, shall be placed in escrow by the individual or organization responsible for payment of such salary. Payment of such salary into escrow shall continue for the duration of the appeal or for the period of time during which such salary would be otherwise due, whichever is shorter. Upon the final reversal of such person's conviction on appeal, the amounts in escrow shall be paid to such person. Upon the final sustaining of that person's conviction on appeal, the amounts in escrow shall be returned to the individual or organization responsible for payments of those amounts. Upon final reversal of such person's conviction, such person shall no longer be barred by this statute from assuming any position from which such person was previously barred.

BONDING

Sec. 412. (a) Every fiduciary of an employee benefit plan and every person who handles funds or other property of such a plan (hereafter in this section referred to as "plan official") shall be bonded as provided in this section; except that—

(1) where such plan is one under which the only assets from which benefits are paid are the general assets of a union or of an employer, the administrator, officers, and employees of such plan shall be exempt from the bonding requirements of this section, and

(2) no bond shall be required of a fiduciary (or of any director, officer, or employee of such fiduciary) if such fiduciary—

(A) is a corporation organized and doing business under the laws of the United States or of any State;

(B) is authorized under such laws to exercise trust powers or to conduct an insurance business;

(C) is subject to supervision or examination by Federal or State authority; and

(D) has at all times a combined capital and surplus in excess of such a minimum amount as may be established by regulations issued by the Secretary, which amount shall be at least $1,000,000. Paragraph (2) shall apply to a bank or other financial institution which is authorized to exercise trust powers and the deposits of which are not insured by the Federal Deposit Insurance Corporation, only if such bank or institution meets bonding or similar requirements under State law which the Secretary determines are at least equivalent to those imposed on banks by Federal law.

The amount of such bond shall be fixed at the beginning of each fiscal year of the plan. Such amount shall be not less than 10 per centum of the amount of funds handled. In no case shall such bond be less than $1,000 nor more than $500,000, except that the Secretary, after due notice and opportunity for hearing to all interested parties, and after consideration of the record, may prescribe an amount in excess of $500,000, subject to the 10 per centum limitation of the preceding sentence. For purposes of fixing the amount of such bond, the amount of funds handled shall be determined by the funds handled by the person, group, or class to be covered by such bond and by their predecessor or predecessors, if any, during the preceding reporting year, or if the plan has no preceding reporting year, the amount of funds to be handled during the current reporting year by such person, group, or class, estimated as provided in regulations of the Secretary. Such bond shall provide protection to the plan against loss by reason of acts of fraud or dishonesty on the part of the plan official, directly or through connivance with others. Any bond shall have as surety thereon a corporate surety company which is an acceptable surety on Federal bonds under authority granted by the Secretary of the Treasury pursuant to sections 6 through 13 of title 6, United States Code. Any bond shall be in a form or of a type approved by the Secretary, including individual bonds or schedule or blanket forms of bonds which cover a group or class.

(b) It shall be unlawful for any plan official to whom subsection (a) applies, to receive, handle, disburse, or otherwise exercise custody or control of any of the funds or other property of any employee benefit plan, without being bonded as required by subsection (a) and it shall be unlawful for any plan official of such plan, or any other person having authority to direct the performance of such functions, to permit such functions, or any of them, to be performed by any plan official, with respect to whom the requirements of subsection (a) have not been met.

(c) It shall be unlawful for any person to procure any bond required by subsection (a) from any surety or other company or through any agent or broker in whose business operations such plan or any party in interest in such plan has any control or significant financial interest, direct or indirect.

(d) Nothing in any other provision of law shall require any person, required to be bonded as provided in subsection (a) because he handles funds or other property of an employee benefit plan, to be bonded insofar as the handling by such person of the funds or other property of such plan is concerned.

(e) The Secretary shall prescribe such regulations as may be necessary to carry out the provisions of this section including exempting a plan from the requirements of this section where he finds that (1) other bonding arrangements or (2) the overall financial condition of the plan would be adequate to protect the interests of the beneficiaries and participants. When, in the opinion of the Secretary, the administrator of a plan offers adequate evidence of the financial responsibility of the plan, or that other bonding arrangements would provide adequate protection of the beneficiaries and participants, he may exempt such plan from the requirements of this section.

LIMITATION OF ACTIONS

Sec. 413. No action may be commenced under this title with respect to a fiduciary's breach of any responsibility, duty, or obligation under this part, or with respect to a violation of this part, after the earlier of—

(1) six years after (A) the date of the last action which constituted a part of the breach or violation, or (B) in the case of an omission, the latest date on which the fiduciary could have cured the breach or violation, or

(2) three years after the earliest date on which the plaintiff had actual knowledge of the breach or violation;

except that in the case of fraud or concealment, such action may be commenced not later than six years after the date of discovery of such breach or violation.

EFFECTIVE DATE

Sec. 414. (a) Except as provided in subsections (b), (c), and (d), this part shall take effect on January 1, 1975.

(b)(1) The provisions of this part authorizing the Secretary to promulgate regulations shall take effect on the date of enactment of this Act.

(2) Upon application of a plan, the Secretary may postpone until not later than January 1, 1976, the applicability of any provision of sections 402, 403 (other than 403(c)), 405 (other than 405(a) and (d)), and 410(a), as it applies to any plan in existence on the date of enactment of this Act if he determines such postponement is (A) necessary to amend the instrument establishing the plan under which the plan is maintained and (B) not adverse to the interest of participants and beneficiaries.

(3) This part shall take effect on the date of enactment of this Act with respect to a plan which terminates after June 30, 1974, and before January 1, 1975, and to which at the time of termination section 4021 applies.

(c) Section 406 and 407(a) (relating to prohibited transactions) shall not apply—

(1) until June 30, 1984, to a loan of money or other extension of credit between a plan and a party in interest under a binding contract in effect on July 1, 1974 (or pursuant to renewals of such a contract), if such loan or other extension of credit remains at least as favorable to the plan as an arm's-length transaction with an unrelated party would be, and if the execution of the contract, the making of the loan, or the extension of credit was not, at the time of such execution, making, or extension, a prohibited transaction (within the meaning of section 503(b) of the Internal Revenue Code of 1954 or the corresponding provisions of prior law);

(2) until June 30, 1984, to a lease or joint use of property involving the plan and a party in interest pursuant to a binding contract in effect on July 1, 1974 (or pursuant to renewals of such a contract), if such lease or joint use remains at least as favorable to the plan as an arm's-length transaction with an unrelated party would be and if the execution of the contract was not, at the time of such execution, a prohibited transaction (within the meaning of section 503(b) of the Internal Revenue Code of 1986 or the corresponding provisions of prior law);

(3) until June 30, 1984, to the sale, exchange, or other disposition of property described in paragraph (2) between a plan and a party in interest if—

(A) in the case of a sale, exchange, or other disposition of the property by the plan to the party in interest, the plan receives an amount which is not less than the fair market value of the property at the time of such disposition; and

(B) in the case of the acquisition of the property by the plan, the plan pays an amount which is not in excess of the fair market value of the property at the time of such acquisition;

(4) until June 30, 1977, to the provision of services, to which paragraphs (1), (2), and (3) do not apply between a plan and a party in interest—

(A) under a binding contract in effect on July 1, 1974 (or pursuant to renewals of such contract), or

(B) if the party in interest ordinarily and customarily furnished such services on June 30, 1974, if such provision of services remains at least as favorable to the plan as an arm's-length transaction with an unrelated party would be and if such provision of services was not, at the time of such provision, a prohibited transaction (within the meaning of section 503(b) of the Internal Revenue Code of 1954) or the corresponding provisions of prior law; or

(5) the sale, exchange, or other disposition of property which is owned by a plan on June 30, 1974, and all times thereafter, to a party in interest, if such plan is required to dispose of such property in order to comply with the provisions of section 407(a) (relating to the prohibition against holding excess employer securities and employer real property), and if the plan receives not less than adequate consideration.

(d) Any election, or failure to elect, by a disqualified person under section 2003 (c)(1)(B) of this Act shall be treated for purposes of this part (but not for purposes of section 514) as an act or omission occurring before the effective date of this part.

(e) The preceding provisions of this section shall not apply with respect to amendments made to this part in provisions enacted after the date of the enactment of this Act.

Part 5—Administration and Enforcement

CRIMINAL PENALTIES

Sec. 501. Any person who willfully violates any provision of part 1 of this subtitle, or any regulation or order issued under any such provision, shall upon conviction be fined not more than $5,000 or imprisoned not more than one year, or both; except that in the case of such violation by a person not an individual, the fine imposed upon such person shall be a fine not exceeding $100,000.

CIVIL ENFORCEMENT

Sec. 502. (a) A civil action may be brought—

(1) by a participant or beneficiary—

(A) for the relief provided for in subsection (c) of this section, or

(B) to recover benefits due to him under the terms of his plan, to enforce his rights under the terms of the plan, or to clarify his rights to future benefits under the terms of the plan;

(2) by the Secretary, or by a participant, beneficiary or fiduciary for appropriate relief under section 409;

(3) by a participant, beneficiary, or fiduciary (A) to enjoin any act or practice which violates any provision of this title or the terms of the plan, or (B) to obtain other appropriate equitable relief (i) to redress such violations or (ii) to enforce any provisions of this title or the terms of the plan;

(4) by the Secretary or by a participant, or beneficiary for appropriate relief in the case of a violation of 105(c);

(5) except as otherwise provided in subsection (b), by the Secretary (A) to enjoin any act or practice which violates any provision of this title, or (B) to obtain other appropriate equitable relief (i) to redress such violation or (ii) to enforce any provision of this title; [or]

(6) by the Secretary to collect any civil penalty under subsection (i) or (*l*)[.];

(7) by a State to enforce compliance with a qualified medical child support order (as defined in section 609(a)(2)(A)); or

(8) by the Secretary, or by an employer or other person referred to in section 101(f)(1),(A) to enjoin any act or practice which violates subsection (f) of section 101, or (B) to obtain appropriate equitable relief (i) to redress such violation or (ii) to enforce such subsection.

◆ ◆ ◆

[*Editor's Note:* Sections 502(a)(7) and (8) were added by OBRA '93 Section 4301(c)(1). The effective date is August 10, 1993.]

◆ ◆ ◆

(b)(1) In the case of a plan which is qualified under section 401(a), 403(a), or 405(a) of the Internal Revenue Code of 1954 (or with respect to which an application to so qualify has been filed and has not been finally determined) the Secretary may exercise his authority under subsection (a)(5) with respect to a violation of, or the enforcement of, parts 2 and 3 of this subtitle (relating to participation, vesting, and funding) only if—

(A) requested by the Secretary of the Treasury, or

(B) one or more participants, beneficiaries, or fiduciaries, of such plan request in writing (in such manner as the Secretary shall prescribe by regulation) that he exercise such authority on their behalf. In the case of such a request under this paragraph he may exercise such authority only if he determines that such violation affects, or such enforcement is necessary to protect, claims of participants or beneficiaries to benefits under the plan.

(2) The Secretary shall not initiate an action to enforce section 515.

(c)(1) Any administrator (A) who fails to meet the requirements of paragraph (1) or (4) of section 606 or section 101(e)(1) with respect to a participant or beneficiary, or (B) who fails or refuses to comply with a request for any information which such administrator is required by this title to furnish to a participant or beneficiary (unless such failure or refusal results from matters reasonably beyond the control of the administrator) by mailing the material requested to the last known address of the requesting participant or beneficiary within 30 days after such request may in the courts' discretion be personally liable to such participant or beneficiary in the amount of up to $100 a day from the date of such failure or refusal, and the court may in its discretion order such other relief as it deems proper.

(2) The Secretary may assess a civil penalty against any plan administrator of up to $1,000 a day from the date of such plan administrator's failure or refusal to file the annual report required to be filed with the Secretary under section 101(b)(4). For purposes of this paragraph, an annual report that has been rejected under section 104(a)(4) for failure to provide material information shall not be treated as having been filed with the Secretary.

(3) Any employer maintaining a plan who fails to meet the notice requirement of section 101(d) with respect to any participant or beneficiary or who fails to meet the requirements of section 101(e)(2) with respect to any person may in the court's discretion be liable to such participant or beneficiary or to such person in the amount of up to $100 a day from the date of such failure, and the court may in its discretion order such other relief as it deems proper.

(4) *The Secretary may assess a civil penalty of not more than $1,000 for each violation by any person of section 101(f)(1). For purposes of this paragraph, each violation described in subparagraph (A) with respect to any single participant, and each violation described in subparagraph (B) with respect to any single participant or beneficiary, shall be treated as a separate violation. The Secretary and the Secretary of Health and Human Services shall maintain such ongoing consultation as may be necessary and appropriate to coordinate enforcement under this subsection with enforcement under section 1144(c)(8) of the Social Security Act.*

◆ ◆ ◆

[*Editor's Note:* Section 502(c)(4) was added by OBRA '93 Section 4301(c)(2). The effective date is August 10, 1993.]

◆ ◆ ◆

(d)(1) An employee benefit plan may sue or be sued under this title as an entity. Service of summons, subpoena, or other legal process of a court upon a trustee or an administrator of an employee benefit plan in his capacity as such shall constitute service upon the employee benefit plan. In a case where a plan has not designated in the summary plan description of the plan an individual as agent for the service of legal process, service upon the Secretary shall constitute such service. The Secretary, not later than 15 days after receipt of service under the preceding sentence, shall notify the administrator or any trustee of the plan of receipt of such service.

(2) Any money judgment under this title against an employee benefit plan shall be enforceable only against the plan as an entity and shall not be enforceable against any other person unless liability against such person is established in his individual capacity under this title.

(e)(1) Except for actions under subsection (a)(1)(B) of this section, the district courts of the United States shall have exclusive jurisdiction of civil actions under this title brought by the Secretary or by a participant, beneficiary, [or fiduciary.] *fiduciary, or any person referred to in section 101(f)(1).* State courts of competent jurisdiction and district courts of the United States shall have concurrent jurisdiction of actions under [subsection (a)(1)(B) of this section.] *paragraphs (1)(B) and (7) of subsection (a).*

(2) Where an action under this title is brought in a district court of the United States, it may be brought in the district where the plan is administered, where the breach took place, or where a defendant resides or may be found, and process may be served in any other district where a defendant resides or may be found.

◆ ◆ ◆

[*Editor's Note:* Section 502(e)(1) was amended by OBRA '93 Sections 4301(c)(3)(A) and (B).]

◆ ◆ ◆

(f) The district courts of the United States shall have jurisdiction, without respect to the amount in controversy or the citizenship of the parties, to grant the relief provided for in subsection (a) of this section in any action.

(g)(1) In any action under this title (other than an action described in paragraph (2) by a participant, beneficiary, or fiduciary, the court in its discretion may allow a reasonable attorney's fee and costs of action to either party.

(2) In any action under this title by a fiduciary for or on behalf of a plan to enforce section 515 in which a judgment in favor of the plan is awarded, the court shall award the plan—

(A) the unpaid contributions,

(B) interest on the unpaid contributions,

(C) an amount equal to the greater of—

(i) interest on the unpaid contributions, or

(ii) liquidated damages provided for under the plan in an amount not in excess of 20 percent (or such higher percentage as may be permitted under Federal or State law) of the amount determined by the court under subparagraph (A),

(D) reasonable attorney's fees and costs of the action, to be paid by the defendant, and

(E) such other legal or equitable relief as the court deems appropriate. For purposes of this paragraph, interest on unpaid contributions shall be determined by using the rate provided under the plan, or, if none, the rate prescribed under section 6621 of the Internal Revenue Code of 1954.

(h) A copy of the complaint in any action under this title by a participant, beneficiary, or fiduciary (other than an action brought by one or more participants or beneficiaries under subsection (a)(1)(B) which is solely for the purpose of recovering benefits due such participants under the terms of the plan) shall be served upon the Secretary and the Secretary of the Treasury by certified mail. Either Secretary shall have the right in his discretion to intervene in any action, except that the Secretary of the Treasury may not intervene in any action under part 4 of this subtitle. If the Secretary brings an action under subsection (a) on behalf of a participant or beneficiary, he shall notify the Secretary of the Treasury.

(i) In the case of a transaction prohibited by section 406 by a party in interest with respect to a plan to which this part applies, the Secretary may assess a civil penalty against such party in interest. The amount of such penalty may not exceed 5 percent of the amount involved in each such transaction (as defined in section 4975(f)(4) of the Internal Revenue Code of 1986) for each year or part thereof during which the prohibited transaction continues, except that, if the transaction is not corrected (in such manner as the Secretary shall prescribe in regulations which shall be consistent with section 4975(f)(5) of such Code) within 90 days after notice from the Secretary (or such longer period as the Secretary may permit), such penalty may be in an amount not more than 100 percent of the amount involved. This subsection shall not apply to a transaction with respect to a plan described in section 4975(e)(1) of such Code.

(j) In all civil actions under this title, attorneys appointed by the Secretary may represent the Secretary (except as provided in section 518(a) of title 28, United States Code), but all such litigation shall be subject to the direction and control of the Attorney General.

(k) Suits by an administrator, fiduciary, participant, or beneficiary of an employee benefit plan to review a final order of the Secretary, to restrain the Secretary from taking any action contrary to the provisions of this Act, or to compel him to take action required under this title, may be brought in the district court of the United States for the district where the plan has its principal office, or in the United States District Court for the District of Columbia.

(*l*) (1) In the case of—

(A) any breach of fiduciary responsibility under (or other violation of) part 4 by a fiduciary, or

(B) any knowing participation in such a breach or violation by any other person, the Secretary shall assess a civil penalty against such fiduciary or other person in an amount equal to 20 percent of the applicable recovery amount.

(2) For purposes of paragraph (1), the term "applicable recovery amount" means any amount which is recovered from a fiduciary or other person with respect to a breach or violation described in paragraph (1)—

(A) pursuant to any settlement agreement with the Secretary, or

(B) ordered by a court to be paid by such fiduciary or other person to a plan or its participants and beneficiaries in a judicial proceeding instituted by the Secretary under subsection (a)(2) or (a)(5).

(3) The Secretary may, in the Secretary's sole discretion, waive or reduce the penalty under paragraph (1) if the Secretary determines in writing that—

(A) the fiduciary or other person acted resonably and in good faith, or

(B) it is reasonable to expect that the fiduciary or other person will not be able to restore all losses to the plan without severe financial hardship unless such waiver or reduction is granted.

(4) The penalty imposed on a fiduciary or other person under this subsection with respect to any transaction shall be reduced by the amount of any penalty or tax imposed on such fiduciary or other person with respect to such transaction under subsection (i) of this section and section 4975 of the Internal Revenue Code of 1986.

CLAIMS PROCEDURE

Sec. 503. In accordance with regulations of the Secretary, every employee benefit plan shall—

(1) provide adequate notice in writing to any participant or beneficiary whose claim for benefits under the plan has been denied, setting forth the specific reasons for such denial, written in a manner calculated to be understood by the participant, and

(2) afford a reasonable opportunity to any participant whose claim for benefits has been denied for a full and fair review by the appropriate named fiduciary of the decision denying the claim.

INVESTIGATIVE AUTHORITY

Sec. 504. (a) The Secretary shall have the power, in order to determine whether any person has violated or is about to violate any provision of this title or any regulation or order thereunder—

(1) to make an investigation, and in connection therewith to require the submission of reports, books, and records, and the filing of data in support of any information required to be filed with the Secretary under this title, and

(2) to enter such places, inspect such books and records and question such persons as he may deem necessary to enable him to determine the facts relative to such investigation, if he has reasonable cause to believe there may exist a violation of this title or any rule or regulation issued thereunder or if the entry is pursuant to an agreement with the plan.

The Secretary may make available to any person actually affected by any matter which is the subject of an investigation under this section, and to any department or agency of the United States, information concerning any matter which may be the subject of such investigation; except that any information obtained by the Secretary pursuant to section 6103(g) of the Internal Revenue Code of 1954 shall be made available only in accordance with regulations prescribed by the Secretary of the Treasury.

(b) The Secretary may not under the authority of this section require any plan to submit to the Secretary any books or records of the plan more than once in any 12 month period, unless the Secretary has reasonable cause to believe there may exist a violation of this title or any regulation or order thereunder.

(c) For the purposes of any investigation provided for in this title, the provisions of sections 9 and 10 (relating to the attendance of witnesses and the production of books, records, and documents) of the Federal Trade Commission Act (15 U.S.C. 49, 50) are hereby made applicable (without regard to any limitation in such sections respecting persons, partnerships, banks, or common carriers) to the jurisdiction, powers, and duties of the Secretary or any officers designated by him. To the extent he considers appropriate, the Secretary may delegate his investigative functions under this section with respect to insured banks acting as fiduciaries of employee benefit plans to the appropriate Federal banking agency (as defined in section 3(q) of the Federal Deposit Insurance Act (12 U.S.C. 1813(q)).

REGULATIONS

Sec. 505. Subject to title III and section 109, the Secretary may prescribe such regulations as he finds necessary or appropriate to carry out the provisions of this title. Among other things, such regulations may define accounting, technical and trade terms used in such provisions; may prescribe forms; and may provide for the keeping of books and records, and for the inspection of such books and records (subject to section 504(a) and (b)).

COORDINATION AND RESPONSIBILITY OF AGENCIES ENFORCING EMPLOYEE RETIREMENT INCOME SECURITY ACT AND RELATED FEDERAL LAWS

Sec. 506. (a) Coordination With Other Agencies and Departments.—In order to avoid unnecessary expense and duplication of functions among Government agencies, the Secretary may make such arrangements or agreements for cooperation or mutual assistance in the performance of his functions under this title and the functions of any such agency as he may find to be practicable and consistent with law. The Secretary may utilize, on a reimbursable or other basis, the facilities or services of any department, agency, or establishment of the United States or of any State or political subdivision of a State, including the services of any of its employees, with the lawful consent of such department, agency, or establishment; and each department, agency, or establishment of the United States is authorized and directed to cooperate with the Secretary and, to the extent permitted by law, to provide such information and facilities as he may request for his assistance in the performance of his functions under this title. The Attorney General or his representative shall receive from the Secretary for appropriate action such evidence developed in the performance of his functions under this title as may be found to warrant consideration for criminal prosecution under the provisions of this title or other Federal law.

(b) Responsibility for Detecting and Investigating Civil and Criminal Violations of Employee Retirement Income Security Act and Related Federal Laws.—The Secretary shall have the responsibility and authority to detect and investigate and refer, where appropriate, civil and criminal violations related to the provisions of this title and other related Federal laws, including the detection, investigation, and appropriate referrals of related violations of title 18 of the United States Code.

Nothing in this subsection shall be construed to preclude other appropriate Federal agencies from detecting and investigating civil and criminal violations of this title and other related Federal laws.

ADMINISTRATION

Sec. 507. (a) Subchapter II of chapter 5, and chapter 7, of title 5, United States Code (relating to administrative procedure), shall be applicable to this title.

(b) [Omitted]

(c) No employee of the Department of Labor or the Department of the Treasury shall administer or enforce this title or the Internal Revenue Code of 1954 with respect to any employee benefit plan under which he is a participant or beneficiary, any employee organization of which he is a member, or any employer organization in which he has an interest. This subsection does not apply to an employee benefit plan which covers only employees of the United States.

APPROPRIATIONS

Sec. 508. There are hereby authorized to be appropriated such sums as may be necessary to enable the Secretary to carry out his functions and duties under this Act.

SEPARABILITY OF PROVISIONS

Sec. 509. If any provision of this Act, or the application of such provision to any person or circumstances, shall be held invalid, the remainder of this Act, or the application of such provision to persons or circumstances other than those as to which it is held invalid, shall not be affected thereby.

INTERFERENCE WITH RIGHTS PROTECTED UNDER ACT

Sec. 510. It shall be unlawful for any person to discharge, fine, suspend, expel, discipline, or discriminate against a participant or beneficiary for exercising any right to which he is entitled under the provisions of an employee benefit plan, this title, section 3001, or the Welfare and Pension Plans Disclosure Act, or for the purpose of interfering with the attainment of any right to which such participant may become entitled under the plan, this title, or the Welfare and Pension Plans Disclosure Act. It shall be unlawful for any person to discharge, fine, suspend, expel, or discriminate against any person because he has given information or has testified or is about to testify in any inquiry or proceeding relating to this Act or the Welfare and Pension Plans Disclosure Act. The provisions of section 502 shall be applicable in the enforcement of this section.

COERCIVE INTERFERENCE

Sec. 511. It shall be unlawful for any person through the use of fraud, force, violence, or threat of the use of force or violence, to restrain, coerce, intimidate, or attempt to restrain, coerce, or intimidate any participant or beneficiary for the purpose of interfering with or preventing the exercise of any right to which he is or may become entitled under the plan, this title, section 3001, or the Welfare and Pension Plans Disclosure Act. Any person who willfully violates this section shall be fined $10,000 or imprisoned for not more than one year, or both.

ADVISORY COUNCIL

Sec. 512. (a)(1) There is hereby established an Advisory Council on Employee Welfare and Pension Benefit Plans (hereinafter in this section referred to as the

"Council") consisting of fifteen members appointed by the Secretary. Not more than eight members of the Council shall be members of the same political party.

(2) Members shall be persons qualified to appraise the programs instituted under this Act.

(3) Of the members appointed, three shall be representatives of employee organizations (at least one of whom shall be representative of any organization members of which are participants in a multiemployer plan); three shall be representatives of employers (at least one of whom shall be representative of employers maintaining or contributing to multiemployer plans); three representatives shall be appointed from the general public, one of whom shall be a person representing those receiving benefits from a pension plan; and there shall be one representative each from the fields of insurance, corporate trust, actuarial counseling, investment counseling, investment management, and the accounting field.

(4) Members shall serve for terms of three years except that of those first appointed, five shall be appointed for terms of one year, five shall be appointed for terms of two years, and five shall be appointed for terms of three years. A member may be reappointed. A member appointed to fill a vacancy shall be appointed only for the remainder of such term. A majority of members shall constitute a quorum and action shall be taken only by a majority vote of those present and voting.

(b) It shall be the duty of the Council to advise the Secretary with respect to the carrying out of his functions under this Act and to submit to the Secretary recommendations with respect thereto. The Council shall meet at least four times each year and at such other times as the Secretary requests. In his annual report submitted pursuant to section 513(b), the Secretary shall include each recommendation which he has received from the Council during the preceding calendar year.

(c) The Secretary shall furnish to the Council an executive secretary and such secretarial, clerical, and other services as are deemed necessary to conduct its business. The Secretary may call upon other agencies of the Government for statistical data, reports, and other information which will assist the Council in the performance of its duties.

(d)(1) Members of the Council shall each be entitled to receive the daily equivalent of the annual rate of basic pay in effect for grade GS-18 of the General Schedule for each day (including travel time) during which they are engaged in the actual performance of duties vested in the Council.

(2) While away from their homes or regular places of business in the performance of services for Council, members of the Council shall be allowed travel expenses, including per diem in lieu of subsistence, in the same manner as persons employed intermittently in the Government service are allowed expenses under section 5703(b) of title 5 of the United States Code.

(e) Section 14(a) of the Federal Advisory Committee Act (relating to termination) shall not apply to the Council.

RESEARCH, STUDIES, AND ANNUAL REPORT

Sec. 513. (a)(1) The Secretary is authorized to undertake research and surveys and in connection therewith to collect, compile, analyze and publish data, information, and statistics relating to employee benefit plans, including retirement, deferred compensation, and welfare plans, and types of plans not subject to this Act.

(2) The Secretary is authorized and directed to undertake research studies relating to pension plans, including but not limited to (A) the effects of this title upon the provisions and costs of pension plans, (B) the role of private pensions in meeting the economic security needs of the Nation, and (C) the operation of private pension plans including types and levels of benefits, degree of reciprocity or portability, and financial and actuarial characteristics and practices, and methods of encouraging the growth of the private pension system.

(3) The Secretary may, as he deems appropriate or necessary, undertake other studies relating to employee benefit plans, the matters regulated by this title, and the enforcement procedures provided for under this title.

(4) The research, surveys, studies, and publications referred to in this subsection may be conducted directly, or indirectly through grant or contract arrangements.

(b) The Secretary shall submit annually a report to the Congress covering his administration of this title for the preceding year, and including (1) an explanation of any variances or extensions granted under section 110, 207, 303, or 304 and the projected date for terminating the variance; (2) the status of cases in enforcement status; (3) recommendations received from the Advisory Council during the preceding year; and (4) such information, data, research findings, studies, and recommendations for further legislation in connection with the matters covered by this title as he may find advisable.

(c) The Secretary is authorized and directed to cooperate with the Congress and its appropriate committees, subcommittees, and staff in supplying data and any other information, and personnel and services, required by the Congress in any study, examination, or report by the Congress relating to pension benefit plans established or maintained by States or their political subdivisions.

EFFECT ON OTHER LAWS

Sec. 514. (a) Except as provided in subsection (b) of this section, the provisions of this title and title IV shall supersede any and all State laws insofar as they may now or hereafter relate to any employee benefit plan described in section 4(a) and not exempt under section 4(b). This section shall take effect on January 1, 1975.

(b)(1) This section shall not apply with respect to any cause of action which arose, or any act or omission which occurred, before January 1, 1975.

(2)(A) Except as provided in subparagraph (B), nothing in this title shall be construed to exempt or relieve any person from any law of any State which regulates insurance, banking, or securities.

(B) Neither an employee benefit plan described in section 4(a), which is not exempt under section 4(b) (other than a plan established primarily for the purpose of providing death benefits), nor any trust established under such a plan, shall be deemed to be an insurance company or other insurer, bank, trust company, or investment company or to be engaged in the business of insurance or banking for purposes of any law of any State purporting to regulate insurance companies, insurance contracts, banks, trust companies, or investment companies.

(3) Nothing in this section shall be construed to prohibit use by the Secretary of services or facilities of a State agency as permitted under section 506 of this Act.

(4) Subsection (a) shall not apply to any generally applicable criminal law of a State.

(5)(A) Except as provided in subparagraph (B), subsection (a) shall not apply to the Hawaii Prepaid Health Care Act (Haw. Rev. Stat. 393-1 through 393-51).

(B) Nothing in subparagraph (A) shall be construed to exempt from subsection (a)—

(i) any State tax law relating to employee benefit plans, or

(ii) any amendment of the Hawaii Prepaid Health Care Act enacted after September 2, 1974, to the extent it provides for more than the effective administration of such Act as in effect on such date.

(C) Notwithstanding subparagraph (A), parts 1 and 4 of this subtitle, and the preceding sections of this part to the extent they govern matters which are governed by the provisions of such parts 1 and 4, shall supersede the Hawaii Prepaid Health Care Act (as in effect on or after the date of the enactment of this paragraph), but the Secretary may enter into cooperative arrangements under this paragraph and section 506 with officials of the State of Hawaii to assist them in effectuating the policies of provisions of such Act which are superseded by such parts 1 and 4 and the preceding sections of this part.

(6)(A) Notwithstanding any other provision of this section—

(i) in the case of an employee welfare benefit plan which is a multiple employer welfare arrangement and is fully insured (or which is a multiple employer welfare arrangement subject to an exemption under subparagraph (B)), any law of any State which regulates insurance may apply to such arrangement to the extent that such law provides—

(I) standards, requiring the maintenance of specified levels of reserves and specified levels of contributions, which any such plan, or any trust established under such a plan, must meet in order to be considered under such law able to pay benefits in full when due, and

(II) provisions to enforce such standards, and

(ii) in the case of any other employee welfare benefit plan which is a multiple-employer welfare arrangement, in addition to this title, any law of any State which regulates insurance may apply to the extent not inconsistent with the preceding sections of this title.

(B) The Secretary may, under regulations which may be prescribed by the Secretary, exempt from subparagraph (A)(ii), individually or by class, multiple employer welfare arrangements which are not fully insured. Any such exemption may be granted with respect to any arrangement or class of arrangements only if such arrangement or each arrangement which is a member of such class meets the requirements of section 3(1) and section 4 necessary to be considered an employee welfare benefit plan to which this title applies.

(C) Nothing in subparagraph (A) shall affect the manner or extent to which the provisions of this title apply to an employee welfare benefit plan which is not a multiple employer welfare arrangement and which is a plan, fund, or program participating in, subscribing to, or otherwise using a multiple employer welfare arrangement to fund or administer benefits to such plan's participants and beneficiaries.

(D) For purposes of this paragraph, a multiple employer welfare arrangement shall be considered fully insured only if the terms of the arrangement provide for benefits the amount of all of which the Secretary determines are guaranteed under a contract, or policy of insurance, issued by an insurance company, insurance service, or insurance organization, qualified to conduct business in a State.

(7) Subsection (a) shall not apply to qualified domestic relations orders (within the meaning of section 206(d)(3)(B)(i)), *qualified medical child support orders (within the meaning of section 609(a)(2)(A), and the provisions of law referred to in section 609(a)(2)(B)(ii) to the extent enforced by qualified medical child support orders.*

(8) Subsection (a) of this section shall not apply to any State law mandating that an employee benefit plan not include any provision which has the effect of limiting or excluding coverage or payment for any health care for an individual who would otherwise be covered or entitled to benefits or services under the terms of the employee benefit plan, because that individual is provided, or is eligible for, benefits or services pursuant to a plan under title XIX of the Social Security Act, to the extent such law is necessary for the State to be eligible to receive reimbursement under title XIX of that Act.

(8) *Subsection (a) of this section shall not be construed to preclude any State cause of action—*

(A) with respect to which the State exercises its acquired rights under section 609(b)(3) with respect to a group health plan (as defined in section 607(1)), or

(B) for recoupment of payment with respect to items or services pursuant to a State plan for medical assistance approved under title XIX of the Social Security Act which would not have been payable if such acquired rights had been executed before payment with respect to such items or services by the group health plan.

◆ ◆ ◆

[*Editor's Note:* ERISA Section 514(b) was amended by OBRA '93 Section 4301(c)(4). The effective date was August 10, 1993.]

◆ ◆ ◆

(c) For purposes of this section:

(1) The term "State law" includes all laws, decisions, rules, regulations, or other State action having the effect of law, of any State. A law of the United States applicable only to the District of Columbia shall be treated as a State law rather than a law of the United States.

(2) The term "State" includes a State, any political subdivisions thereof, or any agency or instrumentality of either, which purports to regulate, directly or indirectly, the terms and conditions of employee benefit plans covered by this title.

(d) Nothing in this title shall be construed to alter, amend, modify, invalidate, impair, or supersede any law of the United States (except as provided in sections 111 and 507(b)) or any rule or regulation issued under any such law.

DELINQUENT CONTRIBUTIONS

Sec. 515. Every employer who is obligated to make contributions to a multiemployer plan under the terms of the plan or under the terms of a collectively bargained agreement shall, to the extent not inconsistent with law, make such contributions in accordance with the terms and conditions of such plan or such agreement.

APPENDIX 3

SELECTED TEXT OF THE INTERNAL REVENUE CODE APPLYING TO FIDUCIARIES

Contents

Section

Source: Reprinted from *ERISA: The Law and the Code, 1994 Edition,* copyright © 1994, The Bureau of National Affairs, Inc., Washington, D.C.

SEC. 4975. TAX ON PROHIBITED TRANSACTIONS

(a) Initial Taxes on Disqualified Person.—There is hereby imposed a tax on each prohibited transaction. The rate of tax shall be equal to 5 percent of the amount involved with respect to the prohibited transaction for each year (or part thereof) in the taxable period. The tax imposed by this subsection shall be paid by any disqualified person who participates in the prohibited transaction (other than a fiduciary acting only as such).

(b) Additional Taxes on Disqualified Person.—In any case in which an initial tax is imposed by subsection (a) on a prohibited transaction and the transaction is not corrected within the taxable period, there is hereby imposed a tax equal to 100 percent of the amount involved. The tax imposed by this subsection shall be paid by any disqualified person who participated in the prohibited transaction (other than a fiduciary acting only as such).

(c) Prohibited Transaction.—

(1) General Rule.—For purposes of this section, the term "prohibited transaction" means any direct or indirect—

(A) sale or exchange, or leasing, of any property between a plan and a disqualified person;

(B) lending of money or other extension of credit between a plan and a disqualified person;

(C) furnishing of goods, services, or facilities between a plan and a disqualified person;

(D) transfer to, or use by or for the benefit of, a disqualified person of the income or assets of a plan;

(E) act by a disqualified person who is a fiduciary whereby he deals with the income or assets of a plan in his own interest or for his own account; or

(F) receipt of any consideration for his own personal account by any disqualified person who is a fiduciary from any party dealing with the plan in connection with a transaction involving the income or assets of the plan.

(2) Special exemption.—The Secretary shall establish an exemption procedure for purposes of this subsection. Pursuant to such procedure, he may grant a conditional or unconditional exemption of any disqualified person or transaction or class of disqualified persons or transactions, from all or part of the restrictions imposed by paragraph (1) of this subsection. Action under this subparagraph may be taken only after consultation and coordination with the Secretary of Labor. The Secretary may not grant an exemption under this paragraph unless he finds that such exemption is—

(A) administratively feasible,

(B) in the interests of the plan and of its participants and beneficiaries, and

(C) protective of the rights of participants and beneficiaries of the plan.

Before granting an exemption under this paragraph, the Secretary shall require adequate notice to be given to interested persons and shall publish notice in the

Federal Register of the pendency of such exemption and shall afford interested persons an opportunity to present views. No exemption may be granted under this paragraph with respect to a transaction described in subparagraph (E) or (F) of paragraph (1) unless the Secretary affords an opportunity for hearing and makes a determination on the record with respect to the findings required under subparagraphs (A), (B), and (C) of this paragraph, except that in lieu of such hearing the Secretary may accept any record made by the Secretary of Labor with respect to an application for exemption under section 408(a) of title I of the Employee Retirement Income Security Act of 1974.

(3) Special rule for individual retirement accounts.—An individual for whose benefit an individual retirement account is established and his beneficiaries shall be exempt [from] the tax imposed by this section with respect to any transaction concerning such account (which would otherwise be taxable under this section) if, with respect to such transaction, the account ceases to be an individual retirement account by reason of the application of section 408(e)(2)(A) or if section 408(e)(4) applies to such account.

(d) Exemptions.—The prohibitions provided in subsection (c) shall not apply to—

(1) any loan made by the plan to a disqualified person who is a participant or beneficiary of the plan if such loan—

(A) is available to all such participants or beneficiaries on a reasonably equivalent basis,

(B) is not made available to highly compensated employees (within the meaning of section 414(q) of the Internal Revenue Code of 1986) in an amount greater than the amount made available to other employees,

(C) is made in accordance with specific provisions regarding such loans set forth in the plan,

(D) bears a reasonable rate of interest, and

(E) is adequately secured;

(2) any contract, or reasonable arrangement, made with a disqualified person for office space, or legal, accounting, or other services necessary for the establishment or operation of the plan, if no more than reasonable compensation is paid therefor;

(3) any loan to a leveraged employee stock ownership plan (as defined in subsection (e)(7)), if—

(A) such loan is primarily for the benefit of participants and beneficiaries of the plan, and

(B) such loan is at a reasonable rate of interest, and any collateral which is given to a disqualified person by the plan consists only of qualifying employer securities (as defined in subsection (e)(8));

(4) the investment of all or part of a plan's assets in deposits which bear a reasonable interest rate in a bank or similar financial institution supervised by the United States or a State, if such bank or other institution is a fiduciary of such plan and if—

(A) the plan covers only employees of such bank or other institution and employees of affiliates of such bank or other institution, or

(B) such investment is expressly authorized by a provision of the plan or by a fiduciary (other than such bank or institution or affiliates thereof) who is expressly empowered by the plan to so instruct the trustee with respect to such investment;

(5) any contract for life insurance, health insurance, or annuities with one or more insurers which are qualified to do business in a State if the plan pays no more than adequate consideration, and if each such insurer or insurers is—

(A) the employer maintaining the plan, or

(B) a disqualified person which is wholly owned (directly or indirectly) by the employer establishing the plan, or by any person which is a disqualified person with respect to the plan, but only if the total premiums and annuity considerations written by such insurers for life insurance, health insurance, or annuities for all plans (and their employers) with respect to which such insurers are disqualified persons (not including premiums or annuity considerations written by the employer maintaining the plan) do not exceed 5 percent of the total premiums and annuity considerations written for all lines of insurance in that year by such insurers (not including premiums or annuity considerations written by the employer maintaining the plan);

(6) the provision of any ancillary service by a bank or similar financial institution supervised by the United States or a State, if such service is provided at not more than reasonable compensation, if such bank or other institution is a fiduciary of such plan, and if—

(A) such bank or similar financial institution has adopted adequate internal safeguards which assure that the provision of such ancillary service is consistent with sound banking and financial practice, as determined by Federal or State supervisory authority, and

(B) the extent to which such ancillary service is provided is subject to specific guidelines issued by such bank or similar financial institution (as determined by the Secretary after consultation with Federal and State supervisory authority), and under such guidelines the bank or similar financial institution does not provide such ancillary service—

(i) in an excessive or unreasonable manner, and

(ii) in a manner that would be inconsistent with the best interests of participants and beneficiaries of employee benefit plans;

(7) the exercise of a privilege to convert securities, to the extent provided in regulations of the Secretary, but only if the plan receives no less than adequate consideration pursuant to such conversion;

(8) any transaction between a plan and a common or collective trust fund or pooled investment fund maintained by a disqualified person which is a bank or trust company supervised by a State or Federal agency or between a plan and a pooled investment fund of an insurance company qualified to do business in a State if—

(A) the transaction is a sale or purchase of an interest in the fund,

(B) the bank, trust company, or insurance company receives not more than reasonable compensation, and

(C) such transaction is expressly permitted by the instrument under which the plan is maintained, or by a fiduciary (other than the bank, trust company, or insurance company, or an affiliate thereof) who has authority to manage and control the assets of the plan;

(9) receipt by a disqualified person of any benefit to which he may be entitled as a participant or beneficiary in the plan, so long as the benefit is computed and paid on a basis which is consistent with the terms of the plan as applied to all other participants and beneficiaries;

(10) receipt by a disqualified person of any reasonable compensation for services rendered, or for the reimbursement of expenses properly and actually incurred, in the performance of his duties with the plan, but no person so serving who already receives full-time pay from an employer or an association of employers, whose employees are participants in the plan, or from an employee organization whose members are participants in such plan shall receive compensation from such fund, except for reimbursement of expenses properly and actually incurred;

(11) service by a disqualified person as a fiduciary in addition to being an officer, employee, agent, or other representative of a disqualified person;

(12) the making by a fiduciary of a distribution of the assets of the trust in accordance with the terms of the plan if such assets are distributed in the same manner as provided under section 4044 of title IV of the Employee Retirement Income Security Act of 1974 (relating to allocation of assets);

(13) any transaction which is exempt from section 406 of such Act by reason of section 408(e) of such Act (or which would be so exempt if such section 406 applied to such transaction) or which is exempt from section 406 of such Act by reason of section 408(b) of such Act;

(14) any transaction required or permitted under part 1 of subtitle E of title IV or section 4223 of the Employee Retirement Income Security Act of 1974, but this paragraph shall not apply with respect to the application of subsection (c)(1)(E) or (F); or

(15) a merger of multiemployer plans, or the transfer of assets or liabilities between multiemployer plans, determined by the Pension Benefit Guaranty Corporation to meet the requirements of section 4231 of such Act, but this paragraph shall not apply with respect to the application of subsection (c)(1)(E) or (F).

The exemptions provided by this subsection (other than paragraphs (9) and (12)) shall not apply to any transaction with respect to a trust described in section 401(a) which is part of a plan providing contributions or benefits for employees some or all of whom are owner-employees (as defined in section 401(c)(3)) in which a plan directly or indirectly lends any part of the corpus or income of the plan to, pays any compensation for personal services rendered to the plan to, or acquires for the plan any property from or sells any property to, any such owner-employee, a member of the family (as defined in section 267(c)(4)) of any such owner-employee, or a corporation controlled by any such owner-employee through the ownership, directly or indirectly, of 50 percent or more of the total combined voting power of all classes of stock entitled to vote or 50 percent or more of the total value of shares of all classes of stock of the corporation. For purposes of the preceding sentence, a shareholder-employee (as defined in section 1379, as in effect on the day before the date of the enactment of the Subchapters Revision Act of 1982), a participant or beneficiary of an individual retirement account or an individual retirement annuity as defined in section 408, and an employer or association of employees which establishes such an account or annuity under section 408(c) shall be deemed to be an owner-employee.

(e) Definitions.—

(1) Plan.—For purposes of this section, the term "plan" means a trust described in section 401(a), which forms a part of a plan, or a plan described in section 403(a) which trust or plan is exempt from tax under section 501(a), an individual retirement account described in section 408(a) or an individual retirement annuity described in section 408(b) (or a trust, plan, account, or annuity which, at any time, has been determined by the Secretary to be such a trust, plan, or account).

(2) Disqualified person.—For purposes of this section, the term "disqualified person" means a person who is—

(A) a fiduciary;

(B) a person providing services to the plan;

(C) an employer any of whose employees are covered by the plan;

(D) an employee organization any of whose members are covered by the plan;

(E) an owner, direct or indirect, of 50 percent or more of—

(i) the combined voting power of all classes of stock entitled to vote or the total value of shares of all classes of stock of a corporation,

(ii) the capital interest or the profits interest of a partnership, or

(iii) the beneficial interest of a trust or unincorporated enterprise,

which is an employer or an employee organization described in subparagraph (C) or (D);

(F) a member of the family (as defined in paragraph (6)) of any individual described in subparagraph (A), (B), (C), or (E);

(G) a corporation, partnership, or trust or estate of which (or in which) 50 percent or more of—

(i) the combined voting power of all classes of stock entitled to vote or the total value of shares of all classes of stock of such corporation,

(ii) the capital interest or profits interest of such partnership, or

(iii) the beneficial interest of such trust or estate, is owned directly or indirectly, or held by persons described in subparagraph (A), (B), (C), (D), or (E);

(H) an officer, director (or an individual having powers or responsibilities similar to those of officers or directors), a 10 percent or more shareholder, or a highly compensated employee (earning 10 percent or more of the yearly wages of an employer) of a person described in subparagraph (C), (D), (E), or (G); or

(I) a 10 percent or more (in capital or profits) partner or joint venturer of a person described in subparagraph (C), (D), (E), or (G).

The Secretary, after consultation and coordination with the Secretary of Labor or his delegate, may by regulation prescribe a percentage lower than 50 percent for subparagraphs (E) and (G) and lower than 10 percent for subparagraphs (H) and (I).

(3) Fiduciary.—For purposes of this section, the term "fiduciary" means any person who—

(A) exercises any discretionary authority or discretionary control respecting management of such plan or exercises any authority or control respecting management or disposition of its assets,

(B) renders investment advice for a fee or other compensation, direct or indirect, with respect to any moneys or other property of such plan, or has any authority or responsibility to do so, or

(C) has any discretionary authority or discretionary responsibility in the administration of such plan.

Such term includes any person designated under section 405(c)(1)(B) of the Employee Retirement Income Security Act of 1974.

(4) Stockholdings.—For purposes of paragraphs (2)(E)(i), and (G)(i) there shall be taken into account indirect stockholdings which would be taken into account under section 267(c), except that, for purposes of this paragraph, section 267(c)(4) shall be treated as providing that the members of the family of an individual are the members within the meaning of paragraph (6).

(5) Partnerships; trusts.—For purposes of paragraphs (2)(E)(ii) and (iii), (G)(ii) and (iii), and (I) the ownership of profits or beneficial interests shall be determined in accordance with the rules for constructive ownership of stock provided in section 267(c) (other than paragraph (3) thereof), except that section 267(c)(4) shall be treated as providing that the members of the family of an individual are the members within the meaning of paragraph (6).

(6) Members of family.—For purposes of paragraph (2)(F), the family of any individual shall include his spouse, ancestor, lineal descendant, and any spouse of a lineal descendant.

(7) Employee stock ownership plan.—The term "employee stock ownership plan" means a defined contribution plan—

(A) which is a stock bonus plan which is qualified, or a stock bonus and a money purchase plan both of which are qualified under section 401(a) and which are designed to invest primarily in qualifying employer securities; and

(B) which is otherwise defined in regulations prescribed by the Secretary.

A plan shall not be treated as an employee stock ownership plan unless it meets the requirements of section 409(h), section 409(o), and, if applicable, section 409(n) and, if the employer has a registration-type class of securities (as defined in section 409(e)(4)), it meets the requirements of section 409(e).

(8) Qualifying employer security.—The term "qualifying employer security" means an employer security within the meaning of section 409(*l*).

If any moneys or other property of a plan are invested in shares of an investment company registered under the Investment Company Act of 1940, the investment shall not cause that investment company or that investment company's investment adviser or principal underwriter to be treated as a fiduciary or a disqualified person for purposes of this section, except when an investment company or its investment adviser or principal underwriter acts in connection with a plan covering employees of the investment company, its investment adviser, or its principal underwriter.

(9) Section made applicable to withdrawal liability payment funds.—

(A) In general.—The term "plan" includes a trust described in section 501(c)(22).

(B) Disqualified person.—In the case of any trust to which this section applies by reason of subparagraph (A), the term "disqualified person" includes any person who is a disqualified person with respect to any plan to which such trust is permitted to make payments under section 4223 of the Employee Retirement Income Security Act of 1974.

(f) Other Definitions and Special Rules.—For purposes of this section—

(1) Joint and several liability.—If more than one person is liable under subsection (a) or (b) with respect to any one prohibited transaction, all such persons shall be jointly and severally liable under such subsection with respect to such transaction.

(2) Taxable period.—The term "taxable period" means, with respect to any prohibited transaction, the period beginning with the date on which the prohibited transaction occurs and ending on the earliest of—

(A) the date of mailing of a notice of deficiency with respect to the tax imposed by subsection (a) under section 6212,

(B) the date on which the tax imposed by subsection (a) is assessed, or

(C) the date on which correction of the prohibited transaction is completed.

(3) Sale or exchange; encumbered property.—A transfer of real or personal property by a disqualified person to a plan shall be treated as a sale or exchange if the property is subject to a mortgage or similar lien which the plan assumes or if it is subject to a mortgage or similar lien which a disqualified person placed on the property within the 10-year period ending on the date of the transfer.

(4) Amount involved.—The term "amount involved" means, with respect to a prohibited transaction, the greater of the amount of money and the fair market value of the other property given or the amount of money and the fair market value of the other property received; except that, in the case of services described in paragraphs (2) and (10) of subsection (d) the amount involved shall be only the excess compensation. For purposes of the preceding sentence, the fair market value—

(A) in the case of the tax imposed by subsection (a), shall be determined as of the date on which the prohibited transaction occurs; and

(B) in the case of the tax imposed by subsection (b), shall be the highest fair market value during the taxable period.

(5) Correction.—The terms "correction" and "correct" mean, with respect to a prohibited transaction, undoing the transaction to the extent possible, but in any case placing the plan in a financial position not worse than that in which it would be if the disqualified person were acting under the highest fiduciary standards.

(g) Application of Section.—This section shall not apply—

(1) in the case of a plan to which a guaranteed benefit policy (as defined in section 401(b)(2)(B) of the Employee Retirement Income Security Act of 1974) is issued, to any assets of the insurance company, insurance service, or insurance organization merely because of its issuance of such policy;

(2) to a governmental plan (within the meaning of section 414(d)); or

(3) to a church plan (within the meaning of section 414(e)) with respect to which the election provided by section 410(d) has not been made.

In the case of a plan which invests in any security issued by an investment company registered under the Investment Company Act of 1940, the assets of such plan shall be deemed to include such security but shall not, by reason of such investment, be deemed to include any assets of such company.

(h) Notification of Secretary of Labor.—Before sending a notice of deficiency with respect to the tax imposed by subsection (a) or (b), the Secretary shall notify the Secretary of Labor and provide him a reasonable opportunity to obtain a correction of the prohibited transaction or to comment on the imposition of such tax.

(i) Cross Reference.—For provisions concerning coordination procedures between Secretary of Labor and Secretary of Treasury with respect to application of tax imposed by this section and for authority to waive imposition of the tax imposed by subsection (b), see section 3003 of the Employee Retirement Income Security Act of 1974.

Appendix 4

Final Department of Labor Regulations Applying to Fiduciaries

29 CFR Part 2550

PART 2550—RULES AND REGULATIONS FOR FIDUCIARY RESPONSIBILITY

Sec. 2550.403a-1—Establishment of trust.

(a) In general. Except as otherwise provided in Sec. 403b-1, all assets of an employee benefit plan shall be held in trust by one or more trustees pursuant to a written trust instrument.

(b) Specific applications.

(1) The requirements of paragraph (a) of this section will not fail to be satisfied merely because securities of a plan are held in the name of a nominee or in street name, provided such securities are held on behalf of the plan by:

(i) A bank or trust company that is subject to supervision by the United States or a State, or a nominee of such bank or trust company;

(ii) A broker or dealer registered under the Securities Exchange Act of 1934, or a nominee of such broker or dealer; or

(iii) A "clearing agency," as defined in Sec. 3(a)(23) of the Securities Exchange Act of 1934, or its nominee.

(2) Where a corporation described in Sec. 501(c)(2) of the Internal Revenue Code holds property on behalf of a plan, the requirements of paragraph (a) of this section are satisfied with respect to such property if all the stock of such corporation is held in trust on behalf of the plan by one or more trustees.

(3) If the assets of an entity in which a plan invests include plan assets by reason of the plan's investment in the entity, the requirements of paragraph (a) of this section are satisfied with respect to such investment if the indicia of ownership of the plan's interest in the entity are held in trust on behalf of the plan by one or more trustees.

(c) Requirements concerning trustees. The trustee or trustees referred to in paragraphs (a) and (b) shall be either named in the trust instrument or in the plan instrument described in Sec. 402(a) of the Act, or appointed by a person who is a named fiduciary (within the meaning of Sec. 402(a)(2) of the Act). Upon acceptance of being named or appointed, the trustee or trustees shall have exclusive authority and discretion to manage and control the assets of the plan, except to the extent that:

(1) The plan instrument or the trust instrument expressly provides that the trustee or trustees are subject to the direction of a named fiduciary who is not a trustee, in which case the trustees shall be subject to the proper directions of such fiduciary which are made in accordance with the terms of the plan and which are not contrary to the provisions of Title I of the Act of Chapter XXV of this Title, or

(2) Authority to manage, acquire or dispose of assets of the plan is delegated to one or more investment managers (within the meaning of Sec. 3(38) of the Act) pursuant to Sec. 402(c)(3) of the Act.

Promulgated: 47 Fed. Reg. 21247 (5/18/82).

Sec. 2550.403b-1—Exemptions from trust requirement.

(a) Statutory exemptions. The requirements of Sec. 403(a) of the Act and Sec. 403a-1 shall not apply—

(1) To any assets of a plan which consist of insurance contracts or policies issued by an insurance company qualified to do business in a State;

(2) To any assets of such an insurance company or any assets of a plan which are held by such an insurance company;

(3) To a plan—

(i) Some or all of the participants of which are employees described in Sec. 401(c)(1) of the Internal Revenue Code of 1954; or

(ii) Which consists of one or more individual retirement accounts described in Sec. 408 of the Internal Revenue Code of 1954. To the extent that such plan's assets are held in one or more custodial accounts which qualify under section 401(f) or 408(h) of such Code, whichever is applicable;

(4) To a contract established and maintained under Sec. 403(b) of the Internal Revenue Code of 1954 to the extent that the assets of the contract are held in one or more custodial accounts pursuant to Sec. 403(b)(7) of such Code.

(5) To any plan, fund or program under which an employer, all of whose stock is directly or indirectly owned by employees, former employees or their beneficiaries, proposes through an unfunded arrangement to compensate retired employees for benefits which were forfeited by such employees under a pension plan maintained by a former employer prior to the date such pension plan became subject to the Act.

Promulgated: 47 Fed. Reg. 21247 (5/18/82).

Sec. 2550.404a-1—Investment duties.

(a) In general. Section 404(a)(1)(B) of the Employee Retirement Income Security Act of 1974 (the Act) provides, in part, that a fiduciary shall discharge his duties with respect to a plan with the care, skill, prudence, and diligence under the circumstances then prevailing that a prudent man acting in a like capacity and familiar with such matters would use in the conduct of an enterprise of a like character and with like aims.

(b) Investment duties.

(1) With regard to an investment or investment course of action taken by a fiduciary of an employee benefit plan pursuant to his investment duties, the requirements of Sec. 404(a)(1)(B) of the Act set forth in subsection (a) of this section are satisfied if the fiduciary:

(i) Has given appropriate consideration to those facts and circumstances that, given the scope of such fiduciary's investment duties, the fiduciary knows or should know are relevant to the particular investment or investment course of action involved, including the role the investment or investment course of action plays in that portion of the plan's investment portfolio with respect to which the fiduciary has investment duties; and

(ii) Has acted accordingly.

(2) For purposes of paragraph (b)(1) of this section, "appropriate consideration" shall include, but is not necessarily limited to,

(i) A determination by the fiduciary that the particular investment or investment course of action is reasonably designed, as part of the portfolio (or, where applicable, that portion of the plan portfolio with respect to which the fiduciary has investment duties), to further the purposes of the plan, taking into consideration the risk of loss and the opportunity for gain (or other return) associated with the investment or investment course of action, and

(ii) Consideration of the following factors as they relate to such portion of the portfolio:

(A) The composition of the portfolio with regard to diversification;

(B) The liquidity and current return of the portfolio relative to the anticipated cash flow requirements of the plan; and

(C) The projected return of the portfolio relative to the funding objectives of the plan.

(3) An investment manager appointed, pursuant to the provisions of Sec. 402(c)(3) of the Act, to manage all or part of the assets of a plan, may, for purposes of compliance with the provisions of paragraphs (b)(1) and (2) of this section, rely on, and act upon the basis of, information pertaining to the plan provided by or at the direction of the appointing fiduciary, if—

(i) Such information is provided for the stated purpose of assisting the manager in the performance of his investment duties, and

(ii) The manager does not know and has no reason to know that the information is incorrect.

(c) Definitions. For purposes of this section:

(1) The term "investment duties" means any duties imposed upon, or assumed or undertaken by, a person in connection with the investment of plan assets which make or will make such person a fiduciary of an employee benefit plan or which are performed by such person as a fiduciary of an employee benefit plan as defined in Sec. 3(21)(A) (i) or (ii) of the Act.

(2) The term "investment course of action" means any series or program of investments or actions related to a fiduciary's performance of his investment duties.

(3) The term "plan" means an employee benefit plan to which Title I of the Act applies.

Promulgated: 44 Fed. Reg. 37225 (6/26/79).

Sec. 2550.404b-1—Maintenance of the indicia of ownership of plan assets outside the jurisdiction of the district courts of the United States.

(a) No fiduciary may maintain the indicia of ownership of any assets of a plan outside the jurisdiction of the district courts of the United States, unless:

(1) Such assets are: (i) Securities issued by a person, as defined in Sec. 3(9) of the Employee Retirement Income Security Act of 1974 (Act) (other than an individual), which is not organized under the laws of the United States or a State and does not have its principal place of business within the United States; (ii) securities issued by a government other than the government of the United States or of a State, or any political subdivision, agency or instrumentality of such a government; (iii) securities issued by a person, as defined in Sec. 3(9) of the Act (other than an individual), the principal trading market for which securities is outside the jurisdiction of the district courts of the United States; or (iv) currency issued by a government other than the government of the United States if such currency is maintained outside the jurisdiction of the district courts of the United States solely as an incident to the purchase, sale or maintenance of securities described in paragraph (a)(1) of this section; and

(2)(i) Such assets are under the management and control of a fiduciary which is a corporation or partnership organized under the laws of the United States or a State, which fiduciary has its principal place of business within the United States and which is—

(A) A bank as defined in Sec. 202(a)(2) of the Investment Advisers Act of 1940 that has, as of the last day of its most recent fiscal year, equity capital in excess of $1,000,000;

(B) An insurance company which is qualified under the laws of more than one State to manage, acquire, or dispose of any asset of a plan, which company has, as of the last day of its most recent fiscal year, net worth in excess of $1,000,000 and which is subject to supervision and examination by the State authority having supervision over insurance companies; or

(C) An investment adviser registered under the Investment Advisers Act of 1940 that has, as of the last day of its most recent fiscal year, total client assets under its management and control in excess $50,000,000 and either (1) shareholders' or partners' equity in excess of $750,000 or (2) all of its obligations and liabilities assumed or guaranteed by a person described in paragraph (a)(2)(i) (A), (B), or (C)(1) or (a)(2)(ii)(A)(2) of this section; or

(ii) Such indicia of ownership are either

(A) In the physical possession of, or, as a result of normal business operations, are in transit to the physical possession of, a person which is organized under the laws of the United States or a State, which person has its principal place of business in the United States and which is—

(*1*) A bank as defined in Sec. 202(a)(2) of the Investment Advisers Act of 1940 that has, as of the last day of its most recent fiscal year, equity capital in excess of $1,000,000;

(*2*) A broker or dealer registered under the Securities Exchange Act of 1934 that has, as of the last day of its most recent fiscal year, net worth in excess of $750,000; or

(*3*) A broker or dealer registered under the Securities Exchange Act of 1934 that has all of its obligations and liabilities assumed or guaranteed by a person described in paragraph (a)(2)(i) (A), (B), or (C)(1) or (a)(2)(ii)(A)(2) of this section; or

(B) Maintained by a broker or dealer, described in paragraph (a)(2)(ii)(A) (2) or (3) of this section, in the custody of an entity designated by the Securities and Exchange Commission as a "satisfactory control location" with respect to such broker or dealer pursuant to Rule 15c3-3 under the Securities Exchange Act of 1934, provided that:

(1) Such entity holds the indicia of ownership as agent for the broker or dealer, and

(2) Such broker or dealer is liable to the plan to the same extent it would be if it retained the physical possession of the indicia of ownership pursuant to paragraph (a)(2)(ii)(A) of this section.

(C) Maintained by a bank described in paragraph (a)(2)(ii)(A)(1), in the custody of an entity that is a foreign securities depository, foreign clearing agency which acts as a securities depository, or foreign bank, which entity is supervised or regulated by a government agency or regulatory authority in the foreign jurisdiction having authority over such depositories, clearing agencies or banks, provided that:

(1) The foreign entity holds the indicia of ownership as agent for the bank;

(2) The bank is liable to the plan to the same extent it would be if it retained the physical possession of the indicia of ownership within the United States;

(3) The indicia of ownership are not subject to any right, charge, security interest, lien or claim of any kind in favor of the foreign entity except for their safe custody or administration;

(4) Beneficial ownership of the assets represented by the indicia of ownership is freely transferable without the payment of money or value other than for safe custody or administration; and

(5) Upon request by the plan fiduciary who is responsible for the selection and retention of the bank, the bank identifies to such fiduciary the name, address

and principal place of business of the foreign entity which acts as custodian for the plan pursuant to this paragraph (a)(2)(ii)(C), and the name and address of the governmental agency or other regulatory authority that supervises or regulates that foreign entity.

(b) Notwithstanding any requirement of paragraph (a) of this section, a fiduciary with respect to a plan may maintain in Canada the indicia of ownership of plan assets which are attributable to a contribution made on behalf of a plan participant who is a citizen or resident of Canada, if such indicia of ownership must remain in Canada in order for the plan to qualify for and maintain tax exempt status under the laws of Canada or to comply with other applicable laws of Canada or any Province of Canada.

(c) For purposes of this regulation:

(1) The term "management and control" means the power to direct the acquisition or disposition through purchase, sale, pledging, or other means; and

(2) The term "depository" means any company, or agency or instrumentality of government, that acts as a custodian of securities in connection with a system for the central handling of securities whereby all securities of a particular class or series of any issuer deposited within the system are treated as fungible and may be transferred, loaned, or pledged by bookkeeping entry without physical delivery of securities certificates.

Promulgated: 42 Fed. Reg. 54124 (10/4/77).

Amended: 46 Fed. Reg. 1267 (1/6/81).

Sec. 2550.404c-1 ERISA section 404(c) plans.

(a) In General.

(1) Section 404(c) of the Employee Retirement Income Security Act of 1974 (ERISA or the Act) provides that if a pension plan that provides for individual accounts permits a participant or beneficiary to exercise control over assets in his account and that participant or beneficiary in fact exercises control over assets in his account, then the participant or beneficiary shall not be deemed to be a fiduciary by reason of his exercise of control and no person who is otherwise a fiduciary shall be liable for any loss, or by reason of any breach, which results from such exercise of control. This section describes the kinds of plans that are "ERISA section 404(c) plans," the circumstances in which a participant or beneficiary is considered to have exercised independent control over the assets in his account as contemplated by section 404(c), and the consequences of a participant's or beneficiary's exercise of control.

(2) The standards set forth in this section are applicable solely for the purpose of determining whether a plan is an ERISA section 404(c) plan and whether a particular transaction engaged in by a participant or beneficiary of such plan is afforded relief by section 404(c). Such standards, therefore, are not intended to be applied in determining whether, or to what extent, a plan which does not meet the requirements for an ERISA section 404(c) plan or a fiduciary with respect to such a plan satisfies the fiduciary responsibility or other provisions of Title I of the Act.

(b) ERISA section 404(c) plans—

(1) *In general.* An "ERISA section 404(c) Plan" is an individual account plan described in section 3(34) of the Act that:

(i) Provides an opportunity for a participant or beneficiary to exercise control over assets in his individual account (see paragraph (b)(2) of this section); and

(ii) Provides a participant or beneficiary an opportunity to choose, from a broad range of investment alternatives, the manner in which some or all of the assets in his account are invested (see paragraph (b)(3) of this section).

(2) *Opportunity to exercise control.*

(i) a plan provides a participant or beneficiary an opportunity to exercise control over assets in his account only if:

(A) Under the terms of the plan, the participant or beneficiary has a reasonable opportunity to give investment instructions (in writing or otherwise, with opportunity to obtain written confirmation of such instructions) to an identified plan fiduciary who is obligated to comply with such instructions except as otherwise provided in paragraph (b)(2)(ii)(B) and (d)(2)(ii) of this section; and

(B) The participant or beneficiary is provided or has the opportunity to obtain sufficient information to make informed decisions with regard to investment alternatives available under the plan, and incidents of ownership appurtenant to such investments. For purposes of this subparagraph, a participant or beneficiary will not be considered to have sufficient investment information unless—

(1) The participant or beneficiary is provided by an identified plan fiduciary (or a person or persons designated by the plan fiduciary to act on his behalf):

(i) An explanation that the plan is intended to constitute a plan described in section 404(c) of the Employee Retirement Income Security Act, and title 29 of the Code of Federal Regulations Section 2550.440c-1, and that the fiduciaries of the plan may be relieved of liability for any losses which are the direct and necessary result of investment instructions given by such participant or beneficiary;

(ii) A description of the investment alternatives available under the plan and, with respect to each designated investment alternative, a general description of the investment objectives and risk and return characteristics of each such alternative, including information relating to the type and diversification of assets comprising the portfolio of the designed investment alternative;

(iii) Identification of any designated investment managers;

(iv) An explanation of the circumstances under which participants and beneficiaries may give investment instructions and explanation of any specified limitations on such instructions under the terms of the plan, including any restrictions on transfer to or from a designated investment alternative, and any restrictions on the exercise of voting, tender and similar rights appurtenant to a participant's or beneficiary's investment in an investment alternative;

(v) A description of any transaction fees and expenses which affect the participant's or beneficiary's account balance in connection with purchases or sales of interests in investment alternatives (e.g., commissions, sales load, deferred sales charges, redemption or exchange fees);

(vi) The name, address, and phone number of the plan fiduciary (and, if applicable, the person or persons designated by the plan fiduciary to act on his behalf) responsible for providing the information described in paragraph (b)(2)(i)(B)(2) upon request of a participant or beneficiary and a description of the information described in paragraph (b)(2)(i)(B)(2) which may be obtained on request;

(vii) In the case of plans which offer an investment alternative which is designed to permit a participant or beneficiary to directly or indirectly acquire or sell any employer security (employer security alternative), a description of the procedures established to provide for the confidentiality of information relating to the purchase, holding and sale of employer securities, and the exercise of voting, tender and similar rights, by participants and beneficiaries, and the name, address and phone number of the plan fiduciary responsible for monitoring compliance with the procedures (see paragraphs (d)(2)(ii)(E)(4) (vii), (viii) and (ix) of this section); and

(viii) In the case of an investment alternative which is subject to the Securities Act of 1933, and in which the participant or beneficiary has no assets invested, immediately following the participant's or beneficiary's initial investment, a copy of the most recent prospectus provided to the plan. This condition will be deemed satisfied if the participant or beneficiary has been provided with a copy of such most recent prospectus immediately prior to the participant's or beneficiary's initial investment in such alternative;

(ix) Subsequent to an investment in a investment alternative, any materials provided to the plan relating to the exercise of voting, tender or similar rights which are incidental to the holding in the account of the participant or beneficiary of an ownership interest in such alternative to the extent that such rights are passed through to participants and beneficiaries under the terms of the plan, as well as a description of or reference to plan provisions relating to the exercise of voting, tender or similar rights.

(2) The participants or beneficiary is provided by the identified plan fiduciary (or a person or persons designated by the plan fiduciary to act on his behalf), either directly or upon request, the following information, which shall be based on the latest information available to the plan:

(i) A description of the annual operating expenses of each designated investment alternative (e.g., investment management fees, administrative fees, transaction costs) which reduce the rate of return to participants and beneficiaries, and the aggregate amount of such expenses expressed as a percentage of average net assets of the designated investment alternative;

(ii) Copies of any prospectuses, financial statements and reports, and of any other materials relating to the investment alternatives available under the plan, to the extent such information is provided to the plan;

(iii) A list of the assets comprising the portfolio of each designated investment alternative which constitute plan assets within the meaning of 29 CFR 2510.3-101, the value of each such asset (or the proportion of the investment alternative which it comprises), and, with respect to each such asset which is a fixed rate investment contract issued by a bank, savings and loan association or insurance company, the name of the issuer of the contract, the term of the contract and the rate of return on the contract;

(iv) Information concerning the value of shares or units in designated investment alternatives available to participants and beneficiaries under the plan, as well as the past and current investment performance of such alternatives, determined, net of expenses, on a reasonable and consistent basis; and

(v) Information concerning the value of shares or units in designated investment alternatives held in the account of the participant or beneficiary.

(ii) A plan does not fail to provide an opportunity for a participant or beneficiary to exercise control over his individual account merely because it—

(A) Imposes charges for reasonable expenses. A plan may charge participants' and beneficiaries' accounts for the reasonable expenses of carrying out investment instructions, provided that procedures are established under the plan to periodically inform such participants and beneficiaries of actual expenses incurred with respect to their respective individual accounts;

(B) Permits a fiduciary to decline to implement investment instructions by participants and beneficiaries. A fiduciary may decline to implement participant and beneficiary instructions which are described at paragraph (d)(2)(ii) of this section, as well as instructions specified in the plan, including instructions—

(1) Which would result in a prohibited transaction described in ERISA section 406 or section 4975 of the Internal Revenue Code, and

(2) Which would generate income that would be taxable to the plan;

(C) Imposes reasonable restrictions on frequency of investment instructions. A plan may impose reasonable restrictions on the frequency with which participants and beneficiaries may give investment instructions. In no event, however, is such a restriction reasonable unless, with respect to each investment alternative made available by the plan, it permits participants and beneficiaries to give investment instructions with a frequency which is appropriate in light of the market volatility to which the investment alternative may reasonably be expected to be subject, provided that—

(1) At least three of the investment alternatives made available pursuant to the requirements of paragraph (b)(3)(i)(B) of this section, which constitute a broad range of investment alternatives, permit participants and beneficiaries to give investment instructions no less frequently than once within any three month period; and

(2)(i) At least one of the investment alternatives meeting the requirements of paragraph (b)(2)(ii)(C)(1) of this section permits participants and beneficiaries to give investment instructions with regard to transfers into the investment alternative as frequently as participants and beneficiaries are permitted to give investment instructions with respect to any investment alternative made available by the plan which permits participants and beneficiaries to give investment instructions more frequently than once within any three month period; or

(ii) With respect to each investment alternative which permits participants and beneficiaries to give investment instructions more frequently than once within any three month period, participants and beneficiaries are permitted to direct their investments from such alternative into an income producing, low risk, liquid fund, subfund, or account as frequently as they are permitted to give investment instructions with respect to each such alternative and, with respect to such fund, subfund or account, participants and beneficiaries are permitted to direct investments from the fund, subfund or account to an investment alternative meeting the requirements of paragraph (b)(2)(ii)(C)(1) as frequently as they are permitted to give investment instructions with respect to that investment alternative; and

(3) With respect to transfers from an investment alternative which is designed to permit a participant or beneficiary to directly or indirectly acquire or sell any employer security (employer security alternative) either:

(i) All of the investment alternatives meeting the requirements of paragraph (b)(2)(ii)(C)(1) of this section must permit participants and beneficiaries to give investment instructions with regard to transfers into each of the investment alternatives as frequently as participants and beneficiaries are permitted to give investment instructions with respect to the employer security alternative; or

(ii) Participants and beneficiaries are permitted to direct their investments from each employer security alternative into an income producing, low risk, liquid fund, subfund, or account as frequently as they are permitted to give investment instructions with respect to such employer security alternative and, with respect to such fund, subfund, or account, participants and beneficiaries are permitted to direct investments from the fund, subfund or account to each investment alternative meeting the requirements of paragraph (b)(2)(ii)(C)(1) as frequently as they are permitted to give investment instructions with respect to each such investment alternative.

(iii) Paragraph (c) of this section describes the circumstances under which a participant or beneficiary will be considered to have exercised independent control with respect to a particular transaction. (3) Broad range of investment alternatives. (i) A plan offers a broad range of investment alternatives only if the available investment alternatives are sufficient to provide the participant or beneficiary with a reasonable opportunity to:

(A) Materially affect the potential return on amounts in his individual account with respect to which he is permitted to exercise control and the degree of risk to which such amounts are subject;

(B) Choose from at least three investment alternatives:

(1) Each of which is diversified;

(2) Each of which has materially different risk and return characteristics;

(3) Which in the aggregate enable the participant or beneficiary by choosing among them to achieve a portfolio with aggregate risk and return characteristics at any point within the range normally appropriate for the participant or beneficiary; and

(4) Each of which when combined with investments in the other alternatives tends to minimize through diversification the overall risk of a participant's or beneficiary's portfolio;

(C) Diversify the investment of that portion of his individual account with respect to which he is permitted to exercise control so as to minimize the risk of large losses, taking into account the nature of the plan and the size of participants' or beneficiaries' accounts. In determining whether a plan provides the participant or beneficiary with a reasonable opportunity to diversify his investments, the nature of the investment alternatives offered by the plan and the size of the portion of the individual's account over which he is permitted to exercise control must be considered. Where such portion of the account of any participant or beneficiary is so limited in size that the opportunity to invest in look-through investment vehicles is the only prudent means to assure an opportunity to achieve appropriate diversification, a plan may satisfy the requirements of this paragraph only by offering look-through investment vehicles.

(ii) Diversification and look-through investment vehicles. Where look-through investment vehicles are available as investment alternatives to participants and beneficiaries, the underlying investments of the look-through investment vehicles shall be considered in determining whether the plan satisfies the requirements of subparagraphs (b)(3)(i)(B) and (b)(3)(i)(C).

(c) Exercise of control.

(1) *In general.*

(i) Sections 404(c)(1) and 404(c)(2) of the Act and paragraphs (a) and (d) of this section apply only with respect to a transaction where a participant or beneficiary has exercised independent control in fact with respect to the investment of assets in his individual account under an ERISA section 404(c) plan.

(ii) For purposes of sections 404(c)(1) and 4040(c)(2) of the Act and paragraphs (a) and (d) of this section, a participant or beneficiary will be deemed to have exercised control with respect to the exercise of voting, tender and similar rights appurtenant to the participant's or beneficiary's ownership interest in an investment alternative, provided that the participant's or beneficiary's investment in the investment alternative was itself the result of an exercise of control, the participant or beneficiary was provided a reasonable opportunity to give instruction with respect to such incidents of ownership, including the provision of the information described in paragraph (b)(2)(i)(B)(1)(ix) of this section, and the participant or beneficiary has not failed to exercise control by reason of the circumstances described in paragraph (c)(2) with respect to such incidents of ownership.

(2) *Independent control.* Whether a participant or beneficiary has exercised independent control in fact with respect to a transaction depends on the facts and circumstances of the particular case. However, a participant's or beneficiary's exercise of control is not independent in fact if:

(i) The participant or beneficiary is subjected to improper influence by a plan fiduciary or the plan sponsor with respect to the transaction;

(ii) A plan fiduciary has concealed material non-public facts regarding the investment from the participant or beneficiary, unless the disclosure of such information by the plan fiduciary to the participant or beneficiary would violate any provision of federal law or any provision of state law which is not preempted by the Act; or

(iii) The participant or beneficiary is legally incompetent and the responsible plan fiduciary accepts the instructions of the participant or beneficiary knowing him to be legally incompetent.

(3) *Transactions involving a fiduciary.* In the case of a sale, exchange or leasing of property (other than a transaction described in paragraph (d)(2)(ii)(E) of this section) between an ERISA section 404(c) plan and a plan fiduciary or an affiliate of such a fiduciary, or a loan to a plan fiduciary or an affiliate of such a fiduciary, the participant or beneficiary will not be deemed to have exercised independent control unless the transaction is fair and reasonable to him. For purposes of this paragraph (c)(3), a transaction will be deemed to be fair and reasonable to a participant or beneficiary if he pays no more than, or receives no less than, adequate consideration (as defined in section 3(18) of the Act) in connection with the transaction.

(4) *No obligation to advise.* A fiduciary has no obligation under part 4 of Title I of the Act to provide investment advice to a participant or beneficiary under an ERISA section 404(c) plan.

(d) Effect of independent exercise of control—

(1) *Participant or beneficiary not a fiduciary.* If a participant or beneficiary of an ERISA section 404(c) plan exercises independent control over assets in his individual account in the manner described in paragraph (c), then such participant or beneficiary is not a fiduciary of the plan by reason of such exercise of control.

(2) *Limitation on liability of plan fiduciaries.*

(i) If a participant or beneficiary of an ERISA section 404(c) plan exercises independent control over assets in his individual account in the manner described in paragraph (c), then no other person who is a fiduciary with respect to such plan shall be liable for any loss, or with respect to any breach of part 4 of Title I of the Act, that is the direct and necessary result of that participant's or beneficiary's exercise of control.

(ii) Paragraph (d)(2)(i) does not apply with respect to any instruction, which if implemented—

(A) Would not be in accordance with the documents and instruments governing the plan insofar as such documents and instruments are consistent with the provisions of Title I of ERISA;

(B) Would cause a fiduciary to maintain the indicia of ownership of any assets of the plan outside the jurisdiction of the district courts of the United States other than as permitted by section 404(b) of the Act and 29 CFR 2550.404b-1;

(C) Would jeopardize the plan's tax qualified status under the Internal Revenue Code;

(D) Could result in a loss in excess of a participant's or beneficiary's account balance; or

(E) Would result in a direct or indirect:

(1) Sale, exchange, or lease of property between a plan sponsor or any affiliate of the sponsor and the plan except for the acquisition or disposition of any interest in a fund, subfund or portfolio managed by a plan sponsor or an affiliate of the sponsor, or the purchase or sale of any qualifying employer security (as defined in section 407(d)(5) of the Act) which meets the conditions of section 408(e) of ERISA and section (d)(2)(ii)(E)(4) below;

(2) Loan to a plan sponsor or any affiliate of the sponsor;

(3) Acquisition or sale of any employer real property (as defined in section 407(d)(2) of the Act); or

(4) Acquisition or sale of any employer security except to the extent that:

(i) Such securities are qualifying employer securities (as defined in section 407(d)(5) of the Act);

(ii) Such securities are stock or an equity interest in a publicly traded partnership (as defined in section 7704(b) of the Internal Revenue Code of 1986), but only if such partnership is an existing partnership as defined in section 10211(c)(2)(A) of the Revenue Act of 1987 (Public Law 100-203);

(iii) Such securities are publicly traded on a national exchange or other generally recognized market;

(iv) Such securities are traded with sufficient frequency and in sufficient volume to assure that participant and beneficiary directions to buy or sell the security may be acted upon promptly and efficiently;

(v) Information provided to shareholders of such securities is provided to participants and beneficiaries with accounts holding such securities;

(vi) Voting, tender and similar rights with respect to such securities are passed through to participants and beneficiaries with accounts holding such securities;

(vii) Information relating to the purchase, holding, and sale of securities, and the exercise of voting, tender and similar rights with respect to such securities by participants and beneficiaries, is maintained in accordance with procedures which are designed to safeguard the confidentiality of such information, except to the extent necessary to comply with Federal laws or state laws not preempted by the Act;

(viii) The plan designates a fiduciary who is responsible for ensuring that: The procedures required under subparagraph (d)(2)(ii)(E)(4) (vii) are sufficient to safeguard the confidentiality of the information described in that subparagraph, such procedures are being followed, and the independent fiduciary required by subparagraph (d)(2)(ii)(E)(4)(ix) is appointed; and

(ix) An independent fiduciary is appointed to carry out activities relating to any situations which the fiduciary designated by the plan for purposes of subparagraph (d)(2)(ii)(E)(4)(viii) determines involve a potential for undue employer influence upon participants and beneficiaries with regard to the direct or indirect exercise of shareholder rights. For purposes of this subparagraph, a fiduciary is not independent if the fiduciary is affiliated with any sponsor of the plan.

(iii) The individual investment decisions of an investment manager who is designated directly by a participant or beneficiary or who manages a look-through investment vehicle in which a participant or beneficiary has invested are not direct and necessary results of the designation of the investment manager or of investment in the look-through investment vehicle. However, this paragraph (d)(2)(iii) shall not be construed to result in liability under section 405 of ERISA with respect to a fiduciary (other than the investment manager) who would otherwise be relieved of liability by reason of section 404(c)(2) of the Act and paragraph (d) of this section.

(3) *Prohibited Transactions.* The relief provided by section 404(c) of the Act and this section applies only to the provisions of part 4 of title I of the Act. Therefore, nothing in this section relieves a disqualified person from the taxes imposed by sections 4975 (a) and (b) of the Internal Revenue Code with respect to the transactions prohibited by section 4975(c)(1) of the Code.

(e) Definitions. For purposes of this section:

(1) Look-through investment vehicle means:

(i) An investment company described in section 3(a) of the Investment Company Act of 1940, or a series investment company described in section 18(f) of the 1940 Act or any of the segregated portfolios of such company;

(ii) A common or collective trust fund or a pooled investment fund maintained by a bank or similar institution, a deposit in a bank or similar institution, or a fixed rate investment contract of a bank or similar institution;

(iii) A pooled separate account or a fixed rate investment contract of an insurance company qualified to do business in a State; or

(iv) Any entity whose assets include plan assets by reason of a plan's investment in the entity;

(2) Adequate consideration has the meaning given it in section 3(18) of the Act and in any regulations under this title;

(3) An affiliate of a person includes the following:

(i) Any person directly or indirectly controlling, controlled by, or under common control with the person;

(ii) Any officer, director, partner, employee, an employee of an affiliated employer, relative (as defined in section 3(15) of ERISA), brother, sister, or spouse of a brother or sister, of the person; and

(iii) Any corporation or partnership of which the person is an officer director or partner.

For purposes of this paragraph (e)(3), the term "control" means, with respect to a person other than an individual, the power to exercise a controlling influence over the management or policies of such person.

(4) A designated investment alternative is a specific investment identified by a plan fiduciary as an available investment alternative under the plan.

(f) Examples. The provisions of this section are illustrated by the following examples. Examples (5) through (11) assume that the participant has exercised independent control with respect to his individual account under an ERISA section 404(c) plan described in paragraph (b) and has not directed a transaction described in paragraph (d)(2)(ii).

(1) Plan A is an individual account plan described in section 3(34) of the Act. The plan states that a plan participant or beneficiary may direct the plan administrator to invest any portion of his individual account in a particular diversified equity fund managed by an entity which is not affiliated with the plan sponsor, or any other asset administratively feasible for the plan to hold. However, the plan provides that the plan administrator will not implement certain listed instructions for which plan fiduciaries would not be relieved of liability under section 404(c) (see paragraph (d)(2)(ii)). Plan participants and beneficiaries are permitted to give investment instructions during the first week of each month with respect to the equity fund and at any time with respect to other investments. The plan provides for the pass-through of voting, tender and similar rights incidental to the holding in the account of a participant or beneficiary of an ownership interest in the equity fund or any other investment alternative available under the plan. The plan administrator of plan A provides each participant and beneficiary with the information described in subparagraphs (i), (ii), (iii), (iv), (v), (vi) and (vii) of paragraph (b)(2)(i)(B)(1) upon their entry into the plan, and provides updated information in the event of any material change in the information provided. Immediately following an investment by a participant or beneficiary in the equity fund, the plan administrator provides a copy of the most recent prospectus received from the fund to the investing participant or beneficiary. Immediately following any investment by a participant or beneficiary in any other investment alternative which is subject to the Securities Act of 1933, the plan administrator provides the participant or beneficiary with the most recent prospectus received from that investment alternative (see paragraph (b)(2)(i)(B)(1)(viii)). Finally, subsequent to any investment by a participant or beneficiary, the plan administrator forwards to the investing participant or beneficiary any materials provided to the plan relating to the exercise of voting, tender or similar rights attendant to ownership of an interest in such investment (see paragraph (b)(2)(i)(B)(1)(ix)). Upon request, the plan administrator provides each participant or beneficiary with copies of any prospectuses, financial statements and reports, and any other materials relating to the investment alternatives available under the plan which are received by the plan (see paragraph (b)(2)(i)(B)(2)(ii)). Also upon request, the plan administrator provides each participant and beneficiary with the other information required by paragraph (b)(2)(i)(B)(2) with respect to the equity fund, which is a designated investment alternative, including information concerning the latest available value of the participant's or beneficiary's interest in the equity fund (see paragraph (b)(2)(i)(B)(2)(v)). Plan A meets the requirements of paragraphs (b)(2)(i)(B)(1) and (2) of this section regarding the provision of investment information.

Note: The regulation imposes no additional obligation on the administrator to furnish or make available materials relating to the companies in which the equity fund invests (e.g., prospectuses, proxies, etc.).

(2) Plan C is an individual account plan described in section 3(34) of the Act under which participants and beneficiaries may choose among three investment alternatives which otherwise meet the requirements of paragraph (b) of this section. The plan permits investment instruction with respect to each investment alternative only on the first 10 days of each calendar quarter, i.e. January 1-10, April 1-10, July 1-10 and October 1-10. Plan C satisfies the condition of paragraph (b)(2)(ii)(C)(1) that instruction be permitted not less frequently than once within any three month period, since there is not any three month period during which control could not be exercised.

(3) Assume the same facts as in paragraph (f)(2), except that investment instruction may only be given on January 1, April 4, July 1 and October 1. Plan C is not an ERISA section 404(c) plan because it does not satisfy the condition of paragraph (b)(2)(ii)(C)(1) that instruction be permitted not less frequently than once within any three month period. Under these facts, there is a three month period, e.g., January 2 through April 1, during which control could not be exercised by participants and beneficiaries.

(4) Plan D is an individual account plan described in section 3(34) of the Act under which participants and beneficiaries may choose among three diversified investment alternatives which constitute a broad range of investment alternatives. The plan also permits investment instruction with respect to an employer securities alternative but provides that a participant or beneficiary can invest no more than 25% of his account balance in this alternative. This restriction does not affect the availability of relief under section 404(c) inasmuch as it does not relate to the three diversified investment alternatives and, therefore, does not cause the plan to fail to provide an opportunity to choose from a broad range of investment alternatives.

(5) A participant, P, independently exercises control over assets in his individual account plan by directing a plan fiduciary, F, to invest 100% of his account balance in a single stock. P is not a fiduciary with respect to the plan by reason of his exercise of control and F will not be liable for any losses that necessarily result from P's investment instruction.

(6) Assume the same facts as in paragraph (f)(5), except that P directs F to purchase the stock from B, who is a party in interest with respect to the plan. Neither P nor F has engaged in a transaction prohibited under section 406 of the Act: P because he is not a fiduciary with respect to the plan by reason of his exercise of control and F because he is not liable for any breach of part 4 of Title I that is the direct and necessary consequence of P's exercise of control. However, a prohibited transaction under section 4975(c) of the Internal Revenue Code may have occurred, and, in the absence of an exemption, tax liability may be imposed pursuant to sections 495 (a) and (b) of the Code.

(7) Assume the same facts as in paragraph (f)(5), except that P does not specify that the stock be purchased from B, and F chooses to purchase the stock from B. In the absence of an exemption, F has engaged in a prohibited transaction described in 406(a) of ERISA because the decision to purchase the stock from B is not a direct or necessary result of P's exercise of control.

(8) Pursuant to the terms of the plan, plan fiduciary F designates three reputable investment managers whom participants may appoint to manage assets in their individual accounts. Participant P selects M, one of the designated managers, to manage the assets in his account. M prudently manages P's account for 6 months after which he incurs losses in managing the account through his imprudence. M has engaged in a breach of fiduciary duty because M's imprudent management of P's account is not a direct or necessary result of P's exercise of control (the choice of M as manager). F has no fiduciary liability for M's imprudence because he has no affirmative duty to advise P (see paragraph (c)(4)) and because F is relieved of co-fiduciary liability by reason of section 404(c)(2) (see paragraph (d)(2)(iii)). F does have a duty to monitor M's performance to determine the suitability of continuing M as an investment manager, however, and M's imprudence would be a factor which F must consider in periodically reevaluating its decision to designate M.

(9) Participant P instructs plan fiduciary F to appoint G as his investment manager pursuant to the terms of the plan which provide P total discretion in choosing an investment manager. Through G's imprudence, G incurs losses in managing P's account. G has engaged in a breach of fiduciary duty because G's imprudent management of P's account is not a direct or necessary result of P's exercise of control (the choice of G as manager). Plan fiduciary F has no fiduciary liability for G's imprudence because F has no obligation to advise P (see paragraph (c)(4)) and because F is relieved of co-fiduciary liability for G's actions by reason of section 404(c)(2) (see paragraph (d)(2)(iii)).

In addition, F also has no duty to determine the suitability of G as an investment manager because the plan does not designate G as an investment manager.

(10) Participant P directs a plan fiduciary, F, a bank, to invest all of the assets in his individual account in a collective trust fund managed by F that is designed to be invested solely in a diversified portfolio of common stocks. Due to economic conditions, the value of the common stocks in the bank collective trust fund declines while the value of publicly-offered fixed income obligations remains relatively stable. F is not liable for any losses incurred by P solely because his individual account was not diversified to include fixed income obligations. Such losses are the direct result of P's exercise of control; moreover, under paragraph (c)(4) of this section F has no obligation to advise P regarding his investment decisions.

(11) Assume the same facts as in paragraph (f)(10) except that F, in managing the collective trust fund, invests the assets of the fund solely in a few highly speculative stocks. F is liable for losses resulting from its imprudent investment in the speculative stocks and for its failure to diversify the assets of the account. This conduct involves a separate breach of F's fiduciary duty that is not a direct or necessary result of P's exercise of control (see paragraph (d)(2)(iii)).

(g) Effective date.

(1) In general. Except as provided in paragraph (g)(2), this section is effective with respect to transactions occurring on or after the first day of the second plan year beginning on or after October 13, 1992.

(2) This section is effective with respect to transactions occurring under a plan maintained pursuant to one or more collective bargaining agreements between employee representatives and one or more employers ratified before October 13, 1992 after the later of the date determined under paragraph (g)(1) or the date on which the last collective bargaining agreement terminates. For purposes of this paragraph (g)(2), any extension or renegotiation of a collective bargaining agreement which is ratified on or after October 13, 1992 is to be disregarded in determining the date on which the agreement terminates.

(3) Transactions occurring before the date determined under subparagraph (g)(1) or (2) of this section, as applicable, are governed by section 404(c) of the Act without regard to the regulation.

Promulgated: 57 Fed. Reg. 49906 (10/13/92).

Sec. 2550.407a-1—General rule for the acquisition and holding of employer securities and employer real property.

(a) In general. Section 407(a)(1) of the Employee Retirement Income Security Act of 1974 (the Act) states that except as otherwise provided in Sec. 407 and Sec. 414 of the Act, a plan may not acquire or hold any employer security which is not a qualifying employer security or any employer real property which is not qualifying employer real property. Section 406(a)(1)(E) prohibits a fiduciary from knowingly causing a plan to engage in a transaction which constitutes a direct or indirect acquisition, on behalf of a plan, of any employer security or employer real property in violation of Sec. 407(a), and Sec. 406(a)(2) prohibits a fiduciary who has authority or discretion to control or manage assets of a plan to permit the plan to hold any employer security or employer real property if he knows or should know that holding such security or real property violates Sec. 407(a).

(b) Requirements applicable to all plans. A plan may hold or acquire only employer securities which are qualifying employer securities and employer real property which is qualifying employer real property. A plan may not hold employer securities and employer real property which are not qualifying employer securities and qualifying employer real property, except to the extent that:

(1) The employer security is held by a plan which has made an election under Sec. 407(c)(3) of the Act; or

(2) The employer security is a loan or other extension of credit which satisfies the requirements of Sec. 414(c)(1) of the Act or the employer real property is leased to the employer pursuant to a lease which satisfies the requirements of Sec. 414(c)(2) of the Act.

Promulgated: 42 Fed. Reg. 47201 (9/20/77); 42 Fed. Reg. 59842 (11/22/77).

Sec. 2550.407a-2—Limitation with respect to the acquisition of qualifying employer securities and qualifying employer real property.

(a) In general. Section 407(a)(2) of the Employee Retirement Income Security Act of 1974 (the Act) provides that a plan may not acquire any qualifying employer security or qualifying employer real property, if immediately after such acquisition the aggregate fair market value of qualifying employer securities and qualifying employer real property held by the plan exceeds 10% of the fair market value of the assets of the plan.

(b) Acquisition. For purposes of Sec. 407(a) of the Act, an acquisition by a plan of qualifying employer securities or qualifying employer real property shall include, but not be limited to, an acquisition by purchase, by the exchange of plan assets, by the exercise of warrants or rights, by the conversion of a security (except any acquisition pursuant to a conversion exempt under Sec. 408(b)(7) of the Act), by default of a loan where the qualifying employer security or qualifying employer real property was security for the loan, or by the contribution of such securities or real property to the plan. However, an acquisition of a security shall not be deemed to have occurred if a plan acquires the security as a result of a stock dividend or stock split.

(c) Fair market value—Indebtedness incurred in connection with the acquisition of a plan asset. In determining whether a plan is in compliance with the limitation on the acquisition of qualifying employer securities and qualifying employer real property in Sec. 407(a)(2), the limitation on the holding of qualifying employer securities and qualifying employer real property in Sec. 407(a)(3) and Sec. 2550.407a-3 thereunder, and the requirement regarding the disposition of employer securities and employer real property in Sec. 407(a)(4) and Sec. 2550.407a-4 thereunder, the fair market value of total plan assets shall be the fair market value of such assets less the unpaid amount of:

(1) Any indebtedness incurred by the plan in acquiring such assets;

(2) Any indebtedness incurred before the acquisition of such assets if such indebtedness would not have been incurred but for such acquisition; and

(3) Any indebtedness incurred after the acquisition of such assets if such indebtedness would not have been incurred but for such acquisition and the incurrence of such indebtedness was reasonably foreseeable at the time of such acquisition. However, the fair market value of qualifying employer securities and qualifying employer real property shall be the fair market value of such assets without any reduction for the unpaid amount of any indebtedness incurred by the plan in connection with the acquisition of such employer securities and employer real property.

(d) Examples.

(1) Plan assets have a fair market value of $100,000. The plan has no liabilities other than liabilities for vested benefits of participants and does not own any employer securities or employer real property. The plan proposes to acquire qualifying employer securities with a fair market value of $10,000 by paying $1,000 in cash and borrowing $9,000. The fair market value of plan assets would be $100,000 ($100,000 of plan assets less $1,000 cash payment plus $10,000 of employer securities less $9,000 indebtedness), the fair market value of the qualifying employer securities would be $10,000, which is 10% of the fair market value of plan assets. Accordingly, the acquisition would not contravene Sec. 407(a).

(2) Plan assets have a fair market value of $100,000. The plan has liabilities of $20,000 which were incurred in connection with the acquisition of those assets, and does not own any employer securities or employer real property. The plan proposes to pay cash for qualifying employer securities with a fair market value of $10,000. The fair market value of plan assets would be $80,000 ($100,000 of plan assets less $10,000 cash payment plus $10,000 of employer securities less $20,000 indebtedness), the fair market value of the qualifying employer securities would be $10,000, which is 12.5% of the fair market value of plan assets. Accordingly, the acquisition would contravene Sec. 407(a).

Promulgated: 42 Fed. Reg. 47201 (9/20/77).

Sec. 2550.407a-3—Limitation with respect to the holding of qualifying employer securities and qualifying employer real property.

(a) In general.

(1) Section 407(a)(3) of the Employee Retirement Income Security Act of 1974 (the Act) provides that a plan (other than an eligible individual account plan) may not hold, after December 31, 1984, any qualifying employer securities or qualifying employer real property (or both) to the extent that the aggregate fair market value of such securities and property, determined on December 31, 1984, exceeds 10% of the greater of:

(i) The fair market value of the assets of the plan, determined on December 31, 1984, or

(ii) The fair market value of the assets of the plan, determined on January 1, 1975.

(2) Section 407(a)(3)(B) makes Sec. 407(a)(3)(A) inapplicable to a plan which on any date after December 31, 1974, and before January 1, 1985, did not hold qualifying employer securities or qualifying employer real property (or both) the aggregate fair market value of which determined on such date exceeded 10% of the greater of:

(i) The fair market value of the assets of the plan, determined on such date, or

(ii) The fair market value of the assets determined on January 1, 1975.

(b) Ten percent limitation.

(1) The requirement of Sec. 407(a)(3) that a plan hold no more than 10% of the fair market value of its assets in qualifying employer securities or qualifying employer real property (or both) can be met at any time between December 31, 1974, and January 1, 1985. In accordance with Sec. 407(a)(3)(B) of the Act, if at any time between December 31, 1974 and January 1, 1985, the fair market value of qualifying employer securities and qualifying employer real property does not exceed 10% of the fair market value of total plan assets, the plan will be in compliance with the holding requirements of Sec. 407(a)(3), notwithstanding any subsequent increase in such percentage above 10% which occurs as the result of changes in the fair market value of either the qualifying employer securities or qualifying employer real property, or the other assets of the plan. Moreover, if such percentage falls below 10%, the plan may acquire additional qualifying employer securities or qualifying employer real property not to exceed the limitation on such acquisitions contained in Sec. 407(a)(2).

(2) *Example.* On January 1, 1975 a plan holds qualifying employer real property with a fair market value of $200,000 and has total assets with a fair market value of $1,000,000. The plan would have to divest qualifying employer securities or qualifying employer real property with a value of $100,000 to comply with Sec. 407(a)(3). If, however, there is a substantial rise in the market value of the plan's other assets in 1976 and the first quarter of 1977 so that the fair market value of total plan assets on March 31, 1977, is $2,000,000, but the aggregate fair market value of the qualifying employer securities and qualifying employer real property is still $200,000, the 10% holding requirement of Sec. 407(a)(3) would have been met on March 31, 1977. Henceforth, the plan would not be subject to the holding limitations of Sec. 407(a)(3), but only the limitations regarding the acquisition of qualifying employer securities and qualifying employer real property set forth in Sec. 407(a)(2) of the Act. If the plan does not acquire any additional employer securities or employer real property, and if in 1978, the fair market value of other plan assets decreases to $1,500,000 while the fair market value of qualifying employer securities and qualifying employer real property held by the plan remains at $200,000, or even increases to $300,000, the plan will not contravene the holding requirement of Sec. 407(a)(3), inasmuch as the plan was in compliance with that requirement on March 31, 1977. If, on February 1, 1980, the fair market value of total plan assets is $2,500,000 and the fair market value of qualifying employer securities and qualifying employer real property is $200,000, the plan may acquire additional qualifying employer securities and qualifying employer real property in the amount of $50,000.

(c) Fair market value—Indebtedness incurred in connection with the acquisition of a plan asset. In determining whether a plan is in compliance with the limitation on the holding of qualifying employer securities and qualifying employer real property in Sec. 407(a)(3), the fair market value of total plan assets, qualifying employer securities and qualifying employer real property for purposes of Sec. 407(a)(3) and this section shall be determined in accordance with the provisions of Sec. 2550.407a-2(c).

Promulgated: 42 Fed. Reg. 47202 (9/20/77).

Sec. 2550.407a-4—Divestiture of employer securities and real property by December 31, 1979.

(a) In general. Section 407(a)(4)(A) of the Employee Retirement Income Security Act of 1974 (the Act) provides that a plan may not hold, after December 31, 1979, any employer securities or employer real property in excess of the amount specified in regulations promulgated by the Secretary of Labor under Sec. 407(a)(4)(B) of the Act. That section directs the Secretary to prescribe regulations which shall have the effect of requiring a plan to divest 50% of the holdings of employer securities and employer real property which the plan would be required to divest before January 1, 1985, under Sec. 407(a)(3) or 407(c) of the Act.

(b) Fair market value—Indebtedness incurred in connection with the acquisition of a plan asset. In determining whether a plan is in compliance with the requirement regarding the disposition of employer securities and employer real property set forth in Sec. 407(a)(4), the fair market value of total plan assets, employer securities and employer real property for purposes of Sec. 407(a)(4) and this section shall be determined in accordance with the provisions of Sec. 2550.407a-2(c).

(c) Fifty percent divestiture—

(1) *Divestiture which would be required under Sec. 407(a)(3).*

(i) A plan which would be required to divest qualifying employer securities or qualifying employer real property before January 1, 1985, pursuant to Sec. 407(a)(3), and which has not met the requirements of that section by December 31, 1979, will be in compliance with the requirements of Sec. 407(a)(4) of the Act and this section if the plan divests by December 31, 1979, qualifying employer securities and qualifying employer real property which have, on any date between December 31, 1974, and January 1, 1980 (hereafter referred to as the "valuation date"), a fair market value equal to 50% of the amount by which such qualifying employer securities and qualifying employer real property exceed 10% of the fair market value of plan assets as of the valuation date. For purposes of this section, the fair market value of plan assets on the valuation date shall be deemed to be an amount equal to:

(A) The fair market value of the assets of the plan on the valuation date, or

(B) An actuarial estimate of the fair market value of the assets of the plan on any date between December 31, 1979 and January 1, 1985. The actuarial estimate under paragraph (c)(1)(i)(B) of this section must be made in good faith and its basis must be set forth in writing.

(ii) The fair market value of qualifying employer securities and qualifying employer real property which must be divested pursuant to paragraph (c)(1)(i) of this section shall be reduced by an amount equal to the fair market value of any qualifying employer security which is a loan or other extension of credit that satisfies the requirements of Sec. 414(c)(1) of the Act or any qualifying employer real property leased to the employer pursuant to a lease that satisfies the requirements of Sec. 414(c)(2) of the Act.

(iii) *Examples.*

(A) On January 1, 1975, the assets of a plan have a fair market value of $800,000. On December 31, 1977, plan assets have a fair market value of $900,000 and the actuarial estimate of the fair market value of plan assets as of December 31, 1984, is $1,000,000. The plan has chosen December 31, 1977, as the valuation date, and has decided that for purposes of section 407(a)(4) and Sec. 2550.407a-4 the fair market value of plan assets on the valuation date shall be the actuarial estimate of the fair market value of plan assets as of December 31, 1984, which is $1,000,000. The qualifying employer securities and qualifying employer real property held by the plan on December 31, 1977 have a fair market value of $200,000. A qualifying employer security, which has a fair market value of $25,000, is a loan by the plan which meets the conditions of Sec. 414(c)(1) of the Act. The fair market value of qualifying employer securities and qualifying employer real property held by the plan exceed by $100,000, 10% of the greater of the fair market value of plan assets on January 1, 1975, or the valuation date. In order to comply with section 407(a)(4) of the Act and this section, the plan ordinarily would have to divest, by December 31, 1979, $50,000 of qualifying employer securities or qualifying employer real property, which would be 50% of the amount which exceeds 10% of plan assets. However, because qualifying employer securities which have a fair market value of $25,000 are held by the plan pursuant to the transitional rules of section 414(c)(1) of the Act, the plan will have to divest by December 31, 1979, only $25,000 of qualifying employer securities and qualifying employer real property because it may subtract the fair market value of any qualifying employer securities or qualifying employer real property held by the plan which satisfies the requirements of the transitional rules of Sec. 414(c)(1) or (2) of the Act from any amounts which it is required to divest.

(B) Same facts as example (A), except that the plan has $100,000 in indebtedness outstanding, which was incurred in connection with the acquisition of a plan asset (other than qualifying employer securities or qualifying employer real property). For purposes of determining the percentage of plan assets represented by the investment in qualifying employer securities and qualifying employer real property, the fair market value of plan assets on the valuation date is $900,000 ($1,000,000 less $100,000 in indebtedness). The fair market value of qualifying employer securities and qualifying employer real property (i.e., $200,000) held by the plan exceeds 10% (i.e., $90,000) of the fair market value of plan assets by $110,000. In order to comply with Sec. 407(a)(4) of the Act and this section, the plan would be required to divest $30,000 of qualifying employer securities or qualifying employer real property by December 31, 1979, which would be 50% of $110,000, less the fair market value of qualifying employer securities or qualifying employer real property held pursuant to Sec. 414(c) (1) or (2) of the Act.

(2) *Divestiture which would be required under Sec. 407(c).*

(i) Notwithstanding the prohibition of Sec. 407(a)(1)(A) of the Act regarding the holding of employer securities and subject to the limitations of Sec. 407(c)(1) of the Act, Sec. 407(c) permits a plan which has made a valid election under Sec. 407(c)(3) to hold an employer security which is neither a qualifying employer security nor a loan of other extension of credit covered by the transitional provisions of Sec. 414(c)(1) of the Act. An election under Sec. 407(c) must have been made before January 1, 1976, and in accordance with Sec. 2550.407c-3 (41 Fed. Reg. 43726, September 23, 1975). A plan which has made a valid election under Sec. 407(c)(3) will be in compliance with the requirements of Sec. 407(a)(4) of the Act and this section if, by December 31, 1979, the plant divests employer securities which have on any date between December 31, 1974 and January 1, 1980 (hereafter referred to as the "valuation date"), a fair market value determined as of December 31, 1974 equal to 50% of the amount in excess of 10% of the lesser of:

(A) The fair market value of the assets of the plan determined on the valuation date (disregarding any portion of the fair market value of employer securities which is attributable to appreciation of such securities after December 31, 1974) but not less than the fair market value of the plan assets on January 1, 1975, or

(B) An amount equal to the sum of (1) The total amount of the contributions to the plan received after December 31, 1974 and prior to the valuation date, plus (2) The fair market value of the assets of the plan, determined as of January 1, 1975. For purposes of this paragraph (c)(2), the fair market value of plan assets on the valuation date shall be deemed to be an amount equal to (1) the fair market value of the assets of the plan on the valuation date, or (2) an actuarial estimate of the fair market value of the assets of the plan on any date between December 31, 1979 and January 1, 1985. The actuarial estimate must be made in good faith and its basis must be set forth in writing.

(ii) The fair market value of employer securities which must be divested pursuant to this section shall be reduced by an amount equal to the fair market value of any employer security which is a loan or other extension of credit that satisfies the requirements of Sec. 414(c)(1) of the Act.

(iii) *Example.*

(A) A plan has made a valid election under Sec. 407(c) of the Act and has been in compliance with the requirements of Sec. 407(c)(3). On January 1, 1975, total plan assets have a fair market value of $105,000 and employer securities have a fair market value of $15,000. On June 30, 1975, the fair market value of plan assets is $105,000, and the actuarial estimate of the fair market value of plan assets as of December 31, 1984 is $145,000. The plan has chosen June 30, 1975 as the valuation date and has decided that for purposes of Sec. 407(a)(4) and Sec. 2550.407a-4 the fair market value of plan assets on the valuation date shall be the actuarial estimate of the fair market value of assets of December 31, 1984, which is $145,000. No contributions have been made to the plan from December

31, 1974, to June 30, 1975, and the employer securities held by the plan on June 30, 1975, are the same employer securities held on January 1, 1975. Five thousand dollars of employer securities held by the plan is a loan which meets the conditions of Sec. 414(c)(1) of the Act. One thousand dollars of employer securities is neither qualifying employer securities nor a loan or other extension of credit covered by the provisions of Sec. 414(c)(1). Ten percent of the fair market value of plan assets on the valuation date is $14,500; and 10 percent of the sum of the amount of contributions received after December 31, 1974, and prior to July 1, 1975 (nothing, because no contributions were received) plus the fair market value of plan assets on January 1, 1975 ($105,000) is $10,500. Ordinarily, as of December 31, 1979, the plan would have to divest employer securities in excess of 50% of the fair market value of the lesser of these amounts. The fair market value of employer securities held by the plan exceeds the lesser of these amounts by $4,500 and 50% of $4,500 is $2,250. However, because $5,000 of employer securities is a loan covered by the provisions of Sec. 414(c)(1), the amount of employer securities which would have to be divested is reduced by $5,000. Accordingly, the plan is not required to divest any employer securities by December 31, 1979.

(B) A plan has made a valid election under Sec. 407(c) and has been in compliance with the requirements of Sec. 407(c)(3). On January 1, 1975, total plan assets have a fair market value of $100,000 and employer securities have a fair market value of $30,000. On April 30, 1977, the fair market value of total plan assets is $110,000, none of which is attributable to appreciation of employer securities after December 31, 1974. The actuarial estimate of the fair market value of plan assets as of December 31, 1984 is $160,000. Contributions to the plan from December 31, 1974, through April 30, 1977, total $12,000. The plan has chosen April 30, 1977 as the valuation date and has decided that the fair market value of plan assets on the valuation date shall be the actuarial estimate of the fair market value of plan assets as of December 31, 1984, which is $160,000. The employer securities held on April 30, 1977, are the same employer securities held on January 1, 1975. Ten percent of the fair market value of plan assets on the valuation date is $16,000; and 10% of the sum of the amount of contributions received after December 31, 1974, and prior to May 1, 1977, plus the fair market value of plan assets on January 1, 1975, is $11,200. The fair market value of employer securities held by the plan exceeds the lesser of these two amounts by $18,800. In order to comply with Sec. 407(a)(4) of the Act and this section, the plan would be required to divest, by December 31, 1979, $9,400 of employer securities.

Promulgated: 42 Fed. Reg. 47202 (9/20/77).

Sec. 2550.407c-3—Election by plan to utilize the alternate method of calculation of value of employer securities.

(a) In general. If an employee benefit plan holds no employer real property (as defined in Sec. 407(d)(2) of the Employee Retirement Income Security Act of 1974 (the "Act")) on January 1, 1975, it may elect under Sec. 407(c)(3) of the Act to utilize the alternate method of calculation of value of employer securities set forth in Sec. 407(c) of the Act for the purpose of satisfying the requirement of Sec. 407(a)(3) of the Act relating to the limitation on holding by certain employee benefit plans of qualifying employer securities and qualifying employer real property.

(b) Election is irrevocable. An election by a plan under Sec. 407(c)(3) of the Act shall be binding with respect to such plan and, once made, shall be irrevocable.

(c) Procedure for making election—

(1) *Time of election.* An election under this section must be made before January 1, 1976. An election will be deemed to be timely filed only if received at the Office of Employee Benefits Security, Labor-Management Services Administration, U.S. Department of Labor, Washington, D.C. 20216 on or before 5 p.m., December 31, 1975, or, if mailed by certified or registered mail, postmarked prior to January 1, 1976.

(2) *By whom election is to be made.* The election provided by this section may be made only by the plan administrator of the plan.

(3) *Manner of making election.* The plan administrator shall file a statement containing the following information: (i) The name and address of the plan; (ii) the EIN number of the plan; (iii) the WP number of the plan (if any); (iv) the name and address of the plan administrator; (v) a statement that on January 1, 1975, the plan held no employer real property; and (vi) a statement that the plan elects to use the alternate method of valuation of employer securities provided under Sec. 407(c)(3) of the Act.

(d) Limitation on acquisition of employer real property. After making an election under this section, and before January 1, 1985, the plan may not acquire any employer real property.

Promulgated: 40 Fed. Reg. 43726 (9/23/75).

Sec. 2550.407d-5—Definition of the term "qualifying employer security".

(a) In general. For purposes of this section and Sec. 407(d)(5) of the Employee Retirement Income Security Act of 1974 (the Act), the term "qualifying employer security" means an employer security which is:

(1) Stock; or

(2) A marketable obligation, as defined in paragraph (b) of this section and Sec. 407(e) of the Act.

(b) For purposes of paragraph (a)(2) of this section and Sec. 407(d)(5) of the Act, the term "marketable obligation" means a bond, debenture, note, or certificate, or other evidence of indebtedness (hereinafter in this paragraph referred to as "obligation") if:

(1) Such obligation is acquired—

(i) On the market, either—

(A) At the price of the obligation prevailing on a national securities exchange which is registered with the Securities and Exchange Commission, or

(B) If the obligation is not traded on such a national securities exchange, at a price not less favorable to the plan than the offering price for the obligation as established by current bid and asked prices quoted by persons independent of the issuer;

(ii) From an underwriter, at a price—

(A) Not in excess of the public offering price for the obligation as set forth in a prospectus or offering circular filed with the Securities and Exchange Commission, and

(B) At which a substantial portion of the same issue is acquired by persons independent of the issuer; or

(iii) Directly from the issuer at a price not less favorable to the plan than the price paid currently for a substantial portion of the same issue by persons independent of the issuer;

(2) Immediately following acquisition of such obligation,

(i) Not more than 25% of the aggregate amount of obligations issued in such issue and outstanding at the time of acquisition is held by the plan, and

(ii) At least 50% of the aggregate amount referred to in paragraph (A) is held by persons independent of the issuer; and

(3) Immediately following acquisition of the obligation, not more than 25% of the assets of the plan is invested in obligations of the employer or an affiliate of the employer.

Promulgated: 42 Fed. Reg. 44388 (9/2/77).

Sec. 2550.407d-6—Definition of the term "employee stock ownership plan".

(a) In general—

(1) *Type of plan.* To be an "ESOP" (employee stock ownership plan), a plan described in Sec. 407(d)(6)(A) of the Employee Retirement Income Security Act of 1974 (the Act) must meet the requirements of this section. See Sec. 407(d)(6)(B).

(2) *Designation as ESOP.* To be an ESOP, a plan must be formally designated as such in the plan document.

(3) *Retroactive amendment.* A plan meets the requirements of this section as of the date that it is designated as an ESOP if it is amended retroactively to meet, and in fact does meet, such requirements at any of the following times:

(i) 12 months after the date on which the plan is designated as an ESOP;

(ii) 90 days after a determination letter is issued with respect to the qualification of the plan as an ESOP under this section, but only if the determination is requested by the date in paragraph (a)(3)(i) of this section; or

(iii) A later date approved by the Internal Revenue Service district director.

(4) *Addition to other plan.* An ESOP may form a portion of a plan the balance of which includes a qualified pension, profit-sharing, or stock bonus plan which is not an ESOP. A reference to an ESOP includes an ESOP that forms a portion of another plan.

(5) *Conversion of existing plan to an ESOP.* If an existing pension, profit-sharing, or stock bonus plan is converted into an ESOP, the requirements of Sec. 404 of the Act, relating to fiduciary duties, and Sec. 401(a) of the Internal Revenue Code (the Code), relating to requirements for plans established for the exclusive benefit of employees, apply to such conversion. A conversion may constitute a termination of an existing plan. For definition of a termination, see the regulations under Sec. 411(d)(3) of the Code and Sec. 4041(f) of the Act.

(6) *Certain arrangements barred*—(i) Buy-sell agreements. An arrangement involving an ESOP that creates a put option must not provide for the issuance of put options other than as provided under Sec. 2550.408b-3 (j), (k) and (l). Also, an ESOP must not otherwise obligate itself to acquire securities from a particular security holder at an indefinite time determined upon the happening of an event such as the death of the holder.

(b) Plan designed to invest primarily in qualifying employer securities. A plan constitutes an ESOP only if the plan specifically states that it is designed to invest primarily in qualifying employer securities. Thus, a stock bonus plan or a money purchase pension plan constituting an ESOP may invest part of its assets in other than qualifying employer securities. Such plan will be treated the same as other stock bonus plans or money purchase pension plans qualified under Sec. 401(a) of the Code with respect to those investments.

(c) Regulations of the Secretary of the Treasury. A plan constitutes an ESOP for a plan year only if it meets such other requirements as the Secretary of the Treasury may prescribe by regulation under Sec. 4975(e)(7) of the Code. (See 26 CFR 54.4975-11).

Promulgated: 42 Fed. Reg. 44388 (9/2/77).

Sec. 2550.408b-1—General statutory exemption for loans to plan participants and beneficiaries who are parties in interest with respect to the plan.

(a)(1) In general. Section 408(b)(1) of the Employee Retirement Income Security Act of 1974 (the Act or ERISA) exempts from the prohibitions of Sec. 406(a), 406(b)(1) and 406(b)(2) loans by a plan to parties in interest who are participants or beneficiaries of the plan, provided that such loans:

(i) Are available to all such participants and beneficiaries on a reasonably equivalent basis;

(ii) Are not made available to highly compensated employees, officers or shareholders in an amount greater than the amount made available to other employees;

(iii) Are made in accordance with specific provisions regarding such loans set forth in the plan;

(iv) Bear a reasonable rate of interest; and

(v) Are adequately secured. The Internal Revenue Code (the Code) contains parallel provisions to Sec. 408(b)(1) of the Act. Effective, December 31, 1978, Sec. 102 of Reorganization Plan No. 4 of 1978 (43 FR 47713, October 17, 1978) transferred the authority of the Secretary of the Treasury to promulgate regulations of the type published herein to the Secretary of Labor. Therefore, all references herein to Sec. 408(b)(1) of the Act should be read to include reference to the parallel provisions of Sec. 4975(d)(1) of the Code.

Section 1114(b)(15)(B) of the Tax Reform Act of 1986 amended Sec. 408(b)(1)(B) of ERISA by deleting the phrase "highly compensated employees, officers or shareholders" and substituting the phrase "highly compensated employees (within the meaning of Sec. 414(q) of the Internal Revenue Code of 1986)." Thus, for plans with participant loan programs which are subject to the amended Sec. 408(b)(1)(B), the requirements of this regulation should be read to conform with the amendment.

(2) *Scope.* Section 408(b)(1) of the Act does not contain an exemption from acts described in Sec. 406(b)(3) of the Act (prohibiting fiduciaries from receiving consideration for their own personal account from any party dealing with a plan in connection with a transaction involving plan assets). If a loan from a plan to a participant who is a party in interest with respect to that plan involves an act described in Sec. 406(b)(3), such an act constitutes a separate transaction which is not exempt under Sec. 408(b)(1) of the Act. The provisions of Sec. 408(b)(1) are further limited by Sec. 408(d) of the Act (relating to transactions with owner-employees and related persons).

(3) *Loans.*

(i) Section 408(b)(1) of the Act provides relief from the prohibitions of Sec. 406(a), 406(b)(1) and 406(b)(2) for the making of a participant loan. The term "participant loan" refers to a loan which is arranged and approved by the fiduciary administering the loan program primarily in the interest of the participant and which otherwise satisfies the criteria set forth in Sec. 408(b)(1) of the Act. The existence of a participant loan or participant loan program will be determined upon consideration of all relevant facts and circumstances. Thus, for example, the mere presence of a loan document appearing to satisfy the requirements of Sec. 408(b)(1) will not be dispositive of whether a participant loan exists where the subsequent administration of the loan indicates that the parties to the loan agreement did not intend the loan to be repaid. Moreover, a loan program containing a precondition designed to benefit a party in interest (other than the participant) is not afforded relief by Sec. 408(b)(1) or this regulation. In this regard, Sec. 408(b)(1) recognizes that a program of participant loans, like other plan investments, must be prudently established and administered for the exclusive purpose of providing benefits to participants and beneficiaries of the plan.

(ii) For the purpose of this regulation, the term "loan" will include any renewal or modification of an existing loan agreement, provided that, at the time of each such renewal or modification, the requirements of Sec. 408(b)(1) and this regulation are met.

(4) *Examples.* The following examples illustrate the provisions of Sec. 2550.408b-1(a).

Example (1): T, a trustee of plan P, has exclusive discretion over the management and disposition of plan assets. As a result, T is a fiduciary with respect to P under Sec. 3(21)(A) of the Act and a party in interest with respect to P pursuant to Sec. 3(14)(A) of the Act. T is also a participant in P. Among T's duties as fiduciary is the administration of a participant loan program which meets the requirements of Sec. 408(b)(1) of the Act. Pursuant to strict objective criteria stated under the program, T, who participates in all loan decisions, receives a loan on the same terms as other participants. Although the exercise of T's discretion on behalf of himself may constitute an act of self-dealing described in Sec. 406(b)(1), Sec. 408(b)(1) provides an exemption from Sec. 406(b)(1). As a result, the loan from P to T would be exempt under Sec. 408(b)(1), provided the conditions of that section are otherwise satisfied.

Example (2): P is a plan covering all the employees of E, the employer who established and maintained P. F is a fiduciary with respect to P and an officer of E. The plan documents governing P give F the authority to establish a participant loan program in accordance with Sec. 408(b)(1) of the Act. Pursuant to an arrangement with E, F establishes such a program but limits the use of loan funds to investments in a limited partnership which is established and maintained by E as general partner. Under these facts, the loan program and any loans made pursuant to this program are outside the scope of relief provided by Sec. 408(b)(1) because the loan program is designed to operate for the benefit of E. Under the circumstances described, the diversion of plan assets for E's benefit would also violate sections 403(c)(1) and 404(a) of the Act.

Example (3): Assume the same facts as in Example 2, above, except that F does not limit the use of loan funds. However, E pressures his employees to borrow funds under P's participant loan program and then reloan the loan proceeds to E. F, unaware of E's activities, arranges and approves the loans. If the loans meet all the conditions of Sec. 408(b)(1), such loans will be exempt under that section. However, E's activities would cause the entire transaction to be viewed as an indirect transfer of plan assets between P and E, who is a party in interest with respect to P, but not the participant borrowing from P. By coercing the employees to engage in loan transactions for its benefit, E has engaged in separate transactions that are not exempt under Sec. 408(b)(1). Accordingly, E would be liable for the payment of excise taxes under Sec. 4975 of the Code.

Example (4): Assume the same facts as in Example 2, above, except that, in return for structuring and administering the loan program as indicated, E agrees to pay F an amount equal to 10% of the funds loaned under the program. Such a payment would result in a separate transaction not covered by Sec. 408(b)(1). This transaction would be prohibited under Sec. 406(b)(3) since F would be receiving consideration from a party in connection with a transaction involving plan assets.

Example (5): F is a fiduciary with respect to plan P. D is a party in interest with respect to plan P. Section 406(a)(1)(B) of the Act would prohibit F from causing P to lend money to D. However, F enters into an agreement with Z, a plan participant, whereby F will cause P to make a participant loan to Z with the express understanding that Z will subsequently lend the loan proceeds to D. An examination of Z's credit standing indicates that he is not creditworthy and would not, under normal circumstances, receive a loan under the conditions established by the participant loan program. F's decision to approve the participant loan to Z on the basis of Z's prior agreement to lend the money to D violates the exclusive purpose requirements of sections 403(c) and 404(a). In effect, the entire transaction is viewed as an indirect transfer of plan assets between P and D, and not a loan to a participant exempt under Sec. 408(b)(1). Z's lack of credit standing would also cause the transaction to fail under Sec. 408(b)(1)(A) of the Act.

Example (6): F is a fiduciary with respect to Plan P. Z is a plan participant. Z and D are both parties in interest with respect to P. F approves a participant loan to Z in accordance with the conditions established under the participant loan program. Upon receipt of the loan, Z intends to lend the money to D. If F has approved this loan solely upon consideration of those factors which would be considered in a normal commercial setting by an entity in the business of making comparable loans, Z's subsequent use of the loan proceeds will not affect the determination of whether loans under P's program satisfy the conditions of Sec. 408(b)(1).

Example (7): A is the trustee of a small individual account plan. D, the president of the plan sponsor, is also a participant in the plan. Pursuant to a participant loan program meeting the requirements of Sec. 408(b)(1), D applies for a loan to be secured by a parcel of real property. D does not intend to repay the loan; rather, upon eventual default, he will permit the property to be foreclosed upon and transferred to the plan in discharge of his legal obligation to repay the loan. A, aware of D's intention, approves the loan. D fails to make two consecutive quarterly payments of principal and interest under the note evidencing the loan thereby placing the loan in default. The plan then acquires the real property upon foreclosure. Such facts and circumstances indicate that the payment of money from the plan to D was not a participant loan eligible for the relief afforded by Sec. 408(b)(1). In effect, this transaction is a prohibited sale or exchange of property between a plan and a party in interest from the time D receives the money.

Example (8): Plan P establishes a participant loan program. All loans are subject to the condition that the borrowed funds must be used to finance home purchases. Interest rates on the loans are the same as those charged by a local savings and loan association under similar circumstances. A loan by P to a participant to finance a home purchase would be subject to the relief provided by Sec. 408(b)(1) provided that the conditions of 408(b)(1) are met. A participant loan program which is established to make loans for certain stated purposes (e.g., hardship, college tuition, home purchases, etc.) but which is not otherwise designed to benefit parties in interest (other than plan participants) would not, in itself, cause such program to be ineligible for the relief provided by Sec. 408(b)(1). However, fiduciaries are cautioned that operation of a loan program with limitations may result in loans not being made available to all participants and beneficiaries on a reasonably equivalent basis.

(b) Reasonably Equivalent Basis.

(1) Loans will not be considered to have been made available to participants and beneficiaries on a reasonably equivalent basis unless:

(i) Such loans are available to all plan participants and beneficiaries without regard to any individual's race, color, religion, sex, age or national origin;

(ii) In making such loans, consideration has been given only to those factors which would be considered in a normal commercial setting by an entity in the business of making similar types of loans. Such factors may include the applicant's creditworthiness and financial need; and

(iii) An evaluation of all relevant facts and circumstances indicates that, in actual practice, loans are not unreasonably withheld from any applicant.

(2) A participant loan program will not fail the requirement of paragraph (b)(1) of this Sec. or Sec. 2550.408b-1(c) if the program establishes a minimum loan amount of up to $1,000, provided that the loans granted meet the requirements of Sec. 2550.408b-1(f).

(3) *Examples.* The following examples illustrate the provisions of Sec. 2550.408b-1(b)(1):

Example (1): T, a trustee of plan P, has exclusive discretion over the management and disposition of plan assets. T's duties include the administration of a participant loan program which meets the requirements of Sec. 408(b)(1) of the Act. T receives a participant loan at a lower interest rate than the rate made available to other plan participants of similar financial condition or creditworthiness with similar security. The loan by P to T would not be covered by the relief provided by Sec. 408(b)(1) because loans under P's program are not available to all plan participants on a reasonably equivalent basis.

Example (2): Same facts as in example 1, except that T is a member of a committee of trustees responsible for approving participant loans. T pressures the committee to refuse loans to other qualified participants in order to assure that the assets allocated to the participant loan program would be available for a loan by P to T. The loan by P to T would not be covered by the relief provided by Sec. 408(b)(1) since participant loans have not been made available to all participants and beneficiaries on a reasonably equivalent basis.

Example (3): T is the trustee of plan P, which covers the employees of E. A, B and C are employees of E, participants in P, and friends of T. The documents governing P provide that T, in his discretion, may establish a participant loan program meeting certain specified criteria. T institutes such a program and tells A, B and C of his decision. Before T is able to notify P's other participants and beneficiaries of the loan program, A, B, and C file loan applications which, if approved, will use up substantially all of the funds set aside for the loan program. Approval of these applications by T would represent facts and circumstances showing that loans under P's program are not available to all participants and beneficiaries on a reasonably equivalent basis.

(c) Highly Compensated Employees.

(1) Loans will not be considered to be made available to highly compensated employees, officers or shareholders in an amount greater than the amount made available to other employees if, upon consideration of all relevant facts and circumstances, the program does not operate to exclude large numbers of plan participants from receiving loans under the program.

(2) A participant loan program will not fail to meet the requirement in paragraph (c)(1), of this section, merely because the plan documents specifically governing such loans set forth either (i) a maximum dollar limitation, or (ii) a maximum percentage of vested accrued benefit which no loan may exceed.

(3) If the second alternative in paragraph (3)(c) of this section (maximum percentage of vested accrued benefit) is chosen, a loan program will not fail to meet this requirement solely because maximum loan amounts will vary directly with the size of the participant's accrued benefit.

(4) *Examples.* The following examples illustrate the provisions of Sec. 2550.408b-1(c).

Example (1): The documents governing plan P provide for the establishment of a participant loan program in which the amount of any loan under the program (when added to the outstanding balances of any other loans under the program to the same participant) does not exceed the lesser of (i) $50,000, or (ii) one-half of the present value of that participant's vested accrued benefit under the plan (but not less than $10,000). P's participant loan program does not fail to meet the requirement in Sec. 408(b)(1)(B) of the Act, and would be covered by the relief provided by Sec. 408(b)(1) if the other conditions of that section are met.

Example (2): The documents governing plan T provide for the establishment of a participant loan program in which the minimum loan amount would be $25,000. The documents also require that the only security acceptable under the program would be the participant's vested accrued benefit. A, the plan fiduciary administering the loan program, finds that because of the restrictions in the plan documents only 20 percent of the plan participants, all of whom earn in excess of $75,000 a year, would meet the threshold qualifications for a loan. Most of these participants are high-level supervisors or corporate officers. Based on these facts, it appears that loans under the program would be made available to highly compensated employees in an amount greater than the amount made available to other employees. As a result, the loan program would fail to meet the requirement in Sec. 408(b)(1)(B) of the Act and would not be covered by the relief provided in section 408(b)(1).

(d) Specific Plan Provisions. For the purpose of Sec. 408(b)(1) and this regulation, the Department will consider that participant loans granted or renewed at any time prior to the last day of the first plan year beginning on or after January 1,

1989, are made in accordance with specific provisions regarding such loans set forth in the plan if:

(1) The plan provisions regarding such loans contain (at a minimum) an explicit authorization for the plan fiduciary responsible for investing plan assets to establish a participant loan program; and

(2) For participant loans granted or renewed on or after the last day of the first plan year beginning on or after January 1, 1989, the participant loan program which is contained in the plan or in a written document forming part of the plan includes, but need not be limited to, the following:

(i) The identity of the person or positions authorized to administer the participant loan program;

(ii) A procedure for applying for loans;

(iii) The basis on which loans will be approved or denied;

(iv) Limitations (if any) on the types and amount of loans offered;

(v) The procedure under the program for determining a reasonable rate of interest;

(vi) The types of collateral which may secure a participant loan; and

(vii) The events constituting default and the steps that will be taken to preserve plan assets in the event of such default.

Example (1): Plan P authorizes the trustee to establish a participant loan program in accordance with section 408(b)(1) of the Act. Pursuant to this explicit authority, the trustee establishes a written program which contains all of the information required by Sec. 2550.408b-1(d)(2). Loans made pursuant to this authorization and the written loan program will not fail under Sec. 408(b)(1)(C) of the Act merely because the specific provisions regarding such loans are contained in a separate document forming part of the plan. The specific provisions describing the loan program, whether contained in the plan or in a written document forming part of a plan, do affect the rights and obligations of the participants and beneficiaries under the plan and, therefore, must in accordance with Sec. 102(a)(1) of the Act, be disclosed in the plan's summary plan description.

(e) Reasonable Rate of Interest. A loan will be considered to bear a reasonable rate of interest if such loan provides the plan with a return commensurate with the interest rates charged by persons in the business of lending money for loans which would be made under similar circumstances.

Example (1): Plan P makes a participant loan to A at the fixed interest rate of 8% for 5 years. The trustees, prior to making the loan, contacted two local banks to determine under what terms the banks would make a similar loan taking into account A's creditworthiness and the collateral offered. One bank would charge a variable rate of 10% adjusted monthly for a similar loan. The other bank would charge a fixed rate of 12% under similar circumstances. Under these facts, the loan to A would not bear a reasonable rate of interest because the loan did not provide P with a return commensurate with interest rates charged by persons in the business of lending money for loans which would be made under similar circumstances. As a result, the loan would fail to meet the requirements of Sec. 408(b)(1)(D) and would not be covered by the relief provided by Sec. 408(b)(1) of the Act.

Example (2): Pursuant to the provisions of plan P's participant loan program, T, the trustee of P, approves a loan to M, a participant and party in interest with respect to P. At the time of execution, the loan meets all of the requirements of Sec. 408(b)(1) of the Act. The loan agreement provides that at the end of two years M must pay the remaining balance in full or the parties may renew for an additional two year period. At the end of the initial two year period, the parties agree to renew the loan for an additional two years. At the time of renewal, however, A fails to adjust the interest rate charged on the loan in order to reflect current economic conditions. As a result, the interest rate on the renewal fails to provide a "reasonable rate of interest" as required by Sec. 408(b)(1)(D) of the Act. Under such circumstances, the loan would not be exempt under Sec. 408(b)(1) of the Act from the time of renewal.

Example (3): The documents governing plan P's participant loan program provide that loans must bear an interest rate no higher than the maximum interest rate permitted under State X's usury law. Pursuant to the loan program, P makes a participant loan to A, a plan participant, at a time when the interest rates charged by financial institutions in the community (not subject to the usury limit) for similar loans are higher than the usury limit. Under these circumstances, the loan would not bear a reasonable rate of interest because the loan does not provide P with a return commensurate with the interest rates charged by persons in the business of lending money under similar circumstances. In addition, participant loans that are artificially limited to the maximum usury ceiling then prevailing call into question the status of such loans under sections 403(c) and 404(a) where higher yielding comparable investment opportunities are available to the plan.

(f) Adequate Security.

(1) A loan will be considered to be adequately secured if the security posted for such loan is something in addition to and supporting a promise to pay, which is so pledged to the plan that it may be sold, foreclosed upon, or otherwise disposed of upon default of repayment of the loan, the value and liquidity of which security is such that it may reasonably be anticipated that loss of principal or interest will not result from the loan. The adequacy of such security will be determined in light of the type and amount of security which would be required in the case of an otherwise identical transaction in a normal commercial setting between unrelated parties on arm's-length terms. A participant's vested accrued benefit under a plan may be used as security for a participant loan to the extent of the plan's ability to satisfy the participant's outstanding obligation in the event of default.

(2) For purposes of this paragraph, (i) no more than 50% of the present value of a participant's vested accrued benefit may be considered by a plan as security for the outstanding balance of all plan loans made to that participant; (ii) a plan will be in compliance with paragraph (f)(2)(i) of this section if, with respect to any participant, it meets the provisions of paragraph (f)(2)(i) of this section immediately after the origination of each participant loan secured in whole or in part by that participant's vested accrued benefit; and (iii) any loan secured in whole or in part by a portion of a participant's vested accrued benefit must also meet the requirements of paragraph (f)(1) of this section.

(g) Effective date. This section is effective for all participant loans granted or renewed after October 18, 1989, except with respect to paragraph (d)(2) of this section relating to specific plan provisions. Paragraph (d)(2) of this section is effective for participant loans granted or renewed on or after the last day of the first plan year beginning on or after January 1, 1989.

Promulgated: 54 Fed. Reg. 30520 (7/20/89).

Sec. 2550.408b-2—General statutory exemption for services or office space.

(a) In general. Section 408(b)(2) of the Employee Retirement Income Security Act of 1974 (the Act) exempts from the prohibitions of Sec. 406(a) of the Act payment by a plan to a party in interest, including a fiduciary, for office space or any service (or a combination of services) if: (1) Such office space or service is necessary for the establishment or operation of the plan; (2) such office space or service is furnished under a contract or arrangement which is reasonable; and (3) no more than reasonable compensation is paid for such office space or service. However, Sec. 408(b)(2) does not contain an exemption from acts described in Sec. 406(b)(1) of the Act (relating to fiduciaries dealing with the assets of plans in their own interest or for their own account), Sec. 406(b)(2) of the Act (relating to fiduciaries in their individual or in any other capacity acting in any transaction involving the plan on behalf of a party (or representing a party) whose interests are adverse to the interests of the plan or the interests of its participants or beneficiaries) or Sec. 406(b)(3) of the Act (relating to fiduciaries receiving consideration for their own personal account from any party dealing with a plan in connection with a transaction involving the assets of the plan). Such acts are separate transactions not described in Sec. 408(b)(2). See Sec. 2250.408b-2 (e) and (f) for guidance as to whether transactions relating to the furnishing of office space or services by fiduciaries to plans involve acts described in Sec. 406(b)(1) of the Act. Section 408(b)(2) of the Act does not contain an exemption from other provisions of the Act, such as Sec. 404, or other provisions of law which may impose requirements or restrictions relating to the transactions which are exempt under Sec. 408(b)(2). See, for example, Sec. 401 of the Internal Revenue Code of 1954. The provisions of Sec. 408(b)(2) of the Act are further limited by Sec. 408(d) of the Act (relating to transactions with owner-employees and related persons).

(b) Necessary service. A service is necessary for the establishment or operation of a plan within the meaning of Sec. 408(b)(2) of the Act and Sec. 2550.408b-2(a)(1) if the service is appropriate and helpful to the plan obtaining the service in carrying out the purposes for which the plan is established or maintained. A person providing such a service to a plan (or a person who is a party in interest solely by reason of a relationship to such a service provider described in Sec. 3(14) (F), (G), (H), or (I) of the Act) may furnish goods which are necessary for the establishment or operation of the plan in the course of, and incidental to, the furnishing of such service to the plan.

(c) Reasonable contract or arrangement. No contract or arrangement is reasonable within the meaning of Sec. 408(b)(2) of the Act and Sec. 2550.408b-2(a)(2) if it does not permit termination by the plan without penalty to the plan on reasonably short notice under the circumstances to prevent the plan from becoming locked into an arrangement that has become disadvantageous. A long-term lease which may be terminated prior to its expiration (without penalty to the plan) on reasonably short notice under the circumstances is not generally an unreasonable arrangement merely because of its long term. A provision in a contract or other arrangement which reasonably compensates the service provider or lessor for loss upon early termination of the contract, arrangement or lease is not a penalty. For example, a minimal fee in a service contract which is charged to allow recoupment of reasonable start-up costs is not a penalty. Similarly, a provision in a lease for a termination fee that covers reasonably foreseeable expenses related to the vacancy and reletting of the office space upon early termination of the lease is not a penalty. Such a provision does not reasonably compensate for loss if it provides for payment in excess of actual loss or if it fails to require mitigation of damages.

(d) Reasonable compensation. Section 408(b)(2) of the Act and Sec. 2550.408b-2(a)(3) permit a plan to pay a party in interest reasonable compensation for the provision of office space or services described in Sec. 408(b)(2). Section 2550.408c-2 of these regulations contains provisions relating to what constitutes reasonable compensation for the provision of services.

(e) Transactions with fiduciaries—

(1) *In general.* If the furnishing of office space or a service involves an act described in Sec. 406(b) of the Act (relating to acts involving conflicts of interest by fiduciaries), such an act constitutes a separate transaction which is not exempt under Sec. 408(b)(2) of the Act. The prohibitions of Sec. 406(b) supplement the other prohibitions of Sec. 406(a) of the Act by imposing on parties in interest who are fiduciaries a duty of undivided loyalty to the plans for which they act. These prohibitions are imposed upon fiduciaries to deter them from exercising the authority, control, or responsibility which makes such persons fiduciaries when they have interests which may conflict with the interests of the plans for which they act. In such cases, the fiduciaries have interests in the transactions which may affect the exercise of their best judgment as fiduciaries. Thus, a fiduciary may not use the authority, control, or responsibility which makes such person a fiduciary to cause a plan to pay an additional fee to such fiduciary (or to a person in which such fiduciary has an interest which may affect the exercise of such fiduciary's best judgment as a fiduciary) to provide a service. Nor may a fiduciary use such authority, control, or responsibility to cause a plan to enter into a transaction involving plan assets whereby such fiduciary (or a person in which such fiduciary has an interest which may affect the exercise of such fiduciary's best judgment as a fiduciary) will receive consideration from a third party in connection with such transaction. A person in which a fiduciary has an interest which may affect the exercise of such fiduciary's best judgment as a fiduciary includes, for example, a person who is a party in interest by reason of a relationship to such fiduciary described in Sec. 3(14) (E), (F), (G), (H), or (I).

(2) *Transactions not described in Sec. 406(b)(1).* A fiduciary does not engage in an act described in Sec. 406(b)(1) of the Act if the fiduciary does not use any of the authority, control or responsibility which makes such person a fiduciary to cause a plan to pay additional fees for a service furnished by such fiduciary or to pay a fee for a service furnished by a person in which such fiduciary has an interest which may affect the exercise of such fiduciary's best judgment as a fiduciary. This may occur, for example, when one fiduciary is retained on behalf of a plan by a second fiduciary to provide a service for an additional fee. However, because the authority, control or responsibility which makes a person a fiduciary may be exercised "in effect" as well as in form, mere approval of the transaction by a second fiduciary does not mean that the first fiduciary has not used any of the authority, control or responsibility which makes such person a fiduciary to cause the plan to pay the first fiduciary an additional fee for a service. See paragraph (f) of this section.

(3) *Services without compensation.* If a fiduciary provides services to a plan without the receipt of compensation or other consideration (other than reimbursement of direct expenses properly and actually incurred in the performance of such services within the meaning of Sec. 2550.408c-2(b)(3)), the provision of such services does not, in and of itself, constitute an act described in Sec. 406(b) of the Act. The allowance of a deduction to an employer under Sec. 162 or 212 of the Code for the expense incurred in furnishing office space or services to a plan established or maintained by such employer does not constitute compensation or other consideration.

(f) Examples. the provisions of Sec. 2550.408b-2(e) may be illustrated by the following examples.

Example (1). E, an employer whose employees are covered by plan P, is a fiduciary of P. I is a professional investment adviser in which E has no interest which may affect the exercise of E's best judgment as a fiduciary. E causes P to retain I to provide certain kinds of investment advisory services of a type which causes I to be a fiduciary of P under Sec. 3(21)(A)(ii) of the Act. thereafter, I proposes to perform for additional fees portfolio evaluation services in addition to the services currently provided. The provision of such services is arranged by I and approved on behalf of the plan by E. I has not engaged in an act described in Sec. 406(b)(1) of the Act, because I did not use any of the authority, control or responsibility which makes I a fiduciary (the provision of investment advisory services) to cause the plan to pay I additional fees for the provision of the portfolio evaluation services. E has not engaged in an act which is described in Sec. 406(b)(1). E, as the fiduciary who has the responsibility to be prudent in his selection and retention of I and the other investment advisers of the plan, has an interest in the purchase by the plan of portfolio evaluation services. However, such an interest is not an interest which may affect the exercise of E's best judgment as a fiduciary.

Example (2). D, a trustee of plan P with discretion over the management and disposition of plan assets, relies on the advice of C, a consultant to P, as to the investment of plan assets, thereby making C a fiduciary of the plan. On January

1, 1978, C recommends to D that the plan purchase an insurance policy from U, an insurance company which is not a party in interest with respect to P. C thoroughly explains the reasons for the recommendation and makes a full disclosure concerning the fact that C will receive a commission from U upon the purchase of the policy of P. D considers the recommendation and approves the purchase of the policy by P. C receives a commission. Under such circumstances, C has engaged in an act described in Sec. 406(b)(1) of the Act (as well as sections 406(b) (2) and (3) of the Act) because C is in fact exercising the authority, control or responsibility which makes C a fiduciary to cause the plan to purchase the policy. However, the transaction is exempt from the prohibited transaction provisions of Sec. 406 of the Act, if the requirements of Prohibited Transaction Exemption 77-9 are met.

Example (3). Assume the same facts as in Example (2) except that the nature of C's relationship with the plan is not such that C is a fiduciary of P. The purchase of the insurance policy does not involve an act described in Sec. 406(b)(1) of the Act (or sections 406(b) (2) or (3) of the Act) because such sections only apply to acts by fiduciaries.

Example (4). E, an employer whose employees are covered by plan P, is a fiduciary with respect to P. A, who is not a party in interest with respect to P, persuades E that the plan needs the services of a professional investment adviser and that A should be hired to provide the investment advice. Accordingly, E causes P to hire A to provide investment advice of the type which makes A a fiduciary under Sec. 2510.3-21(c)(1)(ii)(B). Prior to the expiration of A's first contract with P, A persuades E to cause P to renew A's contract with P to provide the same services for additional fees in view of the increased costs in providing such services. During the period of A's second contract, A provides additional investment advice services for which no additional charge is made. Prior to the expiration of A's second contract, A persuades E to cause P to renew his contract for additional fees in view of the additional services A is providing. A has not engaged in an act described in Sec. 406(b)(1) of the Act, because A has not used any of the authority, control or responsibility which makes A a fiduciary (the provision of investment advice) to cause the plan to pay additional fees for A's services.

Example (5). F, a trustee of plan P with discretion over the management and disposition of plan assets, retains C to provide administrative services to P of the type which makes C a fiduciary under Sec. 3(21)(A)(iii). Thereafter, C retains F to provide for additional fees actuarial and various kinds of administrative services in addition to the services F is currently providing to P. Both F and C have engaged in an act described in Sec. 406(b)(1) of the Act. F, regardless of any intent which he may have had at the time he retained C, has engaged in such an act because F has, in effect, exercised the authority, control or responsibility which makes F a fiduciary to cause the plan to pay F additional fees for the services. C, whose continued employment by P depends on F, has also engaged in such an act, because C has an interest in the transaction which might affect the exercise of C's best judgment as a fiduciary. As a result, C has dealt with plan assets in his own interest under Sec. 406(b)(1).

Example (6). F, a fiduciary of plan P with discretionary authority respecting the management of P, retains S, the son of F, to provide for a fee various kinds of administrative services necessary for the operation of the plan. F has engaged in an act described in Sec. 406(b)(1) of the Act because S is a person in whom F has an interest which may affect the exercise of F's best judgment as a fiduciary. Such act is not exempt under Sec. 408(b)(2) of the Act irrespective of whether the provision of the services by S is exempt.

Example (7). T, one of the trustees of plan P, is president of bank B. The bank proposes to provide administrative services to P for a fee. T physically absents himself from all consideration of B's proposal and does not otherwise exercise any of the authority, control or responsibility which makes T a fiduciary to cause the plan to retain B. The other trustees decide to retain B. T has not engaged in an act described in Sec. 406(b)(1) of the Act. Further, the other trustees have not engaged in an act described in Sec. 406(b)(1) merely because T is on the board of trustees of P. This fact alone would not make them have an interest in the transaction which might affect the exercise of their best judgment as fiduciaries.

Promulgated: 42 Fed. Reg. 32390 (6/24/77).

Sec. 2550.408b-3—Loans to Employee Stock Ownership Plans.

(a) Definitions. When used in this section, the terms listed below have the following meanings:

(1) *"ESOP"*. The term "ESOP" refers to an employee stock ownership plan that meets the requirements of Sec. 407(d)(6) of the Employee Retirement Income Security Act of 1974 (the Act) and 29 CFR 2550.407d-6. It is not synonymous with "stock bonus plan." A stock bonus plan must, however, be an ESOP to engage in an exempt loan. The qualification of an ESOP under Sec. 401 (a) of the Internal Revenue Code (the Code) and 26 CFR 54.4975-11 will not be adversely affected merely because it engages in a non-exempt loan.

(2) *"Loan"*. The term "loan" refers to a loan made to an ESOP by a party in interest or a loan to an ESOP which is guaranteed by a party in interest. It includes a direct loan of cash, a purchase-money transaction, and an assumption of the obligation of an ESOP. "Guarantee" includes an unsecured guarantee and the use of assets of a party in interest as collateral for a loan, even though the use of assets may not be a guarantee under applicable state law. An amendment of a loan in order to qualify as an exempt loan is not a refinancing of the loan or the making of another loan.

(3) *"Exempt loan"*. The term "exempt loan" refers to a loan that satisfies the provisions of this section. A "non-exempt loan" is one that fails to satisfy such provisions.

(4) *"Publicly traded"*. The term "publicly traded" refers to a security that is listed on a national securities exchange registered under Sec. 6 of the Securities Exchange Act of 1934 (15 U.S.C. 78f) or that is quoted on a system sponsored by a national securities association registered under Sec. 15A(b) of the Securities Exchange Act (15 U.S.C. 78o).

(5) *"Qualifying employer security"*. The term "qualifying employer security" refers to a security described in 29 CFR 2550.407d-5.

(b) Statutory exemption—

(1) *Scope.* Section 408(b)(3) of the Act provides an exemption from the prohibited transaction provisions of sections 406(a) and 406(b)(1) of the Act (relating to fiduciaries dealing with the assets of plans in their own interest or for their own account) and 406(b)(2) of the Act (relating to fiduciaries in their individual or in any other capacity acting in any transaction involving the plan on behalf of a party (or representing a party) whose interests are adverse to the interests of the plan or the interests of its participants or beneficiaries). Section 408(b)(3) does not provide an exemption from the prohibitions of Sec. 406(b)(3) of the Act (relating to fiduciaries receiving consideration for their own personal account from any party dealing with a plan in connection with a transaction involving the income or assets of the plan).

(2) *Special scrutiny of transaction.* The exemption under Sec. 408(b)(3) includes within its scope certain transactions in which the potential for self-dealing by fiduciaries exists and in which the interests of fiduciaries may conflict with the interests of participants. To guard against these potential abuses, the Department of Labor will subject these transactions to special scrutiny to ensure that they are primarily for the benefit of participants and their beneficiaries. Although the transactions need not be arranged and approved by an independent fiduciary, fiduciaries are cautioned to scrupulously exercise their discretion in approving them. For example, fiduciaries should be prepared to demonstrate compliance with the net effect test and the arm's-length standard under paragraphs (c) (2) and (3) of this section. Also, fiduciaries should determine that the transaction is truly arranged primarily in the interest of participants and their beneficiaries rather than, for example, in the interest of certain selling shareholders.

(c) Primary benefit requirements—

(1) *In general.* An exempt loan must be primarily for the benefit of the ESOP participants and their beneficiaries. All the surrounding facts and circumstances, including those described in paragraphs (c) (2) and (3) of this section, will be considered in determining whether such loan satisfies this requirement. However, no loan will satisfy such requirement unless it satisfies the requirements of paragraphs (d), (e) and (f) of this section.

(2) *Net effect on plan assets.* At the time that a loan is made, the interest rate for the loan and the price of securities to be acquired with the loan proceeds should not be such that plan assets might be drained off.

(3) *Arm's-length standard.* The terms of a loan, whether or not between independent parties, must, at the time the loan is made, be at least as favorable to the ESOP as the terms of a comparable loan resulting from arm's-length negotiations between independent parties.

(d) Use of loan proceeds. The proceeds of an exempt loan must be used, within a reasonable time after their receipt, by the borrowing ESOP only for any or all of the following purposes:

(1) To acquire qualifying employer securities.

(2) To repay such loan.

(3) To repay a prior exempt loan. A new loan, the proceeds of which are so used, must satisfy the provisions of this section. Except as provided in paragraphs (i) and (j) of this section or as otherwise required by applicable law, no security acquired with the proceeds of an exempt loan may be subject to a put, call, or other option, or buy-sell or similar arrangement while held by and when distributed from a plan, whether or not the plan is then ESOP.

(e) Liability and collateral of ESOP for loan. An exempt loan must be without recourse against the ESOP. Furthermore, the only assets of the ESOP that may be given as collateral on an exempt loan are qualifying employer securities of two classes: Those acquired with the proceeds of the exempt loan and those that were used as collateral on a prior exempt loan repaid with the proceeds of the current exempt loan. No person entitled to payment under the exempt loan shall have any right to assets of the ESOP other than:

(1) Collateral given for the loan,

(2) Contributions (other than contributions of employer securities) that are made under an ESOP to meet its obligations under the loan, and

(3) Earnings attributable to such collateral and the investment of such contributions. The payments made with respect to an exempt loan by the ESOP during a plan year must not exceed an amount equal to the sum of such contributions and earnings received during or prior to the year less such payments in prior years. Such contributions and earnings must be accounted for separately in the books of account of the ESOP until the loan is repaid.

(f) Default. In the event of default upon an exempt loan, the value of plan assets transferred in satisfaction of the loan must not exceed the amount of default. If the lender is a party in interest, a loan must provide for a transfer of plan assets upon default only upon and to the extent of the failure of the plan to meet the payment schedule of the loan. For purposes of this paragraph, the making of a guarantee does not make a person a lender.

(g) Reasonable rate of interest. The interest rate of a loan must not be in excess of a reasonable rate of interest. All relevant factors will be considered in determining a reasonable rate of interest, including the amount and duration of the loan, the security and guarantee (if any) involved, the credit standing of the ESOP and the guarantor (if any), and the interest rate prevailing for comparable loans. When these factors are considered, a variable interest rate may be reasonable.

(h) Release from encumbrance—

(1) *General rule.* In general, an exempt loan must provide for the release from encumbrance of plan assets used as collateral for the loan under this paragraph. For each plan year during the duration of the loan, the number of securities released must equal the number of encumbered securities held immediately before release for the current plan year multiplied by a fraction. The numerator of the fraction is the amount of principal and interest paid for the year. The denominator of the fraction is the sum of the numerator plus the principal and interest to be paid for all future years. See Sec. 2550.408b-3(h)(4). The number of future years under the loan must be definitely ascertainable and must be determined without taking into account any possible extensions or renewal periods. If the interest rate under the loan is variable, the interest to be paid in future years must be computed by using the interest rate applicable as of the end of the plan year. If collateral includes more than one class of securities, the number of securities of each class to be released for a plan year must be determined by applying the same fraction to each class.

(2) *Special rule.* A loan will not fail to be exempt merely because the number of securities to be released from encumbrance is determined solely with reference to principal payments. However, if release is determined with reference to principal payments only, the following three additional rules apply. The first rule is that the loan must provide for annual payments of principal and interest at a cumulative rate that is not less rapid at any time than level annual payments of such amounts for 10 years. The second rule is that interest included in any payment is disregarded only to the extent that it would be determined to be interest under standard loan amortization tables. The third rule is that subdivision (2) is not applicable from the time that, by reason of a renewal, extension, or refinancing, the sum of the expired duration of the exempt loan, the renewal period, the extension period, and the duration of a new exempt loan exceeds 10 years.

(3) *Caution against plan disqualification.* Under an exempt loan, the number of securities released from encumbrance may vary from year to year. The release of securities depends upon certain employer contributions and earnings under the ESOP. Under 26 CFR 54.4975-11(d)(2) actual allocations to participants' accounts are based upon assets withdrawn from the suspense account. Nevertheless, for purposes of applying the limitations under Sec. 415 of the Code to these allocations, under 26 CFR 54.4975-11(a)(8)(ii) contributions used by the ESOP to pay the loan are treated as annual additions to participants' accounts. Therefore, particular caution must be exercised to avoid exceeding the maximum annual additions under Sec. 415 of the Code. At the same time, release from encumbrance in annually varying numbers may reflect a failure on the part of the employer to make substantial and recurring contributions to the ESOP which will lead to loss of qualification under Sec. 401(a) of the Code. The Internal Revenue Service will observe closely the operation of ESOPs that release encumbered securities in varying annual amounts, particularly those that provide for the deferral of loan payments or for balloon payments. See 26 CFR 54.4975- 7(b)(8)(iii).

(4) *Illustration.* The general rule under paragraph (h)(1) of this section operates as illustrated in the following examples:

Example. Corporation X establishes an ESOP that borrows $750,000 from a bank. X guarantees the loan which is for 15 years at 5% interest and is payable in level annual amounts of $72,256.72. Total payments on the loan are $1,083,850.80. The ESOP uses the entire proceeds of the loan to acquire 15,000 shares of X stock which is used as collateral for the loan. The number of securities to be released for the first year is 1,000 shares, i.e., 15,000 shares × $72,256.72/$1,083,850.80 = 15,000 shares × 1/15. The number of securities to be released for the second year is 1,000 shares, i.e., 14,000 shares × $72,256.72/$1,011,594.08 = 14,000 shares × 1/14. If all loan payments are made as originally scheduled, the number of securities released in each succeeding year of the loan will also be 1,000.

(i) Right of first refusal. Qualifying employer securities acquired with proceeds of an exempt loan may, but need not, be subject to a right of first refusal. However, any such right must meet the requirements of this paragraph. Securities subject to such right must be stock or an equity security, or a debt security convertible into stock or an equity security. Also, they must not be publicly traded at the time the right may be exercised. The right of first refusal must be in favor of the employer, the ESOP, or both in any order of priority. The selling price and other terms under the right must not be less favorable to the seller than the greater of the value of the security determined under 26 CFR 54.4975-11(d)(5), or the purchase price and other terms offered by a buyer, other than the employer or the ESOP, making a good faith offer to purchase the security. The right of first refusal must lapse no later than 14 days after the security holder gives written notice to the holder of the right that an offer by a third party to purchase the security has been received.

(j) Put option. A qualifying employer security acquired with the proceeds of an exempt loan by an ESOP after September 30, 1976, must be subject to a put option if it is not publicly traded when distributed or if it is subject to a trading limitation when distributed. For purposes of this paragraph, a "trading limitation" or a security is a restriction under any Federal or State securities law or any regulation thereunder, or an agreement (not prohibited by this section) affecting the security which would make the security not as freely tradeable as one not subject to such restriction. The put option must be exercisable only by a participant, by the participant's donees, or by a person (including an estate or its distributee) to whom the security passes by reason of a participant's death. (Under this paragraph "participant" means a participant and the beneficiaries of the participant under the ESOP.) The put option must permit a participant to put the security to the employer. Under no circumstances may the put option bind the ESOP. However, it may grant the ESOP an option to assume the rights and obligations of the employer at the time that the put option is exercised. If it is known at the time a loan is made that Federal or state law will be violated by the employer's honoring such put option, the put option must permit the security to be put, in a manner consistent with such law, to a third party (e.g., an affiliate of the employer or a shareholder other than the ESOP) that has substantial net worth at the time the loan is made and whose net worth is reasonably expected to remain substantial.

(k) Duration of put option—

(1) *General rule.* A put option must be exercisable at least during a 15 month period which begins the date the security subject to the put option is distributed by the ESOP.

(2) *Special rule.* In the case of a security that is publicly traded without restriction when distributed but ceases to be so traded within 15 months after distribution, the employer must notify each security holder in writing on or before the tenth day after the date the security ceases to be so traded that for the remainder of the 15-month period the security is subject to a put option. The number of days between the tenth day and the date on which notice is actually given, if later than the tenth day, must be added to the duration of the put option. The notice must inform distributees of the terms of the put options that they are to hold. The terms must satisfy the requirements of paragraphs (j) through (l) of this section.

(l) Other put option provisions—

(1) *Manner of exercise.* A put option is exercised by the holder notifying the employer in writing that the put option is being exercised.

(2) *Time excluded from duration of put option.* The period during which a put option is exercisable does not include any time when a distributee is unable to exercise it because the party bound by the put option is prohibited from honoring it by applicable Federal or State law.

(3) *Price.* The price at which a put option must be exercisable is the value of the security, determined in accordance with paragraph (d)(5) of 26 CFR 54.4975-11.

(4) *Payment terms.* The provisions for payment under a put option must be reasonable. The deferral of payment is reasonable if adequate security and a reasonable interest rate are provided for any credit extended and if the cumulative payments at any time are no less than the aggregate of reasonable periodic payments as of such time. Periodic payments are reasonable if annual installments, beginning with 30 days after the date the put option is exercised, are substantially equal. Generally, the payment period may not end more than 5 years after the date the put option is exercised. However, it may be extended to a date no later than the earlier of 10 years from the date the put option is exercised or the date the proceeds of the loan used by the ESOP to acquire the security subject to such put option are entirely repaid.

(5) *Payment restrictions.* Payment under a put option may be restricted by the terms of a loan, including one used to acquire a security subject to a put option, made before November 1, 1977. Otherwise, payment under a put option must not be restricted by the provisions of a loan or any other arrangement, including the terms of the employer's articles of incorporation, unless so required by applicable state law.

(m) Other terms of loan. An exempt loan must be for a specific term. Such loan may not be payable at the demand of any person, except in the case of default.

(n) Status of plan as ESOP. To be exempt, a loan must be made to a plan that is an ESOP at the time of such loan. However, a loan to a plan formally designated as an ESOP at the time of the loan that fails to be an ESOP because it does not comply with Sec. 401(a) of the Code or 26 CFR 54.4975-11 will be exempt as of the time of such loan if the plan is amended retroactively under Sec. 401(b) of the Code or 26 CFR 54.4975-11(a)(4).

(o) Special rules for certain loans—

(1) *Loans made before January 1, 1976.* A loan made before January 1, 1976, or made afterwards under a binding agreement in effect on January 1, 1976 (or under renewals permitted by the terms of such an agreement on that date) is exempt for the entire period of such loan if it otherwise satisfies the provisions of this section for such period, even though it does not satisfy the following provisions of this section:

(i) The last sentence of paragraph (d);

(ii) Paragraphs (e), (f), and (h) (1) and (2); and

(iii) Paragraphs (i) through (m), inclusive.

(2) *Loans made after December 31, 1975, but before November 1, 1977.* A loan made after December 31, 1975, but before November 1, 1977, or made afterwards under a binding agreement in effect on November 1, 1977 (or under renewals permitted by the terms of such an agreement on that date) is exempt for the entire period of such loan if it otherwise satisfies the provisions of this section for such period even though it does not satisfy the following provisions of this section:

(i) Paragraph (f);

(ii) The three provisions of paragraph (h)(2); and

(iii) Paragraph (i).

(3) *Release rule.* Notwithstanding paragraphs (o) (1) and (2) of this section, if the proceeds of a loan are used to acquire securities after November 1, 1977, the loan must comply by such date with the provisions of paragraph (h) of this section.

(4) *Default rule.* Notwithstanding paragraphs (o) (1) and (2) of this section, a loan by a party in interest other than a guarantor must satisfy the requirements of paragraph (f) of this section. A loan will satisfy these requirements if it is retroactively amended before November 1, 1977, to satisfy these requirements.

(5) *Put option rule.* With respect to a security distributed before November 1, 1977, the put option provisions of paragraphs (j), (k), and (l) of this section will be deemed satisfied as of the date the security is distributed if by December 31, 1977, the security is subject to a put option satisfying such provisions. For purposes of satisfying such provisions, the security will be deemed distributed on the date the put option is issued. However, the put option provisions need not be satisfied with respect to a security that is not owned on November 1, 1977, by a person in whose hands a put option must be exercisable.

Promulgated: 42 Fed. Reg. 44385 (9/2/77); 42 Fed. Reg. 45907 (9/13/77).

Amended: 49 Fed. Reg. 18295 (4/30/84).

Sec. 2550.408b-4—Statutory exemption for investments in deposits of banks or similar financial institutions.

(a) In general. Section 408(b)(4) of the Employee Retirement Income Security Act of 1974 (the Act) exempts from the prohibitions of Sec. 406 of the Act the investment of all or a part of a plan's assets in deposits bearing a reasonable rate of interest in a bank or similar financial institution supervised by the United States or a State, even though such bank or similar financial institution is a fiduciary or other party in interest with respect to the plan, if the conditions of either Sec. 2550.408b-4(b)(1) or Sec. 2550.408b-4(b)(2) are met. Section 408(b)(4) provides an exemption from sections 406(b)(1) of the Act (relating to fiduciaries dealing with the assets of plans in their own interest or for their own account) and 406(b)(2) of the Act (relating to fiduciaries in their individual or in any other capacity acting in any transaction involving the plan on behalf of a party (or representing a party) whose interests are adverse to the interests of the plan or the interests of its participants or beneficiaries), as well as Sec. 406(a)(1), because Sec. 408(b)(4) contemplates a bank or similar financial institution causing a plan for which it acts as a fiduciary to invest plan assets in its own deposits if the requirements of Sec. 408(b)(4) are met. However, it does not provide an exemption from Sec. 406(b)(3) of the Act (relating to fiduciaries receiving consideration for their own personal account from any party dealing with a plan in connection with a transaction involving the assets of the plan). The receipt of such consideration is a separate transaction not described in the statutory exemption. Section 408(b)(4) does not contain an exemption from other provisions of the Act, such as Sec. 404, or other provisions of law which may impose requirements or restrictions relating to the transactions which are exempt under Sec. 408(b)(4) of the Act. See, for example, Sec. 401 of the Internal Revenue Code of 1954 (Code). The provisions of Sec. 408(b)(4) of the Act are further limited by Sec. 408(d) of the Act (relating to transactions with owner-employees and related persons).

(b)(1) *Plan covering own employees.* Such investment may be made if the plan is one which covers only the employees of the bank or similar financial institution, the employees of any of its affiliates, or the employees of both.

(2) *Other plans.* Such investment may be made if the investment is expressly authorized by a provision of the plan or trust instrument or if the investment is expressly authorized (or made) by a fiduciary of the plan (other than the bank or similar financial institution or any of its affiliates) who has authority to make such investments, or to instruct the trustee or other fiduciary with respect to investments, and who has no interest in the transaction which may affect the exercise of such authorizing fiduciary's best judgment as a fiduciary so as to cause such authorization to constitute an act described in Sec. 406(b) of the Act. Any authorization to make investments contained in a plan or trust instrument will satisfy the requirement of express authorization for investments made prior to November 1, 1977. Effective November 1, 1977, in the case of a bank or similar financial institution that invests plan assets in deposits in itself or its affiliates under an authorization contained in a plan or trust instrument, such authorization must name such bank or similar financial institution and must state that such bank or similar financial institution may make investments in deposits which bear a reasonable rate of interest in itself (or in an affiliate).

(3) *Example.* B, a bank, is the trustee of plan P's assets. The trust instruments give the trustees the right to invest plan assets in its discretion. B invests in the certificates of deposit of bank C, which is a fiduciary of the plan by virtue of performing certain custodial and administrative services. The authorization is sufficient for the plan to make such investment under Sec. 408(b)(4). Further, such authorization would suffice to allow B to make investments in deposits in itself prior to November 1, 1977. However, subsequent to October 31, 1977, B may not invest in deposits in itself, unless the plan or trust instrument specifically authorizes it to invest in deposits of B.

(c) Definitions.

(1) The term "bank or similar financial institution" includes a bank (as defined in Sec. 581 of the Code), a domestic building and loan association (as defined in Sec. 7701(a)(19) of the Code), and a credit union (as defined in Sec. 101(6) of the Federal Credit Union Act).

(2) A person is an affiliate of a bank or similar financial institution if such person and such bank or similar financial institution would be treated as members of the same controlled group of corporations or as members of two or more trades or businesses under common control within the meaning of Sec. 414 (b) or (c) of the Code and the regulations thereunder.

(3) The term "deposits" includes any account, temporary or otherwise, upon which a reasonable rate of interest is paid, including a certificate of deposit issued by a bank or similar financial institution.

Promulgated: 42 Fed. Reg. 32392 (6/24/77); 42 Fed. Reg. 36823 (7/18/77).

Sec. 2550.408b-6—Statutory exemption for ancillary services by a bank or similar financial institution.

(a) In general. Section 408(b)(6) of the Employee Retirement Income Security Act of 1974 (the Act) exempts from the prohibitions of Sec. 406 of the Act the provision of certain ancillary services by a bank or similar financial institution (as defined in Sec. 2550.408b-4(c)(1) supervised by the United States or a State to a plan for which it acts as a fiduciary if the conditions of Sec. 2550.408b-6(b) are met. Such ancillary services include services which do not meet the requirements of Sec. 408(b)(2) of the Act because the provision of such services involves an act described in Sec. 406(b)(1) of the Act (relating to fiduciaries dealing with the assets of plans in their own interest or for their own account) by the fiduciary bank or similar financial institution or an act described in Sec. 406(b)(2) of the Act (relating to fiduciaries in their individual or in any other capacity acting in any transaction involving the plan on behalf of a party (or representing a party) whose interests are adverse to the interests of the plan or the interests of its participants or beneficiaries). Section 408(b)(6) provides an exemption from sections 406(b) (1) and (2) because Sec. 408(b)(6) contemplates the provision of such ancillary services without the approval of a second fiduciary (as described in Sec. 2550.408b-2(e)(2)) if the conditions of Sec. 2550.408b-6(b) are met. Thus, for example, plan assets held by a fiduciary bank which are reasonably expected to be needed to satisfy current plan expenses may be placed by the bank in a non-interest-bearing checking account in the bank if the conditions of Sec. 2550.408b-6(b) are met, notwithstanding the provisions of Sec. 408(b)(4) of the Act (relating to investments in bank deposits). However, Sec. 408(b)(6) does not provide an exemption for an act described in Sec. 406(b)(3) of the Act (relating to fiduciaries receiving consideration for their own personal account from any party dealing with a plan in connection with a transaction involving the assets of the plan). The receipt of such consideration is a separate transaction not described in Sec. 408(b)(6). Section 408(b)(6) does not contain an exemption from other provisions of the Act, such as Sec. 404, or other provisions of law which may impose requirements or restrictions relating to the transactions which are exempt under Sec. 408(b)(6) of the Act. See, for example, Sec. 401 of the Internal Revenue Code of 1954. The provisions of Sec. 408(b)(6) of the Act are further limited by Sec. 408(d) of the Act (relating to transactions with owner-employees and related persons).

(b) Conditions. Such service must be provided—

(1) At not more than reasonable compensation;

(2) Under adequate internal safeguards which assure that the provision of such service is consistent with sound banking and financial practice, as determined by Federal or State supervisory authority; and

(3) Only to the extent that such service is subject to specific guidelines issued by the bank or similar financial institution which meet the requirements of Sec. 2550.408b-6(c).

Promulgated: 42 Fed. Reg. 32392 (6/24/77); 42 Fed. Reg. 36823 (7/18/77).

Sec. 2550.408c-2—Compensation for services.

(a) In general. Section 408(b)(2) of the Employee Retirement Income Security Act of 1974 (the Act) refers to the payment of reasonable compensation by a plan to a party in interest for services rendered to the plan. Sec. 408(c)(2) of the Act and Secs. 2550.408c-2(b)(1) through 2550.408c-2(b)(4) clarify what constitutes reasonable compensation for such services.

(b)(1) *General rule.* Generally, whether compensation is "reasonable" under sections 408(b)(2) and (c)(2) of the Act depends on the particular facts and circumstances of each case.

(2) *Payments to certain fiduciaries.* Under sections 408(b)(2) and 408(c)(2) of the Act, the term "reasonable compensation" does not include any compensation to a fiduciary who is already receiving full-time pay from an employer or association of employers (any of whose employees are participants in the plan) or from an employee organization (any of whose members are participants in the plan), except for the reimbursement of direct expenses properly and actually incurred and not otherwise reimbursed. The restrictions of this paragraph (b)(2) do not apply to a party in interest who is not a fiduciary.

(3) *Certain expenses not direct expenses.* An expense is not a direct expense to the extent it would have been sustained had the service not been provided or if it represents an allocable portion of overhead costs.

(4) *Expense advances.* Under sections 408(b)(2) and 408(c)(2) of the Act, the term "reasonable compensation," as applied to a fiduciary or an employee of a plan, includes an advance to such a fiduciary or employee by the plan to cover direct expenses to be properly and actually incurred by such person in the performance of such person's duties with the plan if:

(i) The amount of such advance is reasonable with respect to the amount of the direct expense which is likely to be properly and actually incurred in the immediate future (such as during the next month); and

(ii) The fiduciary or employee accounts to the plan at the end of the period covered by the advance for the expenses properly and actually incurred.

(5) *Excessive compensation.* Under sections 408(b)(2) and 408(c)(2) of the Act, any compensation which would be considered excessive under 26 CFR 1.162-7 (Income Tax Regulations relating to compensation for personal services which constitutes an ordinary and necessary trade or business expense) will not be "reasonable compensation." Depending upon the facts and circumstances of the particular situation, compensation which is not excessive under 26 CFR 1.162-7 may, nevertheless, not be "reasonable compensation" within the meaning of sections 408(b)(2) and 408(c)(2) of the Act.

Promulgated: 42 Fed. Reg. 32393 (6/24/77).

Sec. 2550.408e—Statutory exemption for acquisition or sale of qualifying employer securities and for acquisition, sale, or lease of qualifying employer real property.

(a) General. Section 408(e) of the Employee Retirement Income Security Act of 1974 (the Act) exempts from the prohibitions of Sec. 406(a) and 406(b)(1) and (2) of the Act any acquisition or sale by a plan of qualifying employer securities (as defined in Sec. 407(d)(5) of the Act), or any acquisition, sale or lease by a plan of qualifying employer real property (as defined in Sec. 407(d)(4) of the Act) if certain conditions are met. The conditions are that:

(1) The acquisition, sale or lease must be for adequate consideration (which is defined in paragraph (d) of this section);

(2) No commission may be charged directly or indirectly to the plan with respect to the transaction; and

(3) In the case of an acquisition or lease of qualifying employer real property, or an acquisition of qualifying employer securities, by a plan other than an eligible individual account plan (as defined in Sec. 407(d)(3) of the Act), the acquisition or lease must comply with the requirements of Sec. 407(a) of the Act.

(b) Acquisition. For purposes of Sec. 408(e) and this section, an acquisition by a plan of qualifying employer securities or qualifying employer real property shall include, but not be limited to, an acquisition by purchase, by the exchange of plan assets, by the exercise of warrants or rights, by the conversion of a security, by default of a loan where the qualifying employer security or qualifying employer real property was security for the loan, or in connection with the contribution of such securities or real property to the plan. However, an acquisition of a security shall not be deemed to have occurred if a plan acquires the security as a result of a stock dividend or stock split.

(c) Sale. For purposes of Sec. 408(e) and this section, a sale of qualifying employer real property or qualifying employer securities shall include any disposition for value.

(d) Adequate consideration. For purposes of Sec. 408(e) and this section, adequate consideration means:

(1) In the case of a marketable obligation, a price not less favorable to the plan than the price determined under Sec. 407(e)(1) of the Act; and

(2) In all other cases, a price not less favorable to the plan than the price determined under Sec. 3(18) of the Act.

(e) Commission. For purposes of Sec. 408(e) and this section, the term "commission" includes any fee, commission or similar charge paid in connection with a transaction, except that the term "commission" does not include a charge incurred for the purpose of enabling the appropriate plan fiduciaries to evaluate the desirability of entering into a transaction to which this section would apply, such as an appraisal or investment advisory fee.

Promulgated: 45 Fed. Reg. 51197 (8/1/80).

Sec. 2550.412-1—Temporary bonding requirements.

(a) Pending the issuance of permanent regulations with respect to the bonding provisions under Sec. 412 of the Employee Retirement Income Security Act of 1974 (the Act), any plan official, as defined in Sec. 412(a) of the Act, shall be deemed to be in compliance with the bonding requirements of the Act if he or she is bonded under a bond which would have been in compliance with Sec. 13 of the Welfare and Pension Plans Disclosure Act, as amended (the WPPDA), and with the basic bonding requirements of Subparts A through E of Part 2580, Title 29 CFR, and with the prohibition against bonding by parties interested in the plan contained in Subpart G of Part 2580 of such title, or would be exempt from such bonding requirements because bonding would not be required under the exemption provisions contained in Subpart F of Part 2580 of such title. Part 2580 of this title incorporates material previously designated as Subparts A through E of Part 464, Subpart B of Part 465 and Part 485 of this title of the CFR. The requirements which are set forth in the temporary regulations hereby adopted shall be applicable to all employee benefit plans covered by the Act, including those plans which were not covered by the WPPDA. Thus, for example, the regulations so adopted are applicable to plans containing fewer than 26 participants, although such plans were not covered by the WPPDA.

(b) For the purpose of this temporary regulation, any bond or rider thereto obtained by a plan official which contains a reference to the WPPDA will be construed by the Secretary to refer to the Act: Provided, That the surety company so agrees.

(c) For the purpose of this regulation, (1) any reference to Sec. 13 of the WPPDA or any subsection thereof in the regulations issued under the WPPDA and which are incorporated by reference by this temporary regulation shall be deemed to refer to Sec. 412 of the Act, or the corresponding subsection thereof, (2) where the particular phrases set forth in the Act are not identical to the phrases in the WPPDA and the regulations issued pursuant thereto, the phrases appearing in the Act shall be substituted by operation of law, and (3) where the phrases are identical but the meaning is different, the meaning given such phrases by the Act shall govern. For example, the phrase "administrators, officers, and employees of any employee welfare benefit plan or of any employee pension benefit plan subject to this Act who handle funds or other property of such plan" which appears in Sec. 13 of the WPPDA and the regulations issued thereunder shall be construed to mean, for purposes of this regulation, "plan officials", which is the term appearing in section 412 of the Act, and the terms "employee welfare benefit plan" and "employee pension benefit plan" shall be given the meaning assigned to them by the Act, and not the meaning set forth in the WPPDA.

(d) The requirements of this temporary regulation, as set forth in paragraphs (a) through (c) of this section, shall remain in effect pending the issuance of permanent regulations by the Secretary.

Promulgated: 40 Fed. Reg. 2203 (1/10/75).

Amended: 40 Fed. Reg. 20629 (5/12/75); 50 Fed. Reg. 26706 (6/28/85).

Sec. 2550.414b-1—Guidelines for submission of application for postponement of the effective date of certain fiduciary responsibility provisions.

(a) Purpose. The purpose of this regulation is to issue guidelines to assist applicants seeking postponement of the effective date of certain fiduciary responsibility provisions of the Employee Retirement Income Security Act of 1974 (the Act). In general, the fiduciary responsibility provisions of Part 4 of Title I of the Act are effective on January 1, 1975. However, Sec. 414(b)(2) of the Act provides that for plans in existence on September 2, 1974, the Secretary of Labor (the Secretary) may, upon application, postpone until not later than January 1, 1976, the effective date of certain provisions respecting establishment of plans (Sec. 402), establishment of trusts (Sec. 403, other than subsection (c)), liability for breach by co-fiduciaries (Sec. 405, other than subsections (a) and (d)) and exculpatory clauses (Sec. 41)(a)). Such a postponement shall be allowed where the Secretary determines that the delay is (1) necessary to amend the instrument or instruments under which the plan is established or maintained and (2) not adverse to the interest of plan participants and beneficiaries. It should be noted that under the terms of Sec. 414(b)(2), no postponement may be given for the applicability of the provisions of Sec. 403(c), which precludes plan assets from inuring to the benefit of any employer; Sec. 405(a), which sets forth general rules regarding co-fiduciary liability; and Sec. 405(d), dealing with trustee liability where an investment manager has been appointed in accordance with Sec. 402(c)(3) of the Act. Since the provisions as to which the effective date may be postponed were not required by previously existing Federal law and will necessitate amendment of many existing plans to comply with or take these provisions into account, the Secretary has prepared these guidelines setting forth the application procedure and the kind of information the Secretary will require to make a determination.

(b) Who may submit an application for postponement. Any plan administrator, trustee, named fiduciary, or other individual duly authorized to act on behalf of a plan may apply for a postponement.

(c) Procedure for submitting application. Applications for postponement subject to this regulation shall be sent in duplicate by first-class mail, postage prepaid, to the Office of Employee Benefits Security, Labor-Management Services Administration, U.S. Department of Labor, P.O. Box 176, Washington, D.C. 20044, or shall be delivered by hand to Room 3311, U.S. Department of Labor, 14th Street and Constitution Avenue NW., Washington, D.C. An application submitted by mail shall be deemed to be submitted as of the date of the postmark. See Sec. 2550.414b-1(h) for submittal deadlines.

(d) Format and content of application. In order to enable the Secretary to expeditiously process applications under this regulation, those applications which are submitted in duplicate and which include the following information in the following order will be processed first, and applications which do not contain such information will be disapproved, subject to Sec. 2550.414b- 1(h)(3):

(1) The name of the plan and the name and address of the individual making the application on behalf of the plan (applicant) and the basis for his or her authority to make the application on behalf of the plan;

(2) The WP number assigned to the plan, if it has previously filed under the Welfare and Pension Plans Disclosure Act with the Office of Labor-Management and Welfare Pension Reports of the Department of Labor;

(3) The Employer Identification Number (EIN) assigned by the Internal Revenue Service to the plan sponsor (as defined in Sec. 3(16)(B) of the Act) and, if the plan sponsor has assigned a Plan Identification Number to the plan pursuant to instructions of Internal Revenue Service Form 4848, the Plan Identification Number;

(4) A statement that the plan was in existence on September 2, 1974;

(5) A statement that the method of notification used or to be used will afford reasonable notice to plan participants in accordance with the provisions of Sec. 2550.414b-1(f) of the application for postponement and of their right to file comments under Sec. 2550.414b-1(e);

(6) An enumeration of the specific fiduciary responsibility sections (or provisions of such sections) listed in Sec. 414(b)(2) of the Act for which a postponement of the effective date is requested. If a postponement for all such provisions is sought, the applicant may merely state that a postponement is requested for all provisions listed in Sec. 414(b)(2);

(7) A statement disclosing the reason why a postponement is necessary, the date until which such postponement is requested (see Sec. 2550.414b-1(g), and why such postponement will not be adverse to the interest of plan participants and beneficiaries. If the applicant is requesting a postponement of the applicability of Sec. 410(a) of the Act, a separate explanation should be given of the reasons therefor;

(8) If the plan is an employee pension benefit plan (as defined in Sec. 3(2) of the Act) and is requesting a postponement of the applicability of the provisions of Sec. 403(a) of the Act, a statement that, to the extent that plan assets would otherwise be required to be held in trust under the provisions of Sec. 403 of the Act, such assets that are held by a party in interest are held in a manner that would reasonably be expected to protect the plan against loss resulting from the satisfaction of a creditor's claim against the party in interest;

(9) A statement by the applicant that if any of the material facts contained in or underlying the statements made in the application is discovered by the applicant to be inaccurate, the applicant will promptly notify the Secretary in writing of such inaccuracy specifying the reasons for the inaccuracy; and

(10) A duly notarized certification by the person signing the application for postponement on behalf of the plan that he or she is duly authorized to execute the application on behalf of the plan, and that, under applicable penalties of law, the information in the application is, to the best of his or her knowledge and belief, true, correct and complete.

(e) Comments by participants and beneficiaries. Plan participants and beneficiaries and their authorized representatives may submit written comments respecting any application for postponement made under Sec. 2550.414b-1(d) at any time after such application is filed, specifying any objections which they may have. A collective bargaining representative for a plan participant or beneficiary shall be deemed to be an authorized representative for purposes of this Part. Such comments shall be submitted at any time before the expiration of the period of the postponement to the Office of Employee Benefits Security, Labor-Management Services Administration, U.S. Department of Labor, P.O. Box 176, Washington, D.C. 20044.

(f) Notification to participants.

(1) The applicant shall employ methods reasonably calculated to provide plan participants with notification that an application for postponement has been filed with the Secretary of Labor, describing in language calculated to be understood by the average plan participant the sections (or provisions of sections) of the Act for which the delay has been requested, the date until which such postponement has been requested, the reasons for requesting the postponement, why the postponement will not adversely affect the interest of plan participants and beneficiaries, and stating that plan participants and beneficiaries may comment on the requested postponement by writing to the Office of Employee Benefits Security, Labor-Management Services Administration, U.S. Department of Labor, P.O. Box 176, Washington, D.C. 20044.

(2) Notice must be in writing and must be reasonably calculated to reach a substantial number of plan participants. While there is no prescribed form or method of delivery for adequate notice, and while other forms or methods of delivery may be deemed acceptable under the particular circumstances involved, any of the following shall be deemed adequate notice to plan participants:

(i) The prominent posting, not later than 30 days after the date of application for postponement, of the notification required by paragraph (f)(1) of this section at those locations customarily used by the employer for notices to employees with regard to labor-management relations matters at worksites of plan participants or, if the plan is maintained pursuant to a collective bargaining agreement and notices to employees with regard to labor-management relations matters are ordinarily posted at locations such as local union meeting places, at such locations;

(ii) The mailing by first-class mail, not later than 30 days after the date of the application for postponement, of the notification required by paragraph (f)(1) of this section to the last known address of substantially all plan participants;

(iii) The publishing, not later than 60 days after the date of the application for postponement, of the notification required by paragraph (f)(1) of this section in a publication which is directed to a substantial number of plan participants; or

(iv) The utilization of any combination of the above methods reasonably calculated to so notify a substantial number of plan participants. If the plan is the subject of one or more collective bargaining agreements, the applicant shall also mail the notification required by paragraph (f)(1) of this section by first-class mail, not later than 15 days after the date of application for postponement, to each collective bargaining agent representing participants covered by the plan.

(3) In the case of a plan which applied for a postponement of the applicability of sections 402, 403 (other than 403(c)) and 405 (other than 405(a) and (d)), the application of which has been approved under paragraph (h), and which has not been amended so as to comply with such sections before July 1, 1975, the applicant or any other person authorized to file an application for a plan under paragraph (b) shall employ methods reasonably calculated to provide plan participants and, if the plan is the subject of one or more collective bargaining agreements, each collective bargaining agent representing participants covered by the plan, with notification that the Secretary of Labor has extended postponements of the applicability of those sections to the plan until not later than January 1, 1976. This notification shall comply with the requirements of paragraph (f)(2) of this section.

(g) Length of postponement.

(1) All postponements of the applicability of Sec. 410(a) of the Act approved by the Secretary shall be effective for a period of time not extending beyond June 30, 1975.

(2) All postponements of sections 402, 403 (other than 403(c)) and 405 (other than 405(a) and (d)) of the Act approved by the Secretary shall be effective for a period of time extending through December 31, 1975.

(h) Notification of Secretary's decision with respect to postponement; effect of non-notification.

(1) It is contemplated that notification to applicants of approval or disapproval will be made before January 1, 1975, respecting those applications submitted on or before December 10, 1974;

(2) In the case of applications submitted after December 10, 1974, and before January 1, 1975, notification of approval or disapproval will be made as expeditiously as possible, and in the case of any application submitted on or before December 31, 1974, as to which notification of approval or disapproval has not been made before January 1, 1975, the application shall be deemed to be approved, subject to the provisions of Sec. 2550.414b-1(i).

(3) In any case in which notification of disapproval is made before January 1, 1975, and the disapproval is based on receipt of an incomplete application, the applicant shall have a period of 30 days from the date of such notification to submit an amended application, and the application shall be deemed approved during such period.

(4) Applications will not be accepted after December 31, 1974, except for good cause shown for the failure to submit a timely application.

(i) Revocation or modification of postponement. The Secretary may revoke or modify any postponements approved (or deemed approved) under Sec. 2550.414b-1(h) if, upon receipt of comments or upon investigation (or, in the case of an application received too late for review and notification before January 1, 1975, upon review of the application) he determines that such postponement is not necessary to amend the instrument establishing the plan or is adverse to the interest of participants and beneficiaries. Before issuing any proposed decision of revocation or modification, the Secretary shall give the applicant and any persons who filed comments 45 days written notice of the proposed revocation or modification and the reasons therefor and an opportunity to file comments with respect to the proposed action, in accordance with procedures designated in the notice.

Promulgated: 39 Fed. Reg. 40853 (11/21/74).

Amended: 40 Fed. Reg. 20629 (5/12/75); 40 Fed. Reg. 24897 (6/11/75).

Sec. 2550.414c-1—Transitional rule relating to certain loans or other extensions of credit prior to June 30, 1984.

(a) Before June 30, 1984, sections 406 and 407(a) of the Employee Retirement Income Security Act of 1974 shall not apply with respect to a loan of money or other extension of credit between a plan and a party in interest under a binding contract in effect on July 1, 1974, or pursuant to renewals of such a contract, if such loan or other extension of credit remains at least as favorable to the plan as an arm's-length transaction with an unrelated party would be, and if the execution of the contract, the making of the loan, or the extension of credit was not, at the time of such execution, making, or extension, a prohibited transaction within the meaning of Sec. 503(b) of the Internal Revenue Code of 1954 or the corresponding provisions of prior law.

(b) For purposes of this section,

(1) "Binding contract" means a contract which is binding under applicable state law;

(2) A loan or other extension of credit will not be considered to "remain at least as favorable to the plan as an arm's-length transaction with an unrelated party would be" unless:

(i) Such loan or extension of credit, at the time of the execution of the contract and any renewal, is on terms at least as favorable to the plan as those which reasonably would be expected to exist in the case of an otherwise identical transaction in a normal commercial setting between the plan and the party in interest if they were unrelated parties, and

(ii) The plan requires termination or modification of the contract at such time as, and in such manner and to such extent that, it reasonably would be expected to require such termination or modification in the case of an otherwise identical transaction in a normal commercial setting with the party in interest if they were unrelated parties; and

(3) "Renewal" of a contract means only a renewal which:

(i) The plan reasonably would be expected to agree to in the case of an otherwise identical transaction in a normal commercial setting with the party in interest if they were unrelated parties, and

(ii) Except to the extent required by paragraph (b)(2)(ii) of this section, does not result in any substantial change or modification of the terms of the existing contract.

Promulgated: 46 Fed. Reg. 7322 (1/23/81).

Sec. 2550.414c-2—Transitional rule relating to certain leases or joint uses of property prior to June 30, 1984

(a) Before June 30, 1984, sections 406 and 407(a) of the Employee Retirement Income Security Act of 1974 shall not apply with respect to a lease or joint use of property involving the plan and a party in interest pursuant to a binding contract in effect on July 1, 1974, or pursuant to renewals of such a contract, if such lease or joint use remains at least as favorable to the plan as an arm's length transaction with an unrelated party would be and if the execution of the contract was not, at the time of such execution, a prohibited transaction within the meaning of Sec. 503(b) of the Internal Revenue Code of 1954 or the corresponding provisions of prior law.

(b) For purposes of this section,

(1) "Binding contract" means a contract which is binding under applicable state law;

(2) A lease or joint use of property will not be considered to "remain at least as favorable to the plan as an arm's-length transaction with an unrelated party would be" unless:

(i) The contract for such lease or joint use of property, at the time of the execution and any renewal thereof, is on terms at least as favorable to the plan as those which reasonably would be expected to exist in the case of an otherwise identical transaction in a normal commercial setting between the plan and the party in interest if they were unrelated parties, and

(ii) The plan requires termination or modification of the contract at such time as, and in such manner and to such extent that, it reasonably would be expected to require such termination or modification in the case of an otherwise identical transaction in a normal commercial setting with the party in interest if they were unrelated parties; and

(3) "Renewal" of a contract means only a renewal which:

(i) The plan reasonably would be expected to agree to in the case of an otherwise identical transaction in a normal commercial setting with the party in interest if they were unrelated parties, and

(ii) Except to the extent required by paragraph (b)(2)(ii) of this section, does not result in any substantial change or modification of the terms of the existing contract.

Promulgated: 46 Fed. Reg. 7322 (1/23/81).

Sec. 2550.414c-3—Transitional rule relating to certain sales, exchanges, or other dispositions of property prior to June 30, 1984.

(a) Before June 30, 1984, sections 406 and 407(a) of the Employee Retirement Income Security Act of 1974 shall not apply with respect to a sale, exchange, or other disposition of leased or jointly used property described in 29 CFR 2550.414c-2 between a plan and a party in interest: Provided, That:

(1) In the case of a sale, exchange, or other disposition of such property by the plan to the party in interest, the plan receives an amount which is not less than the fair market value of the property at the time of such disposition; and

(2) In the case of the acquisition of such property by the plan, the plan pays an amount which is not in excess of the fair market value of the property at the time of such acquisition.

(b) For purposes of this section:

(1) The term "property described in 29 CFR 2550.414c-2" means any property subject to a lease or joint use involving a plan and a party in interest under a binding contract in effect on July 1, 1974, or pursuant to renewals of such contracts;

(2) A property will not be regarded as the subject of a lease or joint use between a plan and a party in interest if one or more unrelated persons leases or jointly uses any portion or portions of such property representing a total value equal to or greater than the value of the portion of the property leased to or jointly used by one or more parties in interest. Property leased or jointly used by a party in interest which is subleased to or jointly used with an unrelated party shall not, solely because of such sublease or use, be considered property leased to or jointly used by an unrelated party.

(3)(i) Subject to the provisions of paragraph (b)(3)(ii) of this section, "fair market value" shall be determined by the plan trustee or named fiduciary in light of the facts and circumstances of the particular case.

(ii) In determining the fair market value of leased or jointly used property pursuant to paragraph (b)(3)(i) of this section, the plan trustee or named fiduciary shall not take into account any diminution in value resulting from

(A) Any encumbrance arising out of a lease or joint use which violates any provision of the Act, and

(B) Any encumbrance, arising out of a lease or joint use, to the extent such encumbrance extends beyond June 30, 1984.

(4) The term "property" means any property or part thereof.

Promulgated: 46 Fed. Reg. 7322 (1/23/81).

Sec. 2550.414c-4—Transitional rule for the provision of certain services until June 30, 1977.

(a) In general. Section 414(c)(4) of the Employee Retirement Income Security Act of 1974 (the Act) provides that sections 406 and 407(a) shall not apply to the provision of services before June 30, 1977, between a plan and a party in interest if the three requirements contained in Sec. 414(c)(4) are met. The first requirement is that such services must be provided either (1) under a binding contract in effect on July 1, 1974 (or pursuant to a renewal or modification of such contract), or (2) by a party in interest who ordinarily and customarily furnished such services on June 30, 1974. The second requirement is that the services be provided on terms that remain at least as favorable to the plan as an arm's-length transaction with an unrelated party would be. For this purpose, such services are provided on terms that remain at least as favorable to the plan as an arm's-length transaction with an unrelated party would be, if at the time of execution (or renewal) of such binding contract, the contract (or renewal) is on terms at least as favorable to the plan as an arm's-length transaction with an unrelated party would be. However, if in a normal commercial setting an unrelated party in the position of the plan could be expected to insist upon a renegotiation or termination of a binding contract, the plan must so act. Thus, for example, if a party in interest provides services to a plan on a month-to-month basis, and a party in the position of the plan could be expected to renegotiate the price paid under such contract because of a decline in the fair market value of such services, the plan must so act in order to avoid participation in a prohibited transaction. The third requirement is that the provision of services must not be, or have been, at the time of such provision a prohibited transaction within the meaning of Sec. 503(b) of the Internal Revenue Code of 1954 or the corresponding provisions of prior law. If these three requirements are met, Sec. 406 of the Act will apply neither to services provided before June 30, 1977 (both to customers to whom such services were being provided on June 30, 1974, and to new customers) nor to the receipt of compensation therefor. Thus, if these three requirements are met, Sec. 406 of the Act will not apply until June 30, 1977, to the provision of services to a plan by a party in interest (including a fiduciary) even if such services could not be furnished pursuant to the exemption provisions of Sec. 408(b) (2) or (6) of the Act and Secs. 2250.408b-2 and 2550.408b-6. For example, if the three requirements of Sec. 414(c)(4) of the Act are met, a person serving as a fiduciary to a plan who already receives full-time pay from an employer or an association of employers, whose employees are participants in such plan, or from an employee organization whose members are participants in such plan, may continue to receive reasonable compensation from the plan for services rendered to the plan before June 30, 1977. Similarly, until June 30, 1977, a plan consultant who may be a fiduciary because of the nature of the consultative and administrative services being provided may, if these three requirements are met, continue to cause the sale of insurance to the plan and continue to receive commissions for such sales from the insurance company writing the policy. Further, if the three requirements of Sec. 414(c)(4) of the Act are met, a securities broker-dealer who renders investment advice to a plan for a fee, thereby becoming a fiduciary, may furnish other services to the plan, such as brokerage services, and receive compensation therefor. Also, if a registered representative of such a broker-dealer were a fiduciary, the registered representative may receive compensation, including commissions, for brokerage services performed before June 30, 1977.

(b) Persons deemed to be June 30, 1974, service providers. A party in interest with respect to a plan which did not, on June 30, 1974, ordinarily and customarily furnish a particular service, will nevertheless be considered to have ordinarily and customarily furnished such service on June 30, 1974, for purposes of this section and Sec. 414(c)(4) of the Act, if either of the following conditions are met:

(1) At least 50% of the outstanding beneficial interests of such party in interest are owned directly or through one or more intermediaries by the same person or persons who owned, directly or through one or more intermediaries, at least 50%

of the outstanding beneficial interests of a person who ordinarily and customarily furnished such service on June 30, 1974; or

(2) Control or the power to exercise a controlling influence over the management and policies of such party in interest is possessed, directly or through one or more intermediaries, by the same person or persons who possessed, directly or through one or more intermediaries, control or the power to exercise a controlling influence over the management and policies of a person who ordinarily and customarily furnished such service on June 30, 1974. For purposes of paragraph (b) of this section, a person shall be deemed to be an "intermediary" of another person if at least 50% of the outstanding beneficial interests of such person are owned by such other person, directly or indirectly, or if such other person controls or has the power to exercise a controlling influence over the management and policies of such person.

(c) Examples. The following examples apply the principles enunciated in paragraph (b) of this section.

Example. (1). A owns 50% of the outstanding beneficial interests of ABC Partnership which ordinarily and customarily furnished certain services on June 30, 1974. On July 2, 1974, ABC Partnership was incorporated into ABC Corporation with one class of stock outstanding. A owns 50% of the shares of such stock. ABC Corporation furnishes the same services that were furnished by ABC Partnership on June 30, 1974. ABC Corporation will be deemed to have ordinarily and customarily furnished such services on June 30, 1974, for purposes of Sec. 414(c)(4) of the Act.

Example (2). A and B together own 100% of the beneficial interests of AB Partnership, which ordinarily and customarily furnished certain services on June 30, 1974. On September 1, 1974, AB Partnership was incorporated into AB Corporation with one class of stock outstanding. A and B each own 20% of such outstanding class of stock and together have control over the management and policies of AB Corporation. AB Corporation furnishes the same services that were furnished by AB Partnership on June 30, 1974. AB Corporation will be deemed to have ordinarily and customarily furnished such services on June 30, 1974, for purposes of Sec. 414(c)(4) of the Act.

Example (3). On June 30, 1974, M Corporation was ordinarily and customarily furnishing certain services. On that date, X, Y, and Z together owned 50% of all classes of the outstanding shares of M Corporation. On January 28, 1975, all of the shareholders of M Corporation exchanged their shares in M Corporation for shares of a new N Corporation. As a result of that exchange, X, Y, and Z together own 50% of the common stock of N Corporation, the only class of N Corporation stock outstanding after the exchange. N Corporation furnishes the services formerly furnished by M Corporation. N Corporation will be deemed to have ordinarily and customarily furnished such services on June 30, 1974, for purposes of Sec. 414(c)(4) of the Act.

Example (4). I Corporation ordinarily and customarily furnished certain services on June 30, 1974. On November 3, 1975, I Corporation organizes a wholly-owned subsidiary, S Corporation, which furnishes the same services ordinarily and customarily furnished by I Corporation on June 30, 1974. S Corporation will be deemed to have ordinarily and customarily furnished such services on June 30, 1974, for purposes of Sec. 414(c)(4) of the Act.

Example (5). X Corporation, wholly owned and controlled by A, ordinarily and customarily furnished certain services on June 30, 1974. Y corporation did not perform such services on that date. On January 2, 1976, X Corporation is merged into Y Corporation and, although A received less than 50% of the total outstanding shares of Y Corporation, after such merger A has control over the management and policies of Y Corporation. Y Corporation furnishes the same services that were formerly furnished by X Corporation. Y Corporation will be deemed to have ordinarily and customarily furnished such services on June 30, 1974, for purposes of Sec. 414(c)(4) of the Act.

Promulgated: 42 Fed. Reg. 32393 (6/24/77); 42 Fed. Reg. 36823 (7/8/77).

◆ ◆ ◆

PART 2560—RULES AND REGULATIONS FOR ADMINISTRATION AND ENFORCEMENT

Sec. 2560.502-1—Requests for enforcement pursuant to Sec. 502(b)(2).

(a) Form, content and filing. All requests by participants, beneficiaries, and fiduciaries for the Secretary of Labor to exercise his enforcement authority pursuant to Sec. 502(a)(5), 29 U.S.C. 1132(a)(5), with respect to a violation of, or the enforcement of, parts 2 and 3 of Title I of the Employee Retirement Income Security Act of 1974 (the Act) shall be in writing and shall contain information sufficient to form a basis for identifying the participant, beneficiary, or fiduciary and the plan involved. All such requests shall be considered filed if they are directed to and received by any office or official of the Department of Labor or referred to and received by any such office or official by any party to whom such writing is directed.

(b) Consideration. The Secretary of Labor retains discretion to determine whether any enforcement proceeding should be commenced in the case of any request received pursuant to paragraph (a) of this section, and he may, but shall not be required to, exercise his authority pursuant to Sec. 502(a)(5) of the Act only if he determines that such violation affects, or such enforcement is necessary to protect claims of participants or beneficiaries to benefits under the plan.

Promulgated: 43 Fed. Reg. 50175 (10/27/78).

Sec. 2560.502c-2—Civil penalties under Sec. 502(c)(2).

(a) In general.

(1) Pursuant to the authority granted the Secretary under Sec. 502(c)(2) of the Employee Retirement Income Security Act of 1974, as amended (the Act), the administrator (within the meaning of Sec. 3(16)(A)) of an employee benefit plan (within the meaning of Sec. 3(3) and Sec. 2510.3-1, et seq.) for which an annual report is required to be filed under Sec. 101(b)(4) shall be liable for civil penalties assessed by the Secretary under Sec. 502(c)(2) of the Act in each case in which there is a failure or refusal to file the annual report required to be filed under Sec. 101(b)(4).

(2) For purposes of this section, a failure or refusal to file the annual report required to be filed under Sec. 101(b)(4) shall mean a failure or refusal to file, in whole or in part, that information described in Sec. 103 and Sec. 2520.103-1, et seq., on behalf of the plan at the time and in the manner prescribed therefor.

(b) Amount assessed.

(1) The amount assessed under Sec. 502(c)(2) shall be determined by the Department of Labor, taking into consideration the degree or willfulness of the failure to file the annual report. However, the amount assessed under Sec. 502(c)(2) of the Act shall not exceed $1,000 a day, computed from the date of the administrator's failure or refusal to file the annual report and, except as provided in paragraph (b)(2) of this section, continuing up to the date on which an annual report satisfactory to the Secretary is filed.

(2) If upon receipt of a notice of intent to assess a penalty (as described in paragraph (c) of this section) the administrator files a statement of reasonable cause for the failure to file, in accordance with paragraph (e) of this section, a penalty shall not be assessed for any day from the date the Department serves the administrator with a copy of such notice until the day after the Department serves notice on the administrator of its determination on reasonable cause and its intention to assess a penalty (as described in paragraph (g) of this section).

(3) For purposes of this paragraph, the date on which the administrator failed or refused to file the annual report shall be the date on which the annual report was due (determined without regard to any extension for filing). An annual report which is rejected under Sec. 104(a)(4) for a failure to provide material information shall be treated as a failure to file an annual report when a revised report satisfactory to the Department is not filed within 45 days of the date of the Department's notice of rejection. A penalty shall not be assessed under Sec. 502(c)(2) for any day earlier than the day after the date of an administrator's failure or refusal to file the annual report if a revised filing satisfactory to the Department is not submitted within 45 days of the date of the notice of rejection by the Department.

(c) Notice of intent to assess a penalty. Prior to the assessment of any penalty under Sec. 502(c)(2), the Department shall provide to the administrator of the plan a written notice indicating the Department's intent to assess a penalty under Sec. 502(c)(2), the amount of such penalty, the period to which the penalty applies, and the reason(s) for the penalty.

(d) Waiver of assessed penalty. The Department may waive all or part of the penalty to be assessed under Sec. 502(c)(2) on a showing by the administrator that there was reasonable cause for the failure to file the annual report.

(e) Showing of reasonable cause. Upon issuance by the Department of a notice of intent to assess a penalty, the administrator shall have 30 days from the date of the service of notice, as described in paragraph (i) of this section, to file a statement of reasonable cause for the failure to file a complete annual report or why the penalty, as calculated, should not be assessed. A showing of reasonable cause must be made in the form of a written statement setting forth all the facts alleged as reasonable cause. The statement must contain a declaration by the administrator that the statement is made under the penalties of perjury.

(f) Failure to file a statement of reasonable cause. Failure of an administrator to file a statement of reasonable cause within the 30 day period described in paragraph (e) of this section shall be deemed to constitute a waiver of the right to appear and contest the facts alleged in the notice, and such failure shall be deemed an admission of the facts alleged in the notice for purposes of any proceeding involving the assessment of a civil penalty under Sec. 502(c)(2). Such notice shall then become a final order of the Secretary, within the meaning of Sec. 2570.61(g).

(g) Notice of the determination on statement of reasonable cause.

(1) The Department, following a review of all the facts alleged in support of a complete or partial waiver of the penalty, shall notify the administrator, in writing, of its intention to waive the penalty, in whole or in part, and/or assess a penalty. If it is the intention of the Department to assess a penalty, the notice shall indicate the amount of the penalty, not to exceed the amount described in paragraph (c) of this section.

(2) Except as provided in paragraph (h) of this section, a notice issued pursuant to this paragraph indicating the Department's intention to assess a penalty shall become a final order, within the meaning of Sec. 2570.61(g), 30 days after the date of service of the notice.

(h) Administrative hearing. A notice issued pursuant to paragraph (g) of this section will not become a final order, within the meaning of Sec. 2570.61(g), if, within 30 days from the date of service of the notice, an answer, as defined in Sec. 2570.61(c), is filed in accordance with Sec. 2570.62.

(i) Service of notice.

(1) Service of notice shall be made either:

(i) By delivering a copy to the administrator or representative thereof;

(ii) By leaving a copy at the principal office, place of business, or residence of the administrator or representative thereof; or

(iii) By mailing a copy to the last known address of the administrator or representative thereof.

(2) If service is accomplished by certified mail, service is complete upon mailing. If done by regular mail, service is complete upon receipt by the addressee.

(j) Liability.

(1) If more than one person is responsible as administrator for the failure to file the annual report, all such persons shall be jointly and severally liable with respect to such failure.

(2) Any person against whom a civil penalty has been assessed under Sec. 502(c)(2) pursuant to a final order, within the meaning of Sec. 2570.61(g), shall be personally liable for the payment of such penalty.

(k) Cross-reference. See Secs. 2570.60 through 71 of this chapter for procedural rules relating to administrative hearings under Sec. 502(c)(2) of the Act.

Promulgated: 54 Fed. Reg. 26894 (6/26/89).

Sec. 2560.502i-1— Civil Penalties Under Sec. 502(i).

(a) In general. Section 502(i) of the Employee Retirement Income Security Act of 1974 (ERISA or the Act) permits the Secretary of Labor to assess a civil penalty against a party in interest who engages in a prohibited transaction with respect to an employee benefit plan other than a plan described in Sec. 4975(e)(1) of the Internal Revenue Code (the Code). The initial penalty under Sec. 502(i) is 5% of the total "amount involved" in the prohibited transaction (unless a lesser amount is otherwise agreed to by the parties). However, if the prohibited transaction is not corrected during the "correction period," the civil penalty shall be 100% of the "amount involved" (unless a lesser amount is otherwise agreed to by the parties). Paragraph (b) of this section defines the term "amount involved," paragraph (c) defines the term "correction," and paragraph (d) defines the term "correction period." Paragraph (e) illustrates the computation of the civil penalty under Sec. 502(i). Paragraph (f) is a cross reference to the Department's procedural rules for Sec. 502(i) proceedings.

(b) Amount involved. Section 502(i) of ERISA states that the term "amount involved" in that section shall be defined as it is defined under Sec. 4975(f)(4) of the Code. As provided in 26 CFR 141.4975.13, 26 CFR 53.4941(e)-1(b) is controlling with respect to the interpretation of the term "amount involved" under Sec. 4975 of the Code. Accordingly, the Department of Labor will apply the principles set out at 26 CFR 53.4941(e)-1(b) in determining the "amount involved' in a transaction subject to the civil penalty provided by Sec. 502(i) of the Act and this section.

(c) Correction. Section 502(i) of ERISA states that the term "correction" shall be defined in a manner that is consistent with the definition of that term under Sec. 4975(f)(5) of the Code. As provided in 26 CFR 141.4975-13, 26 CFR 53.4941(e)-1(c) is controlling with respect to the interpretation of the term "correction" for purposes of Sec. 4975 of the Code. Accordingly, the Department of Labor will apply the principles set out in 26 CFR 53.4941(e)-(1)(c) in interpreting the term "correction" under Sec. 502(i) of the Act and this section.

(d) Correction Period.

(1) In general, the "correction period" begins on the date the prohibited transaction occurs and ends 90 days after a final agency order with respect to such transaction.

(2) When a party in interest seeks judicial review within 90 days of a final agency order in an ERISA Sec. 502(i) proceeding, the correction period will end 90 days after the entry of a final order in the judicial action.

(3) The following examples illustrate the operation of this paragraph:

(i) A party in interest receives notice of the Department's intent to impose the Sec. 502(i) penalty and does not invoke the ERISA Sec. 502(i) prohibited transaction penalty proceedings described in Sec. 2570.1 of this chapter within 30 days of such notice. As provided in Sec. 2570.5 of this chapter, the notice of the intent to impose a penalty becomes a final order after 30 days. Thus, the "correction period" ends 90 days after the expiration of the 30 day period.

(ii) A party in interest contests a proposed Sec. 502(i) penalty, but does not appeal an adverse decision of the administrative law judge in the proceeding. As provided in Sec. 2570.10(a) of this chapter, the decision of the administrative law judge becomes a final order of the Department unless the decision is appealed within 20 days after the date of such order. Thus, the correction period ends 90 days after the expiration of such 20 day period.

(iii) The Secretary of Labor issues to a party in interest a decision upholding an administrative law judge's adverse decision. As provided in Sec. 2570.12(b) of this chapter, the decision of the Secretary becomes a final order of the Department immediately. Thus, the correction period will end 90 days after the issuance of the Secretary's order unless the party in interest judicially contests the order within that 90 day period. If the party in interest so contests the order, the correction period will end 90 days after the entry of a final order in the judicial action.

(e) Computation of the Sec. 502(i) penalty.

(1) In general, the civil penalty under Sec. 502(i) is determined by applying the applicable percentage (5% or 100%) to the aggregate amount involved in the transaction. However, a continuing prohibited transaction, such as a lease or a loan, is treated as giving rise to a separate event subject to the sanction for each year (as measured from the anniversary date of the transaction) in which the transaction occurs.

(2) The following examples illustrate the computation of the Sec. 502(i) penalty:

(i) An employee benefit plan purchases property from a party in interest at a price of $10,000. The fair market value of the property is $5,000. The "amount involved" in that transaction, as determined under 26 CFR 53.4941(e)-1(b), is $10,000 (the greater of the amount paid by the plan or the fair market value of the property). The initial 5% penalty under Sec. 502(i) is $500 (5% of $10,000).

(ii) An employee benefit plan executes a four year lease with a party in interest at an annual rental of $10,000 (which is the fair rental value of the property). The amount involved in each year of that transaction, as determined under 26 CFR 53.4941(e)-1(b), is $10,000. The amount of the initial sanction under ERISA Sec. 502(i) would be a total of $5,000: $2,000 ($10,000 × 5% × 4 with respect to the rentals paid in the first year of the lease); $1,500 ($10,000 × 5% × 3 with respect to the second year); $1,000 ($10,000 × 5% × 2 with respect to the third year); $500 ($10,000 × 5% × 1 with respect to the fourth year).

(f) Cross Reference. See Secs. 2570.1-2570.12 of this chapter for procedural rules relating to Sec. 502(i) penalty proceedings.

Promulgated: 53 Fed. Reg. 37476 (9/26/88).

Sec. 2560.503-1—Claims procedure.

(a) Scope and purpose. (1) This section sets out certain minimum requirements for employee benefit plan procedures pertaining to claims by participants and beneficiaries (claimants) for plan benefits, consideration of such claims, and review of claim denials, hereinafter referred to in the aggregate as "claims procedures." Except as otherwise noted, these requirements apply to every employee benefit plan described in Sec. 4(a) and not exempted under Sec. 4(b) of the Employee Retirement Income Security Act of 1974 (the Act).

(b) Obligation to establish a reasonable claims procedure. Every employee benefit plan shall establish and maintain reasonable claims procedures.

(1) A claims procedure will be deemed to be reasonable only if it:

(i) Complies with the provisions of paragraphs (d) through (h) of this section, except to the extent that it is deemed to comply with some or all of such provisions under the authority of paragraph (b)(2) or paragraph (j) of this section.

(ii) Is described in the summary plan description, as required by Sec. 2520.102-3,

(iii) Does not contain any provision, and is not administered in a way, which unduly inhibits or hampers the initiation or processing of plan claims, and

(iv) Provides for informing participants in writing, in a timely fashion, of the time limits set forth in paragraphs (e)(3) and (g)(3) and paragraph (h) of this section.

(2) In the case of a plan established and maintained pursuant to a collective bargaining agreement (other than a plan subject to the provisions of Sec. 302(c)(5) of the Labor Management Relations Act, 1947, concerning joint representation on the board of trustees):

(i) Such plan will be deemed to comply with the provisions of paragraphs (d) through (h) of this section if the collective bargaining agreement pursuant to which the plan is established or maintained sets forth or incorporates by specific reference.

(A) Provisions concerning the filing of benefit claims and the initial disposition of benefit claims, and

(B) A grievance and arbitration procedure to which denied claims are subject.

(ii) Such plan will be deemed to comply with the provisions of paragraphs (g) and (h) of this section (but will not be deemed to comply with paragraphs (d) through (f)) if the collective bargaining agreement pursuant to which the plan is established or maintained sets forth or incorporates by specific reference a grievance and arbitration procedure to which denied claims are subject (but not provisions concerning the final and initial disposition of benefit claims).

(c) Claims procedure for an insured welfare or pension plan.

(1) To the extent that benefits under an employee benefit plan are provided or administered by an insurance company, insurance service, or other similar organization which is subject to regulation under the insurance laws of one or more States, the claims procedure pertaining to such benefits may provide for filing of a claim for benefits with and notice of decision by such company, service or organization.

(2) See paragraph (g) regarding review and final decision on denied claims by insurance companies, insurance services and similar organizations.

(d) Filing of a claim for benefits. For purposes of this section, a claim is a request for a plan benefit by a participant or beneficiary. A claim is filed when the requirements of a reasonable claim filing procedure of a plan have been met. If a reasonable procedure for filing claims has not been established by the plan, a claim shall be deemed filed when a written or oral communication is made by the claimant or the claimant's authorized representative which is reasonably calculated to bring the claim to the attention of:

(1) In the case of a single employer plan, either the organizational unit which has customarily handled employee benefits matters of the employer, or any officer of the employer.

(2) In the case of a plan to which more than one unaffiliated employer contributes, or which is established or maintained by an employee organization, either the joint board, association, committee or other similar group (or any member of any such group) administering the plan, or the person or organizational unit to which claims for benefits under the plan customarily have been referred.

(3) In the case of a plan the benefits of which are provided or administered by an insurance company, insurance service, or other similar organization, which is subject to regulation under the insurance laws of one or more States, the person or organizational unit which handles claims for benefits under the plan or any officer of the insurance company, insurance service, or similar organization.

(4) For purposes of paragraphs (d) (1), (2), and (3) of this section, a communication shall be deemed to have been brought to the attention of an organizational unit if it is received by any person employed in such unit.

(e) Notification to claimant of decision.

(1) If a claim is wholly or partially denied, notice of the decision, meeting the requirements of paragraph (f) of this section, shall be furnished to the claimant within a reasonable period of time after receipt of the claim by the plan.

(2) If notice of the denial of a claim is not furnished in accordance with paragraph (e)(1) of this section within a reasonable period of time, the claim shall be deemed denied and the claimant shall be permitted to proceed to the review stage described in paragraph (g) of this section.

(3) For purposes of paragraphs (e) (1) and (2), of this section, a period of time will be deemed to be unreasonable if it exceeds 90 days after receipt of the claim by the plan, unless special circumstances require an extension of time for processing the claim. If such an extension of time for processing is required, written notice of the extension shall be furnished to the claimant prior to the termination of the initial 90-day period. In no event shall such extension exceed a period of 90 days from the end of such initial period. The extension notice shall indicate the special circumstances requiring an extension of time and the date by which the plan expects to render the final decision.

(f) Content of notice. A plan administrator or, if paragraph (c) of this section is applicable, the insurance company, insurance service, or other similar organization, shall provide to every claimant who is denied a claim for benefits written notice setting forth in a manner calculated to be understood by the claimant:

(1) The specific reason or reasons for the denial;

(2) Specific reference to pertinent plan provisions on which the denial is based;

(3) A description of any additional material or information necessary for the claimant to perfect the claim and an explanation of why such material or information is necessary; and

(4) Appropriate information as to the steps to be taken if the participant or beneficiary wishes to submit his or her claim for review.

(g) Review procedure.

(1) Every plan shall establish and maintain a procedure by which a claimant or his duly authorized representative has a reasonable opportunity to appeal a denied claim to an appropriate named fiduciary or to a person designated by such fiduciary, and under which a full and fair review of the claim and its denial may be obtained. Every such procedure shall include but not be limited to provisions that a claimant or his duly authorized representative may:

(i) Request a review upon written application to the plan;

(ii) Review pertinent documents; and

(iii) Submit issues and comments in writing.

(2) To the extent that benefits under an employee benefit plan are provided or administered by an insurance company, insurance service, or other similar organization which is subject to regulation under the insurance laws of one or more States, the claims procedure pertaining to such benefits may provide for review of and decision upon denied claims by such company, service or organization. In such case, that company, service, or organization shall be the "appropriate named fiduciary" for purposes of this section. In all other cases, the "appropriate named fiduciary" for purposes of this section may be the plan administrator or any other person designated by the plan, provided that such plan administrator or other person is either named in the plan instrument or is identified pursuant to a procedure set forth in the plan as the person who reviews and makes decisions on claim denials.

(3) A plan may establish a limited period within which a claimant must file any request for review of a denied claim. Such time limits must be reasonable and related to the nature of the benefit which is the subject of the claim and to other attendant circumstances. In no event may such a period expire less than 60 days after receipt by the claimant of written notification of denial of a claim.

(h) Decision on review.

(1)(i) A decision by an appropriate named fiduciary shall be made promptly, and shall not ordinarily be made later than 60 days after the plan's receipt of a request for review, unless special circumstances (such as the need to hold a hearing, if the plan procedure provides for a hearing) require an extension of time for processing, in which case a decision shall be rendered as soon as possible, but not later than 120 days after receipt of a request for review.

(ii) In the case of a plan with a committee or board of trustees designated as the appropriate named fiduciary, which holds regularly scheduled meetings at least quarterly, a decision on review shall be made by no later than the date of the meeting of the committee or board which immediately follows the plan's receipt of a request for review, unless the request for review is filed within 30 days preceding the date of such meeting. In such case, a decision may be made by no later than the date of the second meeting following the plan's receipt of the request for review. If special circumstances (such as the need to hold a hearing, if the plan procedure provides for a hearing) require a further extension of time for processing, a decision shall be rendered not later than the third meeting of the committee or board following the plan's receipt of the request for review.

(2) If such an extension of time for review is required because of special circumstances, written notice of the extension shall be furnished to the claimant prior to the commencement of the extension.

(3) The decision on review shall be in writing and shall include specific reasons for the decision, written in a manner calculated to be understood by the claimant, as well as specific references to the pertinent plan provisions on which the decision is based.

(4) The decision on review shall be furnished to the claimant within the appropriate time described in paragraph (h)(1) of this section. If the decision on review is not furnished within such time, the claim shall be deemed denied on review.

(i) Apprenticeship plans. This section does not apply to employee benefit plans which provide solely apprenticeship training benefits.

(j) Qualified Health Maintenance Organizations. Claims procedures with respect to any benefits provided through membership in a qualified health maintenance organization, as defined in Sec. 1310(d) of the Public Health Service Act, as amended, 42 U.S.C. 300e-9(d), shall be deemed to satisfy the requirements of this section with respect to the provision of such benefits to persons who are members of such qualified health maintenance organization, provided those procedures meet the requirements of Sec. 1301 of the Public Health Service Act, as amended 42 U.S.C. 300e and the regulations thereunder.

Promulgated: 42 Fed. Reg. 27426 (5/27/77).

Amended: 46 Fed. Reg. 5884 (1/21/81); 49 Fed. Reg. 18295 (4/30/84).

◆ ◆ ◆

PART 2570—PROCEDURAL REGULATIONS UNDER THE EMPLOYEE RETIREMENT INCOME SECURITY ACT

Subpart A—Procedures for the Assessment of Civil Sanctions Under ERISA §502(i)

Sec. 2570.1—Scope of rules.

The rules of practice set forth in this part are applicable to "prohibited transaction penalty proceedings" (as defined in §2570.2(o) of this part) under §502(i) of the Employee Retirement Income Security Act of 1974. The rules of procedure for administrative hearings published by the Department's Office of Administrative

Law Judges at Part 18 of this Title will apply to matters arising under ERISA §502(i) except as modified by this section. These proceedings shall be conducted as expeditiously as possible, and the parties shall make every effort to avoid delay at each stage of the proceedings.

Promulgated: 53 Fed. Reg. 37476 (9/26/88).

Sec. 2570.2—Definitions.

For prohibited transaction penalty proceedings, this section shall apply in lieu of the definitions in §18.2 of this title:

(a) "Adjudicatory proceeding" means a judicial-type proceeding leading to the formulation of a final order;

(b) "Administrative law judge" means an administrative law judge appointed pursuant to the provisions of 5 U.S.C. 3105;

(c) "Answer" is defined for these proceedings as set forth in §18.5(d)(2) of this title;

(d) "Commencement of proceeding" is the filing of an answer by the respondent;

(e) "Consent agreement" means any written document containing a specified proposed remedy or other relief acceptable to the Department and consenting parties;

(f) "ERISA" means the Employee Retirement Income Security Act of 1974, as amended;

(g) "Final order" means the final decision or action of the Department of Labor concerning the assessment of a civil sanction under ERISA §502(i) against a particular party. Such final order may result from a decision of an administrative law judge or the Secretary, or the failure of a party to invoke the procedures for hearings or appeals under this title. Such a final order shall constitute final agency action within the meaning of 5 U.S.C. 704;

(h) "Hearing" means that part of a proceeding which involves the submission of evidence, either by oral presentation or written submission, to the administrative law judge;

(i) "Notice" means any document, however designated, issued by the Department of Labor which initiates an adjudicatory proceeding under ERISA §502(i);

(j) "Order" means the whole or any part of a final procedural or substantive disposition of a matter under ERISA §502(i);

(k) "Party" includes a person or agency named or admitted as a party to a proceeding;

(l) "Person" includes an individual, partnership, corporation, employee benefit plan, association, exchange or other entity or organization;

(m) "Petition" means a written request, made by a person or party, for some affirmative action;

(n) "Pleading" means the notice, the answer to the notice, any supplement or amendment thereto, and any reply that may be permitted to any answer, supplement or amendment;

(o) "Prohibited transaction penalty proceeding" means a proceeding relating to the assessment of the civil penalty provided for in §502(i) of ERISA;

(p) "Respondent" means the party against whom the Department is seeking to assess a civil sanction under ERISA §502(i);

(q) "Secretary" means the Secretary of Labor and includes, pursuant to any delegation of authority by the Secretary, any assistant secretary (including the Assistant Secretary for Pension and Welfare Benefits), administrator, commissioner, appellate body, board, or other official;

(r) "Solicitor" means the Solicitor of Labor or his or her delegate.

Promulgated: 53 Fed. Reg. 37476 (9/26/88).

Sec. 2570.3—Service: Copies of documents and pleadings.

For prohibited transaction penalty proceedings, this section shall apply in lieu of §18.3 of this title.

(a) General. Copies of all documents shall be served on all parties of record. All documents should clearly designate the docket number, if any, and short title of all matters. All documents to be filed shall be delivered or mailed to the Chief Docket Clerk, Office of Administrative Law Judges, Suite 600, 1111 20th Street N.W., Washington, D.C. 20036, or to the OALJ Regional Office to which the proceeding may have been transferred for hearing. Each document filed shall be clear and legible.

(b) By parties. All motions, petitions, pleadings, briefs or other documents shall be filed with the Office of Administrative Law Judges with a copy including any attachments to all other parties of record. When a party is represented by an attorney, service shall be made upon the attorney. Service of any document upon any party may be made by personal delivery or by mailing a copy to the last known address. The Department shall be served by delivery to the Associate Solicitor, Plan Benefits Security Division, ERISA §502(i) Proceeding, P.O. Box 1914, Washington, D.C. 20013. The person serving the document shall certify to the manner and date of service.

(c) By the Office of Administrative Law Judges. Service of orders, decisions and all other documents, except notices, shall be made by regular mail to the last known address.

(d) Service of notices.

(1) Service of notices shall be made either:

(i) By delivering a copy to the individual, any partner, any officer of a corporation, or any attorney of record;

(ii) By leaving a copy at the principal office, place of business, or residence of such individual, partner, officer or attorney; or

(iii) By mailing a copy to the last known address of such individual, partner, officer or attorney.

(2) If service is accomplished by certified mail, service is complete upon mailing. If done by regular mail, service is complete upon receipt by the addressee.

(e) Form of pleadings.

(1) Every pleading shall contain information indicating the name of the Pension and Welfare Benefits Administration (PWBA) as the agency under which the proceeding is instituted, the title of the proceeding, the docket number (if any) assigned by the Office of Administrative Law Judges and a designation of the type of pleading or paper (e.g., notice, motion to dismiss, etc.). The pleading or paper shall be signed and shall contain the address and telephone number of the party or person representing the party. Although there are no formal specifications for documents, they should be typewritten when possible on standard size 8-1/2 × 11 inch paper.

(2) Illegible documents, whether handwritten, typewritten, photocopied, or otherwise, will not be accepted. Papers may be reproduced by any duplicating process provided all copies are clear and legible.

Promulgated: 53 Fed. Reg. 37476 (9/26/88).

Sec. 2570.4—Parties.

For prohibited transaction penalty proceedings, this section shall apply in lieu of §18.10 of this title.

(a) The term "party" wherever used in these rules shall include any natural person, corporation, employee benefit plan, association, firm, partnership, trustee, receiver, agency, public or private organization, or government agency. A party against whom a civil sanction is sought shall be designated as "respondent." The Department shall be designated as the "complainant."

(b) Other persons or organizations shall be permitted to participate as parties only if the administrative law judge finds that the final decision could directly and adversely affect them or the class they represent, that they may contribute materially to the disposition of the proceedings and their interest is not adequately represented by existing parties, and that in the discretion of the administrative law judge the participation of such persons or organizations would be appropriate.

(c) A person or organization not named as a respondent wishing to participate as a party under this section shall submit a petition to the administrative law judge within fifteen (15) days after the person or organization has knowledge of or should have known about the proceeding. The petition shall be filed with the administrative law judge and served on each person or organization who has been made a party at the time of filing. Such petition shall concisely state:

(1) Petitioner's interest in the proceeding;

(2) How his or her participation as a party will contribute materially to the disposition of the proceeding;

(3) Who will appear for petitioner;

(4) The issues on which petitioner wishes to participate; and

(5) Whether petitioner intends to present witnesses.

(d) Objections to the petition may be filed by a party within fifteen (15) days of the filing of the petition. If objections to the petition are filed, the administrative law judge shall then determine whether petitioners have the requisite interest to be a party in the proceedings, as defined in paragraph (b) of this section, and shall permit or deny participation accordingly. Where petitions to participate as parties are made by individuals or groups with common interests, the administrative law judge may request all such petitioners to designate a single representative, or he or she may recognize one or more of such petitioners. The administrative law judge shall give each such petitioner as well as the parties, written notice of the decision on his or her petition. For each petition granted, the administrative law judge shall provide a brief statement of the basis of the decision. If the petition is denied, he or she shall briefly state the grounds for denial and shall then treat the petition as a request for participation as amicus curiae.

Promulgated: 53 Fed. Reg. 37476 (9/26/88).

Sec. 2570.5—Consequences of default.

For prohibited transaction penalty proceedings, this section shall apply in lieu of §18.5(b) of this title. Failure of the respondent to file an answer within the 30 day time period provided in §18.5 of this title shall be deemed to constitute a waiver of his right to appear and contest the allegations of the notice, and such failure shall be deemed to be an admission of the facts as alleged in the notice for purposes of the prohibited transaction penalty proceeding. Such notice shall then become the final order of the Secretary, except that the administrative law judge may set aside a default entered under this provision where there is proof of defective notice.

Promulgated: 53 Fed. Reg. 37476 (9/26/88).

Sec. 2570.6—Consent order or settlement.

For prohibited transaction penalty proceedings, the following shall apply in lieu of §18.9 of this title.

(a) General. At any time after the commencement of a proceeding, but at least five (5) days prior to the date set for hearing, the parties jointly may move to defer the hearing for a reasonable time to permit negotiation of a settlement or an agreement containing findings and an order disposing of the whole or any part of the proceeding. The allowance of such deferment and the duration thereof shall be in the discretion of the administrative law judge, after consideration of such factors as the nature of the proceeding, the requirements of the public interest, the representations of the parties and the probability of reaching an agreement which will result in a just disposition of the issues involved.

(b) Content. Any agreement containing consent findings and an order disposing of a proceeding or any part thereof shall also provide:

(1) That the order shall have the same force and effect as an order made after full hearing;

(2) That the entire record on which any order may be based shall consist solely of the notice and the agreement;

(3) A waiver of any further procedural steps before the administrative law judge;

(4) A waiver of any right to challenge or contest the validity of the order and decision entered into in accordance with the agreement; and

(5) That the order and decision of the administrative law judge shall be final agency action.

(c) Submission. On or before the expiration of the time granted for negotiations, but, in any case, at least five (5) days prior to the date set for hearing, the parties or their authorized representative or their counsel may:

(1) Submit the proposed agreement containing consent findings and an order to the administrative law judge; or

(2) Notify the administrative law judge that the parties have reached a full settlement and have agreed to dismissal of the action subject to compliance with the terms of the settlement; or

(3) Inform the administrative law judge that agreement cannot be reached.

(d) Disposition. In the event a settlement agreement containing consent findings and an order is submitted within the time allowed therefor, the administrative law judge shall issue a decision incorporating such findings and agreement within thirty (30) days of his receipt of such document. The decision of the administrative law judge shall incorporate all of the findings, terms, and conditions of the settlement agreement and consent order of the parties. Such decision shall become final agency action within the meaning of 5 U.S.C. 704.

(e) Settlement without consent of all parties. In cases in which some, but not all, of the parties to a proceeding submit a consent agreement to the administrative law judge, the following procedure shall apply:

(1) If all of the parties have not consented to the proposed settlement submitted to the administrative law judge, then such non-consenting parties must receive notice, and a copy, of the proposed settlement at the time it is submitted to the administrative law judge;

(2) Any non-consenting party shall have fifteen (15) days to file any objections to the proposed settlement with the administrative law judge and all other parties;

(3) If any party submits an objection to the proposed settlement, the administrative law judge shall decide within thirty (30) days after receipt of such objections whether he shall sign or reject the proposed settlement. Where the record lacks substantial evidence upon which to base a decision or there is a genuine issue of material fact, then the administrative law judge may establish procedures for the purpose of receiving additional evidence upon which a decision on the contested issues may reasonably be based;

(4) If there are no objections to the proposed settlement, or if the administrative law judge decides to sign the proposed settlement after reviewing any such objections, the administrative law judge shall incorporate the consent agreement into a decision meeting the requirements of paragraph (d) of this section.

Promulgated: 53 Fed. Reg. 37476 (9/26/88).

Sec. 2570.7—Scope of discovery.

For prohibited transaction penalty proceedings, this section shall apply in lieu of §18.14 of this title.

(a) A party may file a motion to conduct discovery with the administrative law judge. The motion for discovery shall be granted by the administrative law judge only upon a showing of good cause. In order to establish "good cause" for the purposes of this section, a party must show that the discovery requested relates to a genuine issue as to a material fact that is relevant to the proceeding. The order of the administrative law judge shall expressly limit the scope and terms of discovery to that for which "good cause" has been shown, as provided in this paragraph.

(b) A party may obtain discovery of documents and tangible things otherwise discoverable under paragraph (a) of this section and prepared in anticipation of or for the hearing by or for another party's representative (including his or her attorney, consultant, surety, indemnitor, insurer, or agent) only upon a showing that the party seeking discovery has substantial need of the materials or information in the preparation of his or her case and that he or she is unable without undue hardship to obtain the substantial equivalent of the materials or information by other means. In ordering discovery of such materials when the required showing has been made, the administrative law judge shall protect against disclosure of the mental impressions, conclusions, opinions, or legal theories of an attorney or other representative of a party concerning the proceeding.

Promulgated: 53 Fed. Reg. 37476 (9/26/88).

Sec. 2570.8—Summary decision.

For prohibited transaction penalty proceedings, this section shall apply in lieu of §18.41 of this title.

(a) No genuine issue of material fact.

(1) Where no genuine issue of a material fact is found to have been raised, the administrative law judge may issue a decision which, in the absence of an appeal pursuant to Secs. 2570.10-2570.12 of this part, shall become a final order.

(2) A decision made under this paragraph shall include a statement of:

(i) Findings of fact and conclusions of law, and the reasons therefor, on all issues presented; and

(ii) Any terms and conditions of the rule or order.

(3) A copy of any decision under this paragraph shall be served on each party.

(b) Hearings on issue of fact. Where a genuine question of material fact is raised, the administrative law judge shall, and in any other case may, set the case for an evidentiary hearing.

Promulgated: 53 Fed. Reg. 37476 (9/26/88).

Sec. 2570.9—Decision of the administrative law judge.

For prohibited transaction penalty proceedings, this section shall apply in lieu of §18.57 of this title

(a) Proposed findings of fact, conclusions, and order. Within twenty (20) days of the filing of the transcript of the testimony or such additional time as the administrative law judge may allow, each party pay file with the administrative law judge, subject to the judge's discretion, proposed findings of fact, conclusions of law, and order together with a supporting brief expressing the reasons for such proposals.

Such proposals and brief shall be served on all parties, and shall refer to all portions of the record and to all authorities relied upon in support of each proposal.

(b) Decision of the administrative law judge. Within a reasonable time after the time allowed for the filing of the proposed findings of fact, conclusions of law, and order, or within thirty (30) days after receipt of an agreement containing consent findings and order disposing of the disputed matter in whole, the administrative law judge shall make his or her decision. The decision of the administrative law judge shall include findings of fact and conclusions of law with reasons therefor upon each material issue of fact of law presented on the record. The decision of the administrative law judge shall be based upon the whole record. In a contested case in which the Department and the Respondent have presented their positions to the administrative law judge pursuant to the procedures for prohibited transaction penalty proceedings as set forth in this part, the penalty (if any) which may be included in the decision of the administrative law judge shall be limited to the sanction expressly provided for in §502(i) of ERISA. It shall be supported by reliable and probative evidence. The decision of the administrative law judge shall become final agency action within the meaning of 5 U.S.C. 704 unless an appeal is made pursuant to the procedures set forth in Secs. 2570.10 through 2570.12.

Promulgated: 53 Fed. Reg. 37476 (9/26/88).

Sec. 2570.10—Review by the Secretary.

(a) The Secretary may review a decision of an administrative law judge. Such a review may occur only when a party files a notice of appeal from a decision of an administrative law judge within twenty (20) days of the issuance of such decision. In all other cases, the decision of the administrative law judge shall become final agency action within the meaning of 5 U.S.C. 704.

(b) A notice of appeal to the Secretary shall state with specificity the issue(s) in the decision of the administrative law judge on which the party is seeking review. Such notice of appeal must be served on all parties of record.

(c) Upon receipt of a notice of appeal, the Secretary shall request the Chief Administrative Law Judge to submit to him a copy of the entire record before the administrative law judge.

Promulgated: 53 Fed. Reg. 37476 (9/26/88).

Sec. 2570.11—Scope of review.

The review of the Secretary shall not be a de novo proceeding but rather a review of the record established before the administrative law judge. There shall be no opportunity for oral argument.

Promulgated: 53 Fed. Reg. 37476 (9/26/88).

Sec. 2570.12—Procedures for review by the Secretary.

(a) Upon receipt of a notice of appeal, the Secretary shall establish a briefing schedule which shall be served on all parties of record. Upon motion of one or more of the parties, the Secretary may, in his discretion, permit the submission of reply briefs.

(b) The Secretary shall issue a decision as promptly as possible after receipt of the briefs of the parties. The Secretary may affirm, modify, or set aside, in whole or in part, the decision on appeal and shall issue a statement of reasons and bases for the action(s) taken. Such decision by the Secretary shall be final agency action within the meaning of 5 U.S.C. 704.

Subpart B—Procedures for Filing and Processing Prohibited Transaction Exemption Applications

Sec. 2570.30—Scope of rules.

(a)(1) The rules of procedure set forth in this subpart apply to all applications for exemption which the Department has authority to issue under:

(i) §408(a) of the Employee Retirement Income Security Act of 1974 (ERISA);

(ii) §4975(c)(2) of the Internal Revenue Code of 1986 (the Code) (see Reorganization Plan No. 4 of 1978); or

(iii) The Federal Employees' Retirement System Act of 1986 (FERSA) (5 U.S.C. 8477(c)(3)).

(b) The Department will generally treat any exemption application which is filed solely under §408(a) of ERISA or solely under §4975(c)(2) of the Code as an exemption filed under both §408(a) and §4975(c)(2) if it relates to a transaction that would be prohibited both by ERISA and by the corresponding provisions of the Code.

(c) The procedures set forth in this subpart represent the exclusive means by which the Department will issue administrative exemptions. The Department will not issue exemptions upon oral request alone. Likewise, the Department will not grant exemptions orally. An applicant for an administrative exemption may request and receive oral advice from Department employees in preparing an exemption application. However, such advice does not constitute part of the administrative record and is not binding on the Department in its processing of an exemption application or in its examination or audit of a plan.

Promulgated: 55 Fed. Reg. 32847 (8/10/90).

Sec. 2570.31—Definitions.

For purposes of these procedures, the following definitions apply:

(a) An affiliate of a person means—

(1) Any person directly or indirectly through one or more intermediaries, controlling, controlled by, or under common control with the person;

(2) Any director of, relative of, or partner in, any such person;

(3) Any corporation, partnership, trust, or unincorporated enterprise of which such person is an officer, director, or a 5% or more partner or owner; and

(4) Any employee or officer of the person who—

(i) Is highly compensated (as defined in §4975(e)(2)(H) of the Code), or

(ii) Has direct or indirect authority, responsibility, or control regarding the custody, management, or disposition of plan assets.

(b) A class exemption is an administrative exemption, granted under §408(a) of ERISA, §4975(c)(2) of the Code, and/or 5 U.S.C. 8477(c)(3), which applies to any parties in interest within the class of parties in interest specified in the exemption who meet the conditions of the exemption.

(c) Department means the U.S. Department of Labor and includes the Secretary of Labor or his delegate exercising authority with respect to prohibited transaction exemptions to which this subpart applies.

(d) Exemption transaction means the transaction or transactions for which an exemption is requested.

(e) An individual exemption is an administrative exemption, granted under §408(a) of ERISA, §4975(c)(2) of the Code, and/or 5 U.S.C. 8477(c)(3), which applies only to the specific parties in interest named or otherwise defined in the exemption.

(f) A party in interest means a person described in §3(14) of ERISA or 5 U.S.C. 8477(a)(4) and includes a disqualified person, as defined in §4975(e)(2) of the Code.

(g) Pooled fund means an account or fund for the collective investment of the assets of two or more unrelated plans, including (but not limited to) a pooled separate account maintained by an insurance company and a common or collective trust fund maintained by a bank or similar financial institution.

Promulgated: 55 Fed. Reg. 32847 (8/10/90).

Sec. 2570.32—Persons who may apply for exemptions.

(a) The Department may initiate exemption proceedings on its own motion. In addition, the Department will initiate exemption proceedings upon the application of:

(1) Any party in interest to a plan who is or may be a party to the exemption transaction;

(2) Any plan which is a party to the exemption transaction; or

(3) In the case of an application for an exemption covering a class of parties in interest or a class of transactions, in addition to any person described in paragraphs (a)(1) and (a)(2) of this section, an association or organization representing parties in interest who may be parties to the exemption transaction.

(b) An application by or for a person described in paragraph (a) of this section, may be submitted by the applicant or by his authorized representatives. If the application is submitted by a representative of the applicant, the representative must submit proof of his authority in the form of:

(1) A power of attorney; or

(2) A written certification from the applicant that the representation is authorized.

(c) If the authorized representative of an applicant submits an application for an exemption to the Department together with proof of his authority to file the application as required by paragraph (b) of this section, the Department will direct all correspondence and inquiries concerning the application to the representative unless requested to do otherwise by the applicant.

Promulgated: 55 Fed. Reg. 32847 (8/10/90).

Sec. 2570.33—Applications the Department will not ordinarily consider.

(a) The Department will not ordinarily consider:

(1) An application that fails to include all the information required by Secs. 2570.34 and 2570.35 or otherwise fails to conform to the requirements of these procedures; or

(2) An application for exemption involving a transaction or transactions which are the subject of an investigation for possible violations of part 1 or 4 of subtitle B of title I of ERISA or §8477 or 8478 of FERSA or an application for an exemption involving a party in interest who is the subject of such an investigation or who is a defendant in an action by the Department or the Internal Revenue Service to enforce the above-mentioned provisions of ERISA or FERSA.

(b) If for any reason the Department decides not to consider an exemption application, it will inform the applicant of that decision in writing and of the reasons therefor.

(c) An application for an individual exemption relating to a specific transaction or transactions will ordinarily not be considered separately if the Department is considering a class exemption relating to the same type of transaction or transactions.

Promulgated: 55 Fed. Reg. 32847 (8/10/90).

Sec. 2570.34—Information to be included in every exemption application.

(a) All applications for exemptions must contain the following information:

(1) The name(s) of the applicant(s);

(2) A detailed description of the exemption transaction and the parties in interest for whom an exemption is requested, including a description of any larger integrated transaction of which the exemption transaction is a part;

(3) Whether the affected plan(s) and any parties in interest will be represented by the same person with regard to the exemption application;

(4) Reasons a plan would have for entering into the exemption transaction;

(5) The prohibited transaction provisions from which exemptive relief is requested and the reason why the transaction would violate each such provision;

(6) Whether the exemption transaction is customary for the industry or class involved;

(7) Whether the exemption transaction is or has been the subject of an investigation or enforcement action by the Department or by the Internal Revenue Service; and

(8) The hardship or economic loss, if any, which would result to the person or persons on behalf of whom the exemption is sought, to affected plans, and to their participants and beneficiaries from denial of the exemption.

(b) All applications for exemption must also contain the following:

(1) A statement explaining why the requested exemption would be—

(i) Administratively feasible;

(ii) In the interests of affected plans and their participants and beneficiaries; and

(iii) Protective of the rights of participants and beneficiaries of affected plans.

(2) With respect to the notification of interested persons required by §2570.43:

(i) A description of the interested persons to whom the applicant intends to provide notice;

(ii) The manner in which the applicant will provide such notice; and

(iii) An estimate of the time the applicant will need to furnish notice to all interested persons following publication of a notice of the proposed exemption in the Federal Register.

(3) If an advisory opinion has been requested with respect to any issue relating to the exemption transaction—

(i) A copy of the letter concluding the Department's action on the advisory opinion request; or

(ii) If the Department has not yet concluded its action on the request:

(A) A copy of the request or the date on which it was submitted together with the Department's correspondence control number as indicated in the acknowledgment letter; and

(B) An explanation of the effect of a favorable advisory opinion upon the exemption transaction.

(4) If the application is to be signed by anyone other than an individual party in interest seeking exemptive relief on his own behalf, a statement which—

(i) Identifies the individual who will be signing the application and his position with the applicant; and

(ii) Explains briefly the basis of his familiarity with the matters discussed in the application.

(5)(i) A declaration in the following form: Under penalty of perjury, I declare that I am familiar with the matters discussed in this application and, to the best of my knowledge and belief, the representations made in this application are true and correct.

(ii) This declaration must be dated and signed by:

(A) The applicant himself in the case of an individual party in interest seeking exemptive relief on his own behalf;

(B) A corporate officer or partner where the applicant is a corporation or partnership;

(C) A designated officer or official where the applicant is an association, organization or other unincorporated enterprise;

(D) The plan fiduciary who has the authority, responsibility, and control with respect to the exemption transaction where the applicant is a plan.

(iii) Specialized statements from third-party experts, such as appraisals or analyses of market conditions, submitted to support an application for exemption must also be accompanied by a statement of consent from such expert acknowledging that he or she knows that his or her statement is being submitted to the Department as part of an application for exemption.

(iv) For those applications requiring an independent fiduciary to represent the plan in the exemption transaction, each statement submitted by said independent fiduciary must contain a signed and dated declaration under penalty of perjury that, to the best of said fiduciary's knowledge and belief, the representations made in such statement are true and correct.

(c) An application for exemption may also include a draft of the requested exemption which defines the transaction and parties in interest for which exemptive relief is sought and the specific conditions under which the exemption would apply.

Promulgated: 55 Fed. Reg. 32847 (8/10/90).

Sec. 2570.35—Information to be included in applications for individual exemptions only.

(a) Except as provided in paragraph (c) of this section, every application for an individual exemption must include, in addition to the information specified in §2570.34, the following information:

(1) The name, address, telephone number, and type of plan or plans to which the requested exemption applies;

(2) The Employer Identification Number (EIN) and the plan number (PN) used by such plan or plans in all reporting and disclosure required by the Department;

(3) Whether any plan or trust affected by the requested exemption has ever been found by the Department, the Internal Revenue Service, or by a court to have violated the exclusive benefit rule of §401(a) of the Code, or to have engaged in a prohibited transaction under §503(b) of the Code or corresponding provisions of prior law, §4975(c)(1) of the Code, §406 or 407(a) of ERISA, or 5 U.S.C. 8477(c)(3);

(4) Whether any relief under §408(a) of ERISA, §4975(c)(2) of the Code, or 5 U.S.C. 8477(c)(3) has been requested by, or provided to, the applicant or any of the parties on behalf of whom the exemption is sought and, if so, the exemption application number or the prohibited transaction exemption number;

(5) Whether the applicant or any of the parties in interest involved in the exemption transaction is currently, or has been within the last five years, a defendant in any lawsuit or criminal action concerning such person's conduct as a fiduciary or party in interest with respect to any plan;

(6) Whether the applicant or any of the parties in interest involved in the exemption transaction has, within the last 13 years, been convicted of any crime described in §411 of ERISA;

(7) Whether, within the last five years, any plan affected by the exemption transaction or any party in interest involved in the exemption transaction has been under investigation or examination by, or has been engaged in litigation or a continuing controversy with, the Department, the Internal Revenue Service, the Justice Department, the Pension Benefit Guaranty Corporation, or the Federal Retirement Thrift Investment Board involving compliance with provisions of ERISA, provisions of the Code relating to employee benefit plans, or provisions of FERSA relating to the Federal Thrift Savings Fund. If so, the applicant must submit copies of all correspondence with the Department, the Internal Revenue Service, the Justice Department, the Pension Benefit Guaranty Corporation, or the Federal Retirement Thrift Investment Board regarding the substantive issues involved in the investigation, examination, litigation, or controversy which relate to compliance with the provisions of part 1 or 4 of subtitle B of title I of ERISA, §4975 of the Code, or §8477 or 8478 of FERSA. For this purpose, the term "examination" does not include routine audits conducted by the Department pursuant to §8477(g) of FERSA;

(8) Whether any plan affected by the requested exemption has experienced a reportable event under §4043 of ERISA;

(9) Whether a notice of intent to terminate has been filed under §4041 of ERISA respecting any plan affected by the requested exemption;

(10) Names, addresses, and taxpayer identifying numbers of all parties in interest involved in the subject transaction;

(11) The estimated number of participants and beneficiaries in each plan affected by the requested exemption as of the date of the application;

(12) The percentage of the fair market value of the total assets of each affected plan that is involved in the exemption transaction;

(13) Whether the exemption transaction has been consummated or will be consummated only if the exemption is granted;

(14) If the exemption transaction has already been consummated:

(i) The circumstances which resulted in plan fiduciaries causing the plan(s) to engage in the subject transaction before obtaining an exemption from the Department;

(ii) Whether the transaction has been terminated;

(iii) Whether the transaction has been corrected as defined in Code §4975(f)(5);

(iv) Whether Form 5330, Return of Excise Taxes Related to Employee Benefit Plans, has been filed with the Internal Revenue Service with respect to the transaction; and

(v) Whether any excise taxes due under §4975(a) and (b) of the Code by reason of the transaction have been paid.

(15) The name of every person who has investment discretion over any assets involved in the exemption transaction and the relationship of each such person to the parties in interest involved in the exemption transaction and the affiliates of such parties in interest;

(16) Whether or not the assets of the affected plan(s) are invested in loans to any party in interest involved in the exemption transaction, in property leased to any such party in interest, or in securities issued by any such party in interest, and, if such investments exist, a statement for each of these three types of investments which indicates:

(i) The type of investment to which the statement pertains;

(ii) The aggregate fair market value of all investments of this type as reflected in the plan's most recent annual report;

(iii) The approximate percentage of the fair market value of the plan's total assets as shown in such annual report that is represented by all investments of this type; and

(iv) The statutory or administrative exemption covering these investments, if any.

(17) The approximate aggregate fair market value of the total assets of each affected plan;

(18) The person(s) who will bear the costs of the exemption application and of notifying interested persons; and

(19) Whether an independent fiduciary is or will be involved in the exemption transaction and, if so, the names of the persons who will bear the cost of the fee payable to such fiduciary.

(b) Each application for an individual exemption must also include:

(1) True copies of all contracts, deeds, agreements, and instruments, as well as relevant portions of plan documents, trust agreements, and any other documents bearing on the exemption transaction;

(2) A discussion of the facts relevant to the exemption transaction that are reflected in these documents and an analysis of their bearing on the requested exemption; and

(3) A copy of the most recent financial statements of each plan affected by the requested exemption.

(c) Special rule for applications for individual exemption involving pooled funds:

(1) The information required by paragraphs (a) (8) through (12) of this section is not required to be furnished in an application for individual exemption involving one or more pooled funds;

(2) The information required by paragraphs (a) (1) through (7) and (a) (13) through (19) of this section and by paragraphs (b) (1) through (3) of this section must be furnished by reference to the pooled fund, rather than to the plans participating therein. (For purposes of this paragraph, the information required by paragraph (a) (16) of this section relates solely to other pooled fund transactions with, and investments in, parties in interest involved in the exemption transaction which are also sponsors of plans which invest in the pooled fund.);

(3) The following information must also be furnished—

(i) The estimated number of plans that are participating (or will participate) in the pooled fund; and

(ii) The minimum and maximum limits imposed by the pooled fund (if any) on the portion of the total assets of each plan that may be invested in the pooled fund.

(4) Additional requirements for applications for individual exemption involving pooled funds in which certain plans participate.

(i) This paragraph applies to any application for individual exemption involving one or more pooled funds in which any plan participating therein—

(A) Invests an amount which exceeds 20% of the total assets of the pooled fund, or

(B) Covers employees of:

(I) The party sponsoring or maintaining the pooled fund, or any affiliate of such party, or

(II) Any fiduciary with investment discretion over the pooled fund's assets, or any affiliate of such fiduciary.

(ii) The exemption application must include, with respect to each plan described in paragraph (c)(4)(i) of this section, the information required by paragraphs (a) (1) through (3), (a) (5) through (7), (a) (10), (a) (12) through (16) and, (a) (18) and (19), of this section. The information required by this paragraph must be furnished by reference to the plan's investment in the pooled fund (e.g., the names, addresses and taxpayer identifying numbers of all fiduciaries responsible for the plan's investment in the pooled fund [§2570.35(a) (10)], the percentage of the assets of the plan invested in the pooled fund [§2570.35(a) (12)], whether the plan's investment in the pooled fund has been consummated or will be consummated only if the exemption is granted [§2570.35(a) (13)], etc.).

(iii) The information required by paragraph (c) (4) of this section is in addition to the information required by paragraphs (c) (2) and (3) of this section relating to information furnished by reference to the pooled fund.

(5) The special rule and the additional requirements described in paragraphs (c) (1) through (4) of this section do not apply to an individual exemption request solely for the investment by a plan in a pooled fund. Such an application must provide the information required by paragraphs (a) and (b) of this section.

Promulgated: 55 Fed. Reg. 25286 (6/20/90); (Effective 6/20/90—Interim Regulation).

Sec. 2570.36—Where to file an application.

The Department's prohibited transaction exemption program is administered by the Pension and Welfare Benefits Administration (PWBA). Any exemption application governed by these procedures should be mailed or otherwise delivered to: Exemption Application, PWBA, Office of Exemption Determinations, Division of Exemptions, U.S. Department of Labor, 200 Constitution Avenue NW., Washington, D.C. 20210.

Promulgated: 55 Fed. Reg. 25286 (6/20/90); (Effective 6/20/90—Interim Regulation).

Sec. 2570.37—Duty to amend and supplement exemption applications.

(a) During the pendency of his exemption application, an applicant must promptly notify the Division of Exemptions in writing if he discovers that any material fact or representation contained in his application or in any documents or testimony provided in support of the application is inaccurate, if any such fact or representation changes during this period, or if, during the pendency of the application, anything occurs that may affect the continuing accuracy of any such fact or representation.

(b) If, at any time during the pendency of his exemption application, an applicant or any other party in interest who would participate in the exemption transaction becomes the subject of an investigation or enforcement action by the Department, the Internal Revenue Service, the Justice Department, the Pension Benefit Guaranty Corporation, or the Federal Retirement Thrift Investment Board involving compliance with provisions of ERISA, provisions of the Code relating to employee benefit plans, or provisions of FERSA relating to the Federal Thrift Savings Fund, the applicant must promptly notify the Division of Exemptions.

(c) The Department may require an applicant to provide documentation it considers necessary to verify any statements contained in the application or in supporting materials or documents.

Promulgated: 55 Fed. Reg. 25286 (6/20/90); (Effective 6/20/90—Interim Regulation).

Sec. 2570.38—Tentative denial letters.

(a) If, after reviewing an exemption file, the Department concludes that it will not grant the exemption, it will notify the applicant in writing of its tentative denial of the exemption application. At the same time, the Department will provide a short statement of the reasons for its tentative denial.

(b) An applicant will have 20 days from the date of a tentative denial letter to request a conference under §2570.40 of these procedures and/or to notify the Department of its intent to submit additional information in writing under §2570.39 of these procedures. If the Department does not receive a request for a conference or a notification of intent to submit additional information within that time, it will issue a final denial letter pursuant to §2570.41.

(c) The Department need not issue a tentative denial letter to an applicant before issuing a final denial letter where the Department has conducted a hearing on the exemption pursuant to either §2570.46 or §2570.47 of these procedures.

Promulgated: 55 Fed. Reg. 25286 (6/20/90); (Effective 6/20/90—Interim Regulation).

Sec. 2570.39—Opportunities to submit additional information.

(a) An applicant may notify the Department of its intent to submit additional information supporting an exemption application either by telephone or by letter sent to the address furnished in the applicant's tentative denial letter. At the same time, the applicant should indicate generally the type of information that he will submit.

(b) An applicant will have 30 days from the date of the notification discussed in paragraph (a) of this section to submit in writing all of the additional information he intends to provide in support of his application. All such information must be accompanied by a declaration under penalty of perjury attesting to the truth and correctness of the information provided, which is dated and signed by a person qualified under §2570.34(b)(5) of these procedures to sign such a declaration.

(c) If, for reasons beyond his control, an applicant is unable to submit in writing all the additional information he intends to provide in support of his application within the 30-day period described in paragraph (b) of this section, he may request an extension of time to furnish the information. Such requests must be made before the expiration of the 30-day period and will be granted only in unusual circumstances and for limited periods of time.

(d) If an applicant is unable to submit all of the additional information he intends to provide in support of his exemption application within the 30-day period specified in paragraph (b) of this section, or within any additional period of time granted to him pursuant to paragraph (c) of this section, the applicant may withdraw the exemption application before expiration of the applicable time period and reinstate it later pursuant to §2570.44 of these procedures.

(e) The Department will issue, without further notice, a final denial letter denying the requested exemption pursuant to §2570.41 of these procedures where—

(1) The Department has not received the additional information that the applicant indicated he would submit within the 30-day period described in paragraph (b) of this section, or within any additional period of time granted pursuant to paragraph (c) of this section;

(2) The applicant did not request a conference pursuant to §2570.38(b) of these procedures; and

(3) The applicant has not withdrawn his application as permitted by paragraph (d) of this section.

Promulgated: 55 Fed. Reg. 25286 (6/20/90); (Effective 6/20/90—Interim Regulation).

Sec. 2570.40—Conferences.

(a) Any conference between the Department and an applicant pertaining to a requested exemption will be held in Washington, DC, except that a telephone conference will be held at the applicant's request.

(b) An applicant is entitled to only one conference with respect to any exemption application. An applicant will not be entitled to a conference, however, where the Department has held a hearing on the exemption under either §2570.46 or §2570.47 of these procedures.

(c) Insofar as possible, conferences will be scheduled as joint conferences with all applicants present where:

(1) More than one applicant has requested an exemption with respect to the same or similar types of transactions;

(2) The Department is considering the applications together as a request for a class exemption;

(3) The Department contemplates not granting the exemption; and

(4) More than one applicant has requested a conference.

(d) The Department will attempt to schedule a conference under this section for a mutually convenient time during the 45-day period following the later of—

(1) The date the Department receives the applicant's request for a conference, or

(2) The date the Department notifies the applicant, after reviewing additional information submitted pursuant to §2570.39, that it is still not prepared to propose the requested exemption. If the applicant is unable to attend a conference at any of the times proposed by the Department during this 45-day period or if the applicant fails to appear for a scheduled conference, he will be deemed to have waived his right to a conference unless circumstances beyond his control prevent him from scheduling a conference or attending a scheduled conference within this period.

(e) Within 20 days after the date of any conference held under this section, the applicant may submit to the Department a written record of any additional data, arguments, or precedents discussed at the conference but not previously or adequately presented in writing.

Promulgated: 55 Fed. Reg. 25286 (6/20/90); (Effective 6/20/90—Interim Regulation).

Sec. 2570.41—Final denial letters.

(a) The Department will issue a final denial letter denying a requested exemption where:

(1) The conditions for issuing a final denial letter specified in §2570.38(b) or §2570.39(e) of these procedures are satisfied;

(2) After issuing a tentative denial letter under §2570.38 of this part and considering the entire record in the case, including all written information submitted pursuant to §2570.39 and §2570.40(e) of these procedures, the Department decides not to propose an exemption or to withdraw an exemption already proposed; or

(3) After proposing an exemption and conducting a hearing on the exemption under either §2570.46 or §2570.47 of this part and after considering the entire record in the case, including the record of the hearing, the Department decides to withdraw the proposed exemption.

Promulgated: 55 Fed. Reg. 25286 (6/20/90); (Effective 6/20/90—Interim Regulation).

Sec. 2570.42—Notice of proposed exemption.

If the Department tentatively decides, based on all the information submitted by an applicant, that the exemption should be granted, it will publish a notice of proposed exemption in the Federal Register. The notice will:

(a) Explain the exemption transaction and summarize the information received by the Department in support of the exemption;

(b) Specify any conditions under which the exemption is proposed;

(c) Inform interested persons of their right to submit comments in writing to the Department relating to the proposed exemption and establish a deadline for receipt of such comments;

(d) If the proposed exemption includes relief from the prohibitions of §406(b) of ERISA, §4975(c)(1) (E) or (F) of the Code, or §8477(c)(2) of FERSA, inform interested persons of their right to request a hearing under §2570.46 of this part and establish a deadline for receipt of requests for such hearings.

Promulgated: 55 Fed. Reg. 25286 (6/20/90); (Effective 6/20/90—Interim Regulation).

Sec. 2570.43—Notification of interested persons by applicant.

(a) If, as set forth in the exemption application, the notification that an applicant intends to provide to interested persons upon publication of a notice of proposed exemption in the Federal Register is inadequate, the Department will so inform the applicant and will secure the applicant's written agreement to provide what it considers to be adequate notice under the circumstances.

(b) If a notice of proposed exemption is published in the Federal Register in accordance with §2570.42 of this part, the applicant must notify interested persons of the pendency of the exemption in the manner and time period specified in the application or in any superseding agreement with the Department. Any such notification must include:

(1) A copy of the notice of proposed exemption; and

(2) A supplemental statement in the following form:

You are hereby notified that the United States Department of Labor is considering granting an exemption from the prohibited transaction restrictions of the Employee Retirement Income Security Act of 1974, the Internal Revenue Code of 1986, or the Federal Employees' Retirement System Act of 1986. The exemption under consideration is explained in the enclosed Notice of Proposed Exemption. As a person who may be affected by this exemption, you have the right to comment on the proposed exemption by [date].[1] [If you may be adversely affected by the grant of the exemption, you also have the right to request a hearing on the exemption by [date].][2]

Comments or requests for a hearing should be addressed to: Office of Exemption Determinations, Pension and Welfare Benefits Administration, room ,[3] U.S. Department of Labor, 200 Constitution Avenue NW., Washington, DC 20210, ATTENTION: Application No. .[4]

The Department will make no final decision on the proposed exemption until it reviews all comments received in response to the enclosed notice. If the Department decides to hold a hearing on the exemption before making its final decision, you will be notified of the time and place of the hearing.

(c) The method used to furnish notice to interested persons must be reasonably calculated to ensure that interested persons actually receive the notice. In all cases, personal delivery and delivery by first-class mail will be considered reasonable methods of furnishing notice.

(d) After furnishing the notice required by this section, an applicant must provide the Department with a statement confirming that notice was furnished to the persons and in the manner and time designated in its exemption application or in any superseding agreement with the Department. This statement must be accompanied by a declaration under penalty of perjury attesting to the truth of the information provided in the statement and signed by a person qualified under §2570.34(b)(5) of these procedures to sign such a declaration. No exemption will be granted until such a statement and its accompanying declaration have been furnished to the Department.

[1] The applicant will write in this space the date of the last day of the time period specified in the notice of proposed exemption.

[2] To be added in the case of an exemption that provides relief from §406(b) of ERISA or corresponding sections of the Code or FERSA.

[3] The applicant will fill in the room number of the Division of Exemptions. As of the date of this final regulation, the room number of the Division of Exemptions was N-5671.

[4] The applicant will fill in the exemption application number, which is stated in the notice of proposed exemption, as well as in all correspondence from the Department to the applicant regarding the application.

Promulgated: 55 Fed. Reg. 32847 (8/10/90).

Sec. 2570.44—Withdrawal of exemption applications.

(a) An applicant may withdraw his application for an exemption at any time by informing the Department, either orally or in writing, of his intent to withdraw.

(b) Upon receiving an applicant's notice of intent to withdraw an application for an individual exemption, the Department will confirm by letter the applicant's withdrawal of the application and will terminate all proceedings relating to the application. If a notice of proposed exemption has been published in the Federal Register, the Department will publish a notice withdrawing the proposed exemption.

(c) Upon receiving an applicant's notice of intent to withdraw an application for a class exemption or for an individual exemption that is being considered with other applications as a request for a class exemption, the Department will inform any other applicants for the exemption of the withdrawal. The Department will continue to process other applications for the same exemption. If all applicants for a particular class exemption withdraw their applications, the Department may either terminate all proceedings relating to the exemption or propose the exemption on its own motion.

(d) If, following the withdrawal of an exemption application, an applicant decides to reapply for the same exemption, he may submit a letter to the Department requesting that the application be reinstated and referring to the application number assigned to the original application. If, at the time the original application was withdrawn, any additional information to be submitted to the Department under §2570.39 of these procedures was outstanding, that information must accompany the letter requesting reinstatement of the application. However, the applicant need not resubmit information previously furnished to the Department in connection with a withdrawn application unless reinstatement of the application is requested more than two years after the date of its withdrawal.

(e) Any request for reinstatement of a withdrawn application submitted in accordance with paragraph (d) of this section, will be granted by the Department, and the Department will take whatever steps remained at the time the application was withdrawn to process the application.

Promulgated: 55 Fed. Reg. 32847 (8/10/90).

Sec. 2570.45—Requests for reconsideration.

(a) The Department will entertain one request for reconsideration of an exemption application that has been finally denied pursuant to §2570.41 (a)(2) or (a)(3) of this part if the applicant presents in support of the application significant new facts or arguments, which, for good reason, could not have been submitted for the Department's consideration during its initial review of the exemption application.

(b) A request for reconsideration of a previously denied application must be made within 180 days after the issuance of the final denial letter and must be accompanied by a copy of the Department's final letter denying the exemption and a statement setting forth the new information and/or arguments that provide basis for reconsideration.

(c) A request for reconsideration must also be accompanied by a declaration under penalty of perjury attesting to the truth of the new information provided, which is signed by a person qualified under §2570.34(b)(5) of these procedures to sign such a declaration.

(d) If, after reviewing a request for reconsideration, the Department decides that the facts and arguments presented do not warrant reversal of its original decision to deny the exemption, it will send a letter to the applicant reaffirming that decision.

(e) If, after reviewing a request for reconsideration, the Department decides, based on the new facts and arguments submitted, to reconsider its denial letter, it will notify the applicant of its intent to reconsider the application in light of the new information presented. The Department will then take whatever steps remained at the time it issued its final denial letter to process the exemption application.

(f) If, at any point during its subsequent processing of the application, the Department decides again that the exemption is unwarranted, it will issue a letter affirming its final denial.

Promulgated: 55 Fed. Reg. 32847 (8/10/90).

Sec. 2570.46—Hearings in opposition to exemptions from restrictions on fiduciary self-dealing.

(a) Any interested person who may be adversely affected by an exemption which the Department proposes to grant from the restrictions of §406(b) of ERISA, §4975(c)(1)(E) or (F) of the Code, or §8477(c)(2) of FERSA may request a hearing before the Department within the period of time specified in the Federal Register notice of the proposed exemption. Any such request must state:

(1) The name, address, and telephone number of the person making the request;

(2) The nature of the person's interest in the exemption and the manner in which the person would be adversely affected by the exemption; and

(3) A statement of the issues to be addressed and a general description of the evidence to be presented at the hearing.

(b) The Department will grant a request for a hearing made in accordance with paragraph (a) of this section where a hearing is necessary to fully explore material factual issues identified by the person requesting the hearing. However, the Department may decline to hold a hearing where:

(1) The request for the hearing does not meet the requirements of paragraph (a);

(2) The only issues identified for exploration at the hearing are matters of law; or

(3) The factual issues identified can be fully explored through the submission of evidence in written form.

(c) An applicant for an exemption must notify interested persons in the event that the Department schedules a hearing on the exemption. Such notification must be given in the form, time, and manner prescribed by the Department. Ordinarily, however, adequate notification can be given by providing to interested persons a copy of the notice of hearing published by the Department in the Federal Register within 10 days of its publication, using any of the methods approved in §2570.43(c) of this part.

(d) After furnishing the notice required by paragraph (c) of this section, an applicant must submit a statement confirming that notice was given in the form, manner, and time prescribed. This statement must be accompanied by a declaration under penalty of perjury attesting to the truth of the information provided in the statement, which is signed by a person qualified under §2570.34(b)(5) of these procedures to sign such a declaration.

Promulgated: 55 Fed. Reg. 32847 (8/10/90).

Sec. 2570.47—Other hearings.

(a) In its discretion, the Department may schedule a hearing on its own motion where it determines that issues relevant to the exemption can be most fully or expeditiously explored at a hearing.

(b) An applicant for an exemption must notify interested persons of any hearing on an exemption scheduled by the Department in the manner described in §2570.46(c). In addition, the applicant must submit a statement subscribed as true under penalty of perjury like that required in §2570.46(d).

Promulgated: 55 Fed. Reg. 32847 (8/10/90).

Sec. 2570.48—Decision to grant exemptions.

(a) If, after considering all the facts and representations submitted by an applicant in support of an exemption application, all the comments received in response to a notice of proposed exemption, and the record of any hearing held in connection with the proposed exemption, the Department determines that the exemption should be granted, it will publish a notice in the Federal Register granting the exemption.

(b) A Federal Register notice granting an exemption will summarize the transaction or transactions for which exemptive relief has been granted and will specify the conditions under which such exemptive relief is available.

Promulgated: 55 Fed. Reg. 32847 (8/10/90).

Sec. 2570.49—Limits on the effect of exemptions.

(a) An exemption does not take effect or protect parties in interest from liability with respect to the exemption transaction unless the material facts and representations contained in the application and in any materials and documents submitted in support of the application were true and complete.

(b) An exemption is effective only for the period of time specified and only under the conditions set forth in the exemption.

(c) Only the specific parties to whom an exemption grants relief may rely on the exemption. If the notice granting an exemption does not limit exemptive relief to specific parties, all parties to the exemption transaction may rely on the exemption.

Promulgated: 55 Fed. Reg. 32847 (8/10/90).

Sec. 2570.50—Revocation or modification of exemptions.

(a) If, after an exemption takes effect, changes in circumstances, including changes in law or policy, occur which call into question the continuing validity of the Department's original conclusions concerning the exemption, the Department may take steps to revoke or modify the exemption.

(b) Before revoking or modifying an exemption, the Department will publish a notice of its proposed action in the Federal Register and provide interested persons with an opportunity to comment on the proposed revocation or modification. In addition, the Department will give the applicant at least 30 days notice in writing of the proposed revocation or modification and the reasons therefor and will provide the applicant with the opportunity to comment on the revocation or modification.

(c) Ordinarily the revocation or modification of an exemption will have prospective effect only.

Promulgated: 55 Fed. Reg. 32847 (8/10/90).

Sec. 2570.51—Public inspection and copies.

(a) The administrative record of each exemption application will be open to public inspection and copying at the Public Disclosure Branch, PWBA, U.S. Department of Labor, 200 Constitution Avenue, N.W., Washington, D.C. 20210.

(b) Upon request, the staff of the Public Disclosure Branch will furnish photocopies of an administrative record, or any specified portion of that record, for a specified charge per page.

Promulgated: 55 Fed. Reg. 32847 (8/10/90).

Sec. 2570.52—Effective date.

This regulation is effective with respect to all applications for exemptions filed with the Department under §408(a) of ERISA, §4975(c)(2) of the Code, or 5 U.S.C. 8477(c)(3) at any time on or after September 10, 1990. Applications for exemptions under §408(a) of ERISA and/or §4975 of the Code filed before September 10, 1990, are governed by ERISA Procedure 75-1. Applications for exemption under 5 U.S.C. 8477(c)(3) filed before September 10, 1990, but after December 29, 1988 are governed by part 2585 of chapter XXV of title 29 of the Code of Federal Regulations, (§29 CFR part 2585 as revised July 1, 1990). Applications under 5 U.S.C. 8477(c)(3) filed before December 29, 1988 are governed by ERISA Procedure 75-1.

Promulgated: 55 Fed. Reg. 32847 (8/10/90).

Subpart C—Procedures for the Assessment of Civil Penalties Under ERISA §502(c)(2)

Sec. 2570.60—Scope of rules.

The rules of practice set forth in this subpart are applicable to "502(c)(2) civil penalty proceedings" (as defined in §2570.61(n) of this subpart) under §502(c)(2) of the Employee Retirement Income Security Act of 1974. The rules of procedure for administrative hearings published by the Department's Office of Law Judges at Part 18 of this Title will apply to matters arising under ERISA §502(c)(2) except as modified by this section. These proceedings shall be conducted as expeditiously as possible, and the parties shall make every effort to avoid delay at each stage of the proceedings.

Promulgated: 54 Fed. Reg. 26897 (6/26/89).

Sec. 2570.61—Definitions.

For 502(c)(2) civil penalty proceedings, this section shall apply in lieu of the definitions in §18.2 of this title:

(a) "Adjudicatory proceeding" means a judicial-type proceeding before an administrative law judge leading to the formulation of a final order;

(b) "Administrative law judge" means an administrative law judge appointed pursuant to the provisions of 5 U.S.C. 3105;

(c) "Answer" is defined for these proceedings as set forth in §18.5(d)(1) of this title;

(d) "Commencement of proceeding" is the filing of an answer by the respondent;

(e) "Consent agreement" means any written document containing a specified proposed remedy or other relief acceptable to the Department and consenting parties;

(f) "ERISA" means the Employee Retirement Income Security Act of 1974, as amended;

(g) "Final Order" means the final decision or action of the Department of Labor concerning the assessment of a civil penalty under ERISA §502(c)(2) against a particular party. Such final order may result from a decision of an administrative law judge or the Secretary, the failure of a party to file a statement of reasonable cause described in §2560.502c-2(e) within the prescribed time limits, or the failure of a party to invoke the procedures for hearings or appeals under this title within the prescribed time limits. Such a final order shall constitute final agency action within the meaning of 5 USC 704;

(h) "Hearing" means that part of a proceeding which involves the submission of evidence, either by oral presentation or written submission, to the administrative law judge;

(i) "Order" means the whole or any part of a final procedural or substantive disposition of a matter under ERISA §502(c)(2);

(j) "Party" includes a person or agency named or admitted as a party to a proceeding;

(k) "Person" includes an individual, partnership, corporation, employee benefit plan, association, exchange or other entity or organization;

(l) "Petition" means a written request, made by a person or party, for some affirmative action;

(m) "Pleading" means the notice as defined in §2560.502c-2(g), the answer to the notice, any supplement or amendment thereto, and any reply that may be permitted to any answer, supplement or amendment;

(n) "502(c)(2) civil penalty proceeding" means an adjudicatory proceeding relating to the assessment of a civil penalty provided for in §502(c)(2) of ERISA;

(o) "Respondent" means the party against whom the Department is seeking to assess a civil sanction under ERISA §502(c)(2);

(p) "Secretary" means the Secretary of Labor and includes, pursuant to any delegation of authority by the Secretary, any assistant secretary (including the Assistant Secretary for Pension and Welfare Benefits), administrator, commissioner, appellate body, board, or other official; and

(q) "Solicitor" means the Solicitor of Labor or his or her delegate.

Promulgated: 54 Fed. Reg. 26897 (6/26/89).

Sec. 2570.62—Service: Copies of documents and pleadings.

For 502(c)(2) penalty proceedings, this section shall apply in lieu of §18.3 of this title.

(a) General. Copies of all documents shall be served on all parties of record. All documents should clearly designate the docket number, if any, and short title of all matters. All documents to be filed shall be delivered or mailed to the Chief Docket Clerk, Office of Administrative Law Judges, Suite 700, 1111 20th Street, N.W., Washington, D.C. 20036, or to the OALJ Regional Office to which the proceeding may have been transferred for hearing. Each document filed shall be clear and legible.

(b) By parties. All motions petitions, pleadings, briefs, or other documents shall be filed with the Office of Administrative Law Judges with a copy, including any attachments, to all other parties or record. When a party is represented by an attorney, service shall be made upon the attorney. Service of any document upon any party may be made by personal delivery or by mailing a copy to the last known address. The Department shall be served by delivery to the Associate Solicitor, Plan Benefits Security Division, ERISA §502(c)(2) Proceeding, P.O. Box 1914, Washington, D.C. 20013. The person serving the document shall certify to the manner and date of service.

(c) By the Office of Administrative Law Judges. Service of orders, decisions and all other documents shall be made by regular mail to the last known address.

(d) Form of pleadings.

(1) Every pleading shall contain information indicating the name of the Pension and Welfare Benefits Administration (PWBA) as the agency under which the proceeding is instituted, the title of the proceeding, the docket number (if any) assigned by the Office of Administrative Law Judges and a designation of the type of pleading or paper (e.g., notice, motion to dismiss, etc.). The pleading or paper shall be signed and shall contain the address and telephone number of the party or person representing the party. Although there are no formal specifications for documents, they should be typewritten when possible on standard size 8 1/2 × 11 inch paper.

(2) Illegible documents, whether handwritten, typewritten, photocopies, or otherwise, will not be accepted. Papers may be reproduced by any duplicating process provided all copies are clear and legible.

Promulgated: 54 Fed. Reg. 26897 (6/26/89).

Sec. 2570.63—Parties, how designated.

For 502(c)(2) civil penalty proceedings, this section shall apply in lieu of §18.10 of this title.

(a) The term "party" wherever used in these rules shall include any natural person, corporation, employee benefit plan, association, firm, partnership, trustee, receiver, agency, public or private organization, or government agency. A party against whom a civil penalty is sought shall be designated as "respondent." The Department shall be designated as the "complainant."

(b) Other persons or organizations shall be permitted to participate as parties only if the administrative law judge finds that the final decision could directly and adversely affect them or the class they represent, that they may contribute materially to the disposition of the proceedings and their interest is not adequately represented by existing parties, and that in the discretion of the administrative law judge the participation of such persons or organizations would be appropriate.

(c) A person or organization not named as a respondent wishing to participate as a party under this section shall submit a petition to the administrative law judge within fifteen (15) days after the person or organization has knowledge of or should have known about the proceeding. The petition shall be filed with the administrative law judge and served on each person or organization who has been made a party at the time of filing. Such petition shall concisely state:

(1) Petitioner's interest in the proceeding;

(2) How his or her participation as a party will contribute materially to the disposition of the proceeding;

(3) Who will appear for petitioner;

(4) The issues on which petitioner wishes to participate; and

(5) Whether petitioner intends to present witnesses.

(d) Objections to the petition may be filed by a party within fifteen (15) days of the filing of the petition. If objections to the petition are filed, the administrative law judge shall then determine whether petitioners have the requisite interest to be a party in the proceedings, as defined in paragraph (b) of this section, and shall permit or deny participation accordingly. Where petitions to participate as parties are made by individuals or groups with common interests, the administrative law judge may request all such petitioners to designate a single representative, or he or she may recognize one or more of such petitioners. The administrative law judge shall give each such petitioner as well as the parties, written notice of the decision on his or her petition. For each petition granted, the administrative law judge shall provide a brief statement of the basis of the decision. If the petition is denied, he or she shall briefly state the grounds for denial and shall then treat the petition as a request for participation as amicus curiae.

Promulgated: 54 Fed. Reg. 26897 (6/26/89).

Sec. 2570.64—Consequences of default.

For 502(c)(2) civil penalty proceedings, this section shall apply in lieu of §18.5 (a) and (b) of this title. Failure of the respondent to file an answer to the notice of determination described in §2560.502c-2(g) within the 30-day period provided by §2560.502c-2(h) shall be deemed to constitute a waiver of his or her right to appear and contest the allegations of the notice of determination, and such failure shall be deemed to be an admission of the facts as alleged in the notice for purposes of any proceeding involving the assessment of a civil penalty under §502(c)(2). Such notice shall then become the final order of the Secretary.

Promulgated: 54 Fed. Reg. 26897 (6/26/89).

Sec. 2570.65—Consent order or settlement.

For 502(c)(2) civil penalty proceedings, the following shall apply in lieu of §18.9 of this title.

(a) General. At any time after the commencement of a proceeding, but at least five (5) days prior to the date set for hearing, the parties jointly may move to defer the hearing for a reasonable time to permit negotiation of a settlement or an agreement containing findings and an order disposing of the whole or any part of the proceeding. The allowance of such and the duration thereof shall be in the discretion of the administrative law judge, after consideration of such factors as the nature of the proceeding, the requirements of the public interest, the representations of the parties and the probability of reaching an agreement which will result in a just disposition of the issues involved.

(b) Content. Any agreement containing consent findings and an order disposing of a proceeding or any part thereof shall also provide:

(1) That the order shall have the same force and effect as an order made after full hearing;

(2) That the entire record on which any order may be based shall consist solely of the notice and the agreement;

(3) A waiver of any further procedural steps before the administrative law judge;

(4) A waiver of any right to challenge or contest the validity of the order and decision entered into in accordance with the agreement; and

(5) That the order and decision of the administrative law judge shall be final agency action.

(c) Submission. On or before the expiration of the time granted for negotiations, but, in any case, at least five (5) days prior to the date set for hearing, the parties or their authorized representative or their counsel may:

(1) Submit the proposed agreement containing consent findings and an order to the administrative law judge; or

(2) Notify the administrative law judge that the parties have reached a full settlement and have agreed to dismissal of the action subject to compliance with the terms of the settlement; or

(3) Inform the administrative law judge that agreement cannot be reached.

(d) Disposition. In the event a settlement agreement containing consent findings and an order is submitted within the time allowed therefore, the administrative law judge shall issue a decision incorporating such findings and agreement within thirty (30) days of his receipt of such document. The decision of the administrative law judge shall incorporate all of the findings, terms, and conditions of the settlement agreement and consent order of the parties. Such decision shall become final agency action within the meaning of 5 U.S.C. 704.

(e) Settlement without consent of all parties. In cases in which some, but not all, of the parties to a proceeding submit a consent agreement to the administrative law judge, the following procedure shall apply:

(1) If all of the parties have not consented to the proposed settlement submitted to the administrative law judge, then such non-consenting parties must receive notice, and a copy, of the proposed settlement at the time it is submitted to the administrative law judge;

(2) Any non-consenting party shall have fifteen (15) days to file any objections to the proposed settlement with the administrative law judge and all other parties;

(3) If any party submits an objection to the proposed settlement, the administrative law judge shall decide within thirty (30) days after receipt of such objections whether he shall sign or reject the proposed settlement. Where the record lacks substantial evidence upon which to base a decision or there is a genuine issue of material fact, then the administrative law judge may establish procedures for the purpose of receiving additional evidence upon which a decision on the contested issues may reasonably be based;

(4) If there are no objections to the proposed settlement, or if the administrative law judge decides to sign the proposed settlement after reviewing any such objections, the administrative law judge shall incorporate the consent agreement into a decision meeting the requirements of paragraph (d) of this section.

Promulgated: 54 Fed. Reg. 26897 (6/26/89).

Sec. 2570.66—Scope of discovery.

For 502(c)(2) civil penalty proceedings, this section shall apply in lieu of §18.14 of this title.

(a) A party may file a motion to conduct discovery with the administrative law judge. The motion for discovery shall be granted by the administrative law judge only upon a showing of good cause. In order to establish "good cause" for the purposes of this section, a party must show that the discovery requested relates to a genuine issue as to a material fact that is relevant to the proceeding. The order of the administrative law judge shall expressly limit the scope and terms of discovery to that for which "good cause" has been shown, as provided in this paragraph.

(b) A party may obtain discovery of documents and tangible things otherwise discoverable under paragraph (a) of this section and prepared in anticipation of or for the hearing by or for another party's representative (including his or her attorney, consultant, surety, indemnitor, insurer, or agent) only upon showing that the party seeking discovery has substantial need of the materials or information in the preparation of his or her case and that he or she is unable without undue hardship to obtain the substantial equivalent of the materials or information by other means. In ordering discovery of such materials when the required showing has been made, the administrative law judge shall protect against disclosure of the mental impressions, conclusions, opinions, or legal theories of an attorney or other representatives of a party concerning the proceeding.

Promulgated: 54 Fed. Reg. 26897 (6/26/89).

Sec. 2570.67—Summary decision.

For 502(c)(2) civil penalty proceedings, this section shall apply in lieu of §18.41 of this title.

(a) No genuine issue of material of fact.

(1) Where no issue of a material of fact is found to have been raised, the administrative law judge may issue a decision which, in the absence of an appeal pursuant to Secs. 2570.69 through 71 of this subpart, shall become a final order.

(2) A decision made under this paragraph shall include a statement of:

(i) Findings of fact and conclusions of law, and the reasons therefor, on all issues presented; and

(ii) Any terms and conditions of the rule or order.

(3) A copy of any decision under this paragraph shall be served on each party.

(b) Hearings on issues of fact. Where a genuine question of material of fact is raised, the administrative law judge shall, and in any other case may, set the case for an evidentiary hearing.

Promulgated: 54 Fed. Reg. 26897 (6/26/89).

Sec. 2570.68—Decision of the administrative law judge.

For 502(c)(2) civil penalty proceedings, this section shall apply in lieu of §18.57 of this title.

(a) Proposed findings of fact, conclusions, and order. Within twenty (20) days of the filing of the transcript of the testimony of such additional time as the administrative law judge may allow, each party may file with the administrative law judge, subject to the judge's discretion, proposed findings of fact, conclusions of law, and order together with a supporting brief expressing the reasons for such proposals. Such proposals and briefs shall be served on all parties, and shall refer to all portions of the record and to all authorities relied upon in support of each proposal.

(b) Decision of the administrative law judge. Within a reasonable time after the time allowed for the filing of the proposed findings of fact, conclusions of law, and order, or within thirty (30) days after receipt of an agreement containing consent findings and order disposing of the disputed matter in whole, the administrative law judge shall make his or her decision. The decision of the administrative law judge shall include findings of fact and conclusions of law with reasons therefor upon each material issue of fact or law presented on the record. The decision of the administrative law judge shall be based upon the whole record. In a contested case in which the Department and the Respondent have presented their positions to the administrative law judge pursuant to the procedures for 502(c)(2) civil penalty proceedings as set forth in this subpart, the penalty (if any) which may be included in the decision of the administrative law judge shall be limited to the penalty expressly provided for in §502(c)(2) of ERISA. It shall be supported by reliable and probative evidence. The decision of the administrative law judge shall become final agency action within the meaning of 5 U.S.C. 704 unless an appeal is made pursuant to the procedures set forth in Secs. 2570.69 through 2570.71.

Promulgated: 54 Fed. Reg. 26897 (6/26/89).

Sec. 2570.69—Review by the Secretary.

(a) The Secretary may review a decision of an administrative law judge. Such a review may occur only when a party files a notice of appeal from a decision of an administrative law judge within twenty (20) days of the issuance of such decision. In all other cases, the decision of the administrative law judge shall become final agency action within the meaning of 5 U.S.C. 704.

(b) A notice of appeal to the Secretary shall state with specificity the issue(s) in the decision of the administrative law judge on which the party is seeking review. Such notice of appeal must be served on all parties of record.

(c) Upon receipt of a notice of appeal, the Secretary shall request the Chief Administrative Law Judge to submit to him or her a copy of the entire record before the administrative law judge.

Promulgated: 54 Fed. Reg. 26897 (6/26/89).

Sec. 2570.70—Scope of review.

The review of the Secretary shall not be de novo proceeding but rather a review of the record established before the administrative law judge. There shall be no opportunity for oral argument.

Promulgated: 54 Fed. Reg. 26897 (6/26/89).

Sec. 2570.71—Procedures for review by the Secretary.

(a) Upon receipt of the notice of appeal, the Secretary shall establish a briefing schedule which shall be served on all parties of record. Upon motion of one or more of the parties, the Secretary may, in his or her discretion, permit the submission of reply briefs.

(b) The Secretary shall issue a decision as promptly as possible after receipt of the briefs of the parties. The Secretary may affirm, modify, or set aside, in whole or in part, the decision on appeal and shall issue a statement of reasons and bases for the action(s) taken. Such decision by the Secretary shall be final agency action within the meaning of 5 U.S.C. 704.

Promulgated: 54 Fed. Reg. 26897 (6/26/89).

Subpart D—Procedure for the Assessment of Civil Penalties Under ERISA §502(*l*)

Sec. 2570.80—Scope of rules.

The rules of practice set forth in this subpart are applicable to "502(*l*) civil penalty proceedings" (as defined in §2570.82 of this subpart) under §502(*l*) of the Employee Retirement Income Security Act of 1974 (ERISA or the Act). Refer to 29 CFR 2560.5021 for the definition of the relevant terms of ERISA §502(*l*).

Promulgated: 55 Fed. Reg. 25286 (6/20/90); (Effective 6/20/90—Interim Regulation).

Sec. 2570.81—In general.

Section 502(*l*) of the Employee Retirement Income Security Act of 1974 (ERISA or the Act) requires the Secretary of Labor to assess a civil penalty against a fiduciary who breaches a fiduciary responsibility under, or commits any other violation of, part 4 of Title I of ERISA or any other person who knowingly participates in such breach or violation. The penalty under §502(*l*) is equal to 20% of the "applicable recovery amount" paid pursuant to any settlement agreement with the Secretary or ordered by a court to be paid in a judicial proceeding instituted by the Secretary under §502(a)(2) or (a)(5). The Secretary may, in the Secretary's sole discretion, waive or reduce the penalty if the Secretary determines in writing that:

(a) The fiduciary or other person acted reasonably and in good faith, or

(b) It is reasonable to expect that the fiduciary or other person will not be able to restore all losses to the plan or any participant or beneficiary of such plan without severe financial hardship unless such waiver or reduction is granted. The penalty imposed on a fiduciary or other person with respect to any transaction shall be reduced by the amount of any penalty or tax imposed on such fiduciary or other person with respect to such transaction under §502(i) or §4975 of the Internal Revenue Code of 1986 (the Code).

Promulgated: 55 Fed. Reg. 25286 (6/20/90); (Effective 6/20/90—Interim Regulation).

Sec. 2570.82—Definitions.

For purposes of this section:

(a) 502(*l*) civil penalty proceedings means an adjudicatory proceeding relating to the assessment of a civil penalty provided in §502(*l*) of ERISA;

(b) Notice of assessment means any document, however designated, issued by the Secretary which contains a specified assessment, in monetary terms, of a civil penalty under ERISA §502(*l*). A "notice of assessment" will contain a brief factual description of the violation for which the assessment is being made, the identity of the person being assessed, and the amount of the assessment and the basis for assessing that particular person that particular penalty amount;

(c) Person includes an individual, partnership, corporation, employee benefit plan, association, exchange or other entity or organization;

(d) Petition means a written request, made by a person, for a waiver or reduction of the civil penalty described herein; and

(e) Secretary means the Secretary of Labor and includes, pursuant to any delegation of authority by the Secretary, the Assistant Secretary for Pension and Welfare Benefits, Area Directors for Pension and Welfare Benefits, or Deputy Area Directors for Pension and Welfare Benefits.

Promulgated: 55 Fed. Reg. 25286 (6/20/90); (Effective 6/20/90—Interim Regulation).

Sec. 2570.83—Assessment of civil penalty.

(a) Except as described in Secs. 2570.85 and 2570.86 below, subsequent to the payment of the applicable recovery amount pursuant to either a settlement agreement or a court order, the Secretary shall serve on the person liable for making such payment a notice of assessment of civil penalty equal to 20% of the applicable recovery amount.

(b) Service of such notice shall be made either:

(1) By delivering a copy to the person being assessed; if the person is an individual, to the individual; if the person is a partnership, to any partner; if the person is a corporation, association, exchange, or other entity or organization, to any officer of such entity; if the person is an employee benefit plan, to a trustee of such plan; or to any attorney representing any such person;

(2) By leaving a copy at the principal office, place of business, or residence of such individual, partner, officer, trustee, or attorney; or

(3) By mailing a copy to the last known address of such individual, partner, officer, trustee, or attorney. If service is accomplished by certified mail, service is complete upon mailing. If done by regular mail, service is complete upon receipt by the addressee.

Promulgated: 55 Fed. Reg. 25286 (6/20/90); (Effective 6/20/90—Interim Regulation).

Sec. 2570.84—Payment of civil penalty.

(a) The civil penalty must be paid within 60 days of service of the notice of assessment.

(b) At any time prior to the expiration of the payment period for the assessed penalty, any person who has committed, or knowingly participated in, a breach or violation, or has been alleged by the Secretary to have so committed or participated, may submit a written request for a conference with the Secretary to discuss the calculation of the assessed penalty. A person will be entitled under this section to one such conference per assessment. If such written request is submitted during the 60 day payment period described in subparagraph (a), such a request will not toll the running of that payment period.

(c) The notice of assessment will become a final order (within the meaning of 5 U.S.C. 704) on the first day following the 60 day payment period, subject to any tolling caused by a petition to waive or reduce described in paragraph 2570.85.

Promulgated: 55 Fed. Reg. 25286 (6/20/90); (Effective 6/20/90—Interim Regulation).

Sec. 2570.85—Waiver or reduction of civil penalty.

(a) At any time prior to the expiration of the payment period for the assessed penalty, any person who has committed, or knowingly participated in, a breach or violation, or has been alleged by the Secretary to have so committed or participated, may petition the Secretary to waive or reduce the penalty under this section on the basis that:

(1) The person acted reasonably and in good faith in engaging in the breach or violation; or

(2) The person will not be able to restore all losses to the plan or participant or beneficiary of such plan without severe financial hardship unless such waiver or reduction is granted.

(b) All petitions for waiver or reduction shall be in writing and contain the following information:

(1) The name of the petitioner(s);

(2) A detailed description of the breach or violation which is the subject of the penalty;

(3) A detailed recitation of the facts which support one, or both, of the bases for waiver or reduction described in §2570.85(a) of this part, accompanied by underlying documentation supporting such factual allegations;

(4) A declaration, signed and dated by the petitioner(s), in the following form: Under penalty of perjury, I declare that, to the best of my knowledge and belief, the representations made in this petition are true and correct.

(c) If a petition for waiver or reduction is submitted during the 60 day payment period described in §2570.84(a) above, the payment period for the penalty in question will be tolled pending Departmental consideration of the petition. During such consideration, the applicant is entitled to one conference with the Secretary, but the Secretary, in his or her sole discretion, may schedule or hold additional conferences with the petitioner concerning the factual allegations contained in the petition.

(d) Based solely on his or her discretion, the Secretary will determine whether to grant such a waiver or reduction. Pursuant to the procedure described in §2570.83(b), the petitioner will be served with a written determination informing him or her of the Secretary's decision. Such written determination shall briefly state the grounds for the Secretary's decision, and shall be final and non-reviewable. In the case of a determination not to waive, the payment period for the penalty in question, if previously initiated, will resume as of the date of service of the Secretary's written determination.

Promulgated: 55 Fed. Reg. 25286 (6/20/90); (Effective 6/20/90—Interim Regulation).

Sec. 2570.87—Revision of assessment.

If, based on the procedures described in Secs. 2570.84, 2570.85, or 2570.86, the assessed penalty amount is revised, the person being assessed will receive a revised notice of assessment and will be obligated to pay the revised assessed penalty within the relevant 60 day payment period (as determined by the applicable procedure in Secs. 2570.84, 2570.85, or 2570.86), and, if necessary, any excess penalty payment will be refunded as soon as administratively feasible. The revised notice of assessment will revoke any previously issued notice of assessment with regard to the transaction in question and will become a final order (within the meaning of 5 U.S.C. 704) the later of the first day following the 60 day payment period or the date of its service on the person being assessed, pursuant to the service procedures described in §2570.83(b).

Promulgated: 55 Fed. Reg. 25286 (6/20/90); (Effective 6/20/90—Interim Regulation).

Sec. 2570.88—Effective date.

This section is effective June 20, 1990 and shall apply to assessments under §502(*l*) made by the Secretary after June 20, 1990 based on any breach or violation occurring on or after December 19, 1989.

Promulgated: 55 Fed. Reg. 25286 (6/20/90); (Effective 6/20/90—Interim Regulation).

♦ ♦ ♦

PART 2580—TEMPORARY BONDING RULES

Subpart A—Criteria for Determining Who Must Be Bonded

Sec. 2580.412-1—Statutory provisions.

Section 13(a) of the Welfare and Pension Plans Disclosure Act of 1958, as amended, states, in part, that:

Every administrator, officer and employee of any employee welfare benefit plan or of any employee pension benefit plan subject to this Act who handles funds or other property of such plan shall be bonded as herein provided; except that, where such plan is one under which the only assets from which benefits are paid are the general assets of a union or of an employer, the administrator, officers and employees of such plan shall be exempt from the bonding requirements of this section. * * * Such bond shall provide protection to the plan against loss by reason of acts of fraud or dishonesty on the part of such administrator, officer, or employee, directly or through connivance with others.

Promulgated: 28 Fed. Reg. 14403 (12/27/63).

Amended: 50 Fed. Reg. 26706 (6/28/85).

Sec. 2580.412-2—Plans exempt from the coverage of Sec. 13.

Only completely unfunded plans in which the plan benefits derive solely from the general assets of a union[1] or employer, and in which plan assets are not segregated in any way from the general assets of a union or employer and remain solely within the general assets until the time of distribution of benefits, shall be exempt from the bonding provisions. As such, the language "where such plan is one under which the only assets from which benefits are paid are the general assets of a union or of an employer" shall not be deemed to exempt a plan from the coverage of Sec. 13 if the plan is one in which:

(a) Any benefits thereunder are provided or underwritten by an insurance carrier or service or other organization, or

(b) There is a trust or other separate entity to which contributions are made or out of which benefits are paid, or

(c) Contributions to the plan are made by the employees, either through withholding or otherwise, or from any source other than the employer or union involved, or

(d) There is a separately maintained bank account or separately maintained books and records for the plan or other evidence of the existence of a segregated or separately maintained or administered fund out of which plan benefits are to be provided.

As a general rule, the presence of special ledger accounts or accounting entries for plan funds as an integral part of the general books and records of an employer or union shall not, in and of itself, be deemed sufficient evidence of segregation of plan funds to take a plan out of the exempt category, but shall be considered along with the other factors and criteria discussed above in determining whether the exemption applies. Again, it should be noted, however, that the fact that a plan is not exempt from the coverage of Sec. 13 does not necessarily mean that its administrators, officers or employees are required to be bonded. As stated previously, this will depend in each case on whether or not they "handle" funds or other property of the plan within the meaning of Sec. 13 and under the standards set forth in Sec. 2580.412-6.

[1] For purposes of the exemption discussed in Sec. 2580.412-2, the term "union" shall include "* * * any organization of any kind or any agency or employee representation committee, association, group, or plan, in which employees participate and which exists for the purpose in whole or in part, of dealing with employers concerning an employee welfare or pension benefit plan, or other matters incidental to employment relationships * * *" (29 U.S.C. 302(a)(3)).

Promulgated: 28 Fed. Reg. 14403 (12/27/63).

Amended: 50 Fed. Reg. 26706 (6/28/85).

Sec. 2580.412-3—Plan administrators, officers and employees for purposes of Sec. 13.

(a) Administrator.

(1) For purposes of the bonding provisions, the term "administrator" is defined in the same manner as under Sec. 5 of the Act and refers to:

(i) The person or persons designated by the terms of the plan or the collective bargaining agreement with responsibility for the ultimate control, disposition, or management of the money received or contributed; or

(ii) In the absence of such designation, the person or persons actually responsible for the control, disposition, or management of the money received or contributed, irrespective of whether such control, disposition, or management is exercised directly or through an agent or trustee designated by such person or persons.

(2) Where by virtue of this definition, or regulations, interpretations or opinions issued with respect thereto, the term embodies natural persons such as members of the board of trustees of a trust, the bonding requirements shall apply to such persons.

(3) However, when by virtue of this definition or regulations, interpretations, or opinions issued with respect thereto, the administrator in a given case in an entity such as a partnership, corporation, mutual company, joint stock company, trust, unincorporated organization, union or employees' beneficiary association, the term shall be deemed to apply, in meeting the bonding requirements, only to those natural persons who:

(i) Are vested under the authority of the entity-administrator with the responsibility for carrying out functions constituting control, disposition or management of the money received or contributed within the definition of administrator, or who, acting on behalf of or under the actual or apparent authority of the entity-administrator, actually perform such functions, and who

(ii) "Handle" funds or other property of the plan within the meaning of these regulations.

(b) Officers. For purposes of the bonding provisions, the term "officer" shall include any person designated by the terms of a plan or collective bargaining agreement as an officer, any person performing or authorized to perform executive functions of the plan or any member of a board of trustees or similar governing body of a plan. The term shall include such persons regardless of whether they are representatives of or selected by an employer, employees or an employee organization. In its most frequent application the term will encompass those natural persons appointed or elected as officers of the plan or as members of boards or committees performing executive or supervisory functions for the plan, but who do not fall within the definition of administrator.

(c) Employees. For purposes of the bonding provisions the term "employee" shall, to the extent a person performs functions not falling within the definition of officer or administrator, include any employee who performs work for or directly related to a covered plan, regardless of whether technically he is employed, directly or indirectly, by or for a plan, a plan administrator, a trust, or by an employee organization or employer within the meaning of Sec. 3(3) or 3(4) of the Act.

(d) Other persons covered. For purposes of the bonding provisions, the terms "administrator, officer, or employee" shall include any persons performing functions for the plan normally performed by administrators, officers, or employees of a plan. As such, the terms shall include persons indirectly employed, or otherwise delegated, to perform such work for the plan, such as pension consultants and planners, and attorneys who perform "handling" functions within the meaning of Sec. 2580.412-6. On the other hand, the terms would not include those brokers or independent contractors who have contracted for the performance of functions which are not ordinarily carried out by the administrators, officers, or employees of a plan, such as securities, brokers who purchase and sell securities or armored motor vehicle companies.

Promulgated: 28 Fed. Reg. 14403 (12/27/63).

Amended: 34 Fed. Reg. 5158 (3/13/69); 50 Fed. Reg. 26706 (6/28/85).

Sec. 2580.412-4—"Funds or other property" of a plan.

The affirmative requirement for bonding persons falling within the definition of administrator, officer or employee is applicable only if they handle "funds or other property" of the plan concerned. The term "funds or other property" is intended to encompass all property which is used or may be used as a source for the payment of benefits to plan participants. It does not include permanent assets used in the operation of the plan such as land and buildings, furniture and fixtures or office and delivery equipment used in the operation of the plan. It does include all items in the nature of quick assets, such as cash, checks and other negotiable instruments, government obligations and marketable securities. It also includes all other property or items convertible into cash or having a cash value and held or acquired for the ultimate purpose of distribution to plan participants or beneficiaries. In the case of a plan which has investments, this would include all the investments of the plan even though not in the nature of quick assets, such as land and buildings, mortgages, and securities in closely held corporations. However, in a given case, the question of whether a person was "handling" such "funds or other property" so as to require bonding would depend on whether his relationship to this property was such that there was a risk that he, alone or in connivance with others, could cause a loss of such "funds or other property" through fraud or dishonesty.

Promulgated: 28 Fed. Reg. 14403 (12/27/63).

Amended: 50 Fed. Reg. 26706 (6/28/85).

Sec. 2580.412-5—Determining when "funds or other property" belong to a plan.

With respect to any contribution to a plan from any source, including employers, employees or employee organizations, the point at which any given item or amount becomes "funds or other property" of a plan for purposes of the bonding provisions shall be determined as described in this section.

(a) Where the plan administrator is a board of trustees, person or body other than the employer or employee organization establishing the plan, a contribution to the plan from any source shall become "funds or other property" of the plan at the time it is received by the plan administrator.
Employee contributions collected by an employer and later turned over to the plan administrator would not become "funds or other property" of the plan until receipt by the plan administrator.

(b) Where the employer or employee organization establishing the plan is itself the plan administrator:

(1) Contributions from employees or other persons who are plan participants would normally become "funds or other property" of the plan at the time they are received by the employer or employee organization, except however that contributions made by withholding from employees' salaries shall not be considered "funds or other property" of the plan for purposes of the bonding provisions so long as they are retained in and not segregated in any way from the general assets of the withholding employer or employee organization.

(2) Contributions made to a plan by such employer or employee organization and contributions made by withholdings from employees' salaries would normally become "funds or other property" of the plan if and when they are taken out of the general assets of the employer or employee organization and placed in a special bank account or investment account; or identified on a separate set of books and records; or paid over to a corporate trustee or used to purchase benefits from an insurance carrier or service or other organization; or otherwise segregated, paid out or used for plan purposes, whichever shall occur first. Thus, if a plan is operated by a corporate trustee and no segregation from general assets is made of monies to be turned over to the corporate trustee prior to the actual transmittal of such monies, the contribution represented in the transmission becomes "funds or other property" of the plan at the time of receipt by the corporate trustee. On the other hand, if a special fund is first established from which monies are paid over to the corporate trustee, a given item would become "funds or other property" of the plan at the time it is placed in the special fund.

Similarly, if plan benefits are provided through the medium of an insurance carrier or service or other organization and no segregation from general assets of monies used to purchase such benefits is made prior to turning such monies over to the organization contracting to provide benefits, plan funds or other property come into being at the time of receipt of payment for such benefits by the insurance carrier or service or other organization. In such a case, the "funds or other property" of the plan would be represented by the insurance contract or other obligations to pay benefits and would not be normally subject to "handling". Bonding would not be required for any person with respect to the purchase of such benefits directly from general assets nor with respect to the bare existence of the contract obligation to pay benefits. However, if the particular, arrangement were such that monies derived from, or by virtue of, the contract did subsequently flow back to the plan, bonding may be required if such monies returning to the plan are handled by plan administrators, officers or employees. (Further discussion on bonding of insured plans is contained in Sec. 2580.412-6(b)(7)).

Promulgated: 28 Fed. Reg. 14403 (12/27/63).

Amended: 50 Fed. Reg. 26706 (6/28/85).

Sec. 2580.412-6—Determining when "funds or other property" are "handled" so as to require bonding.

(a) General scope of term.

(1) A plan administrator, officer, or employee shall be deemed to be "handling" funds or other property of a plan, so as to require bonding under Sec. 13, whenever his duties or activities with respect to given funds or other property are such that there is a risk that such funds or other property could be lost in the event of fraud or dishonesty on the part of such person, acting either alone or in collusion with others. While ordinarily, those plan administrators, officers and employees who "handle" within the meaning of Sec. 13 will be those persons with duties related to the receipt, safekeeping and disbursement of funds, the scope of the term "handles" and the prohibitions of paragraph (b) of Sec. 13 shall be deemed to encompass any relationship of an administrator, officer or employee with respect to funds or other property which can give rise to a risk of loss through fraud or dishonesty. This shall include relationships such as those which involve access to funds or other property or decisionmaking powers with respect to funds or property which can give rise to such risk of loss.

(2) Section 13 contains no exemptions based on the amount or value of funds or other property "handled", nor is the determination of the existence of risk of loss based on the amount involved. However, regardless of the amount involved, a given duty or relationship to funds or other property shall not be considered "handling", and bonding is not required, where it occurs under conditions and circumstances in which the risk that a loss will occur through fraud or dishonesty is negligible. This may be the case where the risk of mishandling is precluded by the nature of the funds or other property (e.g., checks, securities or title papers which can not be negotiated by the persons performing duties with respect to them). It may also be the case where significant risk of mishandling in the performance of duties of an essentially clerical character is precluded by fiscal controls.

(b) General criteria for determining "handling". Subject to the application of the basic standard of risk of loss to each situation, general criteria for determining whether there is "handling" so as to require bonding are:

(1) *Physical contact.* Physical contact with cash, checks or similar property generally constitutes "handling". However, persons who from time to time perform counting, packaging, tabulating, messenger or similar duties of an essentially clerical character involving physical contact with funds or other property would not be "handling" when they perform these duties under conditions and circumstances where risk of loss is negligible because of factors such as close supervision and control or the nature of the property.

(2) *Power to exercise physical contact or control.* Whether or not physical contact actually takes place, the power to secure physical possession of cash, checks or similar property through factors such as access to a safe deposit box or similar depository, access to cash or negotiable assets, powers of custody or safekeeping, power to withdraw funds from a bank or other account generally constitutes "handling", regardless of whether the person in question has specific duties in these matters and regardless of whether the power or access is authorized.

(3) *Power to transfer to oneself or a third party or to negotiate for value.* With respect to property such as mortgages, title to land and buildings, or securities, while physical contact or the possibility of physical contact may not, of itself, give rise to risk of loss so as to constitute "handling", a person shall be regarded as "handling" such items where he, through actual or apparent authority, can cause those items to be transferred to himself or to a third party or to be negotiated for value.

(4) *Disbursement.* Persons who actually disburse funds or other property, such as officers or trustees authorized to sign checks or other negotiable instruments, or persons who make cash disbursements, shall be considered to be "handling" such funds or property. Whether other persons who may influence, authorize or direct disbursements or the signing or endorsing of checks or similar instruments will be considered to be "handling" funds or other property shall be determined by reference to the particular duties or responsibilities of such persons as applied to the basic criteria of risk of loss.

(5) *Signing or endorsing checks or other negotiable instruments.* In connection with disbursements or otherwise, any persons with the power to sign or endorse checks or similar instruments or otherwise render them transferable, whether individually or as co-signers with one or more persons, shall each be considered to be "handling" such funds or other property.

(6) *Supervisory or decision making responsibility.* To the extent a person's supervisory or decision making responsibility involves factors in relationship to funds discussed in paragraph (b) (1), (2), (3), (4), or (5) of this section, such persons shall be considered to be "handling" in the same manner as any person to whom the criteria of those paragraphs apply. To the extent that only general responsibility for the conduct of the business affairs of the plan is involved, including such functions as approval of contracts, authorization of disbursements, auditing of accounts, investment decisions, determination of benefit claims and similar responsibilities, such persons shall be considered to be "handling" whenever the facts of the particular case raise the possibility that funds or other property of the plan are likely to be lost in the event of their fraud or dishonesty. The mere fact of general supervision would not necessarily, in and of itself, mean that such persons are "handling." Factors to be accorded weight are the system of fiscal controls, the closeness and continuity of supervision, who is in fact charged with, or actually exercising final responsibility for determining whether specific disbursements, investments, contracts, or benefit claims are bona fide, regular and made in accordance with the applicable trust instrument or other plan documents.

(i) For example, persons having supervisory or decisionmaking responsibility would be "handling" to the extent they:

(a) Act in the capacity of plan "administrator" and have ultimate responsibility for the plan within the meaning of the definition of "administrator" (except to the extent that it can be shown that such persons could not, in fact, cause a loss to the plan to occur through fraud or dishonesty);

(b) Exercise close supervision over corporate trustees or other parties charged with dealing with plan funds or other property; exercise such close control over investment policy that they, in effect, determine all specific investments;

(c) Conduct, in effect, a continuing daily audit of the persons who "handle" funds;

(d) Regularly review and have veto power over the actions of a disbursing officer whose duties are essentially ministerial.

(ii) On the other hand, persons having supervisory or decisionmaking responsibility would not be "handling" to the extent:

(a) They merely conduct a periodic or sporadic audit of the persons who "handle" funds;

(b) Their duties with respect to investment policy are essentially advisory;

(c) They make a broad general allocation of funds or general authorization of disbursements intended to permit expenditures by a disbursing officer who has final responsibility for determining the propriety of any specific expenditure and making the actual disbursement;

(d) A bank or corporate trustee has all the day to day functions of administering the plan;

(e) They are in the nature of a Board of Directors of a corporation or similar authority acting for the corporation rather than for the plan and do not perform specific functions with respect to the operations of the plan.

(7) *Insured plan arrangements.* In many cases, plan contributions made by employers or employee organizations or by withholding from employee's salaries are not segregated from the general assets of the employer or employee organization until payment for purchase of benefits from an insurance carrier or service or other organization. No bonding is required with respect to the payment of premiums or other payments made to purchase such benefits directly from general assets, nor with respect to the bare existence of the contract obligation to pay benefits. Such arrangements would not normally be subject to bonding except to the extent that monies returned by way of benefit payments, cash surrender, dividends, credits or otherwise, and which by the terms of the plan belonged to the plan (rather than to the employer, employee organization, insurance carrier or service or other organization) were subject to "handling" by plan administrators, officers or employees.

Promulgated: 28 Fed. Reg. 14403 (12/27/63).

Amended: 50 Fed. Reg. 26706 (6/28/85).

Subpart B—Scope and Form of the Bond

Sec. 2580.412-7—Statutory provision—scope of the bond.

The statute requires that the bond shall provide protection to the plan against loss by reason of acts of fraud or dishonesty on the part of a plan administrator, officer, or employee, directly or through connivance with others.

Promulgated: 28 Fed. Reg. 14403 (12/27/63).

Amended: 50 Fed. Reg. 26706 (6/28/85).

Sec. 2580.412-8—The nature of the duties or activities to which the bonding requirement relates.

The bond required under Sec. 13 is limited to protection for those duties and activities from which loss can arise through fraud or dishonesty.

It is not required to provide the same scope of coverage that is required in faithful discharge of duties bonds under the Labor-Management Reporting and Disclosure Act of 1959 or in the faithful performance bonds of public officials.

Promulgated: 28 Fed. Reg. 14403 (12/27/63).

Amended: 50 Fed. Reg. 26706 (6/28/85).

Sec. 2580.412-9—Meaning of fraud or dishonesty.

The term "fraud or dishonesty" shall be deemed to encompass all those risks of loss that might arise through dishonest or fraudulent acts in handling of funds as delineated in Sec. 2580.412-6. As such, the bond must provide recovery for loss occasioned by such acts even though no personal gain accrues to the person committing the act and the act is not subject to punishment as a crime or misdemeanor, provided that within the law of the state in which the act is committed, a court would afford recovery under a bond providing protection against fraud or dishonesty. As usually applied under state laws, the term "fraud or dishonesty" encompasses such matters as larceny, theft, embezzlement, forgery, misappropriation, wrongful abstraction, wrongful conversion, willful misapplication or any other fraudulent or dishonest acts. For the purposes of Sec. 13, other fraudulent or dishonest acts shall also be deemed to include acts where losses result through any act or arrangement prohibited by Title 18, section 1954 of the U.S. Code.

Promulgated: 28 Fed. Reg. 14403 (12/27/63).

Amended: 50 Fed. Reg. 26706 (6/28/85).

Sec. 2580.412-10—Individual or schedule or blanket form of bonds.

Section 13 provides that "any bond shall be in a form or of a type approved by the Secretary, including individual bonds or schedule or blanket forms of bonds which cover a group or class". Any form of bond which may be described as individual, schedule or blanket in form or any combination of such forms of bonds shall be acceptable to meet the requirements of Sec. 13, provided that in each case, the form of the bond, in its particular clauses and application, is not inconsistent with meeting the substantive requirements of the statute for the persons and plan involved and with meeting the specific requirements of the regulations in this part. Basic types of bonds in general usage are:

(a) Individual bond. Covers a named individual in a stated penalty.

(b) Name schedule bond. Covers a number of named individuals in the respective amounts set opposite their names.

(c) Position schedule bond. Covers each of the occupants of positions listed in the schedule in the respective amounts set opposite such positions.

(d) Blanket bonds. Cover all the insured's officers and employees with no schedule or list of those covered being necessary and with all new officers and employees bonded automatically, in a blanket penalty which takes two forms—an aggregate penalty bond and a multiple penalty bond which are described below:

(1) The aggregate penalty blanket bond such as the Commercial Blanket Bond; the amount of the bond is available for dishonesty losses caused by persons covered thereunder or losses in which such person is concerned or implicated. Payment of loss on account of any such person does not reduce the amount of coverage available for losses other than those caused by such person or in which he was concerned or implicated.

(2) The multiple penalty bond such as the Blanket Position Bond giving separate coverage on each person for a uniform amount—the net effect being the same as though a separate bond were issued on each person covered thereunder and all of such bonds being for a uniform amount.

Note: For the purpose of Sec. 13 blanket bonds which are either aggregate penalty or multiple penalty in form shall be permissible if they otherwise meet the requirements of the Act and the regulations in this part.

Bonding, to the extent required, of persons indirectly employed, or otherwise delegated, to perform functions for the plan which are normally performed by "administrators, officers, or employees" as described in Sec. 2580.412-3(d) may be accomplished either by including them under individual or schedule bonds or other forms of bonds meeting the requirements of the Act, or naming them in what is known under general trade usage as an "Agents Rider" attached to a Blanket Bond.

Promulgated: 28 Fed. Reg. 14403 (12/27/63).

Amended: 50 Fed. Reg. 26706 (6/28/85).

Subpart C—Amount of the Bond

Sec. 2580.412-11—Statutory provision.

Section 13 requires that the amount of the bond be fixed at the beginning of each calendar, policy or other fiscal year, as the case may be, which constitutes the reporting year of the plan for purposes of the reporting provisions of the Act. The amount of the bond shall be not less than 10 per centum of the amount of funds handled, except that any such bond shall be in at least the amount of $1,000 and no such bond shall be required in an amount in excess of $500,000: Provided, That the Secretary, after due notice and opportunity for hearing to all interested parties, and after consideration of the record, may prescribe an amount in excess of $500,000, which in no event shall exceed 10 per centum of the funds handled. For purposes of fixing the amount of such bond, the amount of funds handled shall be determined by the funds handled by the person, group, or class to be covered by such bond and by their predecessor or predecessors, if any, during the preceding reporting year, or if the plan has no preceding reporting year, the amount of funds to be handled during the current reporting year by such person, group, or class, estimated as provided in the regulations in this part. With respect to persons required to be bonded, Sec. 13 shall be deemed to require the bond to insure from the first dollar of loss up to the requisite bond amount and not to permit the use of deductible or similar features whereby a portion of the risk within such requisite bond amount is assumed by the insured. Any request for variance from these requirements shall be made pursuant to the provisions of Sec. 13(e) of the Act.

Promulgated: 28 Fed. Reg. 14403 (12/27/63).

Amended: 50 Fed. Reg. 26706 (6/28/85).

Sec. 2580.412-12—Relationship of determining the amount of the bond to "handling".

A determination of whether persons falling within the definition of administrator, officer or employee are required to be bonded depends on whether they "handle" funds or other property. Determining the amount of the bond is an aspect of the same process in that it requires a determination of what funds or other property are being handled or what amounts of funds or other property are subject to risk of loss with respect to the duties or powers of an administrator, officer or employee of a covered plan. Once this calculation is made, the required amount for which that person must be covered by a bond, either by himself or as a part of a group or class being bonded under a blanket or schedule bond, is not less than 10% of the amount "handled" or $1,000, whichever is the greater amount, except that no such bond shall be required in an amount greater than $500,000 by virtue of these regulations. (See Sec. 2580.412-17.)

Promulgated: 28 Fed. Reg. 14403 (12/27/63).

Amended: 50 Fed. Reg. 26706 (6/28/85).

Sec. 2580.412-13—The meaning of "funds" in determining the amount of the bond.

The amount of the bond depends on the amount of "funds" "handled", and shall be sufficient to provide bonding protection against risk of loss through fraud or dishonesty for all plan funds, including other property similar to funds or in the nature of funds. As such, the term "funds" shall be deemed to include and be equivalent to "funds and other property" of the plan as described in Sec. 2580.412-4. With respect to any item of "funds or other property" which does not have a cash or readily ascertainable market value, the value of such property may be estimated on such basis as will reasonably reflect the loss the plan might suffer if it were mis-handled.

Promulgated: 28 Fed. Reg. 14403 (12/27/63).

Amended: 50 Fed. Reg. 26706 (6/28/85).

Sec. 2580.412-14—Determining the amount of funds "handled" during the preceding reporting year.

(a) The amount of funds "handled" by each person falling within the definition of administrator, officer, or employee (or his predecessors) during the preceding reporting year shall be the total of funds subject to risk of loss, within the meaning of the definition of "handling" (see Sec. 2580.412-6), through acts of fraud or dishonesty, directly or in connivance with others, by such person or his predecessors during the preceding reporting year. The relationship of the determination of the amount of funds "handled" to the determination of who is "handling" can best be illustrated by a situation that commonly arises with respect to executive personnel of a plan, where a bank or corporate trustee has the responsibility for the receipt, safekeeping, physical handling and investment of a plan's assets and the basic function of the executive personnel is to authorize payments to beneficiaries and payments for services to the corporate trustee, the actuary and the employees of the plan itself. Normally, in any given year, only a small portion of the plan's total assets is disbursed, and the question arises as to whether an administrator or executive personnel are "handling" only the amounts actually disbursed each year or whether they are "handling" the total amounts of the assets. The answer to this question depends on the same basic criterion that governs all questions of "handling", namely, the possibility of loss. If the authorized duties of the persons in question are strictly limited to disbursements of benefits and payments for services, and the fiscal controls and practical realities of the situation are such that these persons cannot gain access to funds which they are not legitimately allowed to disburse, the amount on which the bond is based may be limited to the amount actually disbursed in the reporting year. This would depend, in part, on the extent to which the bank or corporate trustee which has physical possession of the funds also has final responsibility for questioning and limiting disbursements from the plan, and on whether this responsibility is embodied in the original plan instruments. On the other hand, where insufficient fiscal controls exist so that the persons involved have free access to, or can obtain control of, the total amount of the fund, the bond shall reflect this fact and the amount "handled" shall be based on the total amount of the fund. This would generally occur with respect to persons such as the "administrator", regardless of what functions are performed by a bank or corporate trustee, since the "administrator" by definition retains ultimate power to revoke any arrangement with a bank or corporate trustee. In such case, the "administrator" would have the power to commit the total amount of funds involved to his control, unless the plan itself or other specific agreement (1) prevents the "administrator" from so doing or (2) requires that revocation cannot be had unless a new agreement providing for similar controls and limitations on the "handling" of funds is simultaneously entered into.

(b) Where the circumstances of "handling" are such that the total amount of a given account or fund is subject to "handling", the amount "handled" shall include the total of all such funds on hand at the beginning of the reporting year, plus any items received during the year for any reason, such as contributions or income, or items received as a result of sales, investments, reinvestment, interest or otherwise. It would not, however, be necessary to count the same item twice in arriving at the total funds "handled" by a given person during a reporting year. For example, a given person may have various duties or powers involving receipt, safekeeping or disbursement of funds which would place him in contact with the same funds at several times during the same year. Different duties, however, would not make it necessary to count the same item twice in arriving at the total "handled" by him. Similarly, where a person has several different positions with respect to a plan, it would not be necessary to count the same funds each time that they are "handled" by him in these different positions, so long as the amount of the bond is sufficient to meet the 10% requirement with respect to the total funds "handled" by him subject to risk or loss through fraud or dishonesty, whether acting alone or in collusion with others. In general, once an item properly within the category of "funds," has been counted as "handled" by a given person, it need not be counted again even though it should subsequently be "handled" by the same person during the same year.

Promulgated: 28 Fed. Reg. 14403 (12/27/63).

Amended: 50 Fed. Reg. 26706 (6/28/85).

Sec. 2580.412-15—Procedures to be used for estimating the amount of funds to be "handled" during the current reporting year in those cases where there is no preceding reporting year.

If for any reason a plan does not have a complete preceding reporting year, the amount "handled" by persons required to be covered by a bond shall be estimated at the beginning of the calendar, policy or other fiscal year, as the case may be, which would constitute either the operating year or the reporting year of the plan, whichever shall occur first, as follows:

(a) In the case of a plan having a previous experience year, even though it has no preceding reporting year, the estimate of the amount to be "handled" for any person required to be covered shall be based on the experience in the previous year by applying the same standards and criteria as in a plan which has a preceding reporting year. Similarly, where a plan is recently established, but has had, at the time a bond is obtained, sufficient experience to reasonably estimate a complete year's experience for persons required to be bonded, the amount of funds to be "handled" shall be projected to the complete year on the basis of the period in which the plan has had experience, unless, to the knowledge of the plan administrator, the given period of experience is so seasonal or unrepresentative of the complete year's experience as not to provide a reasonable basis for projecting the estimate for the complete year.

(b) Where a plan does not have any prior experience sufficient to allow it to estimate the amount "handled" in the manner outlined in paragraph (a) of this section, the amount to be "handled" by the administrators, officers and employees of the plan during the current reporting year shall be that amount initially required to fund or set up the plan, plus the amount of contributions required to be made under the plan formula from any source during the current reporting year. In most cases, the amount of contributions will be calculated by multiplying the total yearly contribution per participant (required by the plan formula from either employers, employees, employer organizations or any other source) by the number of participants in the plan at the beginning of such reporting year. In cases where the per capita contribution cannot readily be determined, such as in the case of certain insured plans covered by the Act, the amount of contributions shall be estimated on the amount of insurance premiums which are actuarially estimated as necessary to support the plan, or on such other actuarially estimated basis as may be applicable. In the case of a newly formed profit-sharing plan covered by the Act, if the employer establishing the plan has a previous year of experience, the amount of contributions required by the plan formula shall be estimated on the basis of the profits of the previous year.

The amount of the bond shall then be fixed at 10% of this calculation, but not more than $500,000. A bond for such amount shall be obtained in any form the plan desires on all persons who are administrators, officers, or employees of the plan and who "handle" funds or other property of the plan.

Promulgated: 28 Fed. Reg. 14403 (12/27/63).

Amended: 50 Fed. Reg. 26706 (6/28/85).

Sec. 2580.412-16—Amount of bond required in given types of bonds or where more than one plan is insured in the same bond.

(a) As indicated in Sec. 2580.412-10, the Act permits the use of blanket, schedule and individual forms of bonds so long as the amount of the bond penalty is sufficient to meet the requirements of the Act for any person who is an administrator, officer or employee of a plan handling funds or other property of the plan. Such person must be bonded for 10% of the amount he handles, and the amount of the bond must be sufficient to indemnify the plan for any losses in which such person is involved up to that amount.

(b) When individual or schedule bonds are written, the bond amount for each person must represent not less than 10% of the funds "handled" by the named individual or by the person in the position. When a blanket bond is written, the amount of the bond shall be at least 10% of the highest amount handled by any administrator, officer or employee to be covered under the bond. It should also be noted that if an individual or group or class covered under a blanket bond "handle" a large amount of funds or other property, while the remaining bondable persons "handle" only a smaller amount, it is permissible to obtain a blanket bond in an amount sufficient to meet the 10% requirements for all except the individual, group or class "handling" the larger amounts, with respect to whom excess indemnity shall be secured in an amount sufficient to meet the 10% requirement.

(c) The Act does not prohibit more than one plan from being named as insured under the same bond. However, any such bond must allow for recovery by each plan in an amount at least equal to that which would be required if bonded separately. This requirement has application where a person or persons sought to be bonded pursuant to the requirements of Sec. 13 have "handling" functions in more than one plan covered under the bond. Where such is the case, the amount of the bond must be sufficient to cover any such persons having functions in more than one plan for at least 10% of the total amount "handled" by them in all the plans covered under the bond. For example, X is the administrator of two welfare plans run by the same employer and he "handled" $100,000 in the preceding reporting year for Plan A and $500,000 in the preceding reporting year for Plan B. If both plans are covered under the same bond, the amount of the bond with respect to X shall be at least $60,000 or ten percent of the total "handled" by X for both plans covered under the bond in which X has powers and duties of "handling" since Plan B is required to carry bond in at least the amount of $50,000 and Plan A, $10,000.

(d) Additionally, in order to meet the requirement that each plan be protected, it shall be necessary that arrangement be made either by the terms of the bond or rider to the bond or by separate agreement among the parties concerned, that payment of a loss sustained by one of such insureds shall not work to the detriment of any other plan covered under the bond with respect to the amount for which that plan is required to be covered. For example, if Plan A suffered a loss of $30,000 as described above and such loss was recompensed in its entirety by the surety company, it would receive $20,000 more than the $10,000 protection required under Sec. 13, and only $30,000 would be available for recovery with respect to further losses caused by X.

In a subsequently discovered defalcation of $40,000 by X from Plan B, it would be necessary that the bond, rider, or separate agreement provide that such amount of recovery paid to Plan A in excess of the $10,000 for which it is required to be covered, be made available by such insured to, or held for the use of, Plan B in such amount as Plan B would receive if bonded separately. Thus, in the instant case, Plan B would be able to recover the full $40,000 of its loss. Where the funds or other property of several plans are commingled (if permitted by law) with each other or with other funds, such arrangement shall allow recovery to be attributed proportionately to the amount for which each plan is required to be protected. Thus, in the instant case, if funds or other property were commingled, and X caused a loss of these funds through fraud or dishonesty, one-sixth of the loss would be attributable to Plan A and five-sixths of the loss attributable to Plan B.

(e) The maximum amount of any bond with respect to any person in any one plan in $500,000, but bonds covering more than one plan may be required to be over $500,000 in order to meet the requirements of the Act, since persons covered by such a bond may have "handling" functions in more than one plan.

The $500,000 limitations for such persons applies only with respect to each separate plan in which they have such functions. The minimum bond coverage for any administrator, officer, or employee "handling" funds or other property of a plan is $1,000 as respects each plan in which he has "handling" functions.

Promulgated: 28 Fed. Reg. 14403 (12/27/63).

Amended: 50 Fed. Reg. 26706 (6/28/85).

Sec. 2580.412-17—Bonds over $500,000.

The Labor-Management Services Administrator, after due notice and opportunity for hearing to all interested parties, and after consideration of the record, may prescribe an amount in excess of $500,000, which in no event shall exceed 10 per centum of the funds "handled." Any requirement for bonding in excess of $500,000 shall be according to such other regulations as may be prescribed.

Promulgated: 28 Fed. Reg. 14403 (12/27/63).

Amended: 50 Fed. Reg. 26706 (6/28/85).

Subpart D—General Bond Rules

Sec. 2580.412-18—Naming of insureds.

Since Sec. 13 is intended to protect funds or other property of all plans involved, bonds under this section shall allow for enforcement or recovery by those persons usually authorized to act for such plans in such matters. In most cases, the naming of the plan or plans as insured will provide for such recovery. Where it is not clear that such recovery will be provided, however, a rider shall be attached to the bond or separate agreement made among the parties concerned to make certain that any reimbursement collected under the bond will be for the benefit and use of the plan suffering a loss. Such rider or agreement shall always be required as respects any bond (a) where the employer or employee organization is first named joint insured with one or more plans, or (b) two or more plans are named joint insureds under a single bond with the first named acting for all insureds for the purpose of orderly servicing of the bond.

Promulgated: 28 Fed. Reg. 14403 (12/27/63).

Amended: 50 Fed. Reg. 26706 (6/28/85).

Sec. 2580.412-19—Term of the bond, discovery period, other bond clauses.

(a) Term of the bond. The amount of any required bond must in each instance be based on the amount of funds "handled" and must be fixed or estimated at the beginning of the plan's reporting year, that is, as soon after the date when such year begins as the necessary information from the preceding reporting year can practicably be ascertained. This does not mean, however, that a new bond must be obtained each year. There is nothing in the Act that prohibits a bond for a term longer than one year, with whatever advantages such a bond might offer by way of a lower premium. However, at the beginning of each reporting year the bond shall be in at least the requisite amount.

If, for any reason, the bond is below the required level at that time, the existing bond shall either be increased to the proper amount, or a supplemental bond shall be obtained.

(b) Discovery period. A discovery period of no less than one year after the termination or cancellation of the bond is required. Any standard form written on a "discovery" basis, i.e., providing that a loss must be discovered within the bond period as a prerequisite to recovery of such loss, however, will not be required to have a discovery period if it contains a provision giving the insured the right to purchase a discovery period of one year in the event of termination or cancellation and the insured has already given the surety notice that it desires such discovery period.

(c) Other bond clauses. A bond shall not be adequate to meet the requirements of Sec. 13, if, with respect to bonding coverage required under Sec. 13, it contains a clause, or is otherwise, in contravention of the law of the State in which it is executed.

Promulgated: 28 Fed. Reg. 14403 (12/27/63).

Amended: 50 Fed. Reg. 26706 (6/28/85).

Sec. 2580.412-20—Use of existing bonds, separate bonds and additional bonding.

(a) Additional bonding. Section 13 neither prevents additional bonding beyond that required by its terms, nor prescribes the form in which additional coverage may be taken. Thus, so long as a particular bond meets the requirements of the regulations in this part as to the persons required to be bonded and provides coverage for such persons in at least the minimum required amount, additional coverage as to persons or amount may be taken in any form, either on the same or separate bond.

(b) Use of existing bonds. Insofar as a bond currently in use is adequate to meet the requirements of the Act and the regulations in this part or may be made adequate to meet these requirements through rider, modification or separate agreement between the parties, no further bonding is required.

(c) Use of separate bonds. The choice of whether persons required to be bonded should be bonded separately or under the same bond, whether given plans should be bonded separately or under the same bond, whether existing bonds should be used or separate bonds for Welfare and Pension Plans Disclosure Act bonding should be obtained, or whether the bond is underwritten by a single surety company or more than one surety company, either separately or on a cosurety basis, is left to the judgment of the parties concerned, so long as the bonding program adopted meets the requirements of the Act and the regulations in this part.

Promulgated: 28 Fed. Reg. 14403 (12/27/63).

Amended: 50 Fed. Reg. 26706 (6/28/85).

Subpart E—Qualified Agents, Brokers and Surety Companies for the Placing of Bonds

Sec. 2580.412-21—Corporate sureties holding grants of authority from the Secretary of the Treasury.

(a) The provisions of Sec. 13 require that any surety company with which a bond is placed pursuant to that section must be a corporate surety which holds a grant of authority from the Secretary of the Treasury under the Act of July 30, 1947 (6 U.S.C. 6-13), as an acceptable surety on Federal bonds. The Act provides, among other things, that in order for a surety company to be eligible for such grant of authority, it must be incorporated under the laws of the United States or of any State and the Secretary of the Treasury shall be satisfied of certain facts relating to its authority and capitalization. Such grants of authority are evidenced by Certificates of Authority which are issued by the Secretary of the Treasury and which expire on the April 30 following the date of their issuance. A list of the companies holding such Certificates of Authority is published annually in the Federal Register, usually in May or June. Changes in the list, occurring between May 1 and April 30, either by addition to or removal from the list of companies, are also published in the Federal Register following each such change.

(b) Where a surety becomes insolvent and is placed in receivership, or if for any other reason the Secretary of the Treasury determines that its financial condition is not satisfactory to him and he revokes the authority of such company to act as an acceptable surety under the Act of July 30, 1947, the "administrator" of the insured plan shall, upon knowledge of such facts, be responsible for securing a new bond with an acceptable surety.

(c) In obtaining or renewing a bond, the plan administrator shall assure that the surety is one which satisfies the requirements of this section. If the bond is for a term of more than one year, the plan administrator, at the beginning of each reporting year, shall assure that the surety continues to satisfy the requirements of this subpart.

Promulgated: 28 Fed. Reg. 14403 (12/27/63).

Amended: 50 Fed. Reg. 26706 (6/28/85).

Sec. 2580.412-22—Interests held in agents, brokers and surety companies.

Section 13(c) prohibits the placing of bonds, required to be obtained pursuant to Sec. 13, with any surety or other company, or through any agent or broker in whose business operations a plan or any party in interest in a plan has significant control or financial interest, direct or indirect.

An interpretation of this section has been issued (Sec. 2580.412-36 of this chapter).

Promulgated: 28 Fed. Reg. 14403 (12/27/63).

Amended: 50 Fed. Reg. 26706 (6/28/85).

Subpart F—Exemptions

Bonds Placed With Certain Reinsuring Companies

Sec. 2580.412-23—Exemption.

An exemption from the bonding requirements of the Welfare and Pension Plans Disclosure Act is granted by this section whereby bonding arrangements (which otherwise comply with the requirements of Sec. 13 of the Act and the regulations issued thereunder) with companies authorized by the Secretary of the Treasury as acceptable reinsurers on Federal bonds will satisfy the bonding requirements of the Act.

Promulgated: 28 Fed. Reg. 14403 (12/27/63).

Amended: 50 Fed. Reg. 26706 (6/28/85).

Sec. 2580.412-24—Conditions of exemption.

(a) This exemption obtains only with respect to the requirement of Sec. 13(a) of the Act that all bonds required thereunder shall have as surety thereon, a corporate surety company, which is an acceptable surety on Federal bonds under authority granted by the Secretary of the Treasury pursuant to the Act of July 30, 1947 (6 U.S.C. 6-13).

(b) The exemption is granted upon the condition that if for any reason the authority of any such company to act as an acceptable reinsuring company is terminated, the administrator of a plan insured with such company, shall, upon knowledge of such fact, be responsible for securing a new bond with a company acceptable under the Act and the exemptions issued thereunder.

(c) In obtaining or renewing a bond, the plan administrator shall ascertain that the surety is one which satisfies the requirements of the Act and the exemptions thereunder. If the bond is for a term of more than one year, the plan administrator, at the beginning of each reporting year, shall ascertain that the surety continues to do so.

Promulgated: 28 Fed. Reg. 14403 (12/27/63).

Amended: 50 Fed. Reg. 26706 (6/28/85).

Bonds Placed With Underwriters at Lloyds, London

Sec. 2580.412-25—Exemption.

An exemption from the bonding requirements of subsection 13(a) of the Welfare and Pension Plans Disclosure Act is granted by this section whereby arrangements (which otherwise comply with the requirements of Sec. 13 of the Act and the regulations issued thereunder), with the Underwriters at Lloyds, London will satisfy the bonding requirements of the Act.

Promulgated: 28 Fed. Reg. 14403 (12/27/63).

Amended: 50 Fed. Reg. 26706 (6/28/85).

Sec. 2580.412-26—Conditions of exemption.

(a) This exemption obtains only with respect to the requirements of Sec. 13(a) of the Act that all bonds required thereunder shall have as surety thereon, a corporate surety company, which is an acceptable surety on Federal bonds under authority granted by the Secretary of the Treasury, pursuant to the Act of July 30, 1947 (6 U.S.C. 6-13).

(b) This exemption is granted on the following conditions:

(1) Underwriters at Lloyds, London shall continue to be licensed in a state of the United States to enter into bonding arrangements of the type required by the Act.

(2) Underwriters at Lloyds, London, shall file with the Office of Pension and Welfare Benefit Programs two (2) copies of each annual statement required to be made to the Commissioner of Insurance of those states in which Underwriters at Lloyds, London are licensed. Copies of annual statements shall be filed with the Office of Pension and Welfare Benefit Programs within the same period required by the respective states.

(3) All bonding arrangements entered into by Underwriters at Lloyds, London under Sec. 13 of the Act shall contain a "Service of Suit Clause" in substantial conformity with that set forth in the petition for exemption.

Promulgated: 28 Fed. Reg. 14403 (12/27/63).

Amended: 50 Fed. Reg. 26706 (6/28/85).

Banking Institutions Subject to Federal Regulation

Sec. 2580.412-27—Exemption.

An exemption from the bonding requirements of subsections 13(a) and (b) of the Welfare and Pension Plans Disclosure Act is granted whereby banking institutions and trust companies specified in Sec. 2580.412-28 are not required to comply with subsections 13(a) and (b) of the Act, with respect to welfare and pension benefit plans covered by the Act.

Promulgated: 34 Fed. Reg. 5158 (3/13/69).

Amended: 50 Fed. Reg. 26706 (6/28/85).

Sec. 2580.412-28—Conditions of exemption.

This exemption applies only to those banking institutions and trust companies subject to regulation and examination by the Comptroller of the Currency or the Board of Governors of the Federal Reserve System, or the Federal Deposit Insurance Corporation.

Promulgated: 28 Fed. Reg. 14403 (12/27/63).

Amended: 50 Fed. Reg. 26706 (6/28/85).

Savings and Loan Associations Subject to Federal Regulation

Sec. 2580.412-29—Exemption.

An exemption from the bonding requirements of subsections 13(a) and (b) of the Welfare and Pension Plans Disclosure Act is granted whereby savings and loan associations (including building and loan associations, cooperative banks and homestead associations) specified in Sec. 2580.412-30 are not required to comply with subsections 13(a) and (b) of the Act, with respect to welfare and pension benefit plans covered by the Act for the benefit of their own employees, where such a savings and loan association is the administrator of such plans.

Promulgated: 32 Fed. Reg. 6840 (5/4/67).

Amended: 50 Fed. Reg. 26706 (6/28/85).

Sec. 2580.412-30—Conditions of exemption.

This exemption applies only to those savings and loan associations (including building and loan associations, cooperative banks and homestead associations) subject to regulation and examination by the Federal Home Loan Bank Board.

Promulgated: 32 Fed. Reg. 6840 (5/4/67).

Amended: 50 Fed. Reg. 26706 (6/28/85).

Insurance Carriers, Service and Other Similar Organizations

Sec. 2580.412-31—Exemption.

An exemption from the bonding requirements of subsection 13(a) and (b) of the Welfare and Pension Plans Disclosure Act is granted whereby any insurance carrier or service or other similar organization specified in Sec. 2580.412-32 is not required to comply with subsections 13(a) and (b) of the Act with respect to any welfare or pension benefit plan covered by the Act which is established or maintained for the benefit of persons other than the employees of such insurance carrier or service or other similar organization.

Promulgated: 34 Fed. Reg. 5158 (3/13/69).

Amended: 50 Fed. Reg. 26706 (6/28/85).

Sec. 2580.412-32—Conditions of exemption.

This exemption applies only to those insurance carriers, service or other similar organizations providing or underwriting welfare or pension plan benefits in accordance with State law.

Promulgated: 34 Fed. Reg. 5158 (3/13/69).

Amended: 50 Fed. Reg. 26706 (6/28/85).

Subpart G—Prohibition Against Bonding by Parties Interested in the Plan

Sec. 2580.412-33—Introductory statement.

(a) This part discusses the meaning and scope of Sec. 13(c) of the Welfare and Pension Plans Disclosure Act of 1958 (76 Stat. 39, 29 U.S.C. 308d(c)) (hereinafter referred to as the Act). This provision makes it unlawful "for any person to procure any bond [required by the Act] from any surety or other company or through any agent or broker in whose business operations such plan or any party in interest in such plan has any significant control or financial interest, direct or indirect." Because the prohibition contained in this provision is broadly stated, it becomes a matter of importance to determine more specifically the types of arrangements intended to be prohibited.

(b) The provisions of Sec. 13 of the Act, including 13(c) are subject to the general investigatory authority of the Director, Office of Labor-Management and Welfare-Pension Reports, embodied in Sec. 9 of the Act. The correctness of an interpretation of these provisions can be determined finally and authoritatively only by the courts. It is necessary, however, for the Labor-Management Services Administrator to reach informed conclusions as to the meaning of the law to enable him to carry out his statutory duties of administration and enforcement. The interpretations of the Labor-Management Services Administrator contained in this part, which are issued upon the advice of the Solicitor of Labor, indicate the construction of the law which will guide the Labor-Management Services Administrator in performing his duties unless and until he is directed otherwise by authoritative ruling of the courts or unless and until he subsequently decides that his prior interpretation is incorrect. Under Sec. 12 of the Act, the interpretations contained in this part, if relied upon in good faith, will constitute a defense in any action or proceeding based on any Act or omission in alleged violation of Sec. 13(c) of the Act. The omission, however to discuss a particular problem in this part, or in interpretations supplementing it, should not be taken to indicate the adoption of any position by the Labor-Management Services Administrator with respect to such problem or to constitute an administrative interpretation or practice. Interpretations of the Labor-Management Services Administrator with respect to 13(c) are set forth in this part to provide those affected by the provisions of the Act with "a practical guide * * * as to how the office representing the public interest in its enforcement will seek to apply it" (Skidmore v. Swift & Co., 323 U.S. 134, 138).

(c) To the extent that prior opinions and interpretations relating to 13(c) are inconsistent with the principles stated in this part, they are hereby rescinded and withdrawn.

Promulgated: 28 Fed. Reg. 14412 (12/27/63).

Amended: 50 Fed. Reg. 26706 (6/28/85).

Sec. 2580.412-34—General.

The purpose of Sec. 13(c), as shown by its legislative history, is similar to a closely related provision contained in Sec. 502(a) of the Labor-Management Reporting and Disclosure Act of 1959 (73 Stat. 536; 29 U.S.C. 502(a)). The fundamental purpose of Congress under 13(c) is to insure against potential abuses arising from significant financial or other influential interests affecting the objectivity of the plan or parties in interest in the plan and agents, brokers, or surety or other companies, in securing and providing the bond specified in Sec. 13(a). As will be explained more fully below, this prohibition, however, was not intended to preclude the placing of bonds through or with certain parties in interest in plans which provide a variety of services to the plan, one of which is a bonding service.

Promulgated: 28 Fed. Reg. 14412 (12/27/63).

Amended: 50 Fed. Reg. 26706 (6/28/85).

Sec. 2580.412-35—Disqualification of agents, brokers and sureties.

Since 13(c) is to be construed as disqualifying any agent, broker, surety or other company from having a bond placed through or with it, if the plan or any party in interest in the plan has a significant financial interest or control in such agent, broker, surety or other company, a question of fact will necessarily arise in many cases as to whether the financial interest or control held is sufficiently significant to disqualify the agent, broker or surety. Although no rule of guidance can be established to govern each and every case in which this question arises, in general, the essential test is whether the existing financial interest or control held is incompatible with an unbiased exercise of judgment in regard to procuring the bond or bonding the plan's personnel. In regard to the foregoing, it is also to be pointed out that lack of knowledge or consent on the part of persons responsible for procuring bonds with respect to the existence of a significant financial interest or control rendering the bonding arrangement unlawful will not be deemed a mitigating factor where such persons have failed to make a reasonable examination into the pertinent circumstances affecting the procuring of the bond.

Promulgated: 28 Fed. Reg. 14412 (12/27/63).

Amended: 50 Fed. Reg. 26706 (6/28/85).

Sec. 2580.412-36—Application of 13(c) to "party in interest".

(a) Under 13(c), an agent, broker or surety or other company is disqualified from having a bond placed through or with it if a "party in interest" in the plan has any significant control or financial interest in such agent, broker, surety or other company. Sec. 3(13) of the Act defines the term "party in interest" to mean "any administrator, officer, trustee, custodian, counsel, or employee of any employee welfare benefit plan or a person providing benefit plan services to any such plan, or an employer any of whose employees are covered by such a plan or officer or employee or agent of such employer, or an officer or agent or employee of an employee organization having members covered by such plan."

(b) A basic question presented is whether the effect of 13(c) is to prohibit persons from placing a bond through or with any "party in interest" in the plan. The language used in 13(c) appears to indicate that in this connection the intent of Congress was to eliminate those instances where the existing financial interest or control held by the "party in interest" in the agent, broker, surety or other company is incompatible with an unbiased exercise of judgment in regard to procuring the bond or bonding the plan's personnel. Accordingly, not all parties in interest are disqualified from procuring or providing bonds for the plan. Thus where a "party in interest" or its affiliate provides multiple benefit plan services to plans, persons are not prohibited from availing themselves of the bonding services provided by the "party in interest" or its affiliate merely because the plan has already availed itself, or will avail itself, of other services provided by the "party in interest." In this case, it is inherent in the nature of the "party in interest" or its affiliate as an individual or organization providing multiple benefit plan services, one of which is a bonding service, that the existing financial interest or control held is not, in and of itself, incompatible with an unbiased exercise of judgment in regard to procuring the bond or bonding the plan's personnel. In short, there is no distinction between this type of relationship and the ordinary arm's length business relationship which may be established between a plan-customer and an agent, broker or surety company, a relationship which Congress could not have intended to disturb. On the other hand, where a "party in interest" in the plan or an affiliate does not provide a bonding service as part of its general business operations, 13(c) would prohibit any person from procuring the bond through or with any agent, broker, surety or other company, with respect to which the "party in interest" has any significant control or financial interest, direct or indirect. In this case, the failure of the "party in interest" or its affiliate to provide a bonding service as part of its general business operations raises the possibility of less than an arm's length business relationship between the plan and the agent, broker, surety or other company since the objectivity of either the plan or the agent, broker or surety may be influenced by the "party in interest".

(c) The application of the principles discussed in this section is illustrated by the following examples:

Example (1). B, a broker, renders actuarial and consultant service to plan P. B has also procured a group life insurance policy for plan P. B may also place a bond for P with surety company S, provided that neither B nor P has any significant control or financial interest, direct or indirect, in S and provided that neither P nor any other "party in interest" in P, e.g., an officer of the plan, has any significant control or financial interest, direct or indirect, in B or S.

Example (2). I, a life insurance company, has provided a group life insurance policy for plan P. I is affiliated with S, a surety company, and has a significant financial interest or control in S. P is not prohibited from obtaining a bond from S since I's affiliation with S does not ordinarily, in and of itself, affect the objectivity of P in procuring the bond or the objectivity of S in bonding P's personnel. However, if any other "party in interest" as defined in Sec. 3(13) of the Act, such as the employer whose employees are covered by P, should have a significant financial interest or control in S, S could not write the bond for P, since the employer's interest affects the objectivity of P and S.

Promulgated: 28 Fed. Reg. 14412 (12/27/63).

Amended: 50 Fed. Reg. 26706 (6/28/85).

Appendix 5

Donovan v. Bierwirth

538 F. Supp. 463, 2 EBC 2145

DONOVAN v. BIERWIRTH

U.S. District Court,
Eastern District of New York

RAYMOND J. DONOVAN, Secretary of the U.S. Department of Labor, Plaintiff, v. JOHN C. BIERWIRTH, ROBERT G. FREESE, and CARL A. PALADINO, Defendants. JOSEPH W. ULLMAN, LILLIAN E. BALDISSARD, RITA V. HARNER, ANTHONY PANCELLA, JR., KATHLEEN T. CHEW, and BENJAMIN L. CREWS, Intervenor-Defendants, 81 CV 3408, Dec. 3, 1981.

ERISA — PROTECTION OF RIGHTS

Fiduciary Responsibility — Fiduciary Duties — Exclusive Purpose (► 20.210)

Fiduciary Responsibility — Prohibited Transactions — Act on Behalf of Adverse Party (► 20.425)

[1] Pension plan trustees, who were also officers of plan's sponsoring employer or of sponsor's subsidiary, did not commit per se violations of ERISA's exclusive purpose standard either by their failure to abstain from investment decision concerning employer's stock or by mere acquisition of employer stock, as part of plan to avoid takeover by outside corporation, since review of ERISA's statutory scheme and legislative history indicates that ERISA contemplates existence and approval, in certain circumstances, of fiduciaries acting on behalf of plan even though they have dual loyalties, so long as they act exclusively for benefit of beneficiaries and participants and otherwise comply with ERISA Sections 404 and 406.

Fiduciary Responsibility — Fiduciary Duties — Prudence Standard (► 20.225)

[2] Pension plan trustees, who were also officers of plan's sponsoring employer or of sponsor's subsidiary, acted imprudently in purchasing sponsoring employer's stock for pension plan as part of plan to avoid takeover by outside corporation, where trustees' decision was arrived at without thorough independent investigation of basis for decision, where trustees' conduct between date of tender offer and pension plan's purchase of stock evince inability to make independent decisions on behalf of pension plan solely in interest of participants and beneficiaries, and where trustees' conduct was motivated solely by their all consuming-desire to defeat tender offer.

Fiduciary Responsibility — Liability for Breach — In General (► 20.651)

Administration and Enforcement — Remedies — Appointment or Removal of Fiduciaries (► 40.204)

[3] Pension plan trustees, who were also officers of plan's sponsoring employer and who purchased on behalf of plan securities of sponsoring employer as part of plan to avoid takeover by outside corporation, are restrained from buying, selling, or exercising any powers, rights, or other duties on behalf of plan with respect to stock of sponsoring employer, except upon written consent of Secretary of Labor, since Secretary of Labor has shown likelihood of success on merits in action challenging trustees' actions as imprudent, since trustees have manifested inability to separate their corporate loyalty and their loyalty to pension plan, and since manner in which trustees' exercised their judgment with respect to employer stock was so egregiously imprudent that court must infer likelihood of further violations.

On Secretary of Labor's motion for preliminary injunction in action under ERISA against trustees of employer's pension plan alleging that trustees breached their fiduciary duties by expending plan assets to purchase employer stock to fend off tender offer and seeking to enjoin trustees actions that violated ERISA and to secure other equitable relief. Motion granted in part.

Ronald G. Whiting, Deputy Solicitor, Monica Gallagher, Associate Solicitor, Robert N. Eccles, Norman P. Goldberg, Sherwin S. Kaplan, and Jane M. Kheel, Office of the Solicitor, Plan Benefits Security Division, U.S. Labor Department, Washington, D.C., attorneys for Secretary.

Raymond L. Falls, David R. Hyde, Immanuel Kohn, Kenneth W. Orce, and George Wailand, of Cahill, Gordon & Reindel, of New York, N.Y., attorneys for defendants.

Mona N. Glanzer, Bruce R. Nullman, and Martin Gringer, of Rains & Pogrebin, P.C., of Mineola, N.Y., attorneys for intervenor-defendants.

Full Text of Opinion

MISHLER, District Judge.

Plaintiff Raymond J. Donovan, the Secretary of Labor (the "Secretary"), brings this action under the Employee Retirement Income Security Act of 1974 ("ERISA") , 29 U.S.C. §1001 *et seq.*, against the three trustees of the Grumman Corporation Pension Plan (the "Pension Plan") to, *inter alia,* enjoin acts and practices violative of Title I of ERISA and secure other appropriate equitable relief. The gravaman of plaintiff's complaint alleges that each of the individual trustees have breached their fiduciary duties by expending Pension Plan assets for the purchase of Grumman Corporation stock in an effort to fend off the tender offer made for the Grumman Corporation ("Grumman") by The LTV Corporation ("LTV"). The details of those open market purchases made by the Pension Plan on October 12 and 13, 1981 have been recounted in a recent decision by this court, *The LTV Corporation v. Grumman Corporation,* ___F.Supp. ___(E.D.N.Y. October 16, 1981). For the purposes of presentation, we shall once again review the details of those purchases and examine the decision-making process which lead to the purchase decision.

The material facts are either conceded or beyond dispute, and accordingly, this motion did not necessitate an evidentiary hearing. The court has thoroughly reviewed the exhibits and depositions submitted at the time of argument on October 30, 1981 and now makes the following findings of fact and conclusions of law as required by Rule 52(a) of the Federal Rules of Civil Procedure.

I. *FACTS*

On September 24, 1981, The LTV Corporation publicly announced that it was making a tender offer for up to 70% of the Grumman Corporation's outstanding stock and securities convertible into stock conditioned upon acquiring at least 50.01% of Grumman stock on a fully diluted basis. On the day prior to the announcement, Grumman's Chief Executive Officer and Chairman of the Board of Directors, John C. Bierwirth, was informed of LTV's intentions while vacationing on the Mississippi River. He returned to Grumman headquarters at Bethpage, New York midday on the 24th. He did not confer with Grumman personnel concerning the LTV offer until his return. The Grumman Board of Directors convened September 25 and passed a resolution to fight the takeover. Thus, the commencement of Grumman's well orchestrated plan to defeat the LTV tender offer was set into motion.

The Pension Plan held 525,000 shares of Grumman stock prior to the October purchases. The market value of that investment immediately before the tender offer (at $25 per share) was approximately $13,125,000. LTV's offer to purchase Grumman stock for $45 per share presented the Pension Plan with the possibility of realizing a substantial gain on its Grumman investments.

Three days after the Board's decision to oppose the LTV takeover, Mr. Bierwirth, acting as Chairman of the Board, in a letter directed to "Fellow Grummanite(s)," observed the following:

> "We're very optimistic about our chances of defeating the takeover bid. About a third of all shares are held by Grumman's employee investment and pension plans. These plans are managed by Grummanites who will look long and hard at how well their fellow members would be served by selling off Grumman stock."

It was indeed the obligation of the Pension Plan trustees to take a long hard look at how the Plan would be served by tendering its Grumman stock.

Mr. Bierwirth spent approximately 90% of his working hours during the two-week period following his return to

Long Island trying to understand the LTV offer and simultaneously denouncing it through public meetings with reporters, employees and retirees. His decision as a trustee of the Pension Plan to refuse the opportunity to tender was arrived at during a special meeting of the trustees on October 7. The meeting lasted somewhere between one and two hours while the discussion of whether to tender took approximately one-half hour. (Freese dep. at p.30). Other than the trustees, John Mullan, in-house counsel for Grumman, was the only other individual present at the special meeting. John Mullan had not been formally retained by the Pension Plan as counsel. The trustees failed to consult with outside counsel, or any independent investment advisor. In part, they relied on the opinion of Dillon, Read & Co., an investment banking firm retained by Grumman to render an opinion solely on the adequacy of LTV's offering price.

The other Pension Plan trustees are Robert G. Freese and Carl A. Paladino. Approximately fifty percent of Freese's time between the announcement of the tender offer and the actual Pension Plan purchases was devoted toward raising bank credit for the purchase of Grumman common stock by Grumman. Paladino's only activity between September 23 and October 7 involved the preparation of financial material concerning Grumman Aerospace, a subsidiary of Grumman. (Paladino's dep. at pp.13–16). He had neither formally nor informally, prior to the October 7 trustees' meeting, discussed the possibility of a Pension Plan purchase of Grumman stock. (Paladino's dep. at pp.24–25).

The October 7 trustees' meeting commenced with a ten-minute presentation by Mr. Mullan about ERISA, (Freese dep. at pp. 24–25), and culminated in a unanimous vote by the trustees not to tender the Grumman shares already owned by the Pension Plan. Further discussions led to a second decision wherein they voted to purchase up to an additional 1,275,000 shares of Grumman stock. The decision not to tender was announced in a press release on October 8, the same day on which the trustees executed an amendment to the Plan's Trust Agreement providing for indemnification of the trustees by Grumman for liability arising out of any action absent willful misconduct or lack of good faith. The amendment agreement was dated October 7.

The October 7 decision to purchase Grumman stock was conditioned upon approval by the Securities and Exchange Commission of an exemption from Rule 10b–6, 17 C.F.R. §240.10b–6, which prohibits persons interested in a "distribution" of stock from trading in that stock. The exemption was granted on October 9. Nevertheless, no purchases were made until October 12. The trustees hoped that this court would enjoin the LTV tender offer over the following weekend thereby avoiding the Pension Plan purchases at the artificially high prices created by the tender offer, or alternatively, avoiding the purchases altogether. (See Bierwirth dep. at pp.43–44). The injunction did not issue that weekend. The trustees convened briefly on October 12 and, without further discussion on the subject, decided to proceed with their purchases.

The Pension Plan purchased 958,000 shares through Dillon, Read & Co. on October 12. The price ranged from a low of $36 to a high of $39 5/8 at an average price of $38.61 per share. On October 13, Dillon, Read & Co. purchased an additional 200,000 shares on behalf of the Pension Plan at an average price of $36.62 per share.

The trustees offer essentially two theories of defense to the Secretary's claims. First, they believed that the Grumman stock represented a good investment for the Pension Plan. Secondly, they were concerned over the impact of an LTV takeover on the Pension Plan. The latter concern was twofold—that the Grumman Plan might be merged, terminated or otherwise altered to the detriment of its beneficiaries and that LTV's financial health, upon which its pension plans ultimately depend for contribution, was unsound.

II. *DISCUSSION*

In its instant motion for preliminary relief, the Secretary contends that each trustee breached his fiduciary obligation by, *inter alia,* (1) failing to act solely in the interest of the Pension Plan's participants and beneficiaries and for the exclusive purpose of providing benefits to its participants and beneficiaries and defraying reasonable expenses of plan administration, in violation of Section 404(a)(1)(A) of ERISA, 29 U.S.C. §1104(a)(1)(A)[1] and (2) failing to act with the care, skill, prudence and diligence that a prudent man acting in a like capacity and familiar with such matters would use in the conduct of a similar enterprise with similar objectives, in violation of Section 404(a)(1)(B) of ERISA, 29 U.S.C. §1104(a)(1)(B).[2]

The Pension Plan is an employee benefit plan established and maintained by Grumman. The plan is an employee benefit plan within the meaning of Section 3(3) of ERISA, 29 U.S.C. §1002(3) and therefore subject to ERISA rules and regulations pursuant to Section 4(a) of ERISA, 29 U.S.C. §1003(a). The Secretary of Labor has standing to maintain this action under Section 502(a)(2) and (5) of ERISA, 29 U.S.C. §1132(a)(2) and (5). Jurisdiction and venue in this court are proper under Section 502(e)(1) and (2) of ERISA, 29 U.S.C. §1132(e)(1) and (2).

[1] ERISA §404(a)(1)(A), 29 U.S.C. §1104(a)(1)(A) provides as follows:

"Subject to sections 1103(c) and (d), 1342, and 1344 of this title, a fiduciary shall discharge his duties with respect to a plan solely in the interest of the participants and beneficiaries and—

for the exclusive purpose of:

(i) providing benefits to participants and their beneficiaries; and

(ii) defraying reasonable expenses of administering the plan."

[2] ERISA §404(a)(1)(B), 29 U.S.C. §1104(a)(1)(B) provides as follows:

"Subject to sections 1103(c) and (d), 1342, and 1344 of this title, a fiduciary shall discharge his duties with respect to a plan solely in the interest of the participants and beneficiaries and—

with the care, skill, prudence, and diligence under the circumstances then prevailing that a prudent man acting in a like capacity and familiar with such matters would use in the conduct of an enterprise of a like character and with like aims." The Secretary also contends that the trustees have violated ERISA §406(b)(1) and (2), 29 U.S.C. §1106(b)(1) and (2). Even assuming the trustees have committed such violations, the scope of the preliminary relief would be unaffected. Accordingly, we decline the opportunity to pass on these claims.

A. *Dual Loyalties*

Each of the trustees of the Pension Plan is also an officer of Grumman or a Grumman subsidiary. John C. Bierwirth is the Chief Executive Officer and Chairman of the Board of Directors of Grumman; Robert G. Freese is a Senior Vice President and a Director of Grumman; and Carl A. Paladino is a Senior Vice President of Grumman Aerospace Corporation, a subsidiary of Grumman. Each of the trustees is a fiduciary with respect to the Pension Plan within the meaning of Section 3(21)(A) of ERISA, 29 U.S.C. §1002(21)(A).

The alleged violations of ERISA arise from the difficult task presented to defendants during the time of the LTV tender offer of simultaneously serving two masters—Grumman and the Pension Plan. It is argued that the separate loyalties ("dual loyalties") created by their dual employment prevented the trustees from acting exclusively in the Pension Plan's interest. It is further argued that subsequent to LTV's tender offer it was *per se* unlawful for the plan's fiduciaries to act on its behalf because of their dual loyalties, without regard to whether their secondary loyalty (to Grumman) influenced their conduct. It is the latter contention which we now address.

[1] Part 4 of Title I sets forth the fiduciary obligations which the Grumman trustees undertook to faithfully discharge. At the outset, we hold that ERISA contemplates the existence and approval, in certain circumstances, of fiduciaries acting on behalf of a pension plan even though they have dual loyalties. Section 408(c)(3) of ERISA, 29 U.S.C. §1108(c)(3), implicitly authorizes an officer of the sponsor corporation to serve as a pension plan fiduciary by providing that Section 406 of ERISA, 29 U.S.C. §1106 (specifying prohibited transactions), shall not be construed so as "to prohibit any fiduciary . . . from serving as a fiduciary in addition to being an officer, employee agent, or other representative of a party in interest." Further, ERISA section 407, 29 U.S.C. §1107 specifically authorizes a plan to acquire stock of the sponsoring corporation. ERISA therefore necessari-

ly contemplates that trustees, who may be officers of the sponsoring company, may act on behalf of the pension plan in making investment decisions concerning stock of the sponsor corporation in spite of a potential conflict of interests.

A more detailed review of the statutory scheme of ERISA and its legislative history corroborates the foregoing conclusion. As previously stated, ERISA section 408(c)(3), 29 U.S.C. §1108(c)(3), expressly contemplates fiduciaries with dual loyalties. The Conference Report on ERISA states that the statute "makes it *clear* that a party-in-interest may serve as a fiduciary in addition to being an officer . . . ." H.Rep.No. 93–1280, 93d Cong. 2d Sess. at 312, 3 U.S.Code Cong. & Admin.News [1974], p.5092 (emphasis added). The Conference Report also contemplates a number of additional exceptions to the traditional rules governing fiduciary conduct. *See id.*

Having provided for an unorthodox departure from the common law rule against dual loyalties, Congress provided two statutory safeguards to protect plan participants and beneficiaries. First, the statute provides that "a fiduciary shall discharge his duties with respect to a plan *solely* in the interest of the participants and beneficiaries . . . ." Section 404(a)(1) of ERISA, 29 U.S.C. §1104(a)(1) (emphasis added). Therefore, although a trustee may have dual loyalties, when acting on behalf of the fund, his primary loyalty to the fund is to the *only* loyalty which may affect his judgment.

Mindful of the difficulty presented to trustees so situated, Congress enacted Section 406 of ERISA as a further protection for plan participants and beneficiaries. That section prohibits a fiduciary from acting in *certain specified circumstances* in order to prevent him "from being put in a position where he has dual loyalties, and, therefore, . . . cannot act exclusively for the benefit of a plan's participants and beneficiaries." H.Rep.No.93–1280, 93d Cong. 2d Sess. at 309, 3 U.S.Code & Admin.News [1974], p. 5089. The Conference Report's concern with the dangers inherent in the case of a fiduciary with dual loyalties was expressed in connection with ERISA section 406(b)(2), 29 U.S.C. §1106(b)(2), which prohibits fiduciaries from acting "in any transaction involving the plan on behalf of a party (or represent a party) whose interests are *adverse* to the interests of the plan or the interests of its participants or beneficiaries." (emphasis added). If we are to interpret ERISA as incorporating a *per se* prohibition against plan fiduciaries with dual loyalties acting on behalf of the plan, then the specific prohibition enacted to prevent a fiduciary from being placed in a position of dual loyalty is completely superfluous. *See id.* The negative implication, of course, is that Congress intended that fiduciaries with dual loyalties would be permitted to act in all other instances as long as they otherwise comply with ERISA section 404 and the balance of the restrictions found in ERISA section 406.

In construing ERISA, we are mindful of its remedial purposes and are therefore reluctant to depart from the inflexible, well established common law rule which precludes a fiduciary having dual loyalties from asserting the defense "that, although he had conflicting interests, he served his masters equally well or that his primary loyalty was not weakened by the pull of the secondary one." *Woods v. City National Bank & Trust Co.* 312 U.S. 262, 269, 61 S. Ct. 493, 497 (1941), *quoted in, NLRB v. Amax Coal Co.,* ___U.S. ___, 101 S. Ct. 2789, 2794 [2 EBC 1489] (1981). This well established rule naturally followed from the recognition in the courts of chancery of a trustee's "unwavering duty of complete loyalty to the beneficiary of the trust, to the exclusion of the interests of all other parties." *NLRB v. Amax Coal Co.,* ___U.S. at ___, 101 S. Ct. at 2794.

Nevertheless, even at common law, trustees are allowed to trade in securities or other property of an entity with which they are affiliated as long as authorization is provided by the terms of the trust. Restatement (Second) of Trusts §170, comment n. ("[s]uch a purchase is proper . . . if expressly or impliedly authorized by the terms of the trust"). *Accord, e.g., Central Hanover Bank & Trust Co. v. Russell,* 290 N.Y.

593, 48 N.E.2d 704 (1943) (mem.); 2 A.W.Scott, *Law of Trusts* §170.15 at 1340–41 (3d ed. 1967). We find that Section 407 of ERISA is Congress' authorization for a trustee to invest in sponsor corporation stock in spite of dual loyalties and conflicting interests *so long as* (1) he acts exclusively for the benefit of the plan beneficiaries and participants and otherwise complies with ERISA section 404, and (2) his actions are not violative of the proscriptions of ERISA section 406. Thus, the statutory scheme has abrogated the traditional common law rule. However, bearing in mind the purposes of ERISA, we further hold that a trustee having dual loyalties has "an *especial obligation* to act fairly on behalf of those concerned with the results of the action taken." *Withers v. Teachers' Retirement System of the City of New York,* 447 F.Supp. 1248, 1256 (S.D.N.Y. 1978), *aff'd mem.,* 595 F.2d 1210 (2d Cir. 1979) (applying common law principles of fiduciary duty) (emphasis added). The Grumman trustees had that very obligation when dealing with Grumman stock.

Our rejection of the Secretary's contention that the trustees' conduct was *per se* unlawful is not contrary to the Supreme Court's recent decision in *NLRB v. Amax Coal Co.* There, the Court held that the employer-selected trustees of a trust fund created under Section 302(c)(5) of the Labor Management Relations Act of 1947 ("LMRA"), 29 U.S.C. §186(c)(5), were not employer representatives (or agents) "for the purposes of collective bargaining or the adjustment of grievances" within the meaning of Section 8(b)(1)(B) of the National Labor Relations Act, as amended by Section 101 of the LMRA. In so construing Section 8(b)(1)(B), the Court recognized that a trustee complies with his fiduciary obligations under ERISA *so long as* he refrains from engaging in specified prohibited transactions and *acts* "exclusively for the benefit of the plan's participants and beneficiaries." *See NLRB v. Amax Coal Co.,* U.S. at ___, 101 S. Ct. at 2796, *quoting* H.R.Conf. Rep.No. 93–1280, 93d Cong., 2d Sess., 296, 309, 3 U.S.Code Cong. & Admin. News [1974], p.5089. In acknowledging that a trustee might possess a dual and conflicting loyalty to the appointing sponsor of the trust plan, the Court simply stated that the trustee "must overcome" that loyalty. *Id.* at 2796. Finally, the discussion of dual loyalties in the context of an employer-financed trust fund is distinguished from the instant case because ERISA's statutory scheme, unlike the LMRA, clearly contemplates the approval of fiduciaries with dual loyalties.

Accordingly, we find that the trustees of the Pension Plan did not commit *per se* violations of ERISA either by their failure to abstain from the investment decision concerning Grumman stock or by the mere acquisition of Grumman stock. *See Curren v. Freitag,* 432 F.Supp. 668, 672 (S.D.Ill. 1977).

B. *Section 404(a)(1)(B) and the Prudent Man Rule*

1. *The Standard*

The Secretary further argues that even if the trustees were permitted to make investment decisions (the decision to buy, sell, or hold) concerning the Grumman stock in the face of the LTV tender offer, they failed to act prudently as required by ERISA section 404(a)(1)(B). At the outset, we hold that this affirmative statutory duty—the duty to act "with the care, skill, prudence, and diligence under the circumstances then prevailing that a prudent man acting in like capacity and familiar with such matters would use in the conduct of an enterprise of a like character and with like aims"—subsumes the duty "to make an independent inquiry into the merits of a particular investment" decision. *See Fiduciary Standards and the Prudent Man Rule under ERISA,* 88 Harv.L.Rev. (Part 2) 960, 965 (1975).

A review of a fiduciary's independent investigation is one of the well-established yardsticks against which courts have customarily tested fiduciary conduct for prudence. *See, e.g., Withers v. Teachers' Retirement System,* 447 F.Supp. at 1254–55; *In re Talbot's Estate,* 141 Cal.App.2d 309, 296 P.2d 848 (1st Dist. 1956); *In re Clark's Will,* 257 N.Y. 132, 177 N.E. 397 (1931); *In re Kent's Estate,* 146 Misc. 155, 261 N.Y.S. 698 (Sur.Ct. 1932), *aff'd, In re Manufac-*

turers Trust Co., 246 App.Div. 604, 284 N.Y.S. 976 (1935); 3 A.W.Scott, *Law of Trusts*, §227.1 at 1809–11. This same test is properly applied in the instant case to test defendants' conduct. *See Morrissey v. Curran*, 567 F.2d 546, 548–49 & n.9 (2d Cir. 1977).

However, when a fiduciary has dual loyalties, his independent investigation into the basis for an investment decision which presents a potential conflict of interests must be both intensive and scrupulous and must be discharged with the greatest degree of care that could be expected under all the circumstances by reasonable beneficiaries and participants of the plan. Were the rule less stringent we could not be certain that the Cardozian time honored standard for fiduciary behavior—"the punctilio of an honor the most sensitive," *Meinhard v. Salmon*, 247 N.Y. 458, 164 N.E. 545 (1928)—would remain uncompromised. Moreover, this greater standard of care is a natural corollary to the trustee's heightened obligation to act fairly when acting with dual loyalties and is fully consistent with principles of equity and the policies underlying ERISA. *See Gilliam v. Edwards*, 492 F.Supp. 1255, 1261 (D.N.J. 1980) ("To fulfill its curative aim, ERISA should be given a liberal construction to safeguard the interests of the Fund participants and beneficiaries and to preserve the integrity of Fund assets"). A thorough review of the record compels us to find that each of the trustees were woefully remiss in this regard and that the Secretary has satisfied his burden on this motion for a preliminary injunction.

2. *The Standard Applied to the Instant Case*

Defendants contend that they "gave *appropriate consideration* to the factors relevant to ERISA's standard of prudence." (Defendants' Memorandum of Law, dated October 29, 1981) (emphasis added). They argue that their decision to purchase Grumman shares was based upon their *belief* (1) that the Grumman stock presented a unique and substantial opportunity for long-term appreciation and was consistent with the portfolio needs of the Pension Plan and (2) that their decision was designed to further the purposes of the plan and the interests of its beneficiaries.

However, as indicated above, a belief, even a good faith belief, held by the trustees does not insulate them from charges that they have acted imprudently. An examination of the facts in *Withers v. Teachers' Retirement System of the City of New York*, 447 F.Supp. 1248 (S.D.N.Y. 1978), *aff'd mem.*, 595 F.2d 1210 (2d Cir. 1979), illustrates defendants' shortfallings in acting on behalf of the Pension Plan. Even though the Teachers' Retirement System (the "TRS") was not subject to ERISA, as we have previously noted, the same fiduciary principles apply since the trustees in *Withers*, as in the instant case, were subject to common law principles of fiduciary duty. *See Marshall v. Teamsters Local 282 Pension Trust Fund*, 458 F.Supp. 986, 990 (E.D.N.Y. 1978).

In *Withers*, the defendant trustees of the TRS were sued for allegedly having breached their fiduciary obligation to the TRS by authorizing the purchase of $860 million of New York City bonds during the City's financial crisis in November 1975. The bonds were highly speculative and unmarketable. Judge Conner found that the trustees had properly acted since they concluded, after a thorough independent investigation of the facts, that the long term viability of the TRS depended on the investment in New York City bonds. In finding that the trustees had fulfilled the obligation of independent investigation the court noted the following: (1) their conclusion that the bankruptcy of New York City was imminent was based on opinions from *highly reliable sources* and represented the *consensus* of a *broad spectrum* of opinion; (2) they participated in *frequent meetings* with City, State and Municipal Assistance Corporation ("MAC") officials during the summer and fall of 1975 concerning the deteriorating state of the City's finances; (3) in November 1975, there were *frequent meetings* among the trustees and the New York City Comptroller and Corporation Counsel to discuss the problems of the City's budget; (4) they acted on *all* the information available to them and "went to *great lengths* to satisfy themselves of the absence of any reasonable possibility" that investment in City bonds could be avoided, (emphasis added); (5) after concluding investment was necessary, they made every reasonable effort to "secure *maximum protection* for the beneficiaries of the TRS," (emphasis added); (6) the trustees made their decision without succumbing to the pressure exerted by both the Governor's office and by City Hall; and finally, (7) "their decision to invest in the City obligations was . . . forged from *intensive independent analysis* as well as consultation with experts." (emphasis added).

For the purposes of this motion, we shall assume that the interests of the Grumman Pension Plan were identical with those of Grumman. Our inquiry is directed solely to the manner in which the trustees exercised their judgment in committing Pension Plan assets amounting to some $36,988,380 (958,000 shares at an average price of $38.61 per share) on October 12 and $7,324,000 (200,000 shares at an average price of $36.62 per share) on October 13. These purchases represented a substantial commitment of Pension Plan assets which had been estimated to be in excess of $600,000,000 at its most recent valuation.

It is no defense to the Secretary's instant action that the trustees' decision to fight the LTV tender offer with Pension Plan assets might have been in the best interests of the Plan *if* their decision was arrived at without a thorough independent investigation of the basis for that decision. Luck or good fortune is no substitute for a trustee's duty of inquiry.

[2] We find that the trustees acted imprudently in purchasing Grumman stock on October 12 and 13. We further find that their conduct between the date of the LTV tender offer and mid-October evince an inability to make independent decisions on behalf of the Pension Plan solely in the interest of its participants and beneficiaries. We reach these conclusions because the trustees' decisions were made without sufficient inquiry into the facts upon which they based their decisions. We find that their conduct was solely motivated by their all consuming-desire to defeat the tender offer.

The deposition testimony of the three trustees provides overwhelming support for our conclusion. Rather than analyzing the offer, the trustees spent most of their time between September 24 and October 13 fighting the LTV tender offer. Even though it is clear that Bierwirth had, at most, a superficial understanding of the offer on September 25, he voted as a director of Grumman to reject the tender offer that same day. Our conclusion that he failed to understand the offer on the 25th is supported by his own deposition testimony. (Bierwirth dep. at p.9, spent three weeks "trying to understand what the offer was. . . ."). While a reasonable inference is that Bierwirth had no interest in considering the LTV offer regardless of the potential for Grumman or the Pension Plan, Bierwirth would challenge this inference because of his "justifiable reliance" on the Dillon, Read & Co. opinion letter which was presented to the Board of Directors on September 25. We reject that contention out of hand and find that Bierwirth was committed to defeating the LTV takeover prior to the September 25 board meeting for reasons unrelated to the Dillon, Read & Co. opinion letter.

Mr. Thayer, Chairman of the Board of Directors and Chief Executive Officer of the LTV Corporation, testified subject to cross-examination by Grumman in the related case *Grumman Corp. v. The LTV Corp.*, Dkt. CV 81 3156, that Mr. Gavin, President of Grumman and speaking on behalf of Bierwirth, prior to the tender offer, rejected LTV's offer to discuss merger prospects. The Grumman rejection came only one hour after LTV's inquiry. Bierwirth was aware of the merger proposal on September 23 and it appears that he personally rejected the offer for discussions on the subject. (See Bierwirth dep. at p.6). The rejection came notwithstanding the assurance provided by LTV that Bierwirth would have been retained as the Chief Executive Officer of a joint Grumman-Vought Aerospace operation. Nowhere in his deposition testimony did Bierwirth indicate that he opposed the takeover because of the potential anti-trust violations and the related problems of future divestiture.

Mr. Bierwirth served as Grumman's chief public spokesman in opposing the LTV takeover. He spent virtually all of his time in activities related to the takeover which included attending meetings, lobbying in Washington, D.C., appearing on talk shows and discussing the crisis with reporters. His deposition testimony fails to reveal any effort to understand how the Pension Plan, as opposed to Grumman might have been advantaged by tendering its Grumman stock to LTV or how the fund might have been protected in the event of an LTV takeover. His inability to consider, or to request discussions, on the protection of Pension Plan benefits (and the survival of the Grumman plan as an independent plan) stemmed from his fear of a solution which would have seriously compromised his position as an advocate against the LTV takeover on behalf of Grumman. Bierwirth was totally committed to Grumman's resolution to quash the takeover bid.

In deciding as a Pension Plan trustee to reject the tender offer, Bierwirth "was quite interested in Carl Paladino's analysis of LTV . . .," presented at the October 7 trustees' meeting. (Bierwirth dep. at p.33). Paladino, however, was hardly a financial expert with respect to LTV. As previously mentioned, the only work performed by Paladino between September 23 and October 7 was the preparation of financial material on Grumman Aerospace. (Paladino dep. at 16). Paladino's only knowledge of LTV's financial position derived from his examination of the LTV annual report and the LTV 10–K. (Paladino dep. at 36). The trustees did not consult William Parmentier and his investment staff with regard to LTV's financial prospects. The third trustee, Mr. Freese, spent more than half of his time for the three weeks following September 25 arranging a bank line of credit for the future purchase of Grumman stock by Grumman.

Clearly, the trustees spent the abundance of their combined waking hours searching for LTV's Achille's heel and otherwise opposing the tender offer. It would be charitable to say that they "took a long and hard" look at how the takeover might damage the interests of the Pension Plan without endeavoring to make any examination of how its interests might have been advanced. Indeed, there was no real inquiry into the dangers presented to the Pension Plan in the event of a takeover. We find that their conclusions regarding the dangers presented by the takeover were based on conjecture, speculation and unfounded assumptions.

As we have previously mentioned, the trustees never considered that they might strike a deal with LTV which could have protected the Pension Plan. The following inquiry was made of Bierwirth:

> "Q. Was there any consideration as to the existing Pension benefits leaving aside the gratuitous increase, any consideration to tendering subject to attempting to obtain some protection for the basic pension benefits?"

Bierwirth responded by stating one of his many unfounded assumptions:

> "A. I think you would have to say that we were of the opinion that you could not protect, so we did not discuss how we could give partial protection."

(Bierwirth dep. at p.29). LTV having once indicated a willingness to "talk merger" and having publicly pledged that it would not merge or terminate the Grumman Pension Plan (Bierwirth dep. at p.25; Paladino dep. at p.38), there was no basis for believing that the Texas conglomerate would have been unreceptive to discussions concerning security for Grumman Pension Plan participants and beneficiaries.

A host of other examples confirm that the trustees failed to act prudently. They failed to consult with outside, independent counsel.[3] In spite of the numerous and difficult questions presented by the LTV tender offer, we must reiterate that the October 7 meeting

[3] The only counsel available at the October 7 trustees' meeting was John Mullan, in-house counsel to Grumman. The propriety of consulting Grumman's counsel under such circumstances is subject to serious question.

lasted less than two hours with only one-half hour devoted to the decision to reject the offer. The decision not to tender, and thereafter, to purchase, was arrived at without the consultation of an independent investment advisor. Yet, Pension assets were expended with the knowledge that if the trustees' objectives were realized, the Pension Plan would have to absorb substantial short-term losses.[4]

Defendants contend that independent investment advice was unneccessary since the Plan historically handled investiment matters in-house. However, the in-house investment staff was not consulted. Viewing the October 12 and 13 purchases from solely an investment standpoint, i.e., ignoring the alleged impact on the Plan in the event of a takeover, taking notice of the availability in the marketplace of other investments, and considering that Grumman stock was selling at an all time high, the trustees should have also considered the long-term appreciation offered by other stocks with the advice of an investment counselor. It is axiomatic to state that any given investment is sensible only if it is superior to other investments available in the marketplace.

The trustees contend that they had guidance from reliable investment advisors. They cite the July 1981 Lehman Brothers Kuhn Loeb ("Lehman Brothers") research report which recommended the purchase of Grumman common to LTV. The report, however, did not render an opinion on the market value of the Grumman stock and the recommendation was made at a time when Grumman stock was trading at $28 per share. The Lehman Brothers' report was hardly support for the proposition that Grumman stock was worth $45 per share to any investor. The tender offer price naturally included a premium for majority control over Grumman as was evidenced by LTV's condition of purchase (the acquisition of at least 50.01% of Grumman common on a fully-diluted basis). In contrast, the Pension Plan did not seek control. Without further analysis, it is evident that the Lehman Brothers' recommendation, prepared with LTV's unique financial position and business objectives in mind, was inadequate support for the trustees' decision to purchase Grumman stock at $45 per share.

Likewise, the trustees were not justified in relying on the Dillon, Read & Co. opinion prepared for the Grumman Board of Directors, dated September 25, 1981. The opinion letter drafted for the Board expressly noted that Dillon, Read & Co. had "provided investment banking services to Grumman in the past, including acting as a manager of an offering of its convertible subordinated debentures in April, 1980." Dillon, Read & Co. had an obvious interest in Grumman's continuing independence, and therefore, as horn-book law indicates, its opinion should have been subject to some level of scrutiny:

> "In reaching his conclusion [concerning an investment decision, a trustee] may take into consideration advice given to him by attorneys, bankers, brokers and others whom prudent men in the community regard as qualified to give advice. He is not justified, however, in relying wholly upon the advice of others, since it is his duty to exercise his own judgment in the light of the information and advice which he receives. In relying upon the advice of another, he should consider whether the person giving the advice is disinterested. Thus it has been held that in purchasing securities for the trust he is not justified in relying solely on the advice of a broker interested in the sale of the securities."

3 A.W.Scott, *Law of Trusts*, §227.1 at 1809. The two-page opinion letter was reviewed by the Pension Plan trustees at the October 7 meeting.[5] The letter was unaccompanied by any underlying

---

[4] Following the affirmance by the Second Circuit Court of Appeals of our decision enjoining the LTV tender offer, *Grumman v. The LTV Corp.*, ___F.2d ___(2d Cir. 1981), the Pension Plan paper losses exceeded $10 million.

[5] The two-page opinion letter authored by Dillon, Read & Co. upon which defendants so heavily relied was not submitted in opposition to the Secretary's motion until the court, *sua sponte*, made a request to defendants' counsel for its production on November 23, 1981.

financial statistics and no representative from Dillon, Read & Co. was present for questioning. Nevertheless, the trustees relied on a report literally prepared overnight and based on the limited amount of information available at the time of the report's preparation. It was gross negligence, if not bad faith, to rely on such a report prepared some twelve days prior to the October 7 meeting *without any effort* to have Dillon, Read & Co. update their evaluation of LTV's offer.[6]

In connection with the foregoing, the balance of pertinent facts surrounding the trustees' decision compel us to conclude that they in fact proceeded in bad faith. Between the time of the tender offer and the October Pension Plan purchases, they had one goal—to defeat the tender offer. Their policy was one of "conscious avoidance"; they intentionally avoided any inquiries which might have indicated that the success of LTV's tender offer could have been favorable to the Pension Plan.

The trustees had been educated on the complexities of "what goes on in the world of takeovers." (Bierwirth dep. at p.7). Earlier in 1981, Grumman had retained the firm of Skadden, Arps, Slate, Meagher & Flom ("Skadden, Arps") to render such advice. By retaining Skadden, Arps, the Grumman board manifested an understanding of the need to have expert legal advice on matters involving intricate federal statutes and administrative regulations. Each of the trustees were, and are, sophisticated businessmen. Yet, after having been shown pertinent sections of ERISA by Mr. Mullan at the October 7 meeting and after a brief oral presentation concerning the obligations of plan fiduciaries under ERISA, the trustees had no questions. (Paladino dep. at p.30; Freese dep. at pp.24–25). Their lack of concern or curiosity about the intricacies of ERISA and how it might affect the Pension Plan's ability to respond to the tender offer is in sharp contrast to the forward thinking decision of the Grumman directors, including Bierwirth and Freese, in retaining Skadden, Arps for general advice on corporate takeovers. The failure to retain counsel with an expertise in the area of ERISA during the four day period between the October 7 meeting and the massive buying campaign commencing on October 12 is strong evidence of their desire to *avoid* advice that might counsel against pension plan purchases. There was ample time to seek advice and it was no coincidence that the trustees failed to do so. Finally, their execution of the Trust Agreement Amendment dated October 7, 1981 which "clarified" the Pension Plan trustees' right to indemnification (Paladino dep. at p.67; exhibit 2), is a further indication of their awareness of ERISA's intricacies and the need for legal advice on matters related to the Pension Plan defense of the LTV takeover.

The trustees ignored other inquiries which should have been made. Plan fiduciaries have an affirmative duty to "defray[ ] reasonable expenses of administering the plan." §404(a)(1)(A)(ii) of ERISA, 29 U.S.C. §1104(a)(1)(A)(ii). Nevertheless, Paladino and Freese had no knowledge as to whether Dillon, Read & Co. was paid a brokerage commission for executing the October 12 and 13 purchase transactions. (Freese dep. at p.41; Paladino dep. at p.56). While Bierwirth knew that Dillon, Read & Co. was paid seven and a half cents a share, he had no idea whether that commission ($86,850 in total) was standard. (Bierwirth dep. at pp.56–57).

Even assuming, as the trustees contend, that they were entitled to consider the impact on the Pension Plan of a successful LTV tender offer, we decline to detail their lack of prudence in this regard, except as is evident from the following: (1) none of the trustees knew how many pension plans were sponsored by LTV; (2) no effort was made to learn anything about LTV's pension plans; further, Bierwirth and Freese never considered examining the Internal Revenue Service Form 5500 annual report which all pension plans file even though they were aware that such reports are

[6] We also agree with the Secretary that no reliance could be placed upon the press release announcing the New York State Comptroller's decision not to tender the 60,000 Grumman shares held by the state pension plan.

filed; (3) though much was made of the $225 million unfunded pension liability assumed in connection with the LTV acquisition of the Lykes Corporation, the trustees neither knew nor investigated why, when or how it came about; Mr. Freese suspected that the unfunded pension liability was not attributable to LTV mismanagement, and finally; (4) though they claim they were fearful that LTV would merge or terminate the Pension Plan (a) Bierwirth and Freese were aware of public pledges from LTV to the contrary but took no steps to secure such assurances and (b) Paladino admitted no basis for believing that LTV would terminate the Pension Plan.

The conduct of the trustees reflect a silent agreement among them (1) to "see, hear, and speak" nothing positive about the LTV tender offer and avoid any inquiries which might have uncovered facts to the contrary and (2) to isolate themselves from legal advice which might have precluded the Pension Plan from participating in the well orchestrated plan to kill the LTV takeover. The unavoidable conclusion is that the trustees failed to discharge their duty of prudence either diligently or in good faith.

III. *PRELIMINARY RELIEF*

The statutory provisions of ERISA authorize the court to award the relief it deems appropriate upon finding that the fiduciary has breached responsibilities, obligations or duties arising under the statute. In pertinent part, ERISA section 409, 29 U.S.C. §1109(a) provides:

> "Any person who is a fiduciary with respect to a plan who breaches any of the responsibilities, obligations, or duties imposed upon fiduciaries by this subchapter shall be personally liable to make good to such plan any losses to the plan resulting from each such breach, and to restore to such plan any profits of such fiduciary which may have been made through use of assets of the plan by the fiduciary, and shall be subject to such other equitable or remedial relief as the court may deem appropriate, including removal of such fiduciary. . . ."

We find that further proceedings are required in order to fashion the relief which will most suitably promote the interests of the Pension Plan, its participants and its beneficiaries.

The relief requested by the Secretary is the appointment of a receiver *pendente lite* who can independently assess the desirability of disposing or holding the Grumman stock held by the Pension Plan. The Secretary does not object to the continuing service by defendant trustees, *pendente lite,* in all matters except as to the Grumman stock. The identical request for preliminary relief has been made in a related case, *Lawrence v. Grumman Corporation Pension Plan,* Dkt.CV 81 3530, not yet consolidated with this action.

[3] Plaintiff has shown a likelihood of success on his claim that each of the trustees has acted imprudently with respect to their recent investment decisions concerning Grumman stock. They have manifested an inability to separate their corporate loyalty and their loyalty to the Pension Plan. The manner in which they exercised their judgment with respect to the Grumman stock was so egregiously imprudent that we must infer a likelihood of further violations. The very decision to hold Grumman stock makes Grumman a less likely candidate as a takeover target. The conduct of the Pension Plan trustees has demonstrated the difficulty that they have in examining objectively an investment decision which might affect the independence of Grumman.

While it is clear that interim relief pursuant to ERISA section 409 is in order, we are reluctant to fashion such relief without comment from all interested parties. We would consider a number of factors for the purposes of selecting an interim remedy including: "(1) the purposes of the trust; (2) the relative pecuniary advantages to the trust estate of the various remedies; (3) the nature of the interest of each beneficiary; (4) the practical availability of the various remedies; and (5) the extent of the deviation from the terms of the trust required by the adoption of each of the remedies." *Eaves v. Penn,* 587 F.2d 453, 462-63 (10th Cir. 1978), *quoting, Restate-*

ment (Second of Trusts, §214 Comment to Subsection (2,b).

Accordingly, the parties, including the interested parties in the action entitled *Lawrence v. Grumman Corporation Pension Plan,* Dkt. CV 81 3530, as well as any participants and beneficiaries who so desire, are directed to submit recommendations and arguments for the appropriate type of relief on or before December 18, 1981. Until such time as this court fashions further preliminary relief following the aforementioned submission date, John C. Bierwirth, Robert G. Freese and Carl A. Paladino, in their capacity as trustees of the Grumman Corporation Pension Plan, are hereby restrained from buying, selling or exercising any powers, rights or other duties on behalf of said Plan respecting stock or other securities issued by the Grumman Corporation except upon the written consent of the Secretary of Labor, and it is

SO ORDERED.

APPENDIX 6

LABOR DEPARTMENT LETTER ON PROXY VOTING BY PLAN FIDUCIARIES

Source: Reprinted from *BNA Pension Reporter,* Vol. 15, pp. 391–92, Feb. 29, 1988.

Mr. Helmuth Fandl
Chairman of the Retirement Board
Avon Products, Inc.
9 West 57th Street
New York, New York 10019

Feb. 23, 1988

Re: Avon Products, Inc. Employees' Retirement Plan

Dear Mr. Fandl:

The Pension and Welfare Benefits Administration (PWBA) of the Department of Labor is responsible for administration and enforcement of Title I of the Employee Retirement Income Security Act of 1974 (ERISA). Title I establishes standards governing the operation of employee benefit plans and includes fiduciary responsibility rules governing the conduct of plan officials and others who exercise discretionary authority or control with respect to the assets of employee benefit plans, such as the Avon Products, Inc. Employees' Retirement Plan (the Plan), which are subject to ERISA.

PWBA has concluded its investigation of the Plan and of your activities as a fiduciary of the Plan, in connection with certain activities concerning the voting of proxies appurtenant to shares held in the accounts of the Plan's investment managers. The facts adduced during this investigation are not conclusive. However, because of the possibility that violations have occurred, and in view of the recurring nature of this aspect of Plan asset management, we believe that it would be appropriate to apprise you of the Department's views concerning the general fiduciary obligations of a named fiduciary and an investment manager appointed pursuant to section 402(c)(3) of ERISA with respect to the voting of proxies on plan-owned stock. Since we expect that this information will be useful to the other members of the plan's retirement board, and to the investment managers of the Plan, we are providing them with copies of this letter.

I. THE APPLICABLE PROVISIONS OF ERISA

Taken together, the provisions of ERISA sections 402, 403, 404 and 405 are intended to, among other things, provide a basis for certainty regarding the identity and responsibilities of those parties involved in managing and operating the plan, as well as each party's liability for mismanagement.

Section 402(a) of ERISA provides that every employee benefit plan shall be established and maintained pursuant to a written instrument. This instrument must provide for one or more named fiduciaries who have authority to control and manage the operation and administration of the plan. The named fiduciaries may be either named in the plan instrument or chosen, through a procedure specified in the plan, by the plan sponsor.

Section 402(b)(2) of ERISA requires plans to describe any procedure for allocating responsibilities for operation and administration of the plan, including any procedure described in section 405(c)(1).

Section 405(c)(1) of ERISA provides, in part, that the named fiduciaries may designate persons other than named fiduciaries to carry out fiduciary responsibilities (other than trustee responsibilities) under the plan. Section 405(c)(3) of ERISA defines "trustee responsibility" to mean any responsibility provided in the plan's trust instrument to manage or control the assets of the plan, other than a power under the trust instrument of a named fiduciary to appoint an investment manager in accordance with section 402(c)(3).

Section 403(a) of ERISA provides, in part, that all assets of an employee benefit plan must be held in trust by one or more trustees. The trustee(s) must have exclusive authority and discretion to manage and control such assets, with two exceptions: (1) when the plan expressly provides that the trustee(s) are subject to the direction of a named fiduciary who is not a trustee, in which case the trustees are subject to proper directions made in accordance with the terms of the plan and not contrary to ERISA, and (2) when the authority to manage, acquire or dispose of assets of the plan is delegated to one or more investment managers pursuant to section 402(c)(3).

Section 402(c)(3) of ERISA states that a plan may provide that with respect to control or management of plan assets a named fiduciary may appoint an investment manager or managers to manage (including the power to acquire and dispose of) plan assets.

Section 3(38) of ERISA defines "investment manager" as any fiduciary (other than a trustee or named fiduciary) (A) who has the power to manage, acquire, or dispose of any plan asset; (B) who is (i) a registered investment adviser under the Investment Advisers Act of 1940; (88) a bank; or (iii) an insurance company; and (C) who has acknowledged in writing that he is a fiduciary with respect to the plan.

Section 405(c)(2) of ERISA provides, in part, that if a plan expressly provides for a procedure described in section 405(c)(1), and pursuant to such procedure a person is designated to carry out a fiduciary responsibility of a named fiduciary, then such named fiduciary shall not be liable for an act or omission of such person in carrying out such responsibility except to the extent that (A) the named fiduciary violated section 404(a)(1)—(i) with respect to such designation, (ii) with respect to the establishment or implementation of the procedure under 405(c)(1), or (iii) in continuing the designation; or (B) the named fiduciary would otherwise be liable under ERISA section 405(a).

Section 404(a)(1)(B) of ERISA requires a fiduciary to discharge his duties to a plan with the care, skill, prudence and diligence under the circumstances then prevailing that a prudent man acting in a like capacity and familiar with such matters would use in the conduct of an enterprise of a like character and with like aims.

Section 404(a)(1)(D) of ERISA requires a fiduciary to discharge his duties in accordance with the documents and instruments governing the plan insofar as such documents and instruments are consistent with the provisions of Titles I and IV of ERISA.

II. PROXY VOTING BY PLAN FIDUCIARIES

In general, the fiduciary act of managing plan assets which are shares of corporate stock would include the voting of proxies appurtenant to those shares of stock. For example, it is the Department's position that the decision as to how proxies should be voted with regard to the issues presented by the fact pattern are fiduciary acts of plan asset management: a proposal to change the state of incorporation of a corporation in which a plan owned shares (thereby possibly affecting shareholders' rights to participate in the decision-making process of the corporation which, in turn, affects the value of their investment) and a proposal to rescind "poison pill" arrangements with regard to various corporations in which a plan is invested. Moreover, because voting such proxies involves plan asset management, section 403(a) requires that plan trustees have the exclusive authority and responsibility for voting these proxies, unless one of the two exceptions stated in section 403(a) applies.

To the extent that the documents governing the plan permit a named fiduciary to appoint an investment manager pursuant to sections 402(c)(3) and 403(a)(2) of ERISA to manage, acquire, and dispose of plan assets, there would be an ERISA violation if, during the duration of such delegation, either the trustee or the named fiduciary makes the decision how to vote any proxy appurtenant to shares owned by the plan with respect to which the investment manager has investment authority because under the plan documents neither the trustee nor the named fiduciary has authority to make that decision with regard to those shares. Indeed, under such plan provisions if *any* person other than the investment manager (or a person under the fiduciary supervision of the investment manager)[1] were to make the proxy voting decision, there would be a section 404(a)(1)(D) violation because that person does not have that fiduciary authority under the plan. Finally, with limited exceptions[2], the named fiduciary, having delegated such responsibility to the investment manager, no longer has the authority to decide how the investment manager votes proxies and would be engaging in a section 404(a)(1)(D) violation in doing so unless, in delegating such management responsibility to the investment manager, it reserves to itself the right to vote proxies.[3]

Moreover, ERISA contains no provision which would relieve an investment manager of fiduciary liability for any decision he made at the direction of another person. Under ERISA's construct, only trustees are able to relieve themselves of fiduciary responsibility and related liabilities by accepting directions, if plan documents so provide, and then only of such directions are "proper directions" made in accordance with the terms of the plan and not contrary to ERISA. Furthermore, neither section 3(38) nor 405(c) of ERISA grants an investment manager the powers of a named fiduciary to allocate or designate its investment management function for plan assets to other persons so as to relieve itself of its fiduciary responsibilities and related liabilities. Therefore, to the extent that anyone purports to direct an investment manager as to the voting of proxies, or to the extent that an investment manager purports to delegate to another the responsibility for such voting decisions, the manager would not be relieved of its own responsibilities and related liabilities merely because it either follows the direction of some other person, or has delegated the responsibility to some other person. The manager would continue to have full responsibility (and liability) for the exercise of the proxy voting decision.

Finally, the Department notes that section 404(a)(1)(B) requires the named fiduciary appointing the investment manager to periodically monitor the activities of the investment manager with respect to the management of plan assets. In general, this duty would encompass the monitoring of decisions made and actions taken by investment managers with regard to proxy voting. In this regard, it is the opinion of the Department that section 404(a)(1)(B) requires proper documentation of the activities of the investment manager and of the named fiduciary of the plan in monitoring the activities of the investment manager. Specifically, with respect to

[1] If the investment manager attempted to delegate his responsibility for proxy voting to another, the manager would not be relieved of his fiduciary responsibilities and related liabilities with regard to the voting decisions of that delegatee. (See discussion *infra*.)

[2] The general fiduciary responsibility provisions of ERISA, including the co-fiduciary liability provisions, remain applicable to the named fiduciary's continuation of the delegation of asset management to the investment manager. Thus, no violation of section 404(a)(1)(D) would occur to the extent that ERISA's fiduciary responsibility provisions would require the named fiduciary to formally rescind the delegation to preclude the investment manager from engaging in a breach of fiduciary responsibility.

[3] To the extent that a named fiduciary reserves to itself the right to direct the trustee to vote proxies, the investment manager would not have fiduciary responsibility and related liability for the exercise of the vote. Moreover, to the extent the named fiduciary retains the voting rights, it would have full fiduciary responsibility and related liability for the exercise of those rights.

proxy voting, this would require the investment manager or other responsible fiduciary to keep accurate records as to the voting of proxies.[4]

We trust you will find the above information useful in discharging your ERISA responsibilities during the 1988 proxy season and thereafter.

Sincerely,

Alan D. Lebowitz
Deputy Assistant Secretary

[4] Although this letter is concerned with the procedural requirements of ERISA as applied to proxy voting where an investment manager is appointed, the Department wishes to reiterate its longstanding interpretation of the substantive requirements of section 404(a)(1). Section 404(a)(1) requires, among other things, that a fiduciary of a plan act prudently, solely in the interest of the plan's participants and beneficiaries, and for the exclusive purpose of providing benefits to participants and beneficiaries. To act prudently in the voting of proxies (as well as in all other fiduciary matters), a plan fiduciary must consider those factors which would affect the value of the plan's investment. Similarly, the Department has construed the requirements that a fiduciary act solely in the interest of, and for the exclusive purpose of providing benefits to, participants and beneficiaries as prohibiting a fiduciary from subordinating the interests of participants and beneficiaries in their retirement income to unrelated objectives.

Appendix 7

Participant-Directed Retirement Plans Under the Final Section 404(c) Regulations

Source: Reprinted from *BNA Pension Reporter,* Vol. 19, pp. 1825–28, October 19, 1989, by Frank Daniele and Nell Hennessy.

Summary

At long last, the Department of Labor has issued final regulations under Section 404(c) of the Employee Retirement Income Security Act of 1974, as amended. Section 404(c) provides relief from certain fiduciary responsibilities applicable to sponsors of individual account retirement plans that allow participant-directed investments and meet the other requirements of the final regulations (Section 404(c) Plans). In general, if the conditions of the final regulations are satisfied, the plan sponsor or other fiduciary responsible for designating the plan's investment alternatives will not be subject to fiduciary liability under ERISA for plan losses resulting from participants' exercise of investment control over the assets in their accounts.

Regulations under Section 404(c) were originally proposed in 1987. Following widespread criticism from plan sponsors and financial institutions, the regulations were reproposed in 1991. The 1991 proposals, while somewhat more tolerant of customary plan practices, still contained many requirements that would have greatly complicated the administration of participant-directed plans.

The major concerns with the 1991 proposals have largely been addressed. In the area of information disclosure to plan participants, however, the requirements of the final regulations are extensive and detailed. Major substantive changes from the 1991 proposals are noted below:

- The final regulation does not require that in-house managed investment funds (i.e., funds managed by plan sponsors) he designated by a plan fiduciary who is not affiliated with the plan sponsor (an Independent Fiduciary).

- There is more flexibility to meet the requirement that participants be allowed to transfer out of volatile investment alternatives with sufficient frequency.

- An Independent Fiduciary need not be appointed to administer purchases, sales and voting of employer securities unless a designated plan fiduciary determines that the particular activities involving employer securities create a potential for undue employer influence on participants' exercise of their rights as shareholders. The preamble to the final regulations cites tender offers, exchange offers and contested board elections as examples of such activities.

- Where a participant is given the opportunity to exercise voting, tender and similar rights, and has been provided the information necessary to exercise those rights, the participant will he considered to have exercised such rights, regardless of whether they are actually exercised.

- As noted above, extensive information must be furnished *directly* to plan participants, and participants must he advised that a variety of other information will be made available upon request.

Discussion

The following discussion describes in more detail the principal provisions of the final regulations. The complete text of these regulations may be found in the October 13, 1992 issue of the *Federal Register* (19 *BPR* 1759).

Significance of Section 404(c)

In general, persons who exercise authority or control over the investment of employee benefit plan assets are considered fiduciaries under ERISA. ERISA fiduciaries are subject to specific statutory standards of conduct, and may be personally liable for plan losses resulting from a breach of these standards.

In the case of individual account plans that permit participants to exercise control over the assets in their accounts, Section 404(c) provides partial relief from the standards that otherwise govern fiduciary conduct. Provided participants actually exercise control over the assets in their accounts, plan fiduciaries will not be liable for any losses that are the direct result of the participants' exercise of control. The protections of Section 404(c) are available only to plans that allow participant-directed investments, such as Internal Revenue Code Section 401(k) plans, group individual retirement accounts, and most profit sharing plans.

Failure to comply with Section 404(c) does not of itself cause a plan to violate ERISA. Failure to comply means that plan fiduciaries may continue to be responsible under ERISA or participant-directed investments. Whether or not the final regulations are complied with, fiduciaries will need to continue to act prudently in selecting and retaining designated investment alternatives for the plan. The Department has made clear, however, that the requirements of the final regulations apply only for purposes of determining whether a plan is a Section 404(c) Plan. The final regulations were not intended to be applied to determine whether or to what extent a fiduciary with respect to a plan that is not a Section 404(c) Plan satisfies the fiduciary responsibility provisions of ERISA. The preamble to the final regulation indicates that a plan that does not satisfy the Section 404(c) requirements may still have a prudent and well-diversified portfolio.

The open question, however, now that the regulations are final, is how courts will evaluate whether a fiduciary has discharged its responsibilities to participants with respect to participant-directed investments when all requirements of the final regulations have not been satisfied. Because it is unlikely that there will be a definitive answer to this question for several years, compliance with Section 404(c) should be carefully considered by all plan sponsors and other investment fiduciaries.

Effective Date

The Department of Labor has extended the time for bringing plans into compliance with the final regulations. The final regulations apply generally to participant-directed investments occurring on or after the first day of the *second* plan year beginning on or after October 13, 1992 (the date on which the final regulation was published). For calendar year plans, therefore, the final regulations will apply as of the plan year beginning January 1, 1994.

For plans maintained pursuant to one or more collective bargaining agreements ratified prior to October 13, 1992, the final regulations apply to transactions occurring on or after the *later* of (1) the first day of the second plan year beginning on or after October 13, 1992, or (2) the date of termination of the last collective bargaining agreement ratified before October 13, 1992.

Participant-directed transactions occurring prior to the effective date of the final regulations are governed by Section 404(c) without regard to the regulation.

Section 404(c) Requirements

The central requirement of the new regulations is that participants be considered to have exercised meaningful, independent control over the assets in their accounts. In general, in order to satisfy this requirement, a participant must have the opportunity to:

(1) choose from a broad range of investment alternatives that allow diversification within and among such alternatives;
(2) give investment instructions with a frequency that is appropriate in light of the market volatility of the investment alternatives; and
(3) obtain sufficient information to make informed investment decisions.
Each of these requirements is discussed more fully below.

Broad Range of Investment Alternatives

A plan provides a broad range of investment alternatives only if the alternatives afford participants the opportunity to:

(1) materially affect the potential return on assets over which the participant is permitted to exercise control;

(2) choose from at least *three* investment alternatives, each of which is diversified and has materially different risk and return characteristics; and

(3) diversify investments so as to minimize the risk of large losses.

Investment alternatives that are intended to satisfy the "broad range" requirement are considered "Core Alternatives." A Section 404(c) Plan may offer additional investment alternatives that are not Core Alternatives if it provides at least three Core Alternatives. Since each Core Alternative must itself be diversified, certain types of investment funds, such as employer stock funds, cannot qualify as Core Alternatives. Plans that do not designate specific investment alternatives but allow participants to invest in any investment vehicle which is administratively feasible under the plan will automatically satisfy the broad range requirement.

Frequency of Investment instructions

The final regulations contain three requirements concerning the frequency with which participants must be allowed to change investments to and from Core Alternatives:

General Volatility Rule. Like the 1991 proposals, the final regulations permit plans to impose reasonable restrictions on the frequency with which participants may give investment instructions. The regulations provide that restrictions will be "reasonable" only if they permit participants to give investment instructions with a frequency that is appropriate in light of the market volatility to which the investments may reasonably be expected to be subject (the General Volatility Rule).

Three-Month Rule. Under the Three-Month Rule, each of the Core Alternatives must afford participants the opportunity to transfer to another Core Alternative *no less frequently* than once within any three month period. This requirement is applicable only to transfers *among* the Core Alternatives, not to transfers between the Core Alternatives and other investment alternatives. Because of this requirement, certain types of investment vehicles that restrict or prohibit direct transfers to Core Alternatives cannot themselves qualify as Core Alternatives. For example, many fixed-rate investment contracts, such as guaranteed investment contracts and bank investment contracts, contain "equity wash" restrictions requiring that transfers from the fixed-rate contract to another fixed income alternative be made through an equity fund in which the transferred amounts must remain invested for a prescribed minimum time period. If this type of restriction were to preclude direct transfers from the fixed-rate contract to a Core Alternative (*e.g.*, if the prescribed minimum time period for amounts transferred to the equity fund exceeds three months), the fixed-rate contract could not itself serve as a Core Alternative, although it could be offered as an investment alternative in addition to the Core Alternatives. A fixed-rate contract that contains such a restriction could be offered as a Core Alternative if the plan does not have any other fixed income Core Alternative.

Volatile Investment Rule. Under the Volatile Investment Rule, generally, participants must be afforded the opportunity to move from a more volatile investment alternative to a less volatile investment alternative that constitutes one of the Core Alternatives. An investment alternative is considered "more volatile" if it permits transfers *more frequently* than once every three months. The final regulations afford greater flexibility than the 1991 proposals by allowing two alternative methods for meeting this requirement.

(1) **Designated Core Alternative.** Under the first alternative, plans may designate any one of the Core Alternatives (such as a money market fund) to receive transfers from more volatile investment alternatives. Accordingly, the designated Core Alternative must be able to *receive* transfers at least as frequently as the participant can transfer amounts *out* of the more volatile investment. However, in the case of an investment fund involving employer securities, the participant must be afforded the opportunity to direct investments from the employer securities fund into *any* of the Core Alternatives.

(2) **Low-Risk Funds/Accounts.** Under the second alternative, plans are permitted to establish income producing, low-risk, liquid funds, subfunds or accounts to hold transfers from volatile investments pending the opportunity to direct investments into one of the Core Alternatives. The participant must have the opportunity to move out of the interim fund as soon as investment instructions may be given with respect to the Core Alternatives. Plans may require that transfers from an interim fund (other than one that holds assets transferred from an employer securities fund) be made only to a designated Core Alternative. However, in the case of an interim fund that holds assets transferred from an employer securities fund, a participant must be able to direct investments into *any* of the Core Alternatives.

Elimination of Uniformity Requirement. The final regulations eliminate the requirement in the 1991 proposals that frequency restrictions apply uniformly to all plan participants. According to the preamble, this change was made partly in response to the concern of commentators that the uniformity requirement would conflict with proposed requirements for participant-directed "insider" transactions in employer stock under new Rule 16b-3 promulgated by the Securities and Exchange Commission under Section 16 of the Securities Exchange Act of 1934. New Rule 16b-3 generally prevents insiders from effecting transactions in employer stock funds more than once every six months; the restriction is not applicable to employees other than insiders.

The Labor Department has not entirely solved this problem, however, since the preamble states that if the restrictions imposed on insiders are not consistent with the General Volatility Rule, investments by insiders would not be covered by Section 404(c). For example, if insiders are precluded from making transactions in an employer stock fund more than once every six months, but the General Volatility Rule would require the ability to make more frequent transfers, the employer stock fund would not be covered by Section 404(c) with respect to insiders' investments. Ironically, this would appear to give insiders, who are most knowledgeable as a group about employer stock, greater remedies against the fiduciaries of a plan than rank-and-file employees who are not subject to the restrictions but are less likely to have inside information.

Expanded Disclosure Requirements

Under the final regulations, a participant must have the opportunity to obtain sufficient information to make informed investment decisions. According to the preamble, the expansion of this requirement was influenced significantly by comments on the 1991 proposals submitted by the Division of Market Regulation of the SEC. Unlike the 1991 proposals, which generally required only that participants be referred to a source of investment information, the final regulations identify specific information that must be made available to participants.

The final regulations require that certain information concerning the plan and available investment alternatives be furnished *directly* to all participants, and that certain other information be furnished only on request.

The following information must be furnished to all participants:

• an explanation that the plan is intended to constitute a Section 404(c) Plan and that plan fiduciaries may be relieved of liability for losses that are the result of participants' investment instructions;

• a description of *all* designated investment alternatives under the plan (not merely Core Alternatives), including a general description of the investment objectives and risk and return characteristics of each alternative;

• identification of any designated investment managers;

• an explanation of how to give investment instructions, any limits or restrictions on giving instructions (including information as to withdrawal penalties and valuation adjustments), and any restrictions on the exercise of voting, tender or similar rights;

• a description of any transaction fees or expenses that are charged to the participant's account;

• a description of the additional information available on request (discussed below) and the identity of the person or persons responsible for providing that information;

• if the plan provides for investment in employer securities, a description of the procedures established to provide for confidentiality of participants' directions and identification of the plan fiduciary responsible for monitoring compliance with those procedures;

• immediately following the participant's initial investment in an investment alternative subject to the Securities Act of 1933, a copy of the most recent prospectus, unless the prospectus was furnished immediately before the participant's investment; and

• subsequent to an investment, any materials provided to the plan relating to the exercise of voting, tender or similar rights, to the extent such rights are passed through to participants, as well as information describing the nature of pass-through rights available pursuant to the plan.

For plans invested in mutual funds, most of this information will generally be contained in the fund's prospectus.

In addition to the material that must be provided to all participants, the following information must be furnished to a participant on request:

• a description of the annual operating expenses borne by investment alternatives, such as investment management fees;

• copies of any prospectuses, financial statements and reports and other information furnished to the plan relating to an investment alternative;

• a listing of assets comprising the portfolio of an investment alternative that holds "plan assets," the value of such assets, and, in the case of fixed-rate investment contracts issued by a bank, savings and loan association or insurance company, the name of the issuer of the contract, the term of the contract and the rate of return on the contract. This information would not be required for mutual fund assets, which are not considered "plan assets" under ERISA;

• information concerning the value of shares or units in investment alternatives available to participants, as well as information concerning the past and current investment performance of the alternative; and

• information concerning the value of shares or units in investment alternatives *held in the account* of the participant. The preamble provides that, in meeting this requirement, plans may establish reasonable procedures limiting the frequency of requests for account balance information.

Requirement of Affirmative Direction

The final regulations provide that a participant will not be considered to have exercised control over account assets unless the participant has provided affirmative investment instructions with respect to such assets. In certain circumstances, a participant who has signed a written agreement that indicates how account assets are invested in the absence of direction will be considered to have provided affirmative investment instructions as to such assets. Also, with respect to the exercise of voting, tender and similar rights, a participant who is given the opportunity and information necessary to exercise such rights will be considered to have exercised them, even if the participant does not in fact do so. This is a significant departure from the Department's previous litigation position that trustees of an employee stock ownership plan have an affirmative duty to make the voting or tender decision in an ESOP if the participant is given the opportunity to act but declines to do so.

Permissible Limitations on Participant Control

The final regulations provide that the plan fiduciary designated to receive and follow participant investment instructions may decline to follow certain instructions. Examples are instructions which, if implemented, (1) would not be in accordance with plan documents, (2) would cause the indicia of ownership of plan assets to be maintained outside the United States, (3) would jeopardize the plan's tax-qualified status, (4) could result in a loss in excess of the participant's account balance, (5) would cause the plan to engage in certain transactions with the plan sponsor, (6) would result in a prohibited transaction, or (7) would generate income taxable to the plan.

Prohibited Transactions

The preamble to the final regulations clarifies that, in general, a fiduciary will not be liable under ERISA for a participant-directed investment that results in a prohibited transaction. This provision provides only limited relief, however, since the fiduciary would be relieved of liability only for losses incurred for the account of the participant whose direction he is following, and would continue to be liable for any losses incurred with respect to other participants' accounts by reason of the prohibited transaction. For this reason, as discussed above, fiduciaries are permitted to decline instructions that would result in a prohibited transaction. Also, the final regulations indicate that this relief is limited to the prohibited transaction provisions of ERISA, and does not extend to the analogous provisions under Section 4975 of the tax code, which are subject to the jurisdiction of the Treasury Department. The Treasury Department has not issued similar exemptive relief under Section 4975, but has indicated that it is willing to entertain requests for such relief.

The regulations also clarify that a fiduciary is not relieved from liability for losses resulting from a prohibited transaction that results from the fiduciary's exercise of its discretion. For example, if a participant directs a fiduciary to purchase certain securities, and the fiduciary elects to use a party in interest to execute the securities transaction, the fiduciary would be liable with respect to the resulting prohibited transaction (unless an exemption is available).

Investments In Employer Securities

Employer Securities. The 1991 proposals extended Section 404(c) relief to participant-directed investments in employer stock if, among other things, the stock was (i) a "qualifying employer security," (ii) publicly traded on a national exchange or other generally recognized market, and (iii) traded with sufficient frequency and in sufficient volume to assure that directions to buy and sell might be acted upon promptly. Section 404(c) relief was also conditioned on the appointment of an Independent Fiduciary to be responsible for handling all activities relating to participants' purchases, sales and voting of employer securities.

While most of the requirements of the 1991 proposals are retained, the role of an Independent Fiduciary has been significantly modified. In addition, the final regulations provide that Section 404(c) relief extends to equity interests in certain publicly-traded partnerships that constitute qualifying employer securities.

Confidentiality Procedures. Rather than requiring an Independent Fiduciary to handle activities relating to participant-directed investments in employer securities, the final regulations condition Section 404(c) relief on:

(a) the establishment of procedures intended to ensure the confidentiality of information relating to participant-directed transactions involving employer securities, including the exercise of voting, tender and similar rights;

(b) the designation of a plan fiduciary (who need not be independent of the sponsor) responsible for ensuring the adequacy of the procedures and for monitoring compliance with the procedures; and

(c) the appointment of an Independent Fiduciary to carry out any activities that the designated plan fiduciary considers to involve a potential for undue employer influence on participants with respect to the exercise of their rights as shareholders (*e.g.*, tender offers, exchange offers, and contested board elections).

Under the disclosure provisions of the final regulations, discussed above, the plan is required to furnish participants a description of the confidentiality procedures and to identify the plan fiduciary responsible for monitoring compliance with those procedures.

Pass-Through Rights. In addition to the above requirements, voting, tender and similar rights relating to employer securities must be passed through to participants, and participants must receive all information provided to share holders generally. Pass through of voting, tender and similar rights is not required for investment alternatives other than employer securities.

A plan that otherwise meets the requirements of the final regulations will not fail to be a Section 404(c) Plan merely because an employer security investment alternative fails to satisfy these requirements. However, in such cases, plan fiduciaries will not be relieved of liability for employer security investments, even where such investments are participant directed.

Appendix 8

ERISA Class Exemptions Summary Contents

Source: Reprinted from *ERISA Class Exemptions* and *ERISA Class Exemptions 1994 Supplement* by Donald J. Myers, copyrights © 1991 and 1994, The Bureau of National Affairs, Inc., Washington, D.C.

SUMMARY CONTENTS

80-26 Interest Free Loans

80-51 Bank Collective Investment Funds

80-83 Use of Proceeds From Sale of Securities to Reduce or Retire Indebtedness

81-6 Lending of Securities

81-7 Mortgage Pool Investment Trusts (*Amended and Superseded by PTE 83-1*)

81-8 Short-Term Investments

81-82 Guaranteed Contract Separate Accounts

82-63 Compensation to Fiduciaries for Securities Lending Services

82-87 Residential Mortgage Financing Arrangements (*Amended and Superseded by PTE 88-59*)

83-1 Mortgage Pool Investment Trusts (*Amends and Supersedes PTE 81-7*)

84-14 Transactions Determined by Independent Qualified Professional Asset Managers (QPAMs)

84-24 Transactions Involving Insurance Agents and Brokers, Pension Consultants, Insurance and Investment Companies, and Investment Company Principal Underwriters (*Amends and Supersedes PTE 77-9*)

84-46 Recapture of Brokerage Commissions on Behalf of Insurance Company Pooled Separate Accounts (*Replaced by PTE 86-128*)

85-68 Purchase of Customer Notes of Employers (*Replaces PTE 79-9*)

86-128 Executing Securities Transactions and Recapture of Commissions (*Replaces PTE 79-1 and PTE 84-46*)

88-59 Residential Mortgage Financing Arrangements (*Amends and Supersedes PTE 82-87*)

90-1 Insurance Company Pooled Separate Accounts (*Amends and Supersedes PTE 78-19*)

91-38 Bank Collective Investment Funds (*Amends and Supersedes PTE 80-51*)

- Proposed Amendment to PTE 80-51
- Adoption of Amendment
- Correction

91-55 American Eagle Coins

- Proposed Exemption
- Final Exemption
- Correction

92-5 Transfer of Individual Life Insurance and Annuity Contracts to Plans *(Amends and Supersedes PTE 77-7)*

- Proposed Amendment to PTE 77-7
- Adoption of Amendment

92-6 Transfer of Individual Life Insurance and Annuity Contracts From Plans *(Amends and Supersedes PTE 77-8)*

- Proposed Amendment to PTE 77-8

Adoption of Amendment

Correction

93-1 Certain Transactions Involving Individual Retirement Accounts and Plans for Self-Employed Individuals

Proposed Exemption

Solicitation of Comments

Final Exemption

93-2 Receipt of Certain Services in Connection With Individual Retirement Accounts and Plans for Self-Employed Individuals *(Amended and Superseded by PTE 93-33)*

IRS Announcement 90-1

Proposed Exemption

Final Exemption

93-33 Receipt of Certain Services in Connection With Individual Retirement Accounts and Plans for Self-Employed Individuals *(Amends and Supersedes PTE 93-2)*

Proposed Amendment to PTE 93-2

Adoption of Amendment to PTE 93-2

Proposed Amendment to PTE 93-33

Adoption of Amendment to PTE 93-33

94-20 Foreign Exchange Transactions

Solicitation of Comments

Proposed Exemption

Correction

Final Exemption

Appendix: Proposed Exemptions That Have Not Been Granted

I. Life Insurance Company Discretionary Asset Management

II. Guaranteed Contract Separate Accounts; Fiduciary Transactions (*Withdrawn*)

Withdrawal

III. Certain Transactions Involving Individual Retirement Accounts and Plans for Self-Employed Individuals

IV. American Eagle Coins

Appendix 9

ERISA Class Exemptions Topical Index

Source: Reprinted from *ERISA Class Exemptions, 1994 Supplement* by Donald J. Myers, copyright © 1994, The Bureau of National Affairs, Inc., Washington, D.C.

Cumulative Topical Index

(Consolidating Main Volume and 1994 Supplement)

Page references to an exemption are to the first page of the *Federal Register* notice of the final exemption (or proposed exemption). Page references not preceded by "S-" are to the main volume. Where there is a page reference to a part of an exemption or to supplemental material, the page number is in *italics*.

Unless otherwise noted, PTE references in the second column are to the most recent exemptions, which may amend or supersede prior exemptions. References to exemptions that have been amended or superseded, and to proposed exemptions, are included where these may assist the reader in understanding provisions of an exemption or particular legal issues. The following system of indicators is used in the second column:

- brackets: exemptions that have been superseded, replaced, revoked, or withdrawn;
- parentheses: proposed exemptions or proposed amendments;
- asterisk: indicates PTE is "as amended."

References to specific statute sections (e.g., ERISA Section 404(c)) are listed in the first column under the full name of the statute.

A list of Applicants for PTEs is included in a separate section preceding this index.

C

D

O

T

APPENDIX 10

CHRONOLOGY: DEVELOPMENT OF ERISA

Source: Reprinted from *ERISA: The Law and the Code, 1994 Edition,* copyright © 1994, The Bureau of National Affairs, Inc., Washington, D.C.

Development of the Law

The Employee Retirement Income Security Act was signed into law by President Gerald Ford on September 2, 1974, after years of deliberation and intensive debate. The law and related tax code sections have been amended frequently since that time, as outlined below.

1980

The first major changes in the law were enacted in September 1980, when President Jimmy Carter signed the Multiemployer Pension Plan Amendments Act of 1980 (PL 96-364).

Although ERISA itself remained virtually untouched for six years, a number of changes affecting pension and benefit plans were enacted through various tax laws that amended the qualified plan provisions of the Internal Revenue Code.

1981

In 1981, a series of savings incentive bills were introduced in Congress. Proposals were made to raise the limits on deductible contributions to individual retirement accounts and Keogh plans, encourage the adoption of employee stock ownership plans, and change the tax treatment of stock options. The retirement plan proposals and other savings incentive provisions eventually were consolidated and, in August 1981, President Ronald Reagan signed the Economic Recovery Tax Act (PL 97-34).

1982

In May 1982, a bill was introduced in the House to reduce the contribution and benefit limits for qualified corporate plans, modify the rules for integration with Social Security, tighten the rules for loans from plans to key employees, and limit the estate tax exclusion for retirement annuities paid to beneficiaries, among other changes in the pension tax area. Despite opposition from the pension industry, those proposals were modified and rolled into a revenue raising package introduced in an attempt to reduce budget deficits. The revenue package became the Tax Equity and Fiscal Responsibility Act of 1982 (PL 97-248) and was approved by Congress in August 1982 and signed by President Reagan, only a few short months after it was first introduced.

1984

Things were quiet in 1983, but on July 18, 1984, the Deficit Reduction Act (PL 98-369) was enacted, which added and amended tax code provisions in such areas as fringe benefits, cafeteria plans, and employee welfare plans. Several weeks later, on August 23, 1984, the Retirement Equity Act (PL 98-397) was enacted, which amended both tax code and ERISA provisions on vesting, participation, and joint and survivor annuities. Two other benefit laws also were enacted in 1984. PL 98-611 provided a two-year extension of the exclusion from gross income for educational assistance programs and PL 98-612 extended the exclusion for prepaid legal plans for one year.

1985

While Congress began debate on yet another tax reform law in 1985, it focused much of its attention on federal budget deficits, which resulted in passage of the Gramm-Rudman-Hollings balanced budget law (PL 99-177).

1986

Passage of the balanced budget law in 1985 led to some speculation during the early days of 1986 that the law could cause the death of the budget reconciliation bill then under consideration. However, the Consolidated Omnibus Budget Reconciliation Act of 1986 (PL 99-272) was passed by Congress and signed by President Reagan April 7 of that year. COBRA included provisions on continuation of employer-sponsored group health insurance for certain individuals and their dependents. In addition, Title XI of the law amended the single-employer pension plan provisions of ERISA. Title XI is cited as the Single-Employer Pension Plan Amendments Act of 1986.

The Tax Reform Act of 1986 (PL 99-514) was signed by President Reagan on October 22, 1986. The 1986 Tax Reform Act made extensive changes affecting employee pension and welfare benefit plans, including amendments to the rules on non-discrimination, coverage, participation, Social Security integration, vesting, and distributions.

The 99th Congress adjourned without passing a concurrent resolution (HConRes 395) that would have made mostly technical corrections to the 1986 TRA. Most of the earlier problems with the resolution had been worked out, but it was not passed because some members of Congress wanted to include controversial, substantive provisions.

The Omnibus Budget Reconciliation Act of 1986 (PL 99-509) was enacted on October 21, 1986. The law requires continued benefit accruals or allocations for employees who continue to work beyond normal retirement age and requires employers to offer health insurance coverage to retirees and dependents who otherwise would lose coverage because the employer had filed for Chapter 11 bankruptcy.

1987

President Reagan signed the Omnibus Budget Reconciliation Act of 1987 (PL 100-203) on December 22, 1987. The law tightened the funding requirements for defined benefit pension plans and increased the premium that single employer defined benefit plans must pay to guarantee a certain level of benefits. However, provisions that would have made technical corrections were dropped before the 1987 OBRA was signed into law, partly to ensure that the bill would comply with a deficit reduction agreement between the White House and Congress.

1988

President Reagan signed the Technical and Miscellaneous Revenue Act of 1988 on November 10, 1988 (PL 100-647). TAMRA included a number of provisions affecting employee benefits. TAMRA retained the 1989 effective date for the Section 89 non-discrimination rules, but relaxed some compliance issues. TAMRA also amended the tax sanctions for violation of the COBRA requirements, increased the excise tax on reversions of excess plan assets, made certain clarifying amendments to pension plan rules, amended the Section 457 rules, and extended for one year the exclusion from income of benefits from group legal service and educational assistance plans.

1989

On November 15, 1989, President George Bush signed PL 101-140, a law that increased the public debt limit and repealed Section 89. On December 19, 1989, President Bush signed the Omnibus Budget Reconciliation Act of 1989 (PL 101-239). OBRA 1989 modified COBRA health care continuation coverage rules and made numerous technical corrections to prior laws. It also amended civil penalties for fiduciary violations and repealed or limited a number of provisions on employee stock ownership plans.

1990

On November 5, 1990, President Bush signed the Omnibus Budget Reconciliation Act of 1990 (PL 101-508). OBRA 1990 extended tax breaks for tuition assistance and group legal service plans, increased the excise tax on reversions of excess assets to employers from plan terminations, raised plan termination insurance premiums, permitted the transfer of some excess assets to retiree health accounts, and made a number of technical changes such as eliminating obsolete provisions from the tax code.

Also in December 1990, President Bush signed PL 101-540, which was introduced and passed just before Congress adjourned for the November elections. This new law amended Title I of ERISA to require employer securities to include interest in publicly traded partnerships.

1991

Simplification of pension laws, expansion of retirement coverage, concern for the financial health of the Pension Benefit Guaranty Corporation, and reform of the health care system were among the topics discussed by Congress and the Bush administration throughout 1991 and 1992. However, despite the attention, only a few, minor changes to ERISA and its corresponding tax code sections were enacted during the second half of 1991.

On August 15, 1991, President Bush signed the Rural Telephone Cooperative Associations ERISA Amendments Act of 1991 (PL 102-89). The law removes from ERISA's definition of multiple employer welfare arrangements the welfare plans of rural telephone cooperative associations.

On December 15, 1991, President Bush signed emergency supplemental appropriations legislation (PL 102-229), which created a new ERISA subsection 4001(a)(14)(C). The provision was aimed specifically at preventing Carl Icahn, chairman and chief executive officer of Trans World Airlines Inc., from escaping responsibility for TWA's pension plan underfunding.

While the Federal Deposit Insurance Corporation Improvement Act of 1991, signed by President Bush December 19, 1991 (PL 102-242), does not amend ERISA or its corresponding tax code sections, it does contain provisions affecting benefit plans. Under the bill, pass-through coverage by the Federal Deposit Insurance Corporation would be allowed for benefit plan assets placed in well-capitalized financial institutions. However, pass-through coverage for bank investment contracts would be eliminated.

Also, the banking bill specifies that FDIC and other successors to failed financial institutions have the same obligation under ERISA Section 602 to offer group health coverage to former employees as the failed institution would have had if not for its failure.

On December 11, President Bush signed the Tax Extension Act of 1991 (PL 102-227), which extended for six months certain expiring tax provisions, including the provisions covering employer-provided educational assistance, group legal services plans, and health insurance costs of self-employed individuals. However, the six months lapsed without the provisions being extended again or made permanent; the provisions expired at the end of June 1992.

1992

Congress passed two tax bills in 1992 (HR 4210 and HR 11) that would have extended some or all of the expiring provisions, among other things. However, President Bush vetoed both measures. An extension of all three tax breaks was included in HR 4210; the exclusion for group legal services was dropped from HR 11.

Nearly identical pension simplification provisions were included in both HR 4210 and HR 11. In addition, HR 11 would have expanded the availability of IRAs. However, these provisions, although mostly non-controversial, were killed with the veto of the tax bills and did not surface as separate legislation.

Despite the tax bill vetoes, two significant benefit changes were enacted in 1992. On July 3, 1992, President Bush signed unemployment benefits legislation (PL 102-318) that is funded, in part, by a withholding tax on certain pension plan distributions. The law, the Unemployment Compensation Amendments of 1992, allows any portion of most distributions from a qualified pension plan or annuity or a tax-sheltered annuity to be rolled over tax free into an IRA or another qualified plan or annuity. In addition, the law requires qualified plans to permit participants to elect to have any distribution eligible for roll-over treatment transferred directly to an eligible transferee plan designated by the participant.

On October 24, 1992, President Bush signed the Comprehensive National Energy Policy Act of 1992 (PL 102-486), which includes a provision on the funding of health benefits for retired coal miners. The law requires companies who were party to labor agreements with the United Mine Workers of America as far back as 1950 to cover retiree health costs. In addition, excess union pension funds and interest on monies in the abandoned mine land reclamation fund would be transferred to the union's health benefit fund. Also, the law allows excess assets in qualified black lung benefit trusts to be used to pay accident and health premiums for retired miners. Another provision of the law expands the exclusion from taxable income for employer-provided transit subsidies while limiting the exclusion for employer-provided parking.

1993

On August 10, 1993, President Bill Clinton signed the Omnibus Budget Reconciliation Act of 1993 (PL 103-66), which lowered the amount of compensation that could be taken into account in calculating benefit accruals or allocations. OBRA '93 extended retroactively the income tax exclusion for employer-provided educational assistance and the health insurance deduction for self-employed individuals, from June 30, 1992, through December 31, 1993. The law changed the fringe benefit treatment of moving expenses, required group health plans to honor child medical support orders, and required group health plans to continue to offer pediatric vaccines.

Appendix 11

Labor Department Interpretive Bulletin on Economically Targeted Investments

59 FR 32606 (06/23/94)

DEPARTMENT OF LABOR

Pension and Welfare Benefits Administration

29 CFR Part 2509

[Interpretive Bulletin 94-1]

Interpretive Bulletin Relating to the Employee Retirement Income Security Act of 1974

AGENCY: Pension and Welfare Benefits Administration, Labor.

ACTION: Interpretive bulletin.

SUMMARY: This document sets forth the view of the Department of Labor (the Department) concerning the legal standard imposed by sections 403 and 404 of Part 4 of Title I of the Employee Retirement Income Security Act of 1974 (ERISA) with respect to a plan fiduciary's decision to invest plan assets in "economically targeted investments" (ETIs). ETIs are generally defined as investments that are selected for the economic benefits they create in addition to the investment return to the employee benefit plan investor. In this document, the Department states that the requirements of sections 403 and 404 do not prevent plan fiduciaries from deciding to invest plan assets in an ETI if the ETI has an expected rate of return that is commensurate to rates of return of alternative investments with similar risk characteristics that are available to the plan, and if the ETI is otherwise an appropriate investment for the plan in terms of such factors as diversification and the investment policy of the plan.

EFFECTIVE DATE: January 1, 1975.

FOR FURTHER INFORMATION CONTACT: Morton Klevan or S. John Ryan, Pension and Welfare Benefits Administration, U.S. Department of Labor, Washington, DC 20210, telephone (202) 219-9044 or (202) 219-8671 or William W. Taylor, Esq., Plan Benefits Security Division, Office of the Solicitor, U.S. Department of Labor, Washington, DC 20210, telephone (202) 219-4592. These are not toll-free numbers.

SUPPLEMENTARY INFORMATION: In order to provide a concise and ready reference to its interpretations of ERISA, the Department publishes its interpretive bulletins in the Rules and Regulations section of the Federal Register. Published in this issue of the Federal Register is ERISA Interpretive Bulletin 94-1, which clarifies that under ERISA a plan fiduciary may invest plan assets in an "economically targeted investment" (ETI) provided the fiduciary determines that such investment is appropriate for the plan in terms of the same factors that a prudent fiduciary would use in determining whether any other type of investment is appropriate for the plan. The Department is publishing this interpretive bulletin because it believes there is a need to summarize and clarify the guidance which it has provided regarding the fiduciary standards applicable to plan investments generally and to investments in ETIs specifically.

(Sec. 505, Pub. L. 93-406, 88 Stat. 894 (29 U.S.C. 1135))

Background

Several recent articles and reports have indicated that a perception exists within the investment community that investments in ETIs are incompatible with ERISA's fiduciary obligations.[1] In order to eliminate this misperception, the Department is issuing this interpretative bulletin to set forth its understanding of the term ETI, and to clarify its position regarding the application of the fiduciary provisions of Part 4 of Title I of ERISA to a decision to invest in an ETI.

As used in this interpretive bulletin, an ETI is an investment that is selected for the economic benefit it creates, in addition to the investment return to the employee benefit plan investor. ETIs fall within a wide variety of asset categories, including real estate, venture capital and small business investments. Although some of these asset categories may require a longer time to generate significant investment returns, may be less liquid and may not have as much readily available information on their risks and returns as other asset categories, nothing in ERISA precludes trustees and investment managers from considering ETIs in constructing plan portfolios. While some of these asset categories may require special expertise to evaluate, they may be attractive to sophisticated, long-term investors, including many pension plans. The Department has issued a number of letters concerning a fiduciary's ability to consider the collateral effects of an investment.[2] The Department has also granted a variety of prohibited transaction exemptions to both individual plans and pooled investment vehicles involving investments which produce collateral benefits.[3] These letters and exemptions illustrate circumstances under which fiduciaries may consider collateral benefits when investing plan assets.

In responding to these various opinion requests, the Department has established certain broad principles. The Department has stated that arrangements designed to bring areas of investment opportunity which provide collateral benefits to the attention of plan fiduciaries will not in and of themselves violate sections 403 or 404, where the arrangements do not restrict the exercise of the fiduciary's investment

[1] Financing the Future, Report of the Commission to Promote Investment in America's Infrastructure, Feb. 1993; Report of the Work Group on Pension Investments, Advisory Council on Employee Welfare and Pension Benefit Plans, Nov. 1992, p. 19; Maria O'Brien Hylton, Socially Responsible Investing: Doing Good Versus Doing Well in an Inefficient Market, 42 Am. U.L. Rev. 1 (1992).

[2] See, letters from the Department of Labor to Mr. John Kenney, dated June 3, 1980 (A.O. 80-33A); to Mr. George Cox, dated January 16, 1981; to Mr. Theodore Groom, dated January 16, 1981; to The Trustees of the Twin City Carpenters and Joiners Pension Plan, dated May 19, 1981; to Mr. William Chadwick, dated July 21, 1982; to Mr. Daniel O'Sullivan, dated August 2, 1982; to Mr. Ralph Katz; dated March 15, 1982 and October 23, 1985 (A.O. 85-36A); to Mr. William Ecklund, dated December 18, 1985, and January 16, 1986; to Mr. Reed Larson, dated July 14, 1986; to Mr. James Ray, dated July 8, 1988; to Mr. Gregory Ridella, dated December 19, 1988 (A.O. 88-16A); to the Honorable Jack Kemp, dated November 23, 1990; and to Mr. Stuart Cohen, dated May 14, 1993.

[3] See, PTE 76-1, part B, concerning construction loans by multiemployer plans; PTE 84-25, issued to the Pacific Coast Roofers Pension Plan; PTE 85-58, issued to the Northwestern Ohio Building Trades and Employer Construction Industry Investment Plan; PTE 87-20, issued to the Racine Construction Industry Pension Fund; PTE 87-70, issued to the Dayton Area Building and Construction Industry Investment Plan, PTE 88-96, issued to the Real Estate for American Labor A Balcor Group Trust; PTE 89-37, issued to the Union Bank; PTE 93-16, issued to the Toledo Roofers Local No. 134 Pension Plan and Trust, et al.

discretion. For example, in Advisory Opinion 88-16A, the Department considered an arrangement whereby a company and union proposed to make recommendations, for up to 5% of the annual contributions, of investments with the potential for providing collateral benefits to union members. The Department concluded that the arrangement would not be inconsistent with the requirements of sections 403(c) and 404(a)(1) of ERISA, where the investment managers having responsibility with respect to these recommendations retained exclusive investment discretion, and were required to secure, over the long term, the maximum attainable total return on investments consistent with the principles of sound pension fund management.[4] Moreover, the Department stated that in considering such investments plan fiduciaries could be influenced by factors that were not related to the plan's expected investment return, only if such investments were equal or superior to alternative available investments.

Similarly, in a case involving the financing of construction projects, the Department concluded that participation in an organization which presents investment opportunities but does not limit the investment alternatives available to the plans, and does not obligate the plans to invest in any project presented for consideration, does not, in itself, violate any of ERISA's fiduciary standards. Moreover, the Department concluded that in enforcing the plan's rights after making an investment, the fiduciary could consider factors unrelated to the plan's investment return only if, in the fiduciary's judgment, the course of action taken would be at least as economically advantageous to the plan as any alternative course of action.[5]

In other letters, the Department concluded that the requirements of sections 403 and 404 do not exclude the consideration of collateral benefits in a fiduciary's evaluation of a particular investment opportunity. However, existence of such collateral benefits may be decisive in evaluating an investment only if the fiduciary determines that the investment containing the collateral benefits is expected to provide an investment return to the plan commensurate to alternative investments having similar risks.[6]

While the Department has stated that a plan fiduciary may consider collateral benefits in choosing between investments that have comparable risks and rates of return, it has consistently held that fiduciaries who are willing to accept expected reduced returns or greater risks to secure collateral benefits are in violation of ERISA.[7] It follows that, because every investment necessarily causes a plan to forgo other investment opportunities, an investment will not be prudent if it would provide a plan with a lower expected rate of return than available alternative investments with commensurate degrees of risk or is riskier than alternative available investments with commensurate rates of return.

The following interpretive bulletin deals solely with the applicability of the prudence and exclusive purpose requirements of ERISA as applied to fiduciary decisions to invest plan assets in ETIs. The bulletin does not supersede the regulatory

[4] See, letter from the Department of Labor to Mr. Gregory Ridella, dated December 19, 1988 (A.O. 88-16A); see also, letters to Mr. John Kenney, dated June 3, 1980 (A.O. 80-33A); and to Mr. Stuart Cohen, dated May 14, 1993.

[5] See, letter from the Department to Mr. George Cox, dated January 16, 1981.

[6] See, letters from the Department of Labor to Mr. Theodore Groom, dated January 16, 1981; to Mr. Daniel O'Sullivan, dated August 2, 1982; to Mr. James Ray, dated July 8, 1988; and to Mr. Stuart Cohen, dated May 14, 1993.

[7] See, letters from the Department of Labor to the Trustees of the Twin City Carpenters and Joiners Pension Plan, dated May 19, 1981; to Mr. William Ecklund, dated December 18, 1985, and January 16, 1986; to Mr. Reed Larson, dated July 14, 1986; and to the Honorable Jack Kemp, dated November 23, 1990. Also note, that in letters to Mr. Ralph Katz, dated March 15, 1982 and October 23, 1985 (A.O. 85-36A), the Department held that increases to plan assets obtained from an increased contribution level, or other collateral benefits could not be added to the investment return of the plan's investment. Thus, for comparison purposes, the economic evaluation of the investment is limited to its actual return.

standard contained at 29 CFR 2550.404a-1, nor does it address any issues which may arise in connection with the prohibited transaction provisions or the statutory exemptions from those provisions.

List of Subjects in 29 CFR Part 2509

Employee benefit plans, Pensions.

For the reasons set forth in the preamble, Part 2509 of Title 29 of the Code of Federal Regulations is amended as follows:

PART 2509—INTERPRETIVE BULLETINS RELATING TO THE EMPLOYEE RETIREMENT INCOME SECURITY ACT OF 1974

1. The authority citation for part 2509 is revised to read as follows:

Authority: 29 U.S.C. 1135. Section 2509.75-1 is also issued under 29 U.S.C. 1114. Sections 2509.75-10 and 2509.75-2 also issued under 29 U.S.C. 1052, 1053, 1054. Secretary of Labor's Order No. 1-87 (52 FR 13139).

2. Part 2509 is amended by adding a new Sec. 2509.94-1 to read as follows:
Sec. 2509.94-1 Interpretive Bulletin relating to the fiduciary standard under ERISA in considering economically targeted investments.

This Interpretive Bulletin sets forth the Department of Labor's interpretation of sections 403 and 404 of the Employee Retirement Income Security Act of 1974 (ERISA), as applied to employee benefit plan investments in "economically targeted investments" (ETIs), that is, investments selected for the economic benefits they create apart from their investment return to the employee benefit plan. Sections 403 and 404, in part, require that a fiduciary of a plan act prudently, and to diversify plan investments so as to minimize the risk of large losses, unless under the circumstances it is clearly prudent not to do so. In addition, these sections require that a fiduciary act solely in the interest of the plan's participants and beneficiaries and for the exclusive purpose of providing benefits to their participants and beneficiaries. The Department has construed the requirements that a fiduciary act solely in the interest of, and for the exclusive purpose of providing benefits to, participants and beneficiaries as prohibiting a fiduciary from subordinating the interests of participants and beneficiaries in their retirement income to unrelated objectives. With regard to investing plan assets, the Department has issued a regulation, at 29 CFR 2550.404a-1, interpreting the prudence requirements of ERISA as they apply to the investment duties of fiduciaries of employee benefit plans. The regulation provides that the prudence requirements of section 404(a)(1)(B) are satisfied if (1) the fiduciary making an investment or engaging in an investment course of action has given appropriate consideration to those facts and circumstances that, given the scope of the fiduciary's investment duties, the fiduciary knows or should know are relevant, and (2) the fiduciary acts accordingly. This includes giving appropriate consideration to the role that the investment or investment course of action plays (in terms of such factors as diversification, liquidity and risk/return characteristics) with respect to that portion of the plan's investment portfolio within the scope of the fiduciary's responsibility.

Other facts and circumstances relevant to an investment or investment course of action would, in the view of the Department, include consideration of the expected return on alternative investments with similar risks available to the plan. It follows that, because every investment necessarily causes a plan to forgo other investment opportunities, an investment will not be prudent if it would be expected to provide a plan with a lower rate of return than available alternative investments with commensurate degrees of risk or is riskier than alternative available investments with commensurate rates of return.

The fiduciary standards applicable to ETIs are no different than the standards applicable to plan investments generally. Therefore, if the above requirements are met, the selection of an ETI, or the engaging in an investment course of action intended to result in the selection of ETIs, will not violate section 404(a)(1) (A) and (B) and the exclusive purpose requirements of section 403.

Signed at Washington, DC, this 17th day of June 1994.

Olena Berg,
Assistant Secretary, Pension and Welfare Benefit Administration, U.S. Department of Labor.

[FR Doc. 94-15162 Filed 6-22-94; 8:45 am]

Glossary

Accrued benefit. The amount of benefit that a participant in a qualified or nonqualified retirement plan has earned under the plan's terms at a specified time.

Annuity. A contract for the payment of specified or objectively determinable periodic payments over a specified period of time or over the lifetime of the recipient.

Annuitized plan. Either an ongoing pension plan fully or partially funded by annuities, or a terminated plan with pension liabilities funded by annuities. Such plans are exempt from the requirement that plan assets be held in trust and from many fiduciary rules on the investment of those assets. However, the selection of the annuity provider is subject to ERISA's fiduciary standards.

Arm's-length transaction. As required for an exemption request for a transaction between a plan and a party in interest, where the transaction would have the same terms as if the parties were unrelated.

Asset allocation. Determination of what portion of plan assets will be invested in different asset classes. May use computer models to determine which types of investments fulfill the investment objectives without exceeding the acceptable levels of risk.

Benchmark. Also called an index, a benchmark is a standard against which to measure investment performance. For example, benchmarks include the following market indices for common stock, the Standard & Poors 500; for small capitalization stocks, the Wiltshire 5,000; for bonds, the Salomon Bros. bond index; and for foreign stocks, the Europe, Australia, and Far East index.

Beta. Measurement of market sensitivity in a pension fund portfolio, using the Standard & Poors 500 as a guide. Beta is the calculation of the average change in the fund's rate of return for each 1 percent change in the market.

Bonding. Required by fiduciaries and any plan official handling plan assets to protect the plan against loss through acts of fraud or dishonesty, directly or indirectly.

Bonds. Certificates of debt issued by governments, municipalities, and corporations.

Defined benefit plan. Qualified funded pension plan, characterized by a benefit formula of a percentage of compensation multiplied by the years of service. This type of plan is funded by certain schedules, and investment experience is borne by the plan sponsor.

Defined contribution plan. Also called individual account plans, where a participant's benefit is the amount in the account. The participant bears all the risk of gains and losses.

Dedicate liabilities. Matching of bond investments to expected plan payments so that future liabilities are covered despite future changes in the interest rates.

Department of Labor (DOL). Agency assigned to administer and oversee the fiduciary provisions of ERISA. Within the DOL, the Pension and Welfare Benefits Administration reviews exemption requests, develops pension policy, and promulgates regulations.

Disclosure. Provision of plan information to participants and beneficiaries. Includes the summary plan description, summary of material modifications to the plan, explanation of investments for participant-directed individual account plans, copies of annual financial statements, and individual benefit statements explaining the accrued benefit to date and vesting status.

Disqualified person. Used in the Internal Revenue Code to mean party-in-interest, this person will incur penalties if engaged in a prohibited transaction. A disqualified person is defined as a fiduciary; a service provider; an employer whose employees are covered by the plan; a union whose members are covered by the plan; a 50-percent owner; family members of disqualified persons; a 50-percent corporate owner; a 10-percent owner-officer or director; or a 10-percent partner or joint venturer.

Duck test. Used by a court to determine if an individual was a fiduciary by function, even though not named as a fiduciary in the plan. The court held that an individual acting as a fiduciary was in fact a fiduciary—that is, "if it walks like a duck and talks like a duck, it is a duck."

Employer security. Stock issued by employers. Up to 10 percent of plan assets may be invested in employer securities in defined contribution plans, while employee stock ownership plans may invest 100 percent of assets in employer securities.

Equities. Common stock or preferred stock representing ownership in a company.

Employee stock ownership plan (ESOP). An individual account retirement plan that invests primarily in employer securities. In a "leveraged" ESOP, the plan borrows money from a bank with the employer's guarantee. As the employer makes contributions to the plan, the plan repays the loan, and employer securities are released from a holding fund and allocated to participants' accounts.

ERISA. Employee Retirement Income Security Act, first enacted in 1974 and amended often. It preempts state laws relating to employee benefit plans and lays down strict standards for plans that wish to have and maintain tax-favored status.

Fiduciary. Any individual or company that exercises control or management of plan assets and investments, renders investment advice for a fee, or has discretionary authority in the administration of the plan.

Growth stock managers. Investment managers who choose stock with high earnings per share growth or high return on equity.

Health and welfare plans. Plans established by employers or unions to provide participants and beneficiaries with medical, surgical, or hospital care; sickness, accident, disability, or death benefits; unemployment or vacation benefits; apprenticeship or other training programs; or day-care centers, scholarship funds, or prepaid legal services.

Immunized bonds. An investment strategy of combining long- and short-term bonds to reduce the effects of interest rate changes on investment returns.

Income managers. Investment managers that look for companies with dividend yields greater than the Standard & Poors 500 dividend average.

Indemnify. To insure against loss.

Index funds. Passive management strategy that picks securities whose return matches those of the securities in a specific index.

Indicia of ownership. Stock and bond certificates are examples of the indicia or proof of ownership of investments of plan assets that must not be maintained outside the United States.

Internal Revenue Service. Agency that administers the tax portion of ERISA and issues regulations to help plans comply with requirements such as funding, nondiscrimination, distributions, tax-deductible contributions, and excise taxes for noncompliance with regulations.

Investment managers. Individuals or corporations that provide investment management services to plans. May be insurance companies, banks, lawyers, or mutual funds.

Junk bonds. Low-quality securities of companies in leveraged buyouts or takeovers. Repayment of the bonds depends on asset sales of these companies, rather than ongoing business. Payment of interest is not guaranteed.

Liquidity. The ease of converting an investment into cash. Treasury notes are very liquid, for example, while real estate is illiquid.

Market indices. *See also* Benchmark. An index is a measure of a particular market, often given as a percentage of a base year. For example, the Dow Jones Industrial Index of 30 industrial stocks may be quoted as 3,050 on a particular day, showing an increase of 300 percent in stock values from the base year.

Market timing. An investment management strategy of investing in cash and common stocks for optimum return on investment.

Master trustee. A bank or custodial service that holds plan assets. The master trustee makes periodic reports to a plan's fiduciaries, and may offer additional services, such as daily cash management or plan administration.

Multiemployer plan. A plan to which more than one employer is required to contribute and which is maintained through one or more written collective bargaining agreements between unions and employers.

Mutual fund. An open-end investment company where investors pool their assets, buying securities based on a unit price. The investments are managed according to the fund's objective, such as income, growth, or international.

Named fiduciary. The person listed in the plan document as being responsible for the management and operation of the plan.

Normal portfolio. A portfolio of investments considered to be efficient, or of the least risk.

Party in interest. *See also* Disqualified person. A person prohibited by ERISA from entering into certain transactions with a plan. Defined as any fiduciary (including administrators, officers, trustees, or custodians), counsel, or plan employee; a service provider to the plan; an employer of employees covered in the plan; a union whose members are covered in the plan; a 50-percent owner; a relative of any of the above persons (including spouses, ancestors, parents, children, and their spouses); a 50-percent corporate owner; an officer or director owning 10 percent of the shares; or a 10-percent partner or joint venturer.

Passive management. A style of investment management that uses indices or other means to attain an average risk-adjusted rate of return.

Pension Benefit Guaranty Corporation (PBGC). Agency charged with administering the plan termination and benefit guarantees of defined benefit plans. PBGC assesses premiums based on the number of participants in a plan, and maintains separate programs for single-employer plans and multiemployer plans.

Pension plans. Any plan, fund, or program maintained by an employer or a union, or both, that provides retirement income to employees, or defers income until a participant terminates employment. However, severance pay arrangements are treated as welfare plans.

Plan assets. The accumulation of employer and employee contributions and their investment earnings.

Plan expenses. In addition to providing benefits, fiduciaries may pay reasonable plan expenses relating to plan administration, including the cost of office space, office supplies, telephone and utility expenses, postage, bank fees, actuarial, accounting and legal fees, trustee fees, recordkeeping and claims processing fees, and investment management and brokerage fees.

Portfolio insurance. An investment program designed to maintain a minimum rate of return by constantly adjusting the allocation of investments in a portfolio.

Preemption. ERISA supersedes all state laws relating to employee benefit plans, although the insurers of plans funded only by insurance products are subject to state insurance laws.

Procedural prudence. The process of arriving at sound fiduciary decisions, which requires investments to be examined for the risk of loss, the opportunity for return, diversification, liquidity, and current return. The process requires fiduciaries to compare a possible investment with other investments, and to document each step of the examination, comparison, choice of investment, and monitoring process.

Prohibited transaction. A transaction between a plan and a party in interest or disqualified person, unless specifically exempted.

Prohibited transaction exemption. An administrative exemption from the prohibited transaction requirements issued by the Labor Department, issued either as an individual exemption or as a class exemption.

Proxy. A ballot to vote for boards of directors or other company business at a company's annual shareholders' meeting, where the holder of the ballot authorizes someone else to cast votes on behalf of the shareholder.

Prudent man standard. ERISA fiduciary standard for investing and managing plan assets that requires a fiduciary to use the care, skill, prudence, and diligence that a similarly situated, knowledgeable person would use. The courts have interpreted this standard to be a "prudent expert standard."

Real estate funds. Pooled investment vehicles for plans to invest in real estate indirectly, without holding the actual property.

Reporting. Form 5500 and related schedules required to be filed with the Internal Revenue Service by administrators of all pension plans covered by ERISA. A section of the form requires listing of any prohibited transactions engaged in by the plan. Schedule C requires a listing of all service providers, their compensation, and if terminated, their reason for termination. Termination of trustees must also be noted.

Risk. Chance of loss.

Self-dealing. Where a fiduciary personally benefits from a plan transaction.

Settlor decisions. Decisions, such as the decision to establish a plan, which are made for business reasons and are outside the scope of fiduciary responsibility. The courts have determined that other activities are settlor and not fiduciary decisions: termination of welfare and pension plans pursuant to corporate bankruptcy, reduction of unaccrued benefits, and termination of a retiree health plan.

Soft dollars. Credit for directing investments commissions to specific brokers, used by fiduciaries and investment managers plans to "buy" research and ancillary services.

Standard & Poors (S&P) 500. An index prepared by Standard & Poor's Corporation that tracks the price movements of 500 stocks, including industrial, transportation, utility, and finance stocks.

Sweep service. Cash management services offered by trustee banks to employee benefit plans. Helps to ensure interest is earned on cash amounts.

Tactical asset allocation. Investment strategy of putting assets into investments with the best expected return for the lowest risk, based on a computerized formula.

Trustee. Individuals or entities such as banks named in a plan's trust instrument or appointed by the plan's named fiduciary, to manage and control plan assets. Trustees may be directed by the named fiduciary, and if so, are not liable for decisions made by the named fiduciary.

Value stock manager. Value investment managers choose stocks on the basis of low price to earnings ratios or low price to book ratios.

Venture capital. Investment of capital in new business or ventures. Since new business is prone to failure, such investment is considered risky.

Vesting. The nonforfeitable right to plan benefits, usually determined by a participant's years of service with an employer. However, a plan participant who attains the plan's normal retirement age is 100 percent vested in the benefits accrued, despite the years of service with the employer.

Volatility. Sensitivity of an investment to changes in the market. Stocks are considered to be volatile.

Bibliography

Books

Employee Benefits Dictionary (an annotated compendium of frequently used terms) by Virginia L. Briggs, Michael G. Kushner, & Michael J. Schinabeck; 1992, BNA Books.

Employee Benefits Law, by the American Bar Association Section of Labor and Employment Law, BNA Books (supplemented).

ERISA Class Exemptions, by Donald J. Myers, 1991, BNA Books (supplemented).

ERISA Regulations, by Michael G. Kushner, 1993, BNA Books.

ERISA Selected Legislative History, 1992, BNA Books.

ERISA: The Law and the Code, BNA Books (published annually).

Primer on ERISA, by Barbara Coleman, 1993, BNA Books.

Trustees Handbook, 4th ed., A Basic Text on Labor-Management Employee Benefit Plans, ed. by Marc Gertner, International Foundation of Employee Benefit Plans, 1990.

Articles

Benefits Quarterly, "ERISA Fiduciary Issues in Pension Fund Proxy Voting," Fourth Quarter, 1992, pp. 70–78.

Publications

Compensation and Benefits Guide, biweekly newsletter and updates to six-volume loose-leaf reference service, The Bureau of National Affairs, Inc., 1231 25th St., N.W., Washington, DC 20037.

BNA Pension Reporter, weekly, The Bureau of National Affairs, Inc.

Employee Benefit News, monthly, *Benefits Sourcebook*, annually, Enterprise Communications Inc., 1165 Northchase Pkwy. N.E., Suite 350, Marietta, GA, 30067.

Greenwich Report, annually, Greenwich Associates, Greenwich, CT.

Mutual Fund Fact Book, annually, Investment Company Institute, Washington, DC.

Employee Benefit Plan Review, monthly, Charles Spencer & Associates.

Employee Benefits Cases, weekly, The Bureau of National Affairs, Inc.

Employee Benefits Journal, quarterly, The International Foundation of Employee Benefit Plans, P.O. Box 69, Brookfield, WI 53008-0069.

Organizations

American Compensation Association, 14040 N. Northsight Blvd., Scottsdale, AZ 85260.

Employee Benefit Research Institute, 2121 K St, N.W., Washington, DC 20037.

International Foundation of Employee Benefit Plans, P.O. Box 69, Brookfield, WI 53008.

WEB, Inc., a network of professionals working in employee benefits, c/o GSS Inc., 8 South Michigan Ave., Suite 1400, Chicago, IL 60603.

Table of Cases

P

Q

R

S

U

W

Y

INDEX

R

S

T

V

W